Walkin' over Medicine

Walkin' over Medicine

LOUDELL F. SNOW

Westview Press

Boulder • San Francisco • Oxford

Published in 1993 in the United States of America by Westview Press, Inc., 5500 Central Avenue, Boulder, Colorado 80301-2877, and in the United Kingdom by Westview Press, 36 Lonsdale Road, Summertown, Oxford OX2 7EW

Library of Congress Cataloging-in-Publication Data
Snow, Loudell F.
  Walkin' over medicine / Loudell F. Snow.
    p. cm.
  Includes bibliographical references and index.
  ISBN 0-8133-1074-1. — ISBN 0-8133-1799-1 (pbk.) (if published as a paperback)
    1. Afro-Americans—Folklore. 2. Afro-Americans—Medicine.
3. Folk medicine—United States. I. Title.
GR111.A47S695 1993
615.8'82'08996073—dc20   92-37482
                                                                               CIP

Printed and bound in the United States of America

The paper used in this publication meets the requirements of the American National Standard for Permanence of Paper for Printed Library Materials Z39.48-1984.

10 9 8 7 6 5 4 3

This Book Is for Shirley Johnson Bordinat,
Carol Markos, and Gabriel Smilkstein

Three Friends Whose Encouragement
and Support Kept Me from Giving Up

It's so many things we use! I didn't know anything about *medicine,* real medicine, because you know this is all I was brought up with. Why, there's a lotta *weeds* out there *now*; why, you're walkin' over *medicine!* And greens we used, like dandelions. Dandelions is a *wonderful* food. There's so many vitamins out there right now that we're *walkin'* over. We walk *over* medicine, that's right. And the doctors say that people [who] wear copper bracelets for arthritis, that it's no *good* these days! I can't explain *what* it *was* about those remedies; it had to be some good because if it hadn't been some good they wouldn't have been able to provide. I've got copper bracelets *now!* Now, there's somethin' *to* it, 'cause those people made the *way* for *us,* that's right. There's some good in it. And you'd be surprised what you can do with what you have.

—*Interview in Detroit, Michigan, 1978*

Contents

Preface

The material on African-American traditional medicine presented in this book spans a time period of more than 20 years. It is derived from my own community-based studies in Arizona and Michigan, work in two urban prenatal clinics, conversations and written communications with traditional healers, and my several years' experience as a behavioral scientist in a pediatrics clinic. It includes examples of folklore collected by some of my students in a university class and, of course, is augmented by the work of other scholars. The various methods of data collection for my own work—both formal and informal—are briefly reviewed below.

My introduction to the subject was the ethnographic study of health beliefs in a low-income neighborhood of Tucson, Arizona, in 1970–1971. The description and analysis of my findings were presented as my doctoral dissertation to the Department of Anthropology at the University of Arizona. In 1971 I accepted a teaching position at Michigan State University, where I have in the years since taught undergraduates, graduate students, medical students, and medical residents. Many of them have been very helpful in giving me examples of their own knowledge and experience of traditional medicine, some of which are included here.

My Tucson experience kindled a particular interest in the reproductive health of women. This experience was the basis of my first research in Michigan—a pilot project done in collaboration with Dr. Shirley Johnson. We were contacted by the physician-director of a Lansing prenatal clinic who expressed concern about the problems he saw in delivering quality care to the clinic's multiethnic, low-income clientele. Some difficulties he blamed on poor communication; he was *sure*, he said, that many women did not understand many of the terms that were used by clinic staff, yet they never said so. He also felt that the ideas the clinic staff held about what is good for pregnant women were not fully shared by the women in question. In response to his request we developed a questionnaire that covered respondents' understanding of selected medical terminology; their health care experiences; and their knowledge and beliefs about menstruation, venereal disease, childbearing, contraception, pregnancy, abortion, and the menopause. It was administered to a sample of women that, though small (N=31), represented just over half of all women coming in for their first prenatal visit during the summer of 1975. Results showed that many of them did *not* understand the medical terminology in use at the clinic, and as suspected, many of their beliefs were culturally patterned and quite different from those of the doctors and nurses responsible for their care. Most did not have the knowledge needed to allow them to prevent pregnancy if they so wished.

The results were interesting, but the time it took to administer the questionnaire—nearly two hours—precluded its usefulness in any busy medical setting. We therefore developed a short, self-administered form including 38 multiple-choice questions designed to provide a profile of a woman's knowledge of reproduction, including her own contraceptive and reproductive history. Answers to the multiple-choice questions included both the most prevalent misinformation held by respondents in the pilot study and the information seen as correct by clinicians. In the summer of 1978 it was tested at a hospital clinic offering gynecological and obstetrical services in the inner city of Detroit, Michigan. Again, the results showed that many of the 200 women who filled out the questionnaire were misinformed and/or lacked the information about the basic reproductive facts essential to control fertility. A number of the beliefs found in these studies continue to be reported in research done since that time.

Another research interest that had carried over from my Arizona study was that of the recruitment and role of the traditional healer. Several of my Tucson informants had engaged in the healing of others. Some had prepared home remedies for family, friends, and neighbors, and one or two others practiced healing in the context of religious services. One individual, Mother Delphine Carver, was able to make a full-time living from her healing practice. I was not able to locate any such individuals in Lansing, however, so I initially took a different tack. A variety of traditional healers and advisers offer their services through the classified advertisements of newspapers with large numbers of African-American readers. In 1973 and again in 1977 I engaged in research involving correspondence by mail and telephone with a number of the men and women whose names I found in the *Chicago Defender*; I have continued to monitor such advertisements in the *Defender*, the *New York Amsterdam News*, and Detroit's *Michigan Chronicle*. I contacted and spoke with several individuals who advertise in one or more of these publications (including one man from Chicago with whom I have interacted off and on since 1973) as the final chapters of this book were being completed. Since 1987 I have also visited and interviewed traditional healers in Grand Rapids and Pontiac, Michigan, and New Orleans, Louisiana.

Just as physicians write out prescriptions or recommend over-the-counter medicinal preparations for their patients, traditional healer/advisers often suggest the purchase of a variety of items—religious, occult, and medicinal—for use by their clientele. Specialty shops selling herbs, charms, candles, incense, oils, and a variety of booklets outlining their proper use are important sources in the health-seeking behavior of many people; such items are sometimes found for sale in inner-city pharmacies and neighborhood grocery stores as well. I have visited such establishments in Chicago, Detroit, San Francisco, New Orleans, Los Angeles, and New York City.

Since 1978 I have taught an undergraduate course entitled "American Folk Medicine" at Michigan State University; an optional project for students includes the collection of health-related folklore from informants of their choice. These materials are collected in a standardized format and are stored in the Department of Anthropology and have yet to be systematically sorted and filed; in the course of writing this book, however, items contributed by African-American informants were retrieved and reviewed. This information had been gathered from 66 individuals—10 men and 56 women—ranging in age from 18 to 94 years; nearly one-third (30 percent) of the respondents were under 30 years of age. They contributed 350 separate items having to do with health maintenance and promotion, practices seen as dangerous to health, and cures for various ailments. The largest number of items clustered around the adult female reproductive cycle—menstruation, pregnancy and abortion, birth and the postpartum period (N=69, 20 percent of total)—and the next most common category had to do with upper respiratory infections (N=51, 15 percent of total). The remainder included treatments for ailments in every body system as well as such miscellaneous problems as cures for hangovers, nightmares, and a fishbone stuck in the throat.

Much of the information presented in the chapter on the health of infants and children was gathered during the years 1980–1987 in which I spent my Tuesday afternoons observing interactions between the staff—receptionist, nurses, a pediatrics nurse practitioner, attending physician, and residents—and the small patients and their caretakers in a public pediatrics clinic in Lansing, Michigan. The clinic served a multiethnic, low-income population, and I was invited to become a part of the program by the residency director, who felt that many of the problems in delivering good care at the facility were based on cultural differences between clients and staff. My own rather grand title was "behavioral scientist attending," and the hope was that I would be able to ferret out problems based on cultural differences and help to solve them. In order to assure some continuity of care each new resident was assigned his or her own clinic afternoon and a group of families who—except for emergencies—would routinely be seen by that resident on that particular day of the week. This arrangement allowed me to interact with a particular subset of residents over the three years of their training and, as well, to get to know the families they saw. I accompanied residents as they met with families, took histories, and examined babies and children. I heard the questions that family members asked and listened as the nurse or resident gave instructions for the care of the child. After the visit was over and the nurse and resident had left the room, I often remained behind while the child was dressed and the family prepared to go home. And because the clinic was busy and the residents frequently fell behind in their appointments, I often went in to talk with the family *before* their child was examined as well. It was during those times when a nurse or physician was not in the room that I was sometimes asked questions that were not brought up during the official visit. It was very clear that the adults who brought the children in had their own ideas about what information was to be shared with health professionals. It was at this clinic that I first met some of the women who play such an important role in this book: Jacie Burnes, whose husband kept her prisoner for years by working "bad roots"; Janine Jackson, who was glad that the catnip for her grandbaby's colic grew in her backyard; Bernita Washington, who at the age of 16 delivered her first child alone because the midwife did not come; that child, Marya Smith, a grandmother at 32, who thought her home remedy for her grandson's thrush infection was preferable to the drops prescribed by a resident. These women are certainly living proof that traditional health beliefs can and do coexist with orthodox medicine.

All of the men, women, and children who move in and out of the following pages have been given pseudonyms; in rare cases minor details of their lives have been changed to further safeguard their privacy. Some individuals are heard from only once; other more key informants appear in nearly every chapter. Because the information was gathered over a number of years, the names, dates, and locations are provided in parentheses so that the reader will be able to tell when and where an observation was made. If an interaction was brief a comment or quotation was written in field notes, either mine or, in the case of the folklore collection, in those of my students. Longer quotations are taken from interviews I conducted; these were tape-recorded with permission, and I subsequently transcribed the tapes. In some instances they are edited because of length, but they are otherwise reported just as I heard them; I did not, that is, attempt to change any individual's manner of speaking into standard English. My personal feeling is that to have done so would have been an act of intellectual arrogance on my part.

Loudell F. Snow

Acknowledgments

I wish to acknowledge financial support for education and research from the Woodrow Wilson Foundation, the Danforth Foundation, the Brush Foundation, and Michigan State University. Special thanks also go to Dr. Donald W. Weston, former dean of the College of Human Medicine at Michigan State; he provided funds that enabled me to take time off from teaching at a crucial time in the preparation of this book.

Some of the material appearing in these pages was collected by undergraduates, medical students, and graduate students at Michigan State University. In the summer of 1975 many of the interviews with women at a prenatal clinic in Lansing, Michigan, were done by Anne Ferguson (now Ph.D.), Mary Walborn (now M.D.), and Helene Dinerstein Jones (now M.D.); I thank them again. Since 1978 some of the students enrolled in an undergraduate class in American folk medicine have gathered health-related lore from African-American informants as an elective assignment, and I have used some of their findings. Thanks to Morris Schrock, Kimberly Troy, Karen Nelson, Melba Bond, Karen Rumisek, Dan Meijer, Peggy Lawrence, Hilary Waddles, Linda Roy, Kathie Murray, Barry Poupard, Lynn Hanson, Patti Gedris, Mary Hoffman, Julie Hess, Kam Hunter, Alma Fowlkes, Elaine Zawecki, Michele Weinbaum, Lori Galper, Jill Fuhrig, Laurel Singer, Kim Nauman, James Rooker, Annette Fowler, Sherilyn Garrett, Cindy Grueber, Mary Jo Silverstein, Marilyn Schmid, Daniel Delmerico, Sue Olson, Janis Brencher, Pamela Haggerty, and Octavia Cannon.

Special thanks go to those friends and colleagues who have generously provided me with their own insights—sometimes from unpublished materials—into traditional African-American health culture. They are Drs. Eddie Boyd, Margaret Boone, Kathryn Heyer Brimhall, Linda Camino, Carole Hill, Holly Mathews, Daniel Moerman, Alice Murphree, Marilyn Poland, Clarissa Scott, Hazel Weidman, and Ben Wilson.

Finally, of course, my heartfelt thanks to all of those individuals who have shared their stories with me over the years. They have welcomed me into their homes and invited me to share in their faith during church services, their joy at weddings and births and graduations, and their sorrow at funerals. They have taught me that true generosity has nothing to do with money.

L.F.S.

1

I Saw a Shadow Leave Me

His business was dread. People came to him in dread, whispered in dread, wept and pleaded in dread. And dread was what he counseled.

Singly they found their way to his door, wrapped each in a shroud stitched with anger, yearning, pride, vengeance, loneliness, misery, defeat, and hunger. They asked for the simplest of things: love, health, and money. Make him love me. Tell me what this dream means. Help me get rid of this woman. Make my mother give me back my clothes. Stop my left hand from shaking. Keep my baby's ghost off the stove. Break so-and-so's fix. To all of these requests he addressed himself. His practice was to do what he was bid—not to suggest to a party that perhaps the request was unfair, mean, or hopeless.

—Toni Morrison, *The Bluest Eye*

Summer 1982. A hot and sultry evening in South Carolina, that time of day that is charmingly called dusk-dark, and Jacie Burnes was impatiently waiting until full-dark. There would be no moon until after midnight; a good night for another attempt to escape. Her *last* chance; she knew that. She had seen the Devil in her husband's reddened eyes again that morning; knew he intended to kill her this time. She sat in the growing darkness, praying. At last it was time and she woke the four boys who were old enough to walk, shushing them the while. She was careful to let baby Sheela and toddler Rashad sleep; she would have to carry them. If all went well they would not wake during the long walk over the fields to the home of a neighbor. There, God willing, she would be able to use the telephone to call the shelter for battered women whose flier she had seen in a grocery store. If she could just reach her own family in Georgia she would be able to figure out something to do, she thought; some way to get so far away that Big Joe would never be able to find them. So far away that even the magical power of his "roots" would not work. She picked up the babies and set out walking rapidly across the soybean rows, the bigger children giggling at this adventure.

It is a number of weeks later in Michigan and more than 800 miles away from those soybean rows. "There's a woman in Room B that I think you'd enjoy talking to," said the director of the pediatric clinic. "She says her husband kept her a prisoner for 15 years with a curse!" I walked in and saw Jacie Burnes and her brood for the first time; they seemed to fill the small examining room. Jacie was a tall and powerful-looking woman, the dark skin of her face crisscrossed with dozens of small scars. At first glimpse the scars seemed to be patterned in X's, but a closer look showed that the marks were random. I was to learn later that they were the result of battles with her husband over the years of their stormy marriage. At six feet two inches she could usually hold her own when they fought, she said, even though her husband was six feet five and sometimes seemed to be "possessed." But she couldn't always stay *awake*, she went on, and when she was sleeping he had the habit of hitting her in the face with bottles. The scars had been made by broken glass. She was glad to finally meet someone in Michigan who knew about roots, she said. She needed to "talk it out."

The family had arrived in Lansing in early September, and the children who were old enough were soon settled in school. She had rented a large and dilapidated house only a block or so from the clinic and was a regular visitor in seeking health care for her family. Indeed, in the next few months she quickly learned to use the network of social agencies for which she and her children were eligible. It was a very long time, however, before the emotional scars of the past years began to dissipate. She was terrified if anyone so much as *spoke* the words "South Carolina," for example, fearing that their very mention might somehow allow her husband to locate her and the children. And she continued to have difficulty sleeping and to suffer nightmares long after a psychiatric social worker told her she "ought to be over it." This is not meant to suggest that Jacie was a weak woman; quite the contrary. The fact that she had survived her ordeal at all was a measure of her strength. And the fact that her husband had been able to *keep* her isolated in that cabin in the country was in part a measure of *his* strength and his powerful personality. More importantly, perhaps, his control over her illustrated the depth of her belief in magical practices. He had kept her there by "working roots" (a regional term for sorcery).

She had been born 35 years earlier on one of the Sea Islands of coastal Georgia. Her mother had been an unmarried 15-year-old whose own mother had put her out of the house in her displeasure at the pregnancy; the newborn Jacie was "given" to her father's mother to raise. She always knew who her mother was, however, as both families had lived in the area for a long time. In later years her own mother wanted her back but her aunt refused to give her up:

> I was raised by my daddy's mother and his sister and his brother. In the house when I was a kid was [also] my grandmother's great-grand-child by her daughter. My uncle, the one who helped raise me, he went overseas to shrimp-fish in order to have money to send back to us. To British Guiana. He said he was gonna make sure that I get out of school; provide for me along with my cousin, my aunt's daughter's little boy. We was the only two kids in the house. It was a pretty nice environment.
>
> I grew up in an environment that they didn't keep nothin' from me; my grandmother used to tell me things. I knew who my mother was, I

knew who my father was; that was a town that wasn't nothin' but family. Surrounded by those islands. One of those islands what where our root started from, you see; then everybody spreaded out from South to North. My mother, I knew who she was and she knew who I was. But there was a hassle when I was comin' up 'bout who should take care of me and who shouldn't, you know, because of the fact that my mother wanted me back. And my aunt refused to give, you know, me back to her. But I survived it, I survived it.

Jacie's fear of "roots" and "rootwork" was a part of her heritage. She had heard stories of friends and relatives who had been victims of such practices from childhood, and they had made an indelible impression on the little girl. No one in her family doubted that there were individuals with unusual abilities, abilities that could be used to do good *or* harm to others. Indeed, it was believed that she herself might have special powers; there was a question as to whether she had been "born with the veil." And as a child she had experiences that told her it must be true:

Roots. That's the same thing as voodoo; I was raised up to call it *roots*. African tribes learn it. Black magic and voodoo and all this; it's the same thing. Now, some people have it psychologically, like God gave them the *gift* to *know* things. Like if somebody's tryin' to do [something to] you, [they'll] tell you if somethin's wrong. It's really psychological. I, myself would have little *visions*. Now, you hear people say you born with a veil over your eyes and stuff like that, O.K.? I, *myself* have that! My grandmother says that I was, you know. And my mother, she say it weren't nothin' but *fat*. I laugh about it today, but really, I knew when my father was gonna die; I saw this happenin', you know. I knew when my baby *sister* was gonna die; I knew that. I couldn't *'splain* it, I was so young. And when this was actually happenin' to me, I didn't know [what it was].

Her mother had married and had other children and these half-siblings were reared in a separate household. The first of her "little visions" was a chilling episode in which she saw the imminent death of a new baby girl born to her mother. Jacie and her grandmother were visiting the family when it happened:

First time, it was my baby sister. And my baby sister had pneumonia, contact pneumonia. They took her to the hospital. And she fall off the sofa on top of that, and why they took her to the hospital was not because of the pneumonia but because she fell off the sofa. And she hit her head on the sofa. My brother and my sister was takin' care of her, and she fell off the sofa and hit her head. And that night we were around there and my grandmother, she enticed my mother to go ahead and get my stepfather to take the baby to the hospital. She'd cried since she fell and hit her head and wouldn't stop, and my grandmother tried everything and she still wouldn't stop. And I thought somethin' was wrong, too, and I tried to talk to her and tell her. I think I was in

the fourth grade. And I tried to tell her. I tried to tell my grandmother
there was somethin' *wrong,* there was somethin' *wrong.* "Let's get her
to the doctor," that's what I kept sayin'.

The infant was hospitalized for a single day and then the family
was called and told to come and take her home:

> They didn't tell her the baby was gonna die; they just told her to take
> her home. They brought her home and put her in her crib. And so that
> night my grandmother and my aunt and all of us were waitin' around,
> and my other cousins. And we looked at her, and when I *looked* I saw
> a *halo* over her head! She was a beautiful baby. I saw a *halo* over her
> head and I knew God wanted her, you know. And I walked around
> and I was cryin' and I tried to *shield,* you know, what I saw and what
> I felt from people—'cause I was afraid and there was this *chill.* I really
> saw this little old golden *halo* over her head, and I knew she was
> gonna die. And my grandmother went over and looked and said, "Oh,
> Mary, look, I don't think she's breathin'." It wasn't five minutes since I
> saw that halo.

After such an experience how could she doubt that things can happen
that are beyond natural explanation?

She had no reason to doubt that individuals could be born with
special powers, then. It was the use of these powers that differentiated those who possessed them; good people used their abilities to
help others without expecting payment. The root doctors used them
to enrich themselves:

> If something bad is going to happen, definitely I know it. When I was
> comin' up I heard people used to say things, [like] was I born with a
> veil over my *face?* My grandmother, she said she wasn't too sure, so I
> asked my mother. My mother say, "Yeah, but a lot of *fat,*" all across
> my face. [Laughs] But I think my aunt, I remember, she tell me that
> she pretty sure that I *did* have a veil over my face, y'know. Some peo-
> ple use it for *good,* some people for bad. The only way you know, [is
> if] that child grow up and she *talk out* about things.

> Good *or* bad, right! Because some people who take *money* for this, I
> don't think that's right, neither. They take money to *tell* you, y'know.
> They call 'em *root* people; *those* people are the ones who accept money
> for their gift, you see, and I don't think that's fair. 'Cause if they *know*
> things *about* things that're gonna *happen,* about sumpin' gonna happen
> to this person *before* it happen, O.K. Then they *oughta* help this person
> to *stop* things afore it happen. There is some people that believe in
> God so *strongly* [and] loves this gift; they'll just tell you these things
> for *free.* All those things that you wanta *know!*

These experiences, coupled with the fearful tales she heard about
the victims of sorcery from her elders, implanted the deep fear of
being injured by magic that would allow her husband to control her

in later years. One story in particular seems to be important in shaping her belief about the possibility of damaging someone with magic. She certainly had no reason to doubt that it was true; after all, it had happened to her own beloved grandmother. A jealous woman had paid a root doctor to work sorcery on the grandmother but had died without divulging the name of the practitioner she had visited; without this information it would be difficult to have the evil reversed. Nor could ordinary doctors help:

> Doctors can't do nothin' *for* it, y'know. O.K., for instance, I know *this* story; that my *grandmother* was rooted by a *woman* over her own husband. My grandmother's husband, my stepgrandfather. And this lady had did sumpin' to her so she had a *sore* on her leg, you see, and this sore didn't never *heal!* And she went to the doctor, she went different places, and they couldn't do *nothin'* for her! It was a open sore, open through the wall [of her leg]. So she decided to go to a root man, and this man told *her* that somebody had put a *root* on her. 'Cause that's the only thing that he could tell was wrong with her. But the person that put the root on had *died* so she never could get the information from that lady to find out *who* did it. Which root doctor did it, which root person was workin' the root. 'Cause that person that workin' the root can take it *off* you, the only person can take it *off* you. 'Cause every root person don't know the different remedies from *another* root person.
>
> So this man, this other root man, just took a *hunch* of tellin' grandmother what to *do,* you know; what to *use.* And he gave my grandmother some kind of special *salve.* What it was I don't know; he gave her sumpin' to *rub* on it, keep puttin' on it, bathin' in it. And she did it. And sho 'nuff, right before everybody's eyes a snake crawled out of it. And they say it was a snake; whether it was a baby snake, big snake, I don't know. I remember this story when I was little, and I couldn't forget it. Couldn't get it out of my mind, every time somebody mention roots to me. She said it *crawl* outa her sore, crawled outa that opening that was in her *leg,* crawl right clean outa there. And they killed it. They was hittin' at it and it just disappear, just like black magic, like voodoo or whatever.
>
> People just don't know the *power* that black magic *have,* or root *have* because of the fact it just unbelievable. You have to see it to believe it, you see. They say it just crawled out and that sore just healed up, it just *closed,* right then and there. It had me just really afraid of it; that was the hold my husband had on me, that was really the *hold* on me. Because that's why the *power* over me was so *strong,* because of the fact that I had this *fear* of root itself personally. 'Cause of the stories I used to hear from my grandparents *about* root and so I was afraid of it.

The 19-year-old Jacie did not set out to marry a man who would terrorize her, of course. She saw a tall, handsome, and personable man, and she was quickly in love. Her family had also liked him, though her mother thought that a five-year age difference made him a little too "mature" for her daughter. Still, there seemed to be no real obstacles to a marriage. He was "brainy," Jacie later reflected; able to hide his true nature when it was in his interest to do so. So the wedding took place and afterward Joe moved his bride to a remote cabin in the woods of his native South Carolina, 30 miles from the nearest town. It was not long before he revealed himself to be so insanely jealous that he forbade her to have anything to do with anyone. There was no telephone; she was cut off from her family; she was not allowed to make new friends. She was utterly alone.

She found herself living with a man filled with rage and frustration, and she struggled to find an explanation for his changed behavior. He had a hatred of women that now seemed to include her, and as he told her stories of his childhood, she decided that the key to his jealous rages lay in his past. There had been one elderly man who had had a particularly malignant effect on the little boy her husband had been, she felt, and had been instrumental in shaping negative views about the female gender that were only now being fully expressed. It helped some to think that there was a *reason* for it all, and although she was unhappy, she also believed strongly in her marital vows. She had suffered when small as the "given-away" child of an illegitimate union and had always dreamed of having a family of her own; her dream was now threatened but she was determined not to give it up easily. Besides, she thought it was her duty to try and help her husband overcome his problems:

> I thought I should *hang* in there, talk to him, tell him to go ahead and
> see a psychiatrist or get some kind of help. 'Cause I think what's
> wrong with my husband was embedded in him when he was small, really. 'Cause he used to tell me stories how this man, this real old man,
> used to tell him stories when he was comin' up. Stories about how
> Black women was treated during slavery and stuff like that, y'know.
> And a whole lot of things I thought was *wrong* for a young kid, especially a little boy, to be *hearin'* and knowin' about. And what they
> should do when they get up and be a man; all these kinds of things.

> But it stuck with my husband real strong, I pretty sure. 'Cause when I
> *did* have a chance to talk to his mother, his *mother* was extremely
> afraid of him. And his father. When I did meet them, they told me
> something was really wrong psychologically. His father is dead, and his
> mother suffers from asthma real bad, y'know. But she stays outa his
> way because I think she's really afraid of him.

She obviously saw the old man's stories to Joe during his formative years in a negative light. Even more striking to me, however, was the physical abuse that the little boy had endured at the hands of his mother. Jacie herself did not discount the importance of this aspect of his experience, though she did not necessarily view it as abuse. Instead she saw it as a mother's understandable efforts to control a willful and disobedient child. She believed it was the combination of maternal beatings, the old man's stories of sexual domination of women, and the early loss of the grandmother who was the one loving woman in his life that made the adult Joe hate the world. Her husband's ability to be "brainy" enough to hide his true nature when he chose also had roots in his childhood, she felt. The boy *knew* he had to depend on his mother for a period of time, that is, but as soon as he was old enough to be independent his true nature was revealed. And his true nature was that of a man who despised women:

> She used to tell me stories about how when he's small she used to have to beat him two or three times a day, four or five times a day, somethin' like that, you know. 'Cause he was really a rough *child* to *deal* with; she couldn't *cope* with him, y'know. And I was just *shocked* from the things that she said was goin' *on*. Like he'd run away and not come back [when he was] *young*, just four or five or six, and stuff like that. And hang around listenin' to this old man *talk*, and stuff like that. And those things are *embedded* in kids' minds when they're real young.

> I think all those bad things came back on him that he would relive; that they came smashin' down on him. And he was tryin' to get away from 'em and he couldn't get away from 'em and they was all smashin' down on him. Because his own sister and mother told me that when he left home at 17 he went up North and he was a *pimp;* he had prostitutes and stuff like that. So I add those things together [and look at] who he is, and *psychologically* he didn't trust women. He didn't have no kind of respect for 'em.

The beatings were not successful in getting young Joe to behave, however, and finally the mother devised a punishment that even Jacie described as being "dramatic." Still, she viewed the intervention of a grandmother not as rescue but as a form of "spoiling" the boy. It was the death of *this* woman that set the child on his path away from God, she thought. Away from God and toward the Devil and the working of roots. For the rest of his life *he* would control *women*, not the other way around:

> Now whether it was dislike for his mother [I don't know], now the only *dramatic* thing that I heard she did to him when he was comin' up back in the woods was *tie* him to a tree in the hot sun. 'Cause she couldn't control him. She said she was tryin' all kinds of *punishment*, y'know, to *stop* him! And she did do this; tie him in the *yard* to a tree in the sun without givin' him food *or* water. Must be all that day. In the sun.

> And the person that *got* him away from there that he was so crazy about was his grandmother. One of his grandmothers came, his father's mother, used to baby him up. And carry him on her back to church and stuff like that. So she got him away from there. She untied him, told 'em to get him down from there. To *him* that was his *savior!* The only righteous person in the *world!*

Oh, don't mention *God* to him, he'd go off! He say, "*God* takes the *good* peoples away, good people away." So he told me back then that his grandmother was good and God took her away. *Why* didn't He take his mother? And that tore him up psychologically bad; he said that God don't do nothin' but take *good* people away. I think he was sumpin' like nine, eight or nine or ten years old, sumpin' like that, when his grandmother *died*. And it hit him pretty strong. I think it really did hit him. And by her spoilin' him, *dramatically* spoilin' him, when she died it was over. Life was over.

I think he made some kind of *vow*. God told him he *had* to cling to his mother a little bit, 'cause that's the only one he had *left*. And so he didn't *show* all those things he was feelin' towards his mother, he just held 'em inside. So he got up to this age that he *become* a young man, to fool with women, run around with women, *he* just took things psychologically out with those *women!*

And now she was one of those women. Her belief that it was her duty to try and change him must have been further strengthened by the fact that it seemed her only hope. She could not leave if she *wanted* to, he told her. He had gone to a root man for a charm that would keep her there. The isolation continued. Sometime in the first year of her marriage some of her family came to visit but she dared not complain; he had warned her that if she was not careful about what she said he would kill them all. During their stay he was cold and silent but his hostility toward them was made evident. He pointedly left a cocked gun by the door and whenever one of them went to the outdoor privy he picked it up and accompanied them, silently waiting outside until they emerged. During one of these brief absences her mother asked why she did not leave him? But she told her mother that Joe was using roots against her and that he would not hesitate to use them against her loved ones as well. The visit was cut short and was not repeated. Now, in fact, most of her family were even afraid to write to her. She spent her days alone.

Before long she was pregnant with her first child but even that made no difference; she was not allowed to go to the clinic in town for prenatal care. But after much pleading Joe did relent and allow her grandmother to come for the birth:

My grandmother *did* come there, I finally got her, through a letter, to come. *Everybody* in my family was afraid of him. Everybody who knew he was foolin' with roots was afraid of him. My grandmother only [would come to help me]. She probably was afraid of him but she tried to stick by me, and came durin' the time I had my son. It was kind of a nervous period for her, also. But my mother is *dramatically* scared of him, y'know. She didn't even want to write no *letters* to me, because she was scared he was gonna put root on her *handwritin'*. *Anything* of yours they can use, *anything*. Clothing, writin', as long as it's yours, y'know. My mother thought that he could do that to her definitely, so she was dramatically afraid of him. He used it to try to make me *hate* my whole family. I didn't have nobody to correspond with me. I was in a mess; I was really in a mess.

The birth of Little Joe had been difficult, and the grandmother had warned Jacie's husband that Jacie should see a doctor if there were more babies. Perhaps she hoped that Jacie would be able to get help from a doctor or nurse if she was allowed to see them. More babies did follow, but Joe drove Jacie into town to the clinic and sat outside in the car waiting for her, shotgun in his lap. He warned her not to tell anybody anything; if she did he would blow her head off. And *if* he killed her the sheriff knew better than to mess with him; he would never spend a day in jail. She knew that that was true; he had been jailed on several occasions for assaulting others and always came home the next day, laughing. So she said not a word. And if the clinic personnel noticed the cuts and bruises they did not mention them; everybody knew Big Joe Burnes had a temper. Nobody wanted to mess with him.

The years passed and the isolation continued. Every morning before leaving, Big Joe would remind her of the roots that held her there and she made no attempts to leave. Who would help her? Where would she go with all the babies? And she could not be sure that he was *really* gone even in the daytime; sometimes she would look out of a window and see him slipping from tree to tree in the woods behind the cabin, his shotgun in his hand. Time passed and the older children began to go to school and were picked up by a schoolbus, leaving her at home with the little ones. Only a rare trip to town to buy supplies or school clothes for the children broke the monotony. It was on one of these occasions that she saw the flier for the shelter for battered women and committed the telephone number to memory. She did not expect to use it. But every life must have some glimmer of hope.

The only other bright spot was the occasional letter from a cousin in Michigan who, perhaps because of the great distance, was not afraid of Jacie's husband. Perhaps because she did not fear him he, in fact, seemed to fear *her.* Perhaps her courage came from using roots of her own! On one memorable occasion his own belief in magic worked to Jacie's advantage, in fact, when a small package from the Michigan cousin arrived addressed to her. She was allowed to open it and did so to find a Bible and an accompanying note telling her to persevere; God would surely help her sooner or later. Because of his hatred of religion Jacie was sure that her husband would throw the Bible away, but he was afraid to touch it. The cousin would have *expected* him to throw it out, he said, but he was not that stupid. He knew that she had had it rooted. So Jacie was allowed to keep it and found consolation in the hours spent in reading Scriptures.

But her fear of roots continued. Roots worked through handwriting, through photographs, through personal possessions, in food or drink. Only if she saw her husband give a child food or a sip of a drink did Jacie dare to take anything from him; he had never tried to harm them:

> Everything was just comin' to him so *easy,* and I was in a mess. And I wasn't *doin'* nothin' [but] takin' care of my people, tryin' to make *him* happy. And ever'thing was comin' to *me* in a bad way and I just wondered what was goin' *on!* It really affected me pretty bad, but I kept my head together 'cause I didn't drink. If I took a beer it would be there in a can; I wouldn't take nothin' from *him* that was open, y'know, unless I saw him give a sip to one of the kids. It can be done like that also, sumpin' you take from someone to eat or drink. Really, that was a thing that I really worried about; takin' things from him that was open. And most of the time I were locked in the house.

She was not simply a passive prisoner, however. She had fought back over the years and on a number of occasions had made plans to kill him to earn her release. But she was never able to bring herself to do so and it was *this,* finally, that convinced her that he had magical power over her. Otherwise why could she not shoot him dead when she had the opportunity? Why *couldn't* she cut his throat when she stood over his sleeping form, knife in hand? Surely no court would have convicted her! It must be roots. Or diabolical forces at work:

> I tried to kill *him* several times, and he had the nerve to tell me that I couldn't *hurt* him, y'know. That he had fixed my *pictures.* My grandmother sent me some pictures of me that was taken when I was in *high* school. And he say he took 'em and he had 'em fixed. And he believed in roots *strongly;* 'ever'body in South Carolina mostly believes in roots strongly. It was a total shock to me. See, I wasn't afraid of *nobody,* and I wasn't totally afraid of my husband at all until he mentioned this *root* to me. And that started it. Because I had fears completely, dramatically, about roots.

> When I saw that I couldn't even *cut* him when he was asleep or *shoot* him when he was standin' around and he had a gun around, then I *knew* that there was sumpin'. I had a gun when he was asleep; I had a knife right over his throat several times, more than one time. So I think that's why he took a *power* and worked it *stronger.* 'Cause he knew I was on the verge of killin' the first chance I got. And so any of those times he would come after me when *I* was asleep and hit me before I even open my eyes, or when I would have ahold of one of my *babies,* he would come in and I think that he was just *possessed,* like really with the *Devil.* He was really possessed. Like his eyes would change and turn red and all those kind of things.

> And even then he was afraid that I might try to get away and the root might not work and he locked me in the house. And I didn't *have* no friends; this was way back in the woods. And he *dared* anybody to *come* out there! The whole town, *two* small towns were afraid of him. This went on for years after years after years; I just couldn't count the years.

Years after years after years. In fact she had been married for more than ten years and had just had her fifth child when she made the first attempt to escape. After all of this time filled with the fear and the violence and the loneliness what did it take, finally, to empower her to try? It was another of her "little visions." She knew from her childhood experience that when she "saw" someone's death that it soon occurred—but *this* time the vision was of her *own* death. She was sleeping when there appeared before her a woman with a sad face, silently weeping. She woke up and she knew that the woman was herself, crying over her impending death. She realized that she had to take action.

A day or so later she talked Big Joe into leaving the keys to the car, something he had rarely done. School would soon start, she said, and the older children needed new shoes. He cursed but threw the keys at her; she could take the children and buy them shoes but that was *all* she was to do in town. And he would know if she did anything else and he would make her very sorry. After he left for work in his truck she quickly packed up all the children and drove away. But a neighbor woman who was sitting on her front porch saw her speed by with the car loaded with children and belongings, went inside and called Big Joe and told him. He in turn called the sheriff and told him that Jacie was "kidnapping" the children, then ran to his truck and followed her. She was almost at the county line when he overtook her and ran her off the road. The sheriff arrived soon after and despite her protestations suggested that she go home where she belonged; he could not look her in the eye when she begged him to help her. So she told him that her blood would be on his conscience when the inevitable happened, then helplessly drove back to her prison in the woods.

What about the weeping woman in the vision? Did it mean that she was doomed? A few days later there arrived a letter from Michigan, informing her that a beloved cousin of about her own age had recently died. It was obviously this cousin, not herself, who had been the woman in the vision. So life went on and her life resumed its customary pattern. Only now Big Joe watched her more closely than ever and she knew that she would never again be able to get the keys to the car. In a few months she was pregnant again, and with a sixth infant due she stopped thinking about trying to get away. It seemed hopeless. But when the new baby was only two months old she decided to try again. She learned that the old root doctor whom Big Joe had always patronized had died. At first she was even more depressed at this news; she had always heard that if this happened the hex could never be reversed. But then she recalled that her grandmother had been cured by a second root doctor after the death of the first; perhaps what *really* happened was a weakening of the hex at the death of the practitioner who had caused it. Perhaps she had a chance after all if she was able to go before Big Joe found another worker!

Still, the consequences of the old man's death might have remained purely speculative but for one other fact—her husband's behavior had become so extreme that she knew he would soon kill her anyway. She had nothing to lose by trying to get away. He had always been violent and had struck her many times in the past; she had known that this would continue. But in the past he had hit her only with his fists or with the bottles that he smashed in her face when she was sleeping. Her face and body were scarred from some of these beatings and she had suffered at least one more "dramatic" injury, a cracked jaw from a blow from his fist. But recently he had begun striking her with objects so large that she *knew* that his intent was murder; she was only alive because God was protecting her with a physical shield:

> What made me leave this time? The thing really was he was getting worse, really worse. He took a beam that hold houses, what hold houses up, and hit me across my back. And see, *God* put a shield around me. Oh, he done hit me with a gunbarrel and it *bent;* a rifle of cast steel, it *bent.* On my arm. It bent, it just bent. And across my shoulders, it just bent. I knew then that God was protecting me.

She interpreted this divine intervention to mean that God was giving her another chance to get away. And after all, God helps those who help themselves. She knew that she did not have much time; there was no possibility of formulating an elaborate plan. She would have to take her children and simply walk away. She did not tell them what they were going to do, fearing that one of them might let something slip to their father. Instead she anxiously waited through the hot August nights for that time when the moon would be only a sliver. The darkness would make their four-mile journey across the fields more difficult, but she did not dare lead her brood down the road. That would mean passing the house of the woman who had spied on them the first time. What if the woman was sitting on her porch and heard the baby cry? No, they would have to walk.

The fateful day came and Jacie knew that she had to pretend that it was like any other day in their lives. She gave her husband his breakfast, silently listened to his abuse, and calmly told him goodbye. It was a Saturday and she prayed that he would follow his usual pattern and stay in town drinking and gambling until late. The hours passed slowly until it was time to give the children their supper; she fed them more than usual as she was not sure when they would eat again. She bathed them and put them to bed, then sat and waited through the long summer evening. It was dark, finally, and she woke the older children. They must be very quiet, she whispered; they were going to play a game. Jacie picked up the still-sleeping littlest ones and quietly told Little Joe, tall and strong for his 12 years, to carry his four-year-old brother. The other two children followed behind, giggling at this strange and unexpected adventure. They stepped off the porch and began to walk across the fields.

The trip seemed endless. At first she jumped each time a small animal rustled through the vegetation but nothing happened; there was no outcry from an outraged Joe. So they kept on walking slowly, slowly; she and Little Joe burdened down with the smallest children, the other two stumbling over the rows in the dark. It was close to dawn when they finally arrived at the small house that was their destination. Jacie knew that the family who lived here were God-fearing people and hoped that they would allow her to use the telephone. She admonished the tired children to be quiet and knocked on the door. Her knock was answered by the man of the house. She explained her plight and he only nodded; everyone knew about Big Joe Burnes and his temper. He gestured toward the phone while his wife quickly prepared a meal for the sleepy children.

Jacie had memorized the number of the shelter for battered women and made her call. She gave directions to the house and said that it would be necessary to come quickly; her good samaritans would be in danger themselves if anyone saw her and her children there. Before long two cars pulled up into the yard and with a quick "God bless you," for their hosts, Jacie and the children were driven away. The first part of the journey was over. They stayed two or three days at the shelter. Jacie had called her family as soon as possible but it would be a day or so before anyone could come to get them. This time was almost the worst of all, she said later; although the women at the shelter insisted that they were safe she was fearful that her husband would somehow learn their whereabouts. What if someone *had* seen them crossing the fields that night? What if Big Joe had gone to the home of the couple who had helped her and threatened them into telling what they knew? What if his knowledge of *roots* somehow led him to her? But the time passed and at last a call came; her family was waiting for them in a shopping mall just over the county line. She and the children were hidden in a car and an old truck and driven there without incident. She got out of the car and for the first time in years she saw some of her own kin; she had never expected to see anyone she loved again.

The immense power that her fear of her husband's magical control had over her life is dramatically illustrated by what happened next. The children clambered into the waiting van, and she climbed quietly in behind them. Her mother, her sister, and her brother hugged her and then excitedly began questioning her about the escape. How had it happened? How had she managed it? Did she think that Big Joe was on their trail? But she was unable to speak, overwhelmed by the emotions that she was feeling. And especially by what she was *seeing*. Finally her mother asked why she did not respond to their questions— and what was it she was looking at in such a strange way? Quite literally she was watching the personification of the hex leave her body where it had held dominion for so many years:

> I got in the van and I was just choked up, I couldn't say nothin'. I saw my mother and my sister and my brother and they was talkin' *down* to me, and askin' questions, and I couldn't say nothin'. Let me tell you, after all those years. And I looked that way and my mother, she said, "What you lookin' at—don't you hear me talkin' to you?" My mother was talkin' to me.

> *I saw a shadow leave me,* went down those steps, stopped, and looked back like this at me and went off. And that shadow went off, tall-built shadow that left me, and it went off that step and disappeared into thin air. I started talkin'. Didn't stop. I done stayed up all that night, talkin'.

As the tall shadow stopped to look back at her before it stepped off the van it nodded to her once, as if to say goodbye. I had goosebumps, listening—what *was* the shadow, I asked? "It was that *root,* that voodoo, that hex!" And now it was gone.

They quickly drove to the family home in Georgia where the other members of the clan greeted the newcomers excitedly; none had ever expected to see Jacie again. Although she was greatly relieved to be out of South Carolina at last, Jacie continued to be uneasy. Big Joe would *expect* her to go home, she thought. And it would not be long before he came to get them. Obviously she would have to take the children and go. Her family did not demur; they too, were afraid of what Big Joe might do to them in retaliation for helping her escape. Again it was the cousin from Michigan who offered a helping hand; *she* was not afraid of Jacie's husband. Why not bring the children to Lansing? It was decided. Bus tickets were purchased and soon Jacie and her children were on their way North.

The first weeks in Lansing were spent in finding a place to live, seeking out health care so that the children could have their school physicals, and entering the older ones in school. After that Jacie did some things for herself, a luxury after the long years of isolation. She was an extremely intelligent woman who had been so long deprived any sort of intellectual stimulation that she was anxious to "catch up" with all she had missed. She obtained a library card and read avidly, began a journal describing her past experiences, and tried her hand at writing poetry. She looked forward to taking a course herself at the local community college. As time passed with no word from Joe she began finally to relax a bit; perhaps he would not come after them after all. Perhaps they were finally safe.

A year or so passed. The children were brought to the clinic regularly for checkups and when they suffered minor illnesses. But as Little Joe entered adolescence she began to be concerned about his behavior. She still had a good deal of control over the babies and the smaller children, but he was now 13 and he began to "get out of hand." There were far too many ways for children to get into trouble in the city. There had been no temptations in the country, she said. They had been 30 miles from town and the children had no playmates; none of the neighbors had dared let their children come to their home. Now they were in a rundown section of a strange city where unemployed men and women loitered on the streets; even worse were the boys and girls not much older than Little Joe who had dropped out of school. For the first time in his life Little Joe saw children "running wild," as his mother put it—and he loved it. Soon *he* began skipping school, coming home late for dinner, and talking back to Jacie. Even more frightening to her, however, was the fact that he had begun hitting his younger brothers and sisters.

The next time she came to the clinic with some of the smaller children she confided to their physician, a third-year resident, that she did not know what to do about her oldest child. She had less and less control over him all the time; she tried spanking him but he only laughed. Would Jacie be willing to have him seen by one of the psychology interns? Yes, she would. But there was one problem; all of the interns were men and she was not sure she wanted to talk to a man about her child's problems. (Jacie had so little trust in men that she had specifically asked for and been assigned a woman resident for her children; she had been very pleased at the care this young woman had provided for her family over the past year.) A compromise was reached; she would bring Little Joe for evaluation if I was also present in the room when the psychologist was there. For the next few weeks I sat in on these sessions with Jacie, Little Joe, and the psychologist. Little Joe was quiet and polite during these times, and responded to most questions with a smile and a shrug.

One day Jacie came in quite upset and asked if she could see me privately before our hour together. Little Joe's behavior was getting worse, not better, she said, and he had begun to remind her of his father. Worse yet, she feared roots again. After more than a year in Michigan she had begun to feel safe from her husband, but now she began to wonder—could he be influencing his oldest son in some way? She had sent the children's school pictures to their paternal grandmother and perhaps she should not have done that. She had been careful not to include an address, but suppose Big Joe's mother had sent the pictures on to *him?* He might have done something to the picture of his oldest son. She knew that I understood about roots and it was all right to ask what I thought.

There would have been no point in trying to dissuade her of her belief and I did not try. I said only, "But could he do it from so far away?" He couldn't hurt *her* from such a distance, she replied; her faith was too strong. But she didn't know about the boy. After all, "He *looks* just like him and now he's beginning to *act* just like him!" And, she went on, her husband "would do just about anything to get even." It occurred to me that irrespective of what she saw to be the cause of her son's behavior, it could not be helpful for him to be viewed as the incarnation of the man she so hated and feared. It next occurred to me that I had absolutely no notion of what should be done about it. So I asked her permission to tell the psychology intern about her fears, telling her that I thought it important that he know. She had come to trust him over the last weeks and agreed that he could be told.

The subject of roots was never mentioned to Little Joe in that day's session, however. The one thing that I remember of the conversation was the boy's answer to the psychologist's query of whether he admired his father? "Oh yeah," had been the reply. "Everyone's afraid of him!" Neither the psychologist nor I knew at the time that that was to be the final session; Jacie told me later that though she knew the psychology intern was trying to be helpful, she didn't think it would "really work" with her son. In any case, it was soon out of her hands, as over the weekend Little Joe was implicated with some older boys in a stolen-bicycle ring. The police had already been to the house on one or two other occasions to inquire about Little Joe, who had been seen with other children around the scenes of fires in abandoned houses. And there had been the problems at school: truancy, schoolyard fights, disruptive behavior in the classroom. His case was turned over to the juvenile court system and he was transferred to a school for children with behavioral problems.

This latter move was one that was very disturbing to Jacie. How, she asked, could he be expected to learn to behave if he was in a school where *all* the children were problems? All they would do was teach him how to be even worse than he already was! What he *really* needed was to be with good kids who knew how to behave, she protested, not with those who would be sure to lead him into worse trouble. And in a few months, in fact, he proved to be too much for the teachers at the special school as well. He was sent to a facility for disturbed adolescents some miles away; now he would not be coming home at the end of the day. He was allowed to come for home visits only on occasional weekends and, as Jacie had no car and there was no bus service to the place, weeks went by when she did not see her oldest son. This was entirely unnatural, she thought. What kind of people took a young boy away from his mother? For the first time she began to talk of how much better things were "down home." There they *understood* the importance of having your family around when times were hard or things went wrong.

I saw Jacie and her children for the last time over the Christmas holidays. Little Joe had been allowed to come for a short visit but was due to go back to the juvenile home in a day or so. Jacie was very upset over this and again talked about the importance of keeping the children of a family together. She was bitter at what she saw as the harsh treatment of Little Joe by the people in the justice system; if he ended up in prison, she said, *they* would have contributed to it!

She now believed that it had been a mistake to have come all the way to Michigan, even though it had seemed the only course open to her at the time. One of these days, she said, she thought she would "just pack them all up and go home."

And so she did. She had asked me to loan her some magazines and a few days later I drove over to the house only to find it empty. She had apparently seized the opportunity to leave before Little Joe could be taken back to the home. I stopped to see if her cousin knew what had happened, but even she had not been told that Jacie was going. She was not surprised that she had done so, however; she knew how unhappy Jacie had been in recent months. She supposed that she had gone back to her family in Georgia; both of us hoped that she had not gone back to Big Joe. I never heard from her again.

It is likely that many readers will be caught up by the drama of Jacie's story yet still wonder how she, an intelligent woman, could possibly believe in the power of the "roots" that kept her a virtual prisoner for so long. And how could a woman who spoke so easily of psychological factors speak just as easily of magical practices? Such a view fails to consider the importance of cultural beliefs in shaping "reality"—and if one of the functions of a belief system is to make sense of experience, then it must be recognized that Jacie's worked for her. The theme of domestic violence has appeared in various guises in folk tales around the world (Ucko 1991), so perhaps we should not be surprised that Jacie's "story" differs from the "story" of wife abuse that is more familiar in American society. She had *not* internalized the cause for her suffering: that somehow she must have behaved in a manner that brought on the violent behavior; that somehow she deserved it. Instead, she externalized her misfortune; if she was powerless it was because her husband was using a power stronger than *any* human. It was the bad roots that prevented her from leaving, not some weakness within herself.

Help was also orchestrated from without: When Big Joe struck her with a gunbarrel God put up the shield that saved her. And when her situation became intolerable God sent her a message in a vision. "Go now," it seemed to say, "or it will be too late!" Only then was she able to leave. Only then did the tall dark shadow that personified the years of control finally recognize that it had been vanquished, nod civilly to her, and walk down the steps of the van into the dusty streets of a small Southern town.[1]

Notes

1. Sadly, the shadow eventually found her again. Her fear of Big Joe and his roots proved not so strong as her feeling that the family should be reunited. More than five years after she fled the city with her children, I learned what had become of her from one of her Lansing cousins. She had hired him to drive her to South Carolina a year before she had gone for good, he told me. She had

met with Big Joe but refused to tell him where she was living with the children. He had been enraged at this and reportedly said to her, "If I ever see your face again I'll kill you!" She had returned to Lansing, but despite his threat, she took her family and returned to him some months later. The following year another child was born; two years later, yet another. This last baby, however, Big Joe claimed was not his and he shot her. The shotgun blast missed her heart but "messed her up inside" so that she is unable to use the left side of her body. She is now living in Georgia with her mother—the older woman is at last getting to care for her daughter—and her daughter's children. Jacie's husband fled after the attempted murder and has not been found. The cousin shook his head as he told me this; "none of us could believe she went back to him." (East Lansing, Michigan; 1992)

2

You'd Be Surprised What You Can Do with What You Have

What was taken by outsiders to be slackness, slovenliness, or even generosity was in fact a full recognition of the legitimacy of forces other than good ones. They did not believe doctors could heal—for them, none had ever done so. They did not believe death was accidental—life might be, but death was deliberate. They did not believe Nature was ever askew—only inconvenient. Plague and drought were as "natural" as springtime. If milk could curdle, God knows robins could fall. The purpose of evil was to survive it and they determined (without ever knowing they had made up their minds to do it) to survive floods, white people, tuberculosis, famine and ignorance. They knew anger well but not despair, and they didn't stone sinners for the same reason they didn't commit suicide—it was beneath them.

—Toni Morrison, *Sula*

The fact that she had been dead for 40 years was no barrier to the mother of Olive Parsons when she knew she was needed; she simply slipped into her daughter's spare room one night and lay down on the bed for a nap. Olive, past 80 now herself, became aware of her mother's presence when she got up to get a drink of water around midnight. She had been unable to sleep in the heat of the Arizona night, consumed as she was with "worriation" about the recent return to town of a newly divorced granddaughter. She felt the young woman would be unable to care for *herself*, let alone the small children for whom she was responsible. The old lady looked after the children in the afternoon and knew full well that they were not "raised." This she blamed on everything having been made too easy for her granddaughter; the girl had never really had to work and her college education had not properly fitted her for the realities of life. Now she was divorced. No telling if her former husband would help her out, though the courts had said that he must. What if he did not? How would she care for herself? And how on earth would she care for those spoiled children?

A drink of ice water might help her to sleep, Olive thought. But as she went past the closed door of the company bedroom she suddenly stopped. She knew, absolutely *knew* that her long-dead mother was in there, lying on the bed. She waited for a moment, holding her breath, hoping for some sort of sign telling her to open the door and go in. When none came she tiptoed on into the kitchen to get that drink of water. She carefully opened the refrigerator door and took out the bottle as quietly as she could. As she stood and sipped her water she pondered her next move. Should she wait to see if her mother would come out of the room? Should *she* open the door and go in? Again she tiptoed to the closed door and waited outside, longing to see and speak to her mother after so many years. Perhaps she could open the door just a crack and take a peek! But it was so quiet that she decided her mother must be sleeping. "Aw naw, I better not bother her," she said to herself, "she probably needs her rest!" Silently she went back into her own bedroom and got back into bed. Soon she was asleep.

Her mother was gone when she looked into the spare room the next morning, and Olive was happy that the bed had been made up with her prized tie-quilt. Her mother had slept on her best. She was still thrilled and happy over the nocturnal visit when she told me about it a day or so later. "We had *two* parents, but only *one* of them raised us," she said. "She sure raised us; my daddy, he didn't. He *fed* us, but she raised us!" It was being "raised" that had helped Olive herself survive as a young mother left alone with small children many many years before—and, she recalled, there had been a visit from *both* deceased parents to that younger self as well. They had returned in "a dream, a vision or sumpin'," wordlessly doing laundry in an iron kettle over a roaring fire, literally demonstrating to their troubled daughter that she could make a living by taking in washing and ironing. And so she had. Her mother had come back now to let her know that her granddaughter, with guidance, would be all right. The worriation was gone. (Tucson, Arizona; 1970)

Tom and Anna Perry lived in a small house just a few blocks away from Olive Parsons. The two had a reputation in the neighborhood for knowing a lot about healing and for being willing to share this expertise. Anna knew many home remedies and treated most of her family's illnesses herself; although she deplored the fact that many of the plants and herbs she had known back in East Texas were not available in Arizona, she had learned to make do with substitutes. She had been given ground calamus root rolled up in bread balls as a child and had given the same thing to her own children, for example, "to keep them from getting sick." But calamus root does not grow in the desert so she simply bought vitamin tablets instead for Terry, her young foster child. She did not see the vitamins as *better*, just available.

She was quite excited that a shop selling herbal teas had recently opened a few blocks away. She was unacquainted with many of the products there but felt that they must be good because they were "natural." Anna was too shy to ask the proprietor as to their possible health-related uses, however; she still smarted from the time a local pharmacist had laughed when she asked for buzzard grease. But the couple's second son, Gabriel, had just returned from a tour of duty as a marine sergeant in Vietnam, bringing with him an illustrated encyclopedia as a gift for his parents. Anna had unexpectedly—and happily—discovered that there were drawings of many medicinal plants in it, as well as descriptions of which ailments they had formerly been used to treat. She was now systematically paging through the book looking for these drawings, ignoring the "formerly" in the descriptions, and carefully writing down the names to see if they might be available at the new shop on the corner.

Tom's contribution to healing was his ability to do "rubbing" for family members and neighbors, a talent based on the observations he had made during a time when he worked in the office of a chiropractor. This service, he always hastened to assure me, was without charge. But Tom and Anna did not exclude the use of other alternatives in their search for health and healing. Both of them at times requested prayer from the evangelist who lived next door; it was said that Sister Erma had been given "the gift" of healing in a vision. At other times each visited a physician; everybody, said Anna, ought to go to the doctor at least *once* a year. The couple were not, in fact, all that different from the other people in the neighborhood whom I had come to know during the year that I gathered data for my dissertation: It was obvious that there was decision-making about the proper treatment of health problems, including how and by whom. The trouble was it did not seem to me to have any recognizable pattern; certainly it did not have the pattern that *I* would use.

One day toward the end of the time that I had allotted for doing interviews I decided to attack the problem head-on. No more indirect questions! I chose the 54-year-old Tom because he and Anna seemed genuinely interested in helping me with my "big paper." Surely, I thought, he would be willing to tell me if I was on the wrong track. So I took out the familiar notebook and said, "Mr. Perry, there is one thing I don't understand. How do you know that it's time to quit using home remedies and go to the doctor instead?" He smiled patiently. Then he pointed to his chest: "If you have a pain in your heart. That is a very bad place to get a pain." A long pause. "Now, write that down on your paper." He nodded gravely and continued rocking in his chair. Chest pain! *I* nodded happily. He not only *knew* when to go to a doctor but his "referral system," according to my own ideas, was appropriate! Chest pain is indeed a serious matter. But there was more to come. "That," he said firmly, "was for *them!*" He leaned forward. "Now, dear," he said, waving away my notebook, "if you ever *do* get a pain in your heart get yourself some azefitty. Take a piece about as big as the end of your little finger; roll it in a ball, drop it in hot water and drink it. That pain will go away. You do *that* if you ever need to!" He nodded again.

I was speechless. Now I recalled *why* Anna had said that it was important to go to the doctor once a year; she thought that it would tell her if her own home remedies were doing the job. She had gone out of the room when her husband mentioned "azefitty" (asafoetida) and now came back carrying a quart jar of whiskey.[1] She had dasafoetida in the whiskey and added a handful of garlic buds for good measure. She took a teaspoonful of this mixture every other day to "keep healthy," she said, and suggested that I do the same. Didn't I want a taste? I took one whiff and politely refused; I did not tell her that from the smell I figured it would also take the varnish off the furniture. I thanked them both, took my notebook, and went away.

I had thought that my undergraduate degree and three years of graduate courses in anthropology had prepared me to be objective in my research. But I had underestimated the importance of my own background in coloring my views, especially the years that I had spent working as a medical technologist in clinical laboratories. Though I recognized the importance of my informants' cultural background in influencing *their* ideas, I did not yet see that "scientific medicine" was part of my own cultural baggage. I still believed that it was "right" in a way that "traditional medicine," however interesting, could never be. I still presumed that for most illness episodes the majority of people, irrespective of cultural beliefs, would make a "logical" progression from what can be treated at home to what should be treated by the doctor. I still thought that this would include a progression from trials of home remedies to over-the-counter preparations to the doctor's prescription, which I saw as "real" medicine. I had, in fact, learned a valuable lesson that day; it just wasn't the one I had expected. And clearly I still had a lot to learn. (Tucson, Arizona; 1971)

It was 15 years later and very far from Arizona. Another woman was sharing with me her beliefs about curing. "*I* was the doctor in our family," Bernita Washington said as she watered the *Aloe vera* plant on her window sill, "with ten children I had to be! And a pretty good one, too, if I do say so myself," she continued, pleased that her "medicine plant" now had enough new sprouts so that one could be sent home with her visitor. She told me that it has that name because it is good for just about *anything;* she had even learned from a neighbor that a company in Nashville sells aloe juice that will cure cancer! She had not used it as a cancer cure but she did know that the sap is especially good for burns, adding that she also sometimes breaks off a piece of her plant to rub the sap on her forehead when she has one of her "migram" headaches:

> Aloe vera plant, which in the stores is called "medicine plant." O.K., you take the aloe vera plant and you can use it for *headaches*. Clip a piece off and rub all of that what's inside of there, what's inside the plant, just rub it on your head. Now *me,* myself, I have what you call migram headaches and I *never* have found, doctors never have found a

cure for it, you know. But, you can *use* it for that. But sometime it
doesn't work as *well* as *peach tree leaves.* A peach tree that you gather
peaches from, you use the leaves. You pluck the leaves from the trees,
you put them into a rag, a cloth, whatever. And you bind it on your
forehead and tie it around there and just wear it. (Lansing, Michigan;
1986)

She had a personal physician who had prescribed medication for
these headaches but, although she had the prescription filled, she
seldom took it. What she would *really* like was to have a peach tree
in her yard just as she did when she lived in rural Mississippi;
binding the leaves around her aching head was the best remedy she
ever found. But she lived in a run-down rental house in a Michigan
city now, and though she knows that there must be medicinal trees
and plants around, "you'd probably have to go miles and miles and
miles out in the country to find them." And even then they might
be "polluted."

She was warming up to her subject now, commenting that cures
for most ailments can be found right in your own kitchen. She
doesn't have to have peach leaves to bind around her head; salt and
cornmeal will do as well:

For migram headaches, doctors never found a cure for it, so what *I* do,
you go in your *kitchen* and you get I would say about a tablespoonful
of *meal,* what you cook with. O.K., you *brown* the meal, you put it
into a pan and you brown the meal. And you puts about a fourth-tea-
spoonful of salt with the browned meal and you can also bind *that* on
your head. And that is really good; that is a good cure for it.

She had recently heard that Ben-Gay ointment is good to rub on
your forehead for headaches but she had not yet tried this. Still, she
thought that it would probably work. After all, she pointed out, the
TV ads say that the product will take the pain out of sore joints, so
why wouldn't it draw the pain from your head as well? She would
buy some the next time she had some money.

Peach leaf poultice; salt and cornmeal from the kitchen; an over-the-
counter pharmaceutical preparation used far differently than intended
by the manufacturer; a prescription painkiller. It occurred to me once
again that Bernita, who for most of her life has lacked access to
professional medical care, actually had several more choices for her
headaches and other ailments than did I—at least she had several more
choices that she was willing to *use* than did I. And again I asked, as
I have asked many people like her over the years, why she didn't *take*
the medication her physician has prescribed? "You really don't know
what's in it" was the reply. And she did not trust what she did not
know. Sometimes doctors give you the *wrong* medicine, she said. Just
because it's good for one person doesn't mean it's good for everyone.
And sometimes—*often*times, she thought—a doctor's medicine is "too

strong." She much preferred to rummage around in her own kitchen for help; then she knew what she was taking! She referred to her self-treatments as "giving God a chance to heal." People do far too much "running to the doctor" as it is. Not Bernita. The few prescription medicines that she had were kept in her purse; safe, she hoped, from some younger family members who used drugs. And the medicine cabinet in the bathroom contained only a tube of acne cream belonging to a teenaged daughter. (Lansing, Michigan; 1986)

"Oh, that plant is so *pretty!*" Marya Smith was in my office at the university. Marya, who is Bernita's oldest daughter, was herself a mother at the age of 16 and, by 33, a grandmother. We had met a year or so earlier when she accompanied *her* oldest daughter, Josie, to the pediatrics clinic where Josie's infant son, Mikey, was receiving well-baby care. There had been some conflict between mother and daughter on that afternoon about the treatment of Mikey's thrush (oral moniliasis) infection. "*I* am going to use *modern* medicine," Josie had said. "Mama isn't going to use any of her 'slavery medicine' on *my* baby!" Marya had only smiled. Things had been very different for her when Josie herself had been born; Marya had been glad for the help and advice on "those 'old-timey' remedies" she had gotten from her own mother.

We began talking and when I learned that she was quite familiar with traditional Southern birth and postpartum practices I asked her if she would be willing to talk about these sometime to students in a seminar on midwifery. She agreed and on this day she has just finished telling us her own experiences of pregnancy and birth "way out in the country." She and her ten siblings had all been delivered at home by a midwife, and so had five of her own six children. Hadn't she been glad to have that last baby born in the hospital, the students had asked? But no, it was that hospital birth that she found the most frightening, she told us; and the hospital was every bit as awful as she had expected. She agrees with her mother that the old ways are usually best.

Now we are in my office and she is admiring a plant on my desk. As she has refused to take any payment for coming to the seminar I ask her if she would like to take it home? "Oh yes," she quickly says, "I've been needing more plants. Plants are so *useful!*" Having never thought of a pink African violet as anything other than decorative I ask what she means; she replies that houseplants, by virtue of being delicate and alive, can be used as protection from evil. Should someone wish you harm and work magic against you—"using that hoodoo," as she puts it—then the evil can actually enter your home. But if there are *plants* in the house these will die first, and the strength of the evil will be dissipated before it reaches its human target. If plants *continue* to die, of course, then the evil is still there and countersteps must be taken.

Of all of Bernita's ten living children Marya is the one who also suffers the blinding headaches that afflict her mother. But not all headaches are the same, Marya told me later, and if doctors don't understand why they occur then there is always the possibility that they are "unnatural"—caused, that is, by the malignant intentions of another:

> Well, when you go to the doctor and the doctor can't *heal* you, and not able to tell you what's wrong with you, you know it's not natural. 'Cause a natural sickness, a doctor'll be able to tell you what it is. Ulcers, gallstones or nerves, migrams; you know. You have headaches, now; they should be able to tell you what cause headaches. Stress, migrams, whatever. Now you doesn't *have* migrams, you doesn't have stress, and you come up with headaches—and you have 'em over and over and over and they can't do anything to stop 'em. Well, you know it's not natural. Sometimes there's people, God love 'em so much that He'll show 'em sumpin's wrong; that they gotta do sumpin' about it. I believed that the Lord loved me and it wasn't time for me to go. And He let me see what was wrong with me, so I could get help.

And the doctors could *not* do anything to stop them—or indeed even *explain* them! She underwent the most thorough and technologically-sophisticated testing that a nearby medical school had to offer only to be told that they could find "no reason" for her suffering. Marya's unease with the doctors' failure to discover the cause of her problem is not surprising, of course, nor is such unease merely idiosyncratic (Torrey 1972:13–16). As Brody and Yates (1990) have recently noted, "the ability to name something implies the ability to control it. This is true both in magical belief systems, in which words and names have their own intrinsic powers, and in scientific belief systems, in which the power to classify and label is seen as the forerunner of the power to understand and to manipulate."

And God did let her see that the illness that began with one particular series of headaches was unnatural and she then knew that she must go elsewhere for relief; she was finally successfully treated by a healer in Grand Rapids. She might not have had to undergo the long and frustrating search for help, she later said, had she known beforehand what "the power" will do to plants. When one of her own house plants had died under strange circumstances she did not see it as the warning it was:

> O.K, now, when I taken sick, when this lady did this to me, it was Sunday. Tuesday, I had this big old green plant, it was in my living room. When I went to bed that night I looked at my plant, I put the light out and I went upstairs to bed. The plant was green and pretty, big old plant. And that mornin' I came downstairs and it was brown, it had *cooked,* just that brown, overnight. They say if you got a green plant in your house the power will burn the plant up, but if you keep aputtin' plants in, green plants, it cannot get to you until it burn the plant up. Then it's really controllin' *you,* then. Can't no plant live in your house under that. Keep aburnin' the plants, [it'll] keep away from

you. I heard it afterwards, after the plant was burnt up. I was tellin' a lady about how my plant burnt up and we got to talkin'. And I told her about what happened to me and she said, "*That's* why your plant burnt up. Always keep your green plants in your house."

Marya takes no chances now; she has never since gone without a houseful of plants. My African violet was taken home to add to the leafy armor already in her kitchen window, its frilly pink blossoms alert to the slightest nuance of unnatural activity. (Lansing, Michigan; 1983)

Marya had had headaches all her life without attributing them to sorcery; what was different this time? In the view of this outsider she had endured a number of difficult life experiences in a relatively short time and it was this series of misfortunes—coupled with the failure of orthodox medical care to help her—that made her come to interpret her problem as the result of the actions of a woman who wished her harm. Things had begun to go badly at a time when everything in her life had seemed so positive: Her five children were in school; she had a handsome new husband; she had a good job at a local car-manufacturing plant. Her parents and all of her brothers and sisters had finally been brought up from Mississippi to live nearby; she had recently bought a house of her own. This latter was her pride and joy, the down payment possible because she had "hit the numbers."

But she was struck in the head in an accident at the plant where she worked and after that the headaches began to come more frequently, a fact which she attributed to the accident. But the company doctors did not agree; none of their tests revealed anything that could explain them. She was sent to the medical school for a complete workup—including a brain scan—and no organic cause for her pain was found. This failure of the doctors to find a reason was particularly worrisome and she began to wonder if something else—something sinister—might be involved. In any case she could no longer work and when her unemployment benefits ran out she was unable to keep up her mortgage payments. The beloved house was gone. Soon her marriage was placed under a severe strain as well; her husband had been married before but had been separated from his first wife for a number of years. He simply assumed that she had gotten a divorce; she had not. On hearing of his remarriage, in fact, she sent word that not only was he a bigamist but that it was about time he began paying some child support! That wasn't so bad, Marya said, anyone can make a mistake—what troubled her more was the fact that he was unwilling to take steps to remedy the situation—and he had "lost his nature" (become impotent) as well. She had noticed a woman at church looking admiringly at him on several occasions; could *she* somehow have something to do with the troubles?

There was worse to come: Her oldest son, Timmy, dropped out of school, began using drugs and sustained permanent brain damage after the ingestion of angel dust (PCP). When he took his prescribed medication he was quiet and calm; he frequently did *not* take it, however, and then he was violent; on one occasion he had broken a beer bottle over the head of his elderly grandfather. Marya was afraid to leave him home alone with the younger children. The headaches continued. Then a final blow: She had always regretted that she had not completed high school because she became pregnant with her oldest daughter, Josie, at the age of sixteen. Now Josie had come home to announce that *she* was pregnant and was going to drop out of school. The headaches came with increasing frequency.

Marya continued to take the pain medication that had been prescribed for her even though she had lost faith in the physician who had ordered it—it helped with the symptoms, she said, whatever their cause.[2] And she decided that some changes in lifestyle were in order as well: After the loss of her house she believed that God was trying to send her a message about the sin of gambling and she was "saved." Even religious services offered danger as well as solace, however, and what was ostensibly help for yet another headache proved to be just the opposite—it allowed "that lady" to slip her magical poison. Marya had been in church one day and had forgotten her medication; could an usher locate some aspirin for her? But to her horror he obtained it from the woman who had been eyeing Lacey, her husband. Nor was there any way that Marya could publicly refuse to take the pills; that would have been tantamount to an accusation of sorcery. Mere hours later new symptoms began: "It was that Sunday afternoon I started gettin' sick," she says. "The headache left but the nausea in the stomach started and I got worse and worse and worse, and it went on for some weeks. I was sick so long; I don't even remember how long." But one afternoon when she was lying in her bed—nearly too weak to talk and unable to keep food on her stomach—God sent her "a vision," showing her that the woman had deliberately harmed her with the "aspirin." She knew then that she needed the help of a different kind of doctor, and the next day she was driven to see the Reverend Doctor Moses Hastings in Grand Rapids.

And what did the Reverend Hastings do for her that the physicians with their extensive physical evaluations could not? He carefully listened to her fears and made recommendations that both removed the trouble and threw up a protective barrier of faith around her; certainly he did not tell her that there was no reason for her symptoms. He knew all about unnatural illnesses and agreed that that was what had happened; she had been right to seek him out. "He said that this lady had put somethin'—wasn't aspirin—was somethin' that she gave me and my inside [stomach] lining had got thin as tissue paper. And I hadn't got to 'im soon as I did, I would have died. So he gave me some stuff to take for seven mornings. The first day I felt better [and] after seven days I was well." The ingredients of his remedy are simple enough: white milk and white wine and the white of an egg, beaten together with a drop of vanilla for flavor; this would help to line the dangerously thinned lining of her stomach.

But his treatment addressed more than her physical condition: He also gave her sweet-smelling salts for ritual baths to cleanse her system of the curse. He told her to pray for healing, suggested a particular set of scriptural readings and admonished her to sleep with a Bible opened to the 23d Psalm under her mattress. In contrast to the diagnostic testing of her physicians, then, he recommended a combination of symbolically charged behaviors involving all the senses: the oral remedy with its soothing white ingredients; the sweet odor of the purifying baths; the recital of prayers; the reading of Scriptures. And working not just in the daytime but by night as well: "Yea, though I walk through the valley of the shadow of death, I will fear no evil," the Psalm reads, "for Thou art with me." It must have been comforting to know that these words of spiritual power were radiating up through the mattress into her sleeping body. And the Reverend Doctor Hastings had some old-fashioned advice to offer as well: He took into account her social situation and strongly suggested that she find another church to attend.

At the time that he cured Marya the Reverend Hastings was neither a full-time healer nor a full-time minister; he had worked for more than 40 years with the U.S. Postal Service and was nearing retirement. When I met him several years later he had retired and was able to devote more time to his healing ministry. His busy practice was largely based, in fact, on the large numbers of individuals who, like Marya, had failed to find satisfaction in the orthodox medical system:

> Most of 'em come, 90, 95 percent of 'em come in, they just done spun out runnin' to the doctor. And [I'm] just they last hope when they come in. They done spun out of *money,* you know. Don't know of no other way. And I'm always around; always in service somewhere. That's the way it goes.

How did he decide what treatments to use, I asked, especially if the doctors seemed unable to help? Well, he replied, he depended on the advice of "the Spirit":

> Sometime you'd be with a person or person'd come to you for help, and medicine don't seem to do any good. The Spirit of itself will tell you what to go get! And sometime I'll be surprised to myself! But you get it and it tell you how to fix it up. And you take it and [sickness] be gone. You hear the Spirit atalkin' to you, inside. Well, say you got headache. Maybe you been takin' aspirin or something like that, and you been havin' this headache for two or three days. O.K., you come and say, "Well, I've been havin' headache." Maybe a little prayer, you know, just like that, and I'll lay my hand on 'em. And the Spirit will say, "Well,"—you can hear that Spirit talkin'—say, "Well, get some

bakin' soda; mix up some bakin' soda, put it in some warm water."
Soon as you drink it, it's gone like that!

He did not need to advertise for clients, he said. He was kept quite
busy enough. But "there's no need to brag about it. Just thank God
whatever you do; we're here to work for 'im. Whatever He take and
use us to do His work, we ought to be just willing to do it. 'Cause
sooner or later we *all* gonna pass." (Grand Rapids, Michigan; 1987)

Some individuals seem able to avoid contact with both physicians
and the alternative healers who are available. One such woman is
Bernita Washington's neighbor Janine Jackson, who moved to Michigan from her native South Carolina 30 years ago. Mrs. Jackson is a
64-year-old widow who certainly does not lack access to medical care.
A doctor has his office right across the street from her home and
there is a hospital only blocks away. She is the grandmother of
several infants who receive primary care at the pediatrics clinic at
that hospital, in fact. Or, to be more accurate, who receive *some* of
their care there. Though she recognizes the value of "baby shots" to
prevent some health problems she herself treats her grandchildren
for a number of minor infantile ailments. "You'd better go talk to
my mom about that," one son had recently told the bemused pediatrics resident who had inquired about the Vaseline-witchhazel ointment used to treat his daughter Annie's diaper rash.

I went to Janine's home on that particular afternoon to talk with
her about her involvement in the health care of her grandbabies. We
discussed her household cures for problems familiar to all the pediatrics residents at the hospital—her homemade ointment for diaper
rash, the best things to do for colic and earaches, colds, and the
like—but also the best thing to do to bring out "the little red hives."
These are a matter of great concern to many women in the neighborhood, irrespective of whether or not the "baby doctors at the
clinic" have ever heard of them. She was glad that catnip, her
treatment of choice, grew right in her own backyard. And if the
catnip was covered with snow, well, she knew it was available along
with other "old-time" products at a pharmacy only a few blocks
away.

And what about her, did she also treat her own illnesses? I asked.
Yes, she did. And her assessment—and prevention and treatment—of
health problems was almost entirely of a religious nature. She was
one of 14 children in a household where health care was the herbal
remedies of her parents and trusting to "Doctor Jesus." And she was
still depending on Doctor Jesus. She saw sickness as a form of
weakness that is very nearly the same as sin and, as such, as something that is not allowed in her house! Pain and other symptoms
were, in her view, simply a trick of Satan and she simply ordered
him off the premises. I was not surprised to hear that her ideas
about health maintenance were embedded in religious belief, though

I was to learn that her first visit to a physician had been only a few months earlier. Even this visit was not of her own volition; she would never have gone on her own. She had injured her leg in an accident at work and her supervisor had insisted that she be seen by a doctor; when Janine demurred, the supervisor drove her to the emergency room herself. There a "very nice young lady doctor" had had X-rays made and found that nothing was broken, wrote out a prescription for pain medication, and suggested the purchase of an elastic bandage.

Janine herself was not particularly concerned about the pain; she was more interested in *why* the accident had happened at all. She attributed it to her own carelessness and believed that it was this carelessness that had allowed Satan to step into the picture:

> I went to the doctor the first of this year and I hadn't been to a doctor to just check me out for my health or anything, not *ever!* That's the first time I ever gone. And about medicine over the counter, you know, with a *prescription?* First time I ever use a prescription to buy medicine. Just been *healthy.* I never did just say "hurt, hurt," you know. The symptom would *come;* just maybe you have a pain that goes through your leg or something. Headaches I never did have. I always tell 'em I just been a blessed *person!* I think I were livin' by faith and I didn't even rea*lize* it! You know, the *Word* tell us we really don't have to be sick; we don't *supposed* to be sick. You see, when Jesus went to the cross He beared *all* of our sin and all of our sickness.

> But *nowadays,* we let Satan put it back on us! But we don't understand it, so many times, because we haven't learned it. We haven't been under the *teachin'* that we don't have to be sick. You can have what you say. If you say you sick, you *sick!* And if you say you're not, you're not. [If] you're goin' by *faith,* you're not. Well, if you really *sick,* you are sick. But you can just say, "I was *healed!* I was healed 2000 years ago when Jesus went to the cross!" And I guess that's what happened to me, 'cause I never was sick! Umh-huh.

She had bought the elastic bandage for her leg that the physician had suggested, but she never wore it. And she had taken only two doses of her prescription medication before discarding it; she really didn't know why she had bothered to buy it at all. The next time she felt pain in her injured leg she simply ordered it out. "Begone, Satan!!" she said, and the pain was gone. I rather quickly decided *not* to ask for a glass of water to swallow aspirin for back pain that I was experiencing. (Lansing, Michigan; 1986)

These people—Olive Parsons, her neighbors Tom and Anna Perry, Bernita Washington, Bernita's daughter Marya and granddaughter Josie, the Reverend Doctor Moses Hastings, Janine Jackson and her grown children—belong to different generations and have had different life experiences. Some live in more comfortable economic circumstances than do the others. Most have made a move both in geographical location and from a rural to an urban setting. And for most of them education was a luxury that was curtailed because of the need to work and/or early childbearing, the latter a pattern that is continuing in some of their families. Religion is an important part of all of their lives, though not all claim the same church affiliation or attend services on a regular basis.

They have also had differential access to orthodox health care over their lives. Old Olive Parsons was the daughter of a slave and the only doctor in her childhood was her own father. And not just for her and her brothers and sisters. People had called him "the daddy of the herbs," she had told me; people had said that he was "the best there was!" Bernita Washington's life as stepdaughter and then wife of poor sharecroppers in Mississippi only rarely brought her into contact with the few physicians in the county, who were all White. She recalls being taken to a doctor only once during her childhood, when she "fell out" from "typhoid malaria" while picking cotton in the hot sun. And Janine Jackson's parents did the doctoring of *their* brood of children in the South Carolina countryside. Along, of course, with Doctor Jesus.

Perhaps most people would expect that modern health care would be wholeheartedly embraced if and when it is made available to those who have lacked it, but this does not always happen. While she was living, Olive Parsons took pride—and Janine Jackson *still* takes pride—in managing an almost total avoidance of the professional health care system. It is a more important component in the search for health for the others; yet most of them, too, share a rather dim view of the usefulness of biomedicine. Tom and Anna Perry occasionally visited a physician to be sure; but more often they depended on Anna's home remedies. Bernita Washington's handbag contains a number of bottles of prescription medication that she rarely takes; what *she* calls "my medicine cabinet" is a sideboard in her dining room where she keeps epsom salts and the like. Her greatest fear is not that hospital care is not available if she needs it; it is that she will be *taken* to a hospital if she becomes really ill. She is afraid of hospitals and what might happen to her there. And the worst health care experience in *her* life, reports Bernita's daughter Marya Smith, was being taken to a hospital when she hemorrhaged during childbirth. It was far, far worse than giving birth at home with her mother there to hold her hand when the pains were bad.

Some of this mistrust toward institutionalized medicine is explainable, of course, by the kinds of experiences that all of these individuals have encountered as low-income African-Americans in a society where people are *not* created equal. But remembrance and/or expectation of poor treatment by people in positions of authority is not in itself enough to explain their failure to "comply" with suggested medical regimens when orthodox care *is* sought. There is no single reason why this occurs, of course. But all of the people who have been mentioned in these pages, along with those others who will come and go in the pages that follow, share some part of a system of health beliefs that is widely shared in the African-American community. Such a "health culture," to use the term coined by Weidman and her co-researchers, "refers to all phenomena associated with the maintenance of well-being and problems of sickness with which people cope in traditional ways within their own social networks and institutional structures" (Weidman et al. 1978:13). It provides an explanatory system concerning health problems that is consistent with the world view of the group and, as well, the means of gathering a group of caring people around the sick person (see also A. Kleinman, Eisenberg, and Good 1978:251–258). The system recognizes the importance of a sense of mastery and control in contributing to that person's feeling of well-being (Brody and Waters 1980:445–447).

The historical basis of the health culture under consideration in these pages derives from a variety of sources: the knowledge brought by the ancestors who were torn from their homes in Africa; the knowledge of the colonists from Europe; the knowledge of the indigenous inhabitants of the New World. Because there has been an ongoing exchange of ideas among groups from different backgrounds for nearly four centuries there has been a blurring of boundaries; it is not always possible to identify a particular belief or practice as distinctly "African" or "European" or "Native American" in origin. Even when this *is* possible it may not be particularly relevant today: *Sassafras albidum,* for example, still widely valued as a "blood medicine" by both African-Americans and Southern Whites, is a plant native to the New World. It was widely used by a number of American Indian groups when the first colonists arrived, just as it is today in some cases (Vogel 1970:361–365). Many of the beliefs and practices that will be described in the pages that follow, in fact—particularly those involving "natural" illnesses—are also shared by many White Southerners (Murphree 1968:125–143; Nations, Camino, and Walker 1985, 1988; Cook and Baisden 1986; C. Hill 1988:116–121).

In those instances in which it *is* possible to identify a belief or practice as African in origin—that the first child born after a set of twins has special healing powers, for example—it does not necessarily follow that this has been handed down in a purely oral tradition over several hundred years, though it may have been (Holloway 1990). Recent social phenomena are also responsible for an infusion of African-influenced beliefs and practices into the scenario: There are ever-growing numbers of immigrants, for example, Haitians, Bahamians, and Jamaicans, whose cultural backgrounds reflect the greater African influence that survived in other places. And there is the deliberate seeking out of African patterns in personal names, clothing styles, foodways, religious practices, and so on, that is part of the new pride in the African past. Many traditional beliefs are incorporated into the poetry and prose of many African-American authors and are widely disseminated in that way as well. What we find today, then, is a thriving system that represents the coming together and exchange of ideas over time from the peoples of several continents.

It would be wrong to see this as an alternative completely separate from the orthodox medical system, however, or uninfluenced by the popular version of orthodox medicine that is widely transmitted by the mass media. Jacie Burnes was perfectly able to talk about roots and psychology in the same breath, for example. And Marya Smith was perfectly willing to swallow aspirin and a prescribed narcotic *and* the Reverend Hastings' mixture when she was so ill. This intertwining of traditional, popular, and biomedical ideas results in a system that is constantly evolving to accommodate changing needs— it is broad enough to include pathological agents as diverse as sorcery and viruses in the etiology of illness and it is flexible enough to incorporate a new problem such as AIDS (acquired immune deficiency syndrome) when it appears. An understanding of the system as a cultural construct helps to explain why a prescription is filled but the pills not taken; why an elastic bandage is purchased but put away on a shelf without being worn. It helps to explain why medicines are used in ways seen as unusual by health professionals and/or are combined with other items from kitchen cabinets to augment their curative properties. It helps to explain how a tub of water may serve both as an ordinary bath and, if prayed over, becomes part of a healing ritual.

It also clearly extends the list of diagnostic possibilities to which an individual may subscribe: An accident at work may well result in soft tissue damage, but Satan may have helped cause the accident that brought the pain and swelling. Jacie Burnes was a woman subject to the violent attacks of her angry husband, but Big Joe needed the outside power of roots to control her. The infant Mikey's physician believed his thrush was caused by a yeast infection; his grandmother thought the white coating in his mouth was curdled milk resulting from too much formula in his diet. The possibilities of prevention and treatment are also extended: Evil power might slip under the door of a room where a woman is sleeping, but a potted plant in her living room can give fair warning. A physician might be able to help alleviate the insomnia brought on by worry and stress, but so might the shade of a beloved parent, come to help shoulder the burden of anxiety. And above all God can heal anything if He chooses so to do.

The fact that health professionals are not told of these beliefs does not mean that they are not believed and acted on by some patients, of course. And health professionals may not be the only ones who do not know that these beliefs have been brought into play: Even young Josie, who so vehemently disavowed her mother's "slavery medicine" in favor of a pediatrician for her new son, was an unwitting participant. She assumed when she left the baby in her mother's care that Marya was giving the drops prescribed for small Mikey's thrush infection. But Marya did not do so. On the afternoon that I first met the two women the pediatrics resident was frustrated because the yeast infection was not responding to treatment. "Go down there and find out what they are doing to that baby," he said to me crossly. "I *know* they are not giving that medicine!" He was quite right about that. It is not so much that Marya believes that the old ways are *always* best, though she did so in this instance. But Marya is able to pick and choose from a variety of treatments and for some sorts of problems she does not think *any* professional—born healer *or* doctor—is necessary. So on this occasion she had chosen to treat her grandbaby's thrush with a tried-and-true remedy suggested by her own mother. She was mopping out his mouth with his own wet diaper.

It is clear that treatments—even when these are defined by the users themselves as "old-fashioned" or "old-timey"—are *not* always replaced just because something newer is available from doctors. The very fact that they were seen as helpful when other alternatives were not available gives them value; they allowed "the foreparents" to survive. If doctors don't approve, according to Latishia Simmons, they don't even have to know:

> It's so many things we use! I didn't know anything about *medicine,* real medicine, because you know this is all I was brought up with. Why, there's a lotta *weeds* out there *now;* why, you're walkin' over *medicine!* And greens we used, like dandelions. Dandelions is a *wonderful* food. There's so many vitamins out there right now that we're *walkin'* over. We walk *over* medicine, that's right. And the doctors say that people [who] wear copper bracelets for arthritis, that it's no *good* these days! I can't explain *what* it *was* about those remedies; it had to be some good because if it hadn't been some good they wouldn't have been able to provide. I've got copper bracelets *now!* Now, there's somethin' *to* it, 'cause those people made the *way* for *us,* that's right. There's some good in it. And you'd be surprised what you can do with what you have. (Detroit, Michigan; 1978)

The fact is that people quickly learn that some of their beliefs and practices are either not shared or are viewed askance by health professionals. Many individuals choose not to mention them at all, even if directly asked. No one wants to be scolded; no one likes to be laughed at. One result is that many physicians do not really *know* what it is that their patients are doing about their health; another is that patients are labeled difficult or "noncompliant" when they do not follow orders. When alternative practices *are* brought up in clinical settings it is often in a diffident and offhand manner: "What do you think about garlic tea for high blood pressure?" Or, "My grandmother says the baby needs a belly band." Or, "Where I come from we always used to use kerosene and sugar for that." This rather noncommittal presentation of beliefs allows them to be perceived as uncommon and/or idiosyncratic; it does not give to the unknowing listener the idea that they are part of a patterned system. It also means that they may not be taken seriously or may simply be ignored.[3]

But there is far more than simple nostalgia in their continuing appeal. They are part of a system that is *holistic* in the best sense of that unfortunately overused word, so that the healthy individual is seen as possessing an integrated balance of body, mind, and spirit. It places the individual in an everyday world that is also more broadly conceived, so that the natural and the supernatural blend seamlessly. It locates a man, woman, or child in a social context where family is so important that even the line between life and death is more relative than absolute. Thus it is that Marya can understand one headache to be the result of stress and another the result of an envious woman's hex; thus it is that Janine believes that a prayer can be more efficacious than penicillin; thus it is that a woman long dead senses her daughter's misery and hurries to her side. And thus it is that a traditional healer in Grand Rapids who never finished high school is able to relieve a problem when the physicians at a university medical center could not.

The system also continues to exist because, unlike biomedicine, it is not restricted to dealing with matters of health and illness. Instead, an individual who has good health may view this as only one aspect of good fortune, just as he or she sees it as good fortune to possess a good job, enough money, a loving wife or husband, and well-behaved children. Likewise, a serious illness may be viewed as just another example of misfortune, together with inability to find work, the discovery that a spouse is unfaithful, or having too little money to keep a family together. This tendency to lump together domains that are kept conceptually separate in the more scientifically oriented world of biomedicine gives the traditional system an elegance of explanation that, I believe, assures that it will not soon disappear. If good things can be linked together, then perhaps the proper strategies may attract good health *and* money *and* love. And if bad things come in a series then perhaps the illness is *not* a natural one and calls for a visit to a powerful person. A person who, unlike a doctor, can help with the illness *and* lawsuits *and* loneliness.

Too often the good things in life—love, health, money—are chronically in short supply, whether a man or woman lives in a sharecropper's cabin in the Mississippi delta or a project on Chicago's West Side. Too often the bad things in life—sickness, poverty, despair—are present in overabundance, for the unmarried teenaged mother in Detroit as well as the family struggling to make ends meet in Oakland. It is the details that vary. In Mississippi, Bernita and Joseph

Washington raised their family in a shack so tumbledown that wind
and cold and rain came through the holes in the walls; Bernita
constantly worried about her children catching cold. Her home in
Michigan is much better built and she does not have to be concerned
about snow drifting under the doors. But she gets up early each
morning to inspect the yard before any children in her care leave
for school, an inspection that is made again in the afternoon before
they return. She wants to make sure the used needles discarded by
the frequenters of the drug house two doors down are picked up.
Worriation comes in many guises.

The ways of preventing or reversing misfortune may also differ
only in detail. If faith and prayer are efficacious then they will do
their work in a store-front church in Harlem, just as they did in the
tiny living room of Sister Erma, Tom and Anna Perry's evangelist
neighbor. If the fresh herbs available in South Carolina are not to
be found in Newark or Watts, then the health-food store on the
corner may have them in a dried form. If there is no candle store
nearby selling the oils and incenses and candles necessary to keep
the home safe from the entry of evil power they may be purchased
by mail. And if old Olive Parson's dead mother found her way to
a front bedroom in a tiny stucco house in Arizona I expect she would
have located her daughter wherever she was living.

Notes

1. Asafoetida is an offensive-smelling resinous material obtained from the
roots of a number of plants of the genus *Ferula;* it has a long history of use as
a medicinal having the property of "keeping away" illness.

2. The drug was Talwin. I discovered this inadvertently one day when riding
with her and, to my horror, she drove through a red light at a very busy
intersection. I asked her—weakly—if she had not seen that the light was red?
She had not. She had had several minor accidents recently, she said, as her
medicine made her "woozy." She showed me the bottle and when I pointed out
that it was clearly marked to indicate that she should not drive after taking it,
she said that she knew that, but that the pain was so severe that she was willing
to take a chance.

3. This informal divulgence of alternative beliefs and practices makes it difficult
to assess just how common they are in a clinic population. It is also not clear
under what circumstances individuals decide that it is safe to ask about them;
during the eight-year period (1980–1987) of observing patient/practitioner interactions in the pediatrics clinic in Lansing, for example, I could discern no particular
pattern of sharing such information. Some clinic personnel were never asked such
questions; others were. Often I was asked about a home treatment *after* the nurse
or physician had left the room. Sometimes an individual wished to know if I
thought a particular physician would mind the use of home remedies; at other
times my opinion was solicited and I was asked directly *not* to tell a physician
about the question. Individuals newly arrived in the city—especially from the
rural South—often wanted to know if catnip or asafoetida or some other substance
was available locally. It became obvious that patients (or, in this instance, the
mothers, fathers, grandmothers, and other caretakers of the patients) *were* very

selective about to whom such questions were posed—and that they were handled in a variety of ways when they were. They might be listened to with sympathy and responded to in some detail; they might be completely ignored; they might be privately laughed at. Some residents made real efforts to incorporate traditional practices (providing, of course, that they were seen as harmless) into the treatment regimen. Some residents noted questions about home remedies and traditional practices in the chart; some did not. Only rarely, however, were they seen as part of an integrated system of beliefs.

3

The Bible Says Watch
as well as Pray

And he sighed the ancient words that were a dark promise. He said
them all around to the others in the field under the whip, ". . . *buba
yali . . . buba tambi. . . .*"

There was a great outcryin'. The bent backs straighted up. Old and
young who were called slaves and could fly joined hands. Say like they
would ring-sing. But they didn't shuffle in a circle. They didn't sing.
They rose on the air. They flew in a flock that was black against the
heavenly blue. Black crows or black shadows. It didn't matter, they
went so high. Way above the plantation, way over the slavery land. Say
they flew away to *Free-dom.*
> —Virginia Hamilton, *The People Could Fly*

Anna Perry woke one night shaking in terror from the dream she
had just had. She sat up and shook her husband, Tom, awake, "There's
going to be trouble in our family!" Their daughter Lila was in grave
danger. The mother and two sisters of Lila's young husband had
been in the dream, the three women standing before Anna with
unsmiling faces. The older woman had wordlessly held something
out, and Anna had reached out her hand to take it. But when she
saw what it was she dropped it with a scream; it was pure evil
given form in a living creature. Something small, something black,
something furry—"like a black chick." A sure sign, she knew, that
the women meant their daughter harm. Perhaps if they called quickly
to warn her it would not be too late to do something! But Lila did
not heed her parents' advice. There was to be a party in a few days
to celebrate the first anniversary of the marriage, and *of course* she
had to invite her husband's family. "Besides," she told her mother,
"the Bible tells us to forgive." Two weeks later pretty young Lila
was dead—killed, so her mother believed, by sorcery. The Bible *does*
say to forgive, said Anna, but it *also* says to watch as well as pray.
(Tucson, Arizona; 1971)

Another sign was received by Sister Erma Allen, Tom and Anna's
evangelist neighbor, after she learned that her mother was lying near
death in a California hospital. Erma's first thought was that she must
leave at once, and she frantically went through her purse to see if

she had the money to go; she did not. The tiny income she received from disability barely allowed her to pay bills and, as close as it was to the end of the month, she simply did not have the $13.85 required for the bus ticket. Nor was she successful in her efforts to borrow the money from any of her acquaintances; everyone else in the neighborhood was poor, too. She would have to get a job, then, although according to "the rules" she was not supposed to work. The fact that she might lose her disability money seemed unimportant when compared to the need of seeing her mother once more. There would be no problem finding something to do for the time it would take to save up for the ticket—but would her mother live that long? She decided to take it to the Lord. She did not ask that her mother be healed; that was in His hands. What she *did* ask was that He let the sick woman live until she could get there to say goodbye. And could He please send a sign that the request had been granted? But one should give if expecting to receive and Sister Erma pondered what she might do; certainly there was no money for candles or incense or the like. Then it came to her: She could offer the gift of a 24-hour fast and prayer vigil! She fell on her knees by the bed and, staring at the window, began to pray aloud. The hours passed and it was the dark just before dawn when the sign came: The window began to glow with a beautiful and unearthly blue light. "Thank you, Jesus!" Her mother would live until she could reach her side. (Tucson, Arizona; 1971)

A third sign took place in a Louisiana city. Several women sat in the anteroom of Prophetess Mother Mary, exchanging stories about how her advice had helped them in the past. But one sad-faced elderly woman was silent, joining the conversation only when the others asked if *she* had ever seen the great woman. No, this was her first visit, she replied; but her hopes were high. Over the last years she had "been everywhere" seeking help for a curse on her family to no avail, but when she recently heard of the prophetess she decided to try one more time. So she traveled all night by bus from her home in Alabama to seek her out, a trip made at great personal cost. In fact, the price of the ticket represented such an enormous sacrifice that she repeated its exact cost—$59.90—several times. There was only her small widow's pension to live on, she confided, so she had cashed an insurance policy to make the journey. She had come to the right place, the others assured her; it would be worth the cost. But just then the Prophetess Mother Mary came out to say that everyone would have to go home. There had been some unexplained upset, and she was unable to "approach the spirits" under such conditions. "But I came all the way from Alabama on the bus," the old lady remonstrated. "Too bad," was the careless reply, and the prophetess disappeared through the curtain to the back room and did not return. After a moment the others shrugged and stood to leave, but the old woman seemed stunned by this turn of events and continued to sit. Still, she did not seem entirely surprised at what had just happened: There had been a "bad sign" that morning at the bus station. "My eyelid twitched three times while I was waiting for it to be time to come," she said. "I *knew* something wasn't going to go right. I just didn't know it was going to be this." As she rose to leave she shook her head and quietly said once again that the ticket had cost $59.90. She had made the long trip for nothing. (New Orleans, Louisiana; 1988)

The "signs" in the above stories took a variety of forms. One was embedded in a dream; another took the form of a vision during a waking state; a third manifested itself as a bodily twitch. All were unusual occurrences serving to alert the interested parties that something momentous was going to happen. They may have been unsought, as in Anna Perry's dream of the three women with their evil pet, or, as in Sister Erma's petition to the Almighty, represented a conscious and deliberate request to know the future. They also offered a differential potential for intervention; sometimes action can change the foretold course of events, sometimes not. Anna Perry believed that Lila's life might have been saved had the girl only removed herself from the dangerous social milieu she was in. But the old lady in the waiting room of the prophetess had already identified her thrice-twitching eyelid as a "bad sign"; she could only wait and learn what form misfortune would take. Anna Perry, Sister Erma, and the unfortunate old lady each saw their experiences as evidence of the linkage of human lives with some source of power extrinsic to themselves. They understood the unusual events in the context of their own situations; clearly *something* out there possessed a familiarity with the fabric of their daily lives! They had each been given knowledge of something to occur in the immediate future—if action could change the course of events then there was time to plan it. And if there was nothing to be done? Well, at least they had been forewarned and could prepare themselves mentally for what was to come.

It is not difficult for someone who does not share such a view of reality to see their explanations in a more pejorative light, of course. An observer uncomfortable with overtones of the supernatural might say that all such manifestations are internally produced and then mistakenly projected onto the outside world. In this view Anna Perry would merely be a woman already concerned about her daughter's problems with her in-laws, a concern that was expressed symbolically in her dream. Sister Erma's glowing blue light could be considered a visual hallucination occurring during an altered state of consciousness engendered by sleep deprivation, focused concentration, the fast, and her strong wish that her mother live. And who could doubt that the poor and unhappy old lady was anxious as she rode all night on the bus seeking help? Small wonder her eyelid twitched as she sat in the bus station waiting to see the woman who might represent her final hope!

When beliefs are not shared, it is all too easy to decry those that are different from one's own as "just superstition" and therefore not worthy of attention. It is important to keep in mind, then, that superstitious beliefs and behaviors cluster around those areas of life that are of great emotional significance, where outcomes are uncertain, and where guaranteed means to desired ends are not available. There are times when we all long for some knowledge about what will be; there are moments when we all wish for control of the immediate future. And at such times many—perhaps most—people behave in superstitious ways. It should also be remembered that such practices can serve the positive psychological function of giving the individual the feeling of some control over life events, illusory though that feeling might prove to be (Jahoda 1971:146; Singer and Benassi 1981). It has been suggested, in fact, that an individual's sense of mastery and control over an illness or its symptoms plays an important part in producing a positive placebo effect in healing (Brody and Yates 1990).

Because the term *superstition* is so often equated with ignorance, it needs to be emphasized that superstitious beliefs and practices are *not* limited to the poor and undereducated. I have worked in a number of hospitals and other clinical settings over the years and have yet to find one in which some health professionals do not firmly believe that "deaths come in threes," for example. And after 20 years' experience in teaching at the university level I still find it true that many students—undergraduates, graduate students, and medical students alike—indulge in superstitious practices at examination time. Commonly, students will repeat practices associated with success in previous exams: They may sit in the same seat, wear the same shirt or dress, eat the same breakfast, use a "lucky pencil," and so on. They laugh about it, but they do it.[1]

It probably is true, however, that superstitious beliefs and practices are more frequently found when people have little control over their lives. This description certainly fits the African-American underclass; many people are trapped in nigh-impossible living situations that they are powerless to change. The troublesome quality of their life experiences may be expressed indirectly in folk belief; many "signs," that is, are negative ones. There are 54 of these signs in the folklore material collected by my students from African-American respondents, and the majority of these (47/54; 87 percent) indicate misfortune to come. In those that are health related (28/54; 52 percent) it is not good health being prognosticated, for example; most (23/28; 82 percent) are death portents. "If you *think* you hear a bell ring, you will die soon," for example. (Angie Evans, East Lansing, Michigan; 1983) Or, "If you are sick in the hospital and dream you will go home soon, you are about to die." (Carrie Benson, East Lansing, Michigan; 1985) Or, "If a corpse remains warm and limp someone else will die soon." (Frances McNair, East Lansing, Michigan; 1983)

Sometimes such beliefs surface in clinical settings, and when they do they may be viewed askance by health professionals. "But she seems to be an *intelligent* woman," one family practitioner kept repeating as he told me of the woman who had refused the surgical removal of uterine fibroids. What *he* viewed as a completely medical (and secular) situation his patient took to be a tangible sign of divine displeasure. She understood the growths to be the deserved outcome of some unstated sinful behavior on her part and continued to firmly insist that God would heal her should it be His will; no scalpels necessary. My doctor friend was nonplussed at her suggestion that the condition might have been "sent" by God for some past transgression and did not share her conviction that supernatural intervention could remove the offending tumors. Instead, he found her "stubborn" attitude inexplicable; such a rationale for the cause and cure of disease had not been part of his medical training.

I do not mean to imply that her religious belief was unfamiliar to my physician friend; religion is very much a part of our history, after all, even though American society is increasingly secularized. Neither do I intend to say that a physician may not be a religious man or woman—one who may, in fact, *also* believe that misfortune can be caused by an angry God. But if this is so, his or her religious beliefs are generally kept separate from the practice of medicine. A chart entry might read, "Patient believes that his myocardial infarction was a punishment from God," that is; it is unlikely to read, "God has seen fit to strike down this patient with a richly deserved myocardial infarction," even if that is what the physician truly believes. It is also true that religion is not totally divorced from the orthodox medical scene; as everyone knows, hospitals may be owned and operated by religious groups, contain chapels or sanctuaries for prayer, and so on. But the religious part of the setting is kept separate from the arenas of care: A rabbi, priest, or minister allowed into a surgical suite is still required to scrub and to wear a sterile gown, and so on. It should also be noted that such medical/religious affiliations are with recognized mainstream religions; I have been in Roman Catholic, Protestant, and Jewish hospitals with rooms for prayer, for example, but I have yet to visit one with an altar to Shango.

The strongly secular approach that is typical of biomedicine is in stark contrast to a health culture in which the most basic premises include aspects of the spiritual and supernatural. The ideas expressed by Anna Perry, Sister Erma, the old lady in the Louisiana waiting room, and the woman with uterine fibroids fit much more closely into the "personalistic" model put forth by Foster in his discussion of non-Western medical systems (1976). He described personalistic belief systems as those in which disease is "due to the *active, purposeful intervention* of an *agent,* who may be human (a witch or sorcerer), nonhuman (a ghost, an ancestor, an evil spirit), or supernatural (a deity or other very powerful being). The sick person literally is a victim, the object of aggression or punishment directed specifically against him, for reasons that concern him alone." Biomedicine, in contrast, fits much better into Foster's "naturalistic" category, in which health conforms to an equilibrium model. Here disease is "thought to stem, not from the machinations of an angry being, but rather from such *natural forces or conditions* as cold, heat, winds, dampness, and, above all, by an upset in the balance of the basic body elements." African-American traditional medicine incorporates both the naturalistic and personalistic views, and individuals often run into difficulty in discussing the latter with their physicians. These would include both those problems seen as sent or allowed by God, as exemplified by the woman with the uterine fibroids, and the "unnatural" results of sorcery, thought responsible by Tom and Anna in the death of their daughter Lila.

Unfortunately, the same derisive tone that labels the interpretation of personal experience as merely superstition is also found in comparisons of medical belief systems. If one is "modern" then others are, by inference, outmoded; if one is based on "fact" then others must be laced with superstition. It is in these terms that biomedicine is seen as somehow more "true" than any alternative system could possibly be. As Weidman has commented, its legitimation has been part of the process of modernization and reflects the high value that has been placed on scientific endeavor and technological achievement. It is this sanction that renders biomedicine orthodox and all other systems "'traditional' within the contexts of various historical processes" (Weidman 1979a). Such a view, with its emphasis on scientific methods of proof, fails to consider the internal logic of other explanatory models. But most health systems *are* logical and rational systems of thought if the underlying assumptions are known; this does not necessarily mean that these assumptions are "correct," only that they can be viewed as having been reached by the coherent use of reason. Even the surgeon and the faith healer, as Hufford noted, "can rather easily be brought to understand the logic of each other's thought if each will listen to a straightforward description of the assumptions and observations involved. This understanding can lead to a reasonable discussion that can work to the advantage of each, and even more importantly to the advantage of a patient who may be seeking help from both simultaneously" (1984).

The Idea of Power

One way to understand the assumptions underlying the health beliefs put forth by the African-American men and women in this book is, as Glick has suggested, to make explicit the ideas of power they contain. This is "not diffuse unattached power, but power existing as a manifest attribute of persons and of objects in their environment" (1967). The idea is that power makes things happen and thus it can sometimes be used to change the ordinary course of events. In the broadest sense human well-being depends on maintaining a state of balance in relation to the various sources of power: striving to avoid the dangerous and attempting to key into the useful. The wise man or woman neither laughs at nor ignores signs and portents; the wise man or woman pays attention to the power that is being expressed in them. Nor does the wise man or woman take the various sources of power for granted; if they are there why not use them?

To use power one must know where it is located and, as Glick suggested, it is differentially distributed in the world. If the individual is to take full advantage of this fact then he or she must possess the knowledge of where it is and how to use it. When attempts are made to deliberately change what otherwise would be they are by definition "supernatural," of course. The very term contains within it the idea of the extraordinary and in the realm of religious belief it is a concept that will be familiar to most readers. The association of power with disincarnate spiritual entities is well known from the Judeo-Christian-Islamic traditions; because these supernatural beings are intrinsically powerful, humans are in a vulnerable position in their interactions with them. These interactions may be greatly valued *or* greatly feared, dependent both on the good or evil qualities of the supernaturals involved and on the behavior of the individual who comes to their notice.

The underlying assumption is that ultimate power is vested in a God responsible for the construction of the universe; a God believed to maintain a deep interest in His creation. This personal interest includes a continuing regard for each and every man, woman, and child; if asked, God may choose to alter the course of events by direct intervention. He may send a beautiful blue light to let a grieving woman know that her mother will live a little longer. But He may also fill a middle-aged woman's uterus with fibroids to let her know that her sinful behavior has not gone unnoticed. Power is also associated with supernatural beings who are *not* loving and good, of course, and Satan and other evil spirits may also be responsible for misfortune. Appeals to such powerful beings—both good and evil—are frequently in the form of a contract: Heal my child and I will serve You always; give me riches and I will relinquish my soul.[2]

The idea that there are powerful forces in the everyday world that can be directly utilized to bring about wished-for change *without* the intercession of supernatural beings is one that will be much less familiar to many readers.[3] It is recognized that there are people with unusual abilities in the magical arts who may be paid to use these for help or harm—and whose ill-will is only slightly less threatening than that of God or Satan—but it is also believed that many of the principles of magic may be learned by anyone. This belief allows individuals to attempt to manipulate events in their favor while bypassing the dangers inherent in interactions with

powerful beings, be those divine, demonic, *or* human. If done correctly, it is hoped, a magical ritual will produce the desired effect
with no element of choice on the part of the power being used. It
is rather like using electricity: *It* does not decide whether or not it
will be used, nor does it make judgments about the one who wishes
to use it. A profane source of power is devoid of attributes of good
and evil and therefore morally neutral; it is simply energy to be
harnessed toward a desired end. What is *done* with it may be seen
as good or evil, of course, but even that distinction may not be
perfect. What is advantageous to one individual, after all, may be at
the expense of another.

Everyone is free, then, to take advantage of the magical attributes
of such inanimate substances as sulfur, silver, salt, or pepper; all are
more than they seem at first glance. The arcane strength inherent in
certain plant and animal products may also be transmitted to the
man or woman who possesses these: Such portable power is present
in the root that people call High John the Conqueror, for example,
or the more sinister Black Cat Bone. People learn to select various
colors, certain numbers, and left/right-sidedness to add significance
to their actions as well: Three (and its multiple nine) are heard over
and over in beliefs and practices; red is linked with health and black
with evil-doing; the left side is associated with the undesirable.[4]
Even the physical environment may be seen as more powerful in
certain locations, both sacred and profane. An additional aura of
strength may be lent to favors asked or deeds performed in such
ritually charged settings: in a church; by a flowing stream; at a busy
crossroad; in a graveyard at midnight.

Such ritual manipulation of invisible forces in the universe involves magic with its emphasis on instrumentality. Such practice is
commonly divided into *imitative* and *contagious* magic. Imitative
magic is based on the idea that things that are similar are somehow
linked: like follows like. A wished-for outcome may be brought
about, that is, by copying it. A red-colored food is eaten in the belief
that it will build blood, for example, or a knife is placed under the
mattress of a woman who has just delivered an infant to "cut" the
pains of afterbirth.[5] Contagious magic, in contrast, is based on the
premise that things that were once joined together can never be fully
put asunder: The part stands for the whole. A lock of hair or a
fingernail clipping thus represent the individual from which they
were taken. I would add to this definition the idea that things that
were once open can never be fully closed: The fontanel and the navel
are open only in the newborn infant, for example, yet throughout
the lifespan both remain sites of entrance to the body for both
healing and sorcery.[6]

Perhaps the most important point to be remembered is that power
is seen as a transferable commodity—whether gleaned from personal
interaction with a supernatural spirit, contracted for from a conjure
man or woman, or fashioned oneself from items found in nature or

bought in a shop—and that its use is both necessary and expected. The theme of *taking action* is one that is heard over and over when people speak of the problems they experience; there is very little sympathy for the passive individual who does not make some effort to help him- or herself. Knowing where power lies and how to use this knowledge to one's own advantage—whether in matters of health or in anything else—is an important part of managing the difficulties of daily life. Thus one is assured that *something* is available for help at all times. Supplication to the Almighty for aid is understandable as just common sense as well as a demonstration of faith, then. And in this sense using the power in the natural world is simply taking advantage of something God-given to help oneself or one's loved ones. When times are hard who would be so foolish as not to try?

Power in the Natural World

One of the more fundamental differences between biomedicine and African-American traditional medicine is a very different attitude toward the natural world. Whereas the scientist is likely to view natural forces as something to be harnessed by technology to serve humankind, a follower of the traditional system is more likely to see nature as a powerful entity with which one must cooperate to live. People "try to outdo nature," said Wilson Erving, but, "Nature will kill *you,* you won't kill it!" (Tucson, Arizona; 1971) Elderly men and women in the Sea Islands would agree, as "issues of health and health care are approached through a frame of reference that assumes that nature has its own processes and that the actor must understand them and become a part of them, not alter or master them. In this context, the medical practitioner may be seen as a 'meddler' rather than as a healer, particularly when the practitioner gives advice that is contrary to strongly held traditional beliefs" (Blake 1984).

   This linkage between people and the rest of the natural world is so close that whatever happens in nature directly affects human well-being. The wise individual is careful to monitor the effects of such natural phenomena as ambient temperature, the phases of the moon, the signs of the zodiac, and so on. Change in nature is seen as especially problematic, particularly the turning of the seasons. In the fall and in the spring, people say, you have to be careful—in the fall the sap is falling and a time of dormancy beginning—in the spring the sap is rising as life in nature is renewed. This ebb and flow of the life force is echoed in the body. "In the spring the seasons done made their turn; when sap go up, it makes you sick," Bertha Alexander told me. "In the fall when sap go down, it'll make you sick." (Tucson, Arizona; 1970) If one is *already* in poor health the effect of seasonal change is even more dramatic, says Latishia Simmons, reflecting on the home remedies of her childhood:

For tuberculosis, well, they would take *milk,* fresh milk, warm milk
from a cow. What happen if you had tuberculosis, it was very *good* for
it. At that time people didn't have proper medical care, so a person
would *linger,* linger. And when the sap start comin', risin' like in the
spring, now; in April or May. A person who has that disease even
now—I don't know how, it's maybe through God, I don't know—but
somehow a person will have a tendency to *weaken.* And they just spit-
tin' and coughin' until all of their lung, everything is gone. (Detroit,
Michigan; 1978)

The tuberculosis, lying dormant during the months when all nature
is at rest, seems to come back to life right along with the rising sap.
    If the power in nature can adversely affect the body, however,
when properly used it can also be used to strengthen the weak. Said
Bernita Washington about the movement of sap:

I do know that it does make some difference with a *sick* person! I
don't know about a well person. But I do know it does make a difference with a sick person. Say that if a person's *sick,* if the sap is *up,* if
he's takin' the right kind of medicine and doin' the right thing and
havin' the right *activity,* he'll have a chance to really come up better
than he would if the sap goes down, because he goes down with it.
Your body somehow functions like that. (Lansing, Michigan; 1986)

Observations of nature's cycles may also be used in the making of
medicines, as elderly Frances McNair's home-made "pain killer liniment" clearly demonstrates. Her basic recipe contains bitterweed, red
pepper powder, salt, and kerosene; this mixture is allowed to "pickle"
for a time in a large jar and may then be used to rub on any painful
area. If one waits until after the first hard frost and gathers those
plants the frost did not kill to add to the jar, however, then the
liniment will be especially useful for rheumatic joints. Such plants—
unfazed by the cold—will surely be helpful to symptoms brought
on by the cold. (East Lansing, Michigan; 1983)
    The signs of the zodiac may also be perused for their effect on
human lives; this effect may be both generalized and personalized.
The blood is believed to move up and down in the body in tandem
with the changing "moon signs," for example, providing the rationale
for using the almanac to schedule optimal times for dental work or
surgery. "If the Moon is going through the sign which rules that
part of the body where the operation is to be performed," according
to *MacDonald's Farmers Almanac* (1987, n.p.), "defer it for a day or
two until the Moon gets well into the next sign or past it. This will
minimize the danger of complications and not infrequently the
symptoms change so that the operation is avoided." Such general
rules affect everyone and the ability to "read the signs" in an almanac is greatly valued, allowing decision-making to be based on the
positive or negative combinations of the heavenly bodies affecting

physical well-being.[7] Many individuals who use the almanac to monitor their health and select proper times for dental and surgical procedures know that their beliefs are not shared by health professionals, of course. As Bertha Alexander commented to me crisply, "Lotta doctors stand around on their butts laughin' at the signs. They'd do better if they paid attention!" (Tucson, Arizona; 1970)

There is also a more intimate connection between the zodiacal signs and the individual that has to do with the position of the heavenly bodies at the moment of birth. This "birth sign" or "sun sign" provides a special lifelong linkage between each person and these natural forces. Again, knowledge of this linkage provides a blueprint for action, so that both help and threat can be individualized. Each sign is also associated with certain plants and other healing substances, for example, so that knowledge of the birth sign allows the selection of the best possible natural remedy for the afflicted man, woman, or child (Riva 1974). The personal connection between the individual and nature may also be used to do harm, of course, if someone is so disposed. The knowledge that an intended victim is physically vulnerable on certain days can only add potency to magical attack. The Reverend Moses Hastings, who successfully treated Marya Smith for her unnatural headaches, explained:

> See, we all born on the certain moon, certain sign; we born on a sign. What's your sign? Cancer? Yeah, I figured you was, 'cause I could tell [by] your mood you're a Cancer. And as long as a person can't catch that *sign* that you're born on and change that moon, can't never do anything to you. During that sign, during that month of Cancer, or Cancer comes at certain time of the month, [when] Cancer comes in existence. It changes, it comes in there. So if they can't catch that *sign,* they can't nearly do anything to you. They got to know your *sign* before they can harm you, before they can really do anything to do you harm. (Grand Rapids, Michigan; 1987)

Fortunately, the birth sign can also be used to insure protection from unnatural attack, just as it can help one select the proper herbal treatment for a natural illness. Even plain old table salt, said Reverend Hastings, is

> security, always security. Salt will *help* a person if somebody are workin' *against* them and they knows what *sign* they are workin' on, they can block it that way with salt. Some of 'em mostly take salt; take and sprinkle just a little in their shoe. Only during those days, Cancer days. Other lady can't get to you.

Knowing when one is particularly vulnerable is helpful whether the vulnerability stems from an impersonal natural force or the use of that force by an enemy. And, obviously, protective substances need not be outwardly extraordinary, even though they may be intrinsically strong. It is its *ritual* use that turns such mundane stuff into magical protection—and even the poorest man or woman has help as near as the kitchen cabinet. They may be used, along with amulets, oils, incense, and candles to "glaze and transform a hostile environment into a beneficient one" (Davis, Boles, and Tatro 1984).

Power in the Spirit World

The fact that spiritual intervention in illness and healing is not part of the orthodox medical system has already been touched upon. In African-American traditional medicine, in contrast, human well-being depends greatly on maintaining proper relationships with an invisible world of spirits. Unlike impersonal natural forces such as the weather or the signs of the zodiac these are sentient beings, and involvement with them may result in help or harm. The *realness* of the spirit world in everyday life can be startling to the outsider, in fact, as people discuss nocturnal visits of deceased relatives or the most effective measures to remove evil spirits from the premises as casually as they do the visits of neighbors or the removal of trash. Powerful spiritual beings are part of most religious traditions, and belief in the possibility of human interaction with them is well known; in African-American traditional belief such interactions may also take place between living people and the spirits of the once-living.

The concept of a soul or spirit as an integral part of an individual that survives the death of the body is also an important part of the world's major religious traditions, of course. But in African-American traditional culture this belief must be broadened to include the wider historical perspective of Africa. The idea that a person's spirit can remain on or return to earth, retain personality, exhibit volition, and above all maintain an intense interest in surviving family members has a distinctly African flavor (Herskovits 1941:140; Genovese 1974:217; Beck 1975; Levine 1977:58–59; Raboteau 1978:13–16; Baer 1984:114). The belief that death does not end the connection between people—particularly kin—is widely found among African-Americans today. It is a particularly powerful indicator of the importance of family in social life. In one study of social support among single-parent families, for example, researchers were surprised when some mothers "spontaneously listed deceased persons as a part of their network" (Lindblad-Goldberg and Dukes 1985). Nor does this mean simply a fond regard on the part of the living for the memory of the departed: the *revenant*, able to see what is occurring in the lives of the entire kin network, returns to give support, advice, or help to the living (see Hufford 1982:226–228 for a vivid account of a long-dead woman returning to protect her great-granddaughter).

Old Olive Parsons was the first of my informants to tell me of such visits from her deceased relatives but she was certainly not the last. Cassie Seales is a licensed practical nurse who is frequently visited by the shades of her parents. Sometimes these visits are simple demonstrations of their continued love in times of trouble; at other times there is the expectation that she will "see into" the life situations of other kin:

> Any time that something is wrong with some member of the family [they'll come], but never when things are all right. But whenever there's some sort of trouble, if I'm *depressed* or *worried,* they'll come. I was very close to my father. Now if something is wrong in the family, if he wants me to go see about my sister or my brother, he'll come constantly; just constantly bother me until I get on the phone or I'll hear what happened. All I can sense is that something is wrong; it doesn't be long 'til I find out what it is.

His latest visit had been only the day before our conversation, in fact, when he appeared as Cassie was scrubbing the bathroom floor. He *knew* she was worried about the breast biopsy her daughter was to undergo the next day, she felt, and wanted her to know that the girl would be all right. Sometimes one parent or the other will appear to offer her astonishingly practical help. Once when she was ill Cassie's physician prescribed an antibiotic that was to be taken every four hours; she was worn out, however, and had slept through her midnight dose. But minutes later she woke to find her dead mother shaking her by the shoulder and admonishing, "It's time for your medicine!" (Lansing, Michigan; 1973)

Bernita Washington's husband, Joseph, has a special tie to his dead twin, Marcie; the little girl had died suddenly one afternoon when the children were only five years old. But the pair had been close and little Marcie has returned many times over the years, especially if her brother is ill. Joseph is in his sixties now and in 1988 suffered a stroke; sure enough, on the morning that he came home from the hospital he looked up to see the small ghost standing in the doorway, "comin' to see if I was all right." The spirits of the departed are not just aware of present troubles among their living kin, in fact; they may also alleviate concerns of the family about the future. Jackie Forde, for example, was quite anxious about the ill health of her elderly mother who lives in another state. She was vastly relieved, then, when her mother called to tell her she need not worry just yet. The sick woman's *own* deceased mother had appeared with the news that she would live a while longer. She told her that, "It isn't yet my time," Jackie's mother was able to report. "So y'all don't need to worry yourselves none 'bout me for a while yet." (Lansing, Michigan; 1987)

The belief in the continued interaction of the dead with the living is particularly well developed in the Gullah culture of the Sea Islands, where the spirits of all deceased inhabitants are said to "walk" at night. There the continued interest of the dead in the living may be expressed as help *or* trouble; the spirits of the family dead are usually benign and may be said to protect still-living family members. The spirits of those who have died sudden or violent deaths may be "haunting spirits," however, responsible for "fright" symptoms in those who encounter them (Heyer 1981:70). Infants and small children are especially vulnerable to contact with spirits, and a Sea Island funeral may still include the old custom of "passing" them over the casket so they will not be "touched" by the spirit of the departed (Jones-Jackson 1987:73; Blockson 1987; Creel 1990). The decoration of graves with seashells, broken crockery, and personal items may also be seen to "constitute a visual environment that in Afro-American tradition is seen as the world of the spirits, often the spirits of ancestors. Graveyard goods are a statement of homage; their function is to keep a tempestuous soul at rest. Far from being heaps of junk, funeral offerings are sanctified testimonies; material messages of the living intended to placate the potential fury of the deceased" (Vlach 1978:139; see also Jeane 1978 and Creel 1990).

In other instances spirits may be deliberately summoned by the living; in the Sea Islands this summoning ". . . involves rituals whereby spirits, good or evil, are conjured up to offer predictions, kill enemies, or perform cures for problems ranging from broken hearts, infertility, and rheumatism to mental illness and cancer. The spirit of one's ancestors is considered the closest link to the spirits of the 'other' world. Thus, on the Sea Islands as well as in Africa, spirits are asked to intervene on behalf of a living relative . . . " (Jones-Jackson 1987:25). The "symbolic strength" of location may be employed when such a ritual takes place in a cemetery or utilizes such products as grave dirt (M. Bell 1980:334). In Virginia, Linda Camino was allowed to be present while a root doctor (Joe) instructed a client (James) on how to contact a dead relative as part of the cure for the hex that had been placed on him:

> Next Joe asked, "You have anybody close to you that has died?"
>
> James: "One of my brothers."
>
> Joe: "You got someone on the other side. He can tell you what to do, but you got to have a way of getting through to him by way of this world. You got a graveyard near where you live?"
>
> James: "There's one a few blocks off."
>
> Joe: "Now you get some graveyard dirt and get it from a newly dug grave. You take that dirt home with you and put a circle of candles around it, just candles you got in the house, light them and say your brother's name. Then go to bed and your brother will come to you in a dream and he'll tell you what to do." (1986:233)

From his station on "the other side" the brother's spirit possesses knowledge not given to the living—and of course he will come to help his own kin when asked. Grave dirt or "goofer dust" is commercially available if one does not have ready access to a graveyard—or the nerve to steal dirt from a freshly dug grave.

Even living to a ripe old age may be enough to cause a man or woman to be viewed as possessing extraordinary abilities. Elderly people, for example, positioned as they are on the borderline between life and death, already share some of the attributes of the dead. They are nearing that day when they will join the spirit realm and, as if in preparation for that time, their own spirits are seen as loosely attached and able to leave their bodies at will. These disembodied spirits may then seek out those who have treated them badly in order to punish them in their sleep. Tales told of such chilling visitations add special emphasis to the belief that the elderly should be treated with deference.[8] Kathryn Heyer's research on St. Helena Island clearly reveals that such spirits are keenly aware of social rules and intent on seeing that these are followed by community members. Island dwellers say that someone who is guilty of disrespect toward an old person may be "ridden" that night by "hag," the offended elder's spirit. It is particularly rude, for example, to have "looked an old person right in the eye." Even those claiming not to believe the story may avoid looking into the eyes of the old: "They say if you look old people in the eye that they will ride you that night. I don't believe that. I like old people. But when they are too old I can't stand to look in their eyes because they have those desperate-looking eyes. I don't trust them, either. I'll be talking to them, but I always turn my head away. Otherwise they might think I'm looking at them" (1981:68).

The proscription on mocking the elderly may be backed by powerful supernatural sanctions as well. The biblical injunction to "honor thy father and thy mother" is often quoted in support of filial respect, for example. And *no* thinking person would deliberately insult an old person believed skilled in magic. One afternoon Marya Smith was describing how upset her mother, Bernita Washington, always becomes whenever she speaks of *her* own mother's death by "hoodoo" many years ago. Marya herself became visibly agitated as she confessed that she, too, is afraid to speak of such things. In the hope of making her more comfortable I quickly changed the subject by asking her to tell me her earliest memory—as it turned out I could scarcely have made a worse choice:

I remember when I was, I guess, about three years old; I had a little sister I had to take care of when my mom was workin'. And my daddy's mother lived with us. And I remember Grandma, she dipped snuff, and she wanted us to go to this old lady's house to get some snuff. And that lady was blind. And I told Grandma I didn't want to go, 'cause I was 'fraid of the lady. 'Cause she was *blind* and had one glass eye, and she could take this eye out. And I was 'fraid to go to this lady's house. And Grandma said, "Go on and get it, 'cause if you *don't* mind *old* peoples, God will put a curse on you. You have to mind old peoples."

And she said, "And for God's sakes, don't laugh at the lady, because God will put a curse on you." Say, "They shake their hand in your

face, sumpin' will happen to you." And she said that many times older
people, say, shook their hands at children when they was little, 'bout
laughin' at 'em and makin' games at 'em. And they say that 'fore sun-
down you be hollerin' like a dog, and they *would* be. All those things
would happen back then. I think I was about three years old.

An awful choice for such a tiny girl—to be cursed by God for
disobeying one old woman if she did not go—the threat of being
turned into a howling dog by another if she did. And *did* she go
to the old lady's house to borrow the snuff for Grandma, I asked?
"Yes, I went." Clearly the elderly are not without recourse when
badly treated, weak and feeble though their bodies might be.
(Lansing, Michigan; 1983)

Although in her story Marya did not make it explicit—and I, after
my gaffe, did not pursue it—it seems likely that the old lady with
the glass eye was a conjure woman. No ordinary individual, irrespective of age, has the power to make a human being behave as
an animal does. Such terrifying ability *is* attributed to the man or
woman identified as possessing magical powers, however. Animal
symbolism may be employed when such people advertise their abilities in urban newspapers, for example. "Frogs Croak Loudly Serpents
Will Swallow Them Up, Whatever you want done I will do," reads
a classified ad in the *Chicago Defender* (May 24, 1986, p. 47). "Make
'em crawl like a dog & root like a hog," reads another. "What you
want done I do" (*Chicago Defender*, September 23, 1991, p. 24). I
have heard a number of such stories and in each instance the hapless
victim was said to have been transformed into a pitiful creature who
behaved like and/or "howled like a dog" until his or her death.

Power in the Social World

Although the elderly man or woman begins to take on some of
the freedom of the spirit world the fact remains that this potential
is available to anyone who lives long enough; it is *age*, that is, that
renders them unique. In contrast, there are people who are seen as
special for very different reasons. They possess abilities—including
the ability to heal—that set them apart from ordinary people. The
ways in which these abilities are gained and used contrast greatly
with the years of formal learning necessary to become a physician;
in these pages it is possible to provide only a few examples of some
of these. Certain very specific healing methods have been passed
down for centuries in the European tradition, for example, and are
found today among both African-Americans and Southern Whites.
These include the power to stop bleeding, to take away the pain of
burns, and to make warts disappear. Such treatments often include
the recitation of a verbal charm, the use of the ritual numbers three

or nine, and the incorporation of some sort of religious symbolism (Forbes 1966; E. Brandon 1976).

The man or woman known as a "bloodstopper" recites a magical verse as a curing technique; he or she may be called upon for problems ranging from bleeding from minor cuts to postpartum hemorrhage (W. Black 1883:75–94; Dorson 1947; Murphree 1968, 1976; Waller and Killion 1972; Emrich 1972:610; Cooper 1972:77; C. Hill and Mathews 1981; C. Hill 1988:114). The most commonly reported such verse is found in the Bible (Ezekiel 16:6): "And when I passed by thee, and saw thee polluted in thine own blood, I said unto thee *when thou wast* in thy blood, Live; yea, I said unto thee *when thou wast* in thy blood, Live." Sister Erma Allen once told me of having healed a small boy who had cut his head; she had silently said the verse over and over while at the same time applying ice to the wound. How did she know that it was not the *ice* that had stopped the bleeding, I asked? After a pause she reprimanded me gently with, "God sewed it with *His* needle, darlin'." (Tucson, Arizona; 1971)

The "firedrawer" removes the pain of a burn by "drawing the fire" from it; he or she may blow on the burn three times while mentally reciting a verse such as, "Two little angels come from the West—One named Fire and one named Frost, Go away, Fire! Come, Frost!" (S. Black 1883; Cooper 1972). Other versions are, "Out fire, In frost, In the name of Father, Son, and Holy Ghost," and "Under clod, Under clay, God Almighty take the fire away" (Emrich 1972:610–611; see also G. Wilson 1966; E. Brandon 1976; Waller and Killion 1972; C. Hill and Mathews 1981). On St. Helena Island Kathryn Heyer was told of a small boy who had been scalded by boiling water; his distraught parents took him to a physician who treated him with an ointment that seemed not to help. They then decided to take him for treatment to a woman who they had heard could "talk fire out" of burns: "She just sort of rubbed with her hands over him and said something to him—I don't know what. Then she blew several times on him. She said, 'Now he'll be all right directly.' And in just two or three minutes, it seemed, he was down playing with the rest of the young ones, having a fine time" (1981:63). The child's recovery, the parents were convinced, was entirely due to the ministrations of this woman.

There are hundreds of magical treatments for the removal of warts and some of these—as in the cures for bleeding and burns—involve their being prayed over or "talked away" (Hughes 1963; Forbes 1971; Waller and Killion 1972; C. Hill and Mathews 1981; C. Hill 1988:114). The power of the "wart talker" illustrates how beliefs from one group are incorporated into those of another. It is only relatively recently that the wart talking brought to the Sea Islands by German immigrants in the nineteenth century has been taken up by the African-American inhabitants, for example; although all of Heyer's White informants knew of the practice it was familiar only to African-American informants under the age of 45 (Heyer 1981:60–61).

Said one island resident (p. 62): "My dad was a faith healer, but he took warts off, too. Some people will talk a wart off, but my dad did it a little bit differently. He would pray and he had a kind of ritual, too. He took a string and tied nine knots in it and rubbed each knot on the wart until it started hurting. Then he gave you the string and you threw it over your left shoulder without looking back. Then he'd pray over the wart and it just commenced to drop away. Within a week it would be gone."

The man or woman who possesses the knowledge of one or more of the cures described above is sometimes referred to as "having the power"; sometimes the power is seen as inborn, sometimes not. In any case it is believed that the knowledge of these very specific cures may be transmitted to others; it is sometimes said that this may be only to members of the opposite sex who are not blood kin. Sometimes the power is lost after it is taught to the third person, so the individual who "has the power" may wait until late in life before teaching it for the third and final time. Such abilities are particularly useful to have, of course, and knowing how to treat such minor ailments is seen as a specialized sort of first aid.

One may also become a healer, however, without any sort of learning at all. Special abilities may be suddenly and dramatically conferred on an individual during a peak religious experience, for example. Such people often describe hearing a voice that directs them on a certain path; in this sense they are deliberately "chosen." When an elderly Florida midwife was removed from her practice, therefore, her sense of loss was made even keener by her belief that she had been divinely called to her profession. There had been deficiencies found in the midwife bag that she carried and it was also noted that she sometimes worked without pay, further indication that she was failing to comply with regulations. But she had heard the voice and was only doing what she felt she must:

> And out of that bush he heard a voice that said, "Moses, pull the shoes off your feet because the ground that you are standing on is holy ground." That's the spirit that called me. It wasn't for the money I got, it was all right but if they didn't have it, it didn't make me no difference. I loved them just the same because He tole me. I say, "Lord, they done stopped paying me now. Some of them ain't got it and some of them got it and won't pay me. What's you want me to do? Stop?"
>
> "Is you sick? Is you hungry in the heart?" I could hear something. I say, "No."
>
> "Is you naked?"
>
> "No."
>
> "Do what I told you. If they don't ever pay you, I'll give you help and strength and a comfortable home. But, you do what I said."
>
> I got to meet justice one day. Them is the words that He told me. (Dougherty 1982:124)

"The call" often comes to people who are struggling to find answers to their problems; it may be deliberately sought out or appear quite literally as a bolt from the blue. Sister Erma Allen was the recipient of this latter sort of message at a particularly difficult period in her life, and the call was doubly thrilling because it was unexpected. "Erma! Go ye therefore!," the voice in the night had said, and she could only answer, "Yes, Lord." Nor did her lack of education deter her when in later years she heard the voice say, "Lay hands on that one," when she made hospital visits. God's will was far more important that the licensing regulations of the state of Arizona. Sometimes the healing role itself is taken on as part of a contract with the Almighty—for example, for one woman in Miami, who said: "One day I was drunk; my mouth swelled up, and I could not talk. I asked God for his help and healing. I promised that if I were healed, I would change my way of life and serve Him. From that day, I was able to heal bodies" (Weidman et al. 1978:717).

The men and women who are thus chosen to serve are merely the conduit through which divine power flows, and they are expected to use such a gift to help others. Sometimes they function privately and sometimes they go on to become religious leaders whose divinely bestowed talents are used in more public settings; such "faith healing" is a familiar part of American life. Because the healing power is seen as coming from the Almighty it is not surprising that the individuals who have it are thought to be able to cure things beyond the abilities of purely secular medicine. Said Arnella Lewis:

> *See, now, if you have cancer, the doctors can't cure cancer! But if they go prayin' for you, and you have lots of faith, the Lord will cure that cancer! The Lord heals a whole lot of people of things the doctors done give up! While the doctor may give you up, the Lord can come in and deliver you! Put you on your feet! Then whenever the doctor come back and examine you for that particular thing, and he don't see it, why, he'll say, "Well, I know it was there, but I don't know what become of you now!" They'll be amazed theirselves; they want to know what happened! (Tucson, Arizona; 1971) (Snow 1977:82)*

Such healing is often seen as a contractual arrangement between God and the afflicted as well—and woe betide the human partner who fails to live up to the agreement. Such a person, said Sister Erma, had better watch out:

> *Now I know a man right down here that had cancer. And they prayed for him, and the Lord really healed him. And do you know that he's back drinkin' and gamblin'? I saw him Christmas night, and I said, "You forget that good God that healed your body." This is why the Lord doesn't heal ever'body. He said, "Go in peace and sin no more unless a worser thing come upon you." Because when it come, it liable to be*

worser. It could be worser. I believe you can work it so that He get
vexed. It's a bad thing to be whupped under a angry God. (Tucson,
Arizona; 1971) (Snow 1977:57)

Such healing powers are particularly useful in treating those ailments
that are seen as "natural" in origin.

The unfortunate individual whose problems—whether ill health
or any other sort of misfortune—are seen to stem from "unnatural"
activity must usually seek out someone with even more remarkable
abilities. A man or woman will have to be located who has the
spiritual force necessary to deal with the forces of evil as well as of
good. A variety of terms describes such an individual: conjure man
or woman, root doctor, rootworker, hoodoo (or voodoo) man or
woman, spiritualist, and so on. They are often referred to by titles
that combine kinship and religious terms: Mother, Brother, Sister,
Madam, Prophet, Prophetess, Reverend Mother, Evangelist, Bishop,
and the like (Whitten 1962; Jordan 1975; B. Jackson 1976; Weidman
et al. 1978:653; Snow 1978; P. Davis, Boles, and Tatro 1984). The term
Doctor—or *Reverend Doctor*—is more rarely used; you have to
"serve" a *long* time, says Marya Smith, to have that added to your
name! That is how she describes the Reverend Moses Hastings, who
removed the evil spell she was under:

> Not every minister but quite a few of 'em—most all the ones that you
> know are saved—they have the gift of prophecy and they see things.
> And they pray and the Lord shows 'em things about a person. Just any
> minister wouldn't be able to take a spell off; you have to have that spe-
> cial gift from God, like this minister. He been doin' it for 50 years and
> he's very experienced in that. And a minister get in *that* stage, he's
> likely to be call a doctor. And that's what he's called. A doctor.
> (Lansing, Michigan; 1983)

Most people who possess the ability to "see things" and thereby
influence what happens in the future are said to have been born
with such power. Any sort of unusual prenatal occurrence and/or
circumstance of birth may therefore be taken as indication that the
infant is special. The two most commonly reported such events are
the child who is the seventh sibling of the same sex and/or is "born
with the veil" or caul over its face; both have been associated with
special powers for centuries. According to Keith Thomas, the belief
in the powers of a seventh son (better yet, the seventh son of a
seventh son) or seventh daughter (usually referred to as a seventh
sister) was unknown before the sixteenth century; it was widely
disseminated in Europe by modern times (1971:200–202). By the mid-
nineteenth century the belief had clearly been taken up by African-
Americans as well; an 1860 advertisement for patients (Shryock
1966:49–70) reads: "T. Edwards is naturally a Doctor—having a gift
from the Lord. My mother was her mother's seventh daughter, and
I am her seventh son. . . . I am a seven months' child, and walked

seven months after I was born, and have shed my teeth seven times." Such individuals were (and are) often said to be able to communicate with spirits and to possess "second sight," that is, the ability to read the future, positioning them admirably to give advice about all manner of problems (W. Black 1883:136–147; E. Parsons 1923:198; Cameron 1930:54–55; Pickard and Buley 1946:75; G. Wilson 1966; Stekert 1971; de Albuquerque 1979; Roberson 1983:130; Hand 1980:43–56).

Individuals born with power are often described as having been "different" throughout their lives; they may also be differentially treated from their infancy as they are watched for signs of special ability. It is not surprising that they—and those around them—become convinced that they can indeed intervene in the lives of others. Such special children may begin to use their special powers in early childhood: an elderly herbalist from North Carolina, for example, whose unusual qualities were made known to all by the circumstances of her birth, was soon known as "that little medicine thing." Small wonder after the magical fashion in which she was lighted into the world:

> When I was born, I was the seventh one, the seventh sister. And they say the seventh one will be over-endowed in everything. Well, I was the seventh child. When I was born I was born way back in the hard times—way back. We had no lights, but we had a little bit in a lamp. And my daddy went for the doctor, and that was called a midwife and some call her a grannylady. He went and got his mule and cart and went to get the midwife. Meanwhile all of the oil from the lantern burnt out. And he hadn't gotten back by the time the oil burnt out. And my mother was in the dark. When he got back it had got day just like early in the morning. They had a glow—the yard, leaves, and the house glowed—and that light stayed until 10 in the day, and it was brighter than the sun when I was born. [My mother] says that's why I was so different. I was a different child. People talked and I listened and my heart was big enough to hold all that. I talked different—was strong in my talking—I was just born to that. (Baldwin 1984:50)

The importance of birth order in the conferral of power is also illustrated in the findings of Weidman and her coworkers in inner-city Miami; 12 of the 20 Southern Black traditional healers who were interviewed described significant events surrounding their birth as instrumental in their calling.[9] One Spiritualist healer, for example, was reportedly not only born face down with the veil—accompanied by three spirits—but was also the ninth child of a seventh child (1978:718)! Healers/advisers who advertise for clients also frequently mention such events to signal their special abilities; they often claim to be a "seventh son" or "seventh sister," born with power (Snow 1978). An even more direct tie to magical practice is made when such individuals indicate that they are from a geographical area associated with such activities—and just *which* part of the country this is reflects the migration patterns of African-Americans from

South to North. In advertisements in the *New York Amsterdam News,* for example, the person who wishes to signal his or her power is likely to refer to South Carolina (often Beaufort is specifically mentioned); in the *Chicago Defender* or Detroit's *Michigan Chronicle* it is more often stated that the individual is from Louisiana (sometimes New Orleans is specifically mentioned).[10]

Similarly, the belief that a child born with the caul (amniotic membrane) intact possesses special powers is centuries old; it has been reported from many parts of the world, including Africa (Forbes 1966:vii; Herskovits 1941:189). Such a child is frequently referred to having been "born with the veil," and as such is gifted with the ability to "see spirits" or "know things" (E. Parsons 1923:197–198, 206; Puckett 1926:336; Cameron 1930:57; Dorson 1967:62–63; Frankel 1977:42; de Albuquerque 1979; Hand 1980:43–56; Gwaltney 1980:253; Roberson 1983:130; Laguerre 1987:38). Sometimes the special status is passed down through a family: "Babies born with a veil covering their eyes," says one college student, "can see visions and can predict the future." She has one friend who was born with a veil—as was her friend's mother, grandmother, and great-grandmother. The older women reportedly have seen and heard ghosts and predicted the future; the friend, so far, has had one "vision" and several "revealing dreams."[11] (Cristal Fellows, Detroit, Michigan; 1978)

Additional power, it appears, is conferred by a combination of unusual birth events; one woman from Chicago revealed that she was not only a seventh sister but that all seven of the siblings had been born with the veil, for example (Snow 1978). And Joe, the Virginia root doctor who had instructed his conjured client in how to contact his dead brother, assured the man that he would be able to help him because he himself had not only been *born* special, but had once been the victim of a similar problem himself and so knew it from within:

> *You know I was a scrawny kid, always weak, but I could heal. I must have inherited it. I was born with the veil, seventh son of a seventh son. And I was once conjured. That's why I can cure, because I know what it's like myself. The world is a dangerous place, you got to be careful. Yes siree, I am a natural born healer. Now you know the doctors are there for a purpose. She [referring to the researcher], Linda there, has been working with them and she knows they don't know how to cure a conjuration because they had never had one put on them before, they don't understand it. They're city people and white people, never even know a thing about it.* (Camino 1986:234)

And if one veil brings power then being born with several will surely bring more; here, of course, the parallel with the biomedical amniotic membrane is lost in favor of signaling incremental power. One veil or caul is the equivalent of the biomedical amniotic membrane, that is, but there is no biomedical equivalent of there being more than one. This did not stop one root doctor in Miami from declaring to have been not only a seventh child but one born with no fewer than *seven* veils (Weidman et al. 1978:718). The Reverend Moses Hastings was also born with multiple veils and was seen to be different from his playmates as a child:

> Well, I've been told ever since I was little. I can remember quite a ways back, you know; I guess when I was two, three years old. My mother used to say that I was born with two veils over my face. . . . In other words they say when you're born with veils over your face you'll be able to discern *spirits.* You'll be able to discern the *inside* of a person . . . sometime I can see *dead* spirits, I mean people that are passed and gone.

> People always, well, ever since I was [small], peoples always be *shy* of me, you know. You don't have too many friends. Like have a whole lot of playmates and stuff like that. It just sumpin' *about* it when people, when kids or folks do *come* to you when you're small like that. They always come to you for *help,* and how *they* would know *I* wouldn't know. (Grand Rapids, Michigan; 1987)

People *did* know, however, and he began his healing practice as a child. White and African-American children alike frequently asked him to "lay hands" on the bumps and bruises they suffered while playing.

Mother Delphine Carver was also born with a gift and this fact was signaled to the world by a combination of factors. Her grandmother had been a powerful midwife/healer in South Carolina; the older woman had not doubted that one of her descendents would inherit her abilities, and it only remained to be seen just which one it would be. It was revealed to be the infant Delphine when—in the African tradition—she was the first child to be born after a set of twins (Herskovits 1937:201–206, 1941:189; Metraux 1959:146–153; Courlander 1960:31–32; Mintz and Price 1976:24; Laguerre 1987:38–39). The family already *knew* that the coming child was to be special, then, an expectation that was further strengthened when she was heard to cry out three times from the womb. In consequence Mother Delphine began her long healing career before she was able to read and write:

> *I had two brothers, they twins. And I were born behind the twins. Some people believe that twins have the gift. . . . Some people say that I have the gift, because I were born behind two twins. But I don't know; I always had the urge that I could cure anything, I've always felt like that.*

> *But grandmother knew before I were born. I cried three times in my mother's womb before I were born. Then she said, "That's the one! That's the one what's gonna be just exactly like me!" I was fortunate. I was born just exactly with the gift.*

> *My mother told me that I was born with power. I remember when I was five, five years old. 'Cause I never will forget the little stool which she used to use for me to lie my hands on my brothers and sisters. Her or them would have a pain; I could lie my hand on them, and their pain would leave them. She would tell me all along that I was gifted. I was born like that. From God.* (Tucson, Arizona; 1971) (Snow 1977:89)

It must be a formidable experience for a small child to lay a hand on a brother or a sister—or a parent!—and hear them pronounce themselves healed. And that particular small child grew up to be a very charismatic woman indeed (Snow 1973).

Those men and women who have been born with special qualities obviously have the potential to do great good by helping others. But human beings also have the gift of free will, and the choice of what to *do* with "the power" remains with the individual. And what is helpful to one person, of course, may be to the detriment of another. The very fact of magical practice—whether by ordinary people or by those understood *not* to be ordinary—underscores just how helpless many individuals feel in their daily lives. The use of external sources of power offers to those who have little the hope of obtaining those things that are valued but in short supply, whether that be love or health or money. It offers to the weak the opportunity to become stronger and to the strong the wherewithal to hold on to what they have. Power may be used to *get* things, that is—but it must also be used to *keep* them. Even Big Joe Burnes, nearly six-and-a-half feet of meanness, felt the need of a root doctor's help to keep his wife at home.

It is useful to *have* such an individual to turn to when help is needed, then, but it is frightening as well; great knowledge is dangerous and those who have it are viewed with great ambivalence. Mother Delphine certainly saw herself as directly gifted by God, for example; nor was there any doubt that she was widely regarded as a great and powerful healer by many. The waiting room in what she called "my doctor's office" was always filled with people who required her help. But the fact remains that many people were also deathly afraid of her; Ella Thomas once confided to me that if she saw Mother Delphine coming she quickly crossed to the other side of the street to avoid having to speak to her. Everyone agreed that she had the power; they just were not certain what she was going to do with it. Who is to know whether someone who has the knowledge and the inner strength to remove a hex might not also know how to administer one? After all, Lucifer himself was once the brightest of the angels.

Notes

1. In an undergraduate class in the spring of 1991, for example, a young woman sheepishly confided that while taking the Medical College Admissions

Test (MCAT) examinations the week before she and several other students had taken advantage of the break time to go outside the building and scramble around on the ground, looking for four-leaved clovers.

2. A number of West African spirits are included in the pantheon of syncretized New World religions such as *Vodun* and *Santeria*—the Yoruba deity Shango, for example—and belief in their powers has accompanied the recent wave of migrants from the islands of the Caribbean to the mainland. They join the more familiar Judeo-Christian spirits in a list of other-worldly beings with whom humans sometimes interact.

3. Most people do not have difficulty accepting the idea of the supernatural when it is associated with religious phenomena. The fact that religion is such a fundamental part of the fabric of American life makes belief in the satanic or divine familiar even to those who do not themselves subscribe to such thinking. Few people would be surprised if a sick individual (or his or her family) prayed for healing. The idea of magic is very differently viewed, however. The belief in and practice of magic does not have the institutionalized place in American life held by religion and is much more likely to be viewed as superstition; here the label of "supernatural" is pejorative, not sympathetic. The same individual who hangs a St. Christopher medal in the car for protection against accidents, that is, may think it hilarious that someone else wears a silver dime on the body for protection against evil.

4. The age-old connection of "left"with the opposite of what is normal and/or desirable (ranging from the female principle to the diabolical) continues to be made. The following example is a death portent featuring the appearance of an undesirable animal on an undesirable side; in that sense it is negative: "If you are walking along and a snake appears on your left side and raises its head, there will be a death in the family." But it also contains the wherewithal to avert the misfortune: "Death can be defied if you look the snake right back in the eyes." (Etheldean Mitchell, Lansing, Michigan; 1980) The importance of *taking action* is a recurring theme in this health belief system.

5. When college students offer examples of folk belief they frequently include a scientifically based rationale; they seem to be more comfortable with such an explanation of how and why something might "really work." The following anecdote was provided by a young woman who began medical school in the fall of 1990: "When I was a child, I used to have nightmares from watching horror movies, and I would often wake up in tears. My mother told me to put a knife under my pillow and the dreams would be cut in half. Faithfully every night, I did just that from about age 5 to age 11 or 12. I believed it, and it worked. It was probably psychological, but it helped me sleep through the night." (Orlanda Cameron, East Lansing, Michigan; 1990)

6. It was her belief in contagious magic that finally convinced Anna Perry that her pretty young daughter had been magically killed by her mother-in-law. Anna had already been suspicious because of her premonitory dream, suspicions that were confirmed when, after the funeral, the mother-in-law offered to fix Anna's hair. Anna was a woman in her sixties when I knew her, and so fearful of sorcery that not once in her life had she ever had her hair dressed in a beauty salon. There was always the danger that someone would "get hold" of some of her hair, she told me, and use it to harm her. The seemingly kind offer to do her hair was bad enough; when combined with the fact that the mother-in-law was from Louisiana, "the home of hoodoo," Anna had all the proof she needed that Lila's death was "unnatural."

The belief in rootwork and its manifestations would fill an entire book and there is just not room to do the topic justice here. Hyatt's monumental work, for example, reports literally thousands of cases (1970–1978, Vols. 1–5; see M. Bell 1980 for a condensation of Hyatt's work). Although it is used to control every aspect of life, it is the health-related issues that are important here. The most frequent symptoms seem to be: (1) gastrointestinal (as the "poison" is often introduced into the body through the food or drink), (2) changes from normal functioning, or "crazy" behavior—including behaving as does an animal, and (3) the belief in the presence in the body of animals such as snakes, lizards, frogs, scorpions, and the like (in at least some instances the animal in the body takes the form of pseudocyesis or a "demon child").

The clinical literature continues to report the case histories of patients who have presented such beliefs, often to the consternation of their physicians (Clinicopathologic Conference 1967; Snell 1967; Tinling 1967; Freemon and Drake 1967; Kimball 1970; Rocereto 1973; Wintrob 1973; Maduro 1975; Cappannari et al. 1975; Golden 1977; Baer 1981; Hillard 1982; Lyles and Hillard 1982; Lichstein 1982; Pellegrini and Putman 1984; Gray, Baron, and Herman 1985; Brandon 1988). At least some scholars have studied such beliefs as partial fulfillment of the requirements for advanced degrees (see Marshall 1955 for a study of rootwork beliefs in a state mental hospital in Maryland; Cooley 1974 for a study of folk belief in North Carolina; and Cothran 1977 for similar beliefs in Alabama).

Although all of the above-cited articles and theses are interesting they—because of their format—tend to focus on case studies taken out of their social and cultural context. Two recent doctoral dissertations provide that context and allow the reader to understand how such beliefs function in community settings; these are Heyer's work on St. Helena Island (1981) and Camino's research in a Virginia city (1986). All of Camino's informants were acquainted with the features of conjuration, as she calls it, and could tell of at least one instance when it had happened to family or friends. During the 18 months of her fieldwork, in fact, no fewer than 8 of her 54 informants developed a problem which they attributed to it (pp. 178–210). She was allowed to be present at the healing session of one of her informants by a root doctor (pp. 229–239).

7. The belief in the effect of the signs of the zodiac on human health provides an important bridge between rural and urban expressions of traditional medicine. The proprietor of a candle shop in southside Chicago once advised me that—along with the Holy Bible—"the only two medical books" a person needs to stay healthy are the farmers' almanac and Hohman's *Pow-Wows, or, The Long-Lost Friend.* (Lunell Nelson, Chicago, Illinois; 1973) The latter book of magical charms was first published in 1820 and is an important part of the Pennsylvania Dutch healing tradition (Yoder 1976:235–248); it is still available today in shops dealing in occult items. On that particular afternoon Mrs. Nelson sold me a copy of *Pow-Wows* and also asked my date of birth; she then pointed out the many items that would "go along" with Cancer, my birth sign: Grains of Paradise (my own "personal herb"), oils, sachets, incense, and so on, all marked with the sign of Cancer. She also provided me with one of the shop's advertising flyers: "ALWAYS GET WHAT AND WHO YOU WANT," it read, "START NOW WITH FAST-LUCK CANDLES INCENSE OILS AND HERBS."

8. Such nocturnal assaults—known by such folk terms as "Old Hag," "Witchriding" and "Nightmare"—are reported worldwide from a variety of cultures and subcultures. Victims' accounts of such occurrences are remarkably similar and correspond closely to the psychobiological phenomenon known as sleep paralysis. (For a comprehensive account of such assault traditions, see Hufford 1982; see also Simons and Hughes 1985:115–148.) The prevalence of isolated sleep paralysis is reportedly high among African-Americans; in one survey 41 percent of the subjects had experienced at least one episode (C. Bell et al. 1984). A later study revealed that 25 percent of subjects interviewed suffered a recurrent pattern (one or more/month) of such episodes; such frequent episodes were stress related, and individuals were said to suffer from a high prevalence of panic disorder (C. Bell, Dixie-Bell, and Thompson 1986:649–659). When one young college student suffered

such an attack she told her aunt about it; keep a saucer of salt under the bed, the older woman advised, and it will not happen again. She did so and has slept untroubled since. (Hallie Wilmot, Detroit, Michigan; 1984)

9. From 1971 to 1976 the University of Miami's Health Ecology Project gathered health-related data from 100 families from each of the major ethnic groups in the inner city, including Puerto Ricans, Cubans, Haitians, Bahamians, and U.S.-born Southern Blacks; information from this study will be quoted throughout this book. The researchers discovered a variety of traditional healers in the area under study and devoted a chapter of their final report to the subject (Weidman et al. 1978:677-745). They describe the difficulties of obtaining information from and about individuals who often prefer to maintain distance from orthodox institutions: Such individuals often fear legal sanctions for practicing medicine without a license; the collection of fees for their services; and, in the case of Haitian and Cuban religious cults, animal sacrifice (pp. 686-690). The important thing is that people *do* in fact (and not just in Miami) have a wide choice of practitioners of various sorts—practitioners with power—to help them with the problems of daily life (see also Stewart 1971; Hall and Bourne 1973; Jordan 1975; Snow 1978; Baer 1981, 1984; Heyer 1981:123-189; Roberson 1983:155-172; Davis, Boles and Tatro 1984; Camino 1986:208-256; Laguerre 1987:50-63).

10. A Sister Rosemary, for example, is "ONE OF THE 7 SISTERS FROM LOUISIANA WITH POWER FROM GOD," according to a classified advertisement. "Are you sick, suffering, bad luck, hair falling out, need help in any problem," she asks? If so, the reader should know that "I am superior to all other readers. I was born with God given power to help you. I will tell your past as you alone know it, your present as it is your future to come. I help in love, marriage, business, health. One call will convince you" (*Michigan Chronicle,* August 21-27, 1991, p. 6D). At $5.00 for a "reading" a bargain indeed! In December 1991 another of the "Seven Sisters from New Orleans" advertised her services by way of a Lansing, Michigan, radio station; she is located in a nearby small town. Her fee for a reading was quoted as $35.00.

11. This particular belief is another that has recently been incorporated into fiction by an African-American author. In Ansa's *Baby of the Family* (1989) both the doctor and head nurse in a maternity ward in a smalltown Georgia hospital recognize the potential of a newborn girl with a caul; the child's mother, however, is a nonbeliever and refuses to follow the instructions that would free her daughter from a lifetime of seeing spirits.

4

You Brought It on Your Own Self

"But listen, they say you should lay your burdens at the feet of the Lord. They say He'll listen." Sister Madelaine stifled a yawn. "But you have to tell *Him* the truth; that's the only catch there. Else, even *He* can't help you."

"I have laid them everywhere, believe me that is the truth. Starting years ago I went to everybody that would listen. Including Him. But the more I lays them down the heavier they gets. All around me is a great big hush, like before a storm, and when I dream it is just to let witches ride me."

Sister Madelaine raised an eyebrow. "My colledged son will tell you there is no such thing as witches riding people. From Morehouse he learns it is indigestion. Something you ate, the way you are laying in the bed. The circulation of your blood stops and you can't move. While you lay there sweating and not able to move you have nightmares, and when you wake up you think a witch has been riding you. According to my son you wouldn't need a fortuneteller, you'd need a dose of salts."

—Alice Walker, *The Third Life of Grange Copeland*

On a very hot August night Anna Perry called me out to the front porch of her home; she had something to tell me that "the men" should not hear. As we sat on the old porch swing drinking iced tea she admonished me once again on the importance of burning used menstrual pads. I had always been polite, she said, and did not openly disagree with the things she told me. But now it really *was* important that I pay attention; after all, I had a new job teaching at a university in faraway Michigan. *Now* I was going to be "one of the higher ups"; now I would *always* have enemies. Didn't I remember what had happened to Lila?[1] (Tucson, Arizona; 1971)

Ann Lee Dalton poured a spoonful or so of red pepper and some of her own urine into a bucket of hot and soapy water as she prepared to mop the worn linoleum of her kitchen floor. The soap and water would remove the dirt her children have tracked in from the yard, muddy from a spring rain in Michigan. The pepper and urine was a preventive measure which, she believed, "helps to keep bad spirits away." So far it has worked. (Port Huron, Michigan; 1981)

It was Christmas morning and Bernita Washington was lying on her old red couch, suffering from the headache she had had for 24 hours. Her own fault, she says; it was brought on by "neuralgia" from going out in the cold without her head covered. This, coupled with the fact that she had not been careful about what she was eating, had caused her blood "to rise" and the result was pain. She was treating the headache by resting and drinking only black coffee for breakfast. And for the rest of the day? "I'm going to not eat any pork or grease, or too much sweetenin'." She expected to be herself by afternoon when the members of her large family would be dropping in because of the holiday. (Lansing, Michigan; 1986)

Reverend Moses Hastings had just made a pastoral call to a 23-year-old woman dying of AIDS in a nearby hospital. For days she had been distraught at the inconsolable weeping of babies, unaware that no one else in the room could hear their cries. It was the wailing of the seven babies she aborted, Reverend Moses said, the babies that she had not allowed to be born. But she was beyond any help he could give; "All I could do was pray for her." Nor does he pity her. She has to pay, he said, and she is. God was punishing her for the terrible sins she had committed. (Grand Rapids, Michigan; 1987)

These anecdotes deal with a common-sense way to prevent the malicious use of a bodily fluid by the envious; the everyday use of body waste to prevent infestations of evil spirits; a regimen of diet and rest to alleviate the bad headache resulting from injudicious behavior; a terrible death as punishment for a sinful lifestyle. As Glick has stated (1967), "the most important fact about an illness in most medical systems is not the underlying pathological process but the underlying cause. This is such a central consideration that most diagnoses prove to be statements about causation, and most treatments, responses directed against particular causal agents."

As the above examples illustrate, one could safely add that ideas about prevention are *also* statements about causation, with health maintenance a matter of sensible behavior. Anna Perry felt that anything that might make others envious rendered an individual at risk for magical attack. Some people are just like that, she said; "Just put on a few little clothes and they get begrudged-hearted." No need for me to invite misfortune at a time when my system was already weakened by functional bleeding; why not simply burn used menstrual pads? Ann Lee Dalton saw evil spirits as just as likely to contaminate her kitchen as tracked-in dirt; why not prevent both with proper cleansing? Bernita Washington blamed herself for her headache; *she* had knowingly gone out into a Michigan winter day with her head uncovered; *she* had eaten ham and sweet potato pie when she knew she shouldn't. All she could do now was keep her symptoms from getting worse and be more careful next time. And the young woman who was dying as she unwillingly listened to the crying of her dead babies? *She* chose to be a prostitute, said Reverend Hastings; no one made her do it.

Most people will say that the majority of health problems could be avoided if people would only be more careful. Many discussions about illness include statements such as, "But you can keep that from happening, just don't go out in the cold unprotected"; or, "Don't eat all that rich food"; or, "Read your Bible every day." Health in African-American culture fits closely into an equilibrium model in which attention must be paid to all aspects of human experience; health maintenance thus means paying attention to body, mind, and spirit as they respond to constantly changing influences from the external world. Ideally this will result in what Frank has called "a harmonious integration of forces within the person coupled with a corresponding harmony in his relations with other persons and the spirit world" (1977).

The healthy person is able to carry out life's daily tasks with ease. One elderly woman in Virginia defines health, for example, as "feeling good, a good appetite—do what you want, go where you want. I used to work all day, come home, fix dinner, do chores, and go to the oyster house at midnight to shuck oysters all night—that's healthy" (Roberson 1983:102). Health is not merely the absence of disease; to elderly Sea Islanders it means the ability to live independently and meet their own needs:

> *Although signs of decreasing mobility and quickness are acknowledged, we have met respondents in their 60s and 70s who plow and plant several acres of crops every year; even the most aged are proud of their fields. Others, in their 90s, regularly gather pecans for sale each year. They maintain their homes and fences in good order as long as they are able. All of these people, despite ailment and pain, are considered in good health. When one can no longer maintain such independence, one is seen as "failing."* (Blake 1984:38)

Health, then, is the ability to "keep on *keepin'* on," a phrase I first heard from old Olive Parsons many years ago; I have heard it many times since. It means doing what has to be done even in the presence of weakness or pain. It is not a matter of physical function alone; people are expected to "keep on keepin' on" despite lives filled with anxiety about jobs and money and loved ones. This requires a kind of inner strength that will allow the individual to endure in every aspect of living, "almost as though the life force represents an inherent state of 'volume' or 'substance' which should be able to withstand any onslaught from the outer world" (Weidman 1979b).

Theoretically, then, it is possible for an individual—man, woman, child, or the tiniest infant—indeed, even the unborn child—to be in a state of balance with the natural, supernatural, and social environments. But it is also recognized that achieving that balance takes a goodly dose of "Mother Wit." In health matters this means understanding the various sources of threat and what the impact of these would be on body, mind, and spirit. It means knowing how to go about protecting oneself so that the body is kept fit; the mind calm and happy; the spirit free of sin. And health action is imperative: Failure to "take care" will inevitably lead to problems. Little sympathy is wasted on the person whose foolish or careless behavior has resulted in sickness:

> *Lotsa times when people get sick, now take myself. . . . People can get out here and stay out all night and not take their rest, be rest broken, and just keep on doin' it, just keep on doin' it, they gonna get down! Sumpin' gonna happen! And you ain't gonna know what it is! It's your nerves, or you gonna need to be sleepy, you need to sleep, sumpin' gonna happen to ya that you gonna have to go to the doctor. And the doctor gonna tell you you gonna have to slow up. Well, you brought it on your own self.* (Arnella Lewis, Tucson, Arizona; 1971) (Snow 1977:31)

Arnella had learned her lesson the hard way. She had *not* taken care of herself and a few months earlier she had to be "taken off" work as she was suffering from "nerves." She also blamed herself when she later suffered a light stroke; she had eaten too much rich food, she admitted, so that her blood had "boiled up" and given her "blood on the brains."

Her neighbor Olive Parsons was 20 years older than Arnella, but considered herself to be healthy; only her eyesight was failing and that was to be expected. She attributed her long life and good health to the fact that she had *not* subjected her body to such wear and tear; she believed that people got sick if they did not take care:

> *I feel like it's the care that they take of theirselves. That's what I think, I don't know. I feel like they exposes theirselves too much, and don't take enough care of theirself like they should. That's one reason that I can get around and do things now at my age! Now I've worked hard all my life, ever since I started at ten years old. But otherwise I've taken care of myself. And I never was the goin' kind! I didn't work all day, and then goin' half of the night and all like that. . . .* (Tucson, Arizona; 1971) (Snow 1977:31–32)

She also believed that she had remained in good health because she had always relied on her own home remedies. And what did she think of the doctors' medicines? She was proud to be able to say that, "My system ain't never been poisoned up by no medical doctor."

Bernita Washington learned of necessity how to care for the health of herself and her large family. She also had little sympathy for those who fail to take health precautions:

> Well, they become *ill,* they become *ill* and they really think there's something seriously wrong with them when they doesn't do anything to keep themselves *up!* Doesn't do anything to keep the body up! You have to do things; like a lotta people don't think that exercise is necessary. All those things is necessary. Bathin' everyday is necessary. All

those things is necessary. All those things in necessary for your *body!*
That's right, those things is really necessary. (Lansing, Michigan; 1986)

When she was a child, matters of health and illness were nearly
always dealt with at home; there was no money for doctors. Most
of the time *now* her health and that of family members (and not a
few neighbors) she takes care of at home. No sense running to the
doctor all the time, she says. "Lotta times these doctors don't even
know!"

It has been my experience that most individuals know enough to
take care of—and are thought responsible for taking care of—their
own health (see also Weidman et al. 1978:664). Only the very young
are freed of such responsibility; they may be warned that certain
behaviors are dangerous but, being children, they may not pay
attention. Most likely, though, their youthful folly will someday take
its toll. The belief that one will someday have to pay for earlier
excesses is a well-developed theme; somewhere score is being kept.
Sister Erma Allen believed that her arthritis resulted from her childhood play with her brothers and sisters; they were, she said, "bad
kids for jumpin'":

> You know, I have arthritis in my knees. They used to call it rheuma-
> tism. In my knees. When I was a little girl I would ride on the side of
> the car and I jumped off the car, and somehow or other my legs
> swung under and the trailer run over both of my knees. It buried me
> in the sand. Well, my mother didn't take me to the doctor; she didn't
> think it hurt me that much. Well, it *didn't* hurt me that much! Well, I
> guess maybe [it did]. It always do somethin' to the bone or maybe the
> gristle, kneecap or sumpin'. 'Cause me to be stiff in both of my knees.
> I had a fall two or three different times; I had a fall from a horse, had
> a fall from the top of the house. Climbin', when I was a kid. And then
> one time I had a kink in my back from fallin'. My mother would just
> rub it; take some hot water and a towel and just rub it. Well, these
> things cause arthritis; cause me to have arthritis in my spine and arthri-
> tis in my knees. Quite natural; I used to jump from high places. We
> was bad kids for jumpin'. (Tucson, Arizona; 1970)

In her role as evangelist Sister Erma spent a good deal of time at
the hospital that served the indigent population in the city; when
she was not praying for patients she enjoyed simply observing the
hospital routine. Had her life been different, she sometimes said, she
would have liked to have been a doctor. That was not possible, she
knew, but she *could* watch and observe and think about what caused
people to suffer. And 40 years—and 350 pounds—later the "bad kid
for jumpin'" *did* suffer:

> Now, my ankle bothers me from this. And you know, I sit and
> thought about this. *This* is what causes it! It don't bother you until you
> get up. Well, I'll say mine never bothered me really until about 45;

when I got about 45 my knees began to bother me. And then after that my ankles would bother me; then my back flew loose on me. When I went to have a check with the doctor, this is what he found. He said it was arthritis. These things cause sickness; falls that never go to the doctor and [no one] never checked them. Bein' in the country, we were country-raised kids. And *never* think to go to the doctor for ever'thing. My mother was afraid of the doctor. She never took us to the doctor for ever'thing; *she* knew ever'thing to do. She knowed roots and herbs and first one thing and then another to use for us. And that was the cause of havin' rheumatism.

Though a relatively young woman (47 years old when I first met her in 1970) she was in poor health and on disability; she suffered from arthritis, hypertension, and diabetes. The latter I felt contributed to her seeing the glowing blue light after her all-night fast and prayer session on the occasion she asked God for a "sign" that her mother would live (an opinion I kept to myself).

On another day she told me of her practice of fasting for religious merit: "Christmas day I didn't eat a bite; I fast all day Christmas. Usually when I go to the [church] meeting I fast; I go through the revival fastin'. Sometime I go all day; sometime I go three or four days." I had learned from experience not to directly suggest that one of her health practices might be unwise; in this instance I said carefully that I had *heard* that diabetics should not go without eating and had she told her doctor of her fasts? Her answer made it clear that her "connection" with God was far more important that any doctor/patient relationship. "Well, see he can't tell me what to do 'cause I got connection with God. He can't tell me what to do about God. See, it's more important to God than man. Man can't tell me what to do; when God say, 'Put on a fast,' I got to put on a fast."

In the traditional health system it is thought that ill health is bound to—sooner or later—result from the failure to take proper precautions so that these become an important part of daily life for everyone. And sometimes extra help is needed: Heightened vulnerability is associated with the extremes of age so that the very young and the very old are seen as relatively weak. Women in their childbearing years are also at increased risk when their femaleness is expressed in the reproductive cycle. A tiny baby; an elderly man; the menstruating woman—all may need even more protection to stay well. Such protection runs the gamut from common sense avoidance of cold or damp to the use of complex combinations of natural substances enhanced by religious and/or magical symbolism. Such measures are learned from friends and relatives; read about in the printed word; heard on television or radio; spontaneously thought up as the occasion rises. They are designed to help the individual take on strength; they allow a person to feel that in at least part of their life they have responsibility and control. They are Mother Wit in action.

The Body

Followers of the traditional system view the human being as an integration of body, mind, and spirit, all three of which must be in harmony if health is to be maintained. The body must be properly cared for if it is to function normally: cleansed inside and out; kept warm; properly fed; appropriately exercised; adequately rested. The importance of maintaining balance is underscored by the fact that protective measures must themselves be in a kind of state of equilibrium—something seen as good for the body, that is, is just as damaging in excess as it is if it is lacking. Too much exercise harms the body just as much as a slothful lifestyle, for example; and good food is dangerous if too much of it is eaten. It is also important to behave in a way that does not attract undue attention to oneself in spiritual matters and interpersonal relationships. The acquisition of nice things is valued; accumulating *too* much, however, invites divine displeasure or the envy of a neighbor. Unfortunately, the fine line between "not enough" and "too much" is not always easy to assess or maintain. One must always be vigilant.

Failure to take care of the body weakens its defenses and renders its boundaries permeable to a variety of external forces and/or entities. These range from the cold air of a December day to invisible animals introduced by means of a hex; a weakened body is thus made vulnerable to both natural and unnatural problems. Glick's (1967) statement that cause is emphasized over pathological process is clearly demonstrated here, in fact, as a single symptom may be interpreted very differently according to assessment of previous risk. A stroke, for example, may be caused by bathing during a menstrual period; eating too much red meat; worrying so that the blood rushes to the head; a punishment from God; a curse ordered up by an enemy (see also C. Hill and Mathews 1981). The fact that the same symptom may result from a broad range of causes means that diagnosis may also shift from one causal category to another; the assignment of a "natural" cause may give way to an "unnatural" one if the sick person fails to respond to appropriate treatment.

Access to the body's internal environment occurs in a variety of ways. The openness of the major body orifices is obvious, of course, and all of these may be the means of entry for problem-causing agents. The mouth figures prominently in the etiology of illnesses, both in intake of ordinary food and drink and as a route for magically adulterated items. Eyes, nose, and ears give access to microorganisms, cold air, or noxious fumes—but they also allow in fearful sights; the words of someone with a "bad mouth"; and the odors of incense and ritual oils. The skin is also a major entry point for unwanted intrusion when the pores are "open." Other less obvious parts of the body are also vulnerable to intrusion by unwanted entities. The soles of the feet are particularly important as the only body part in direct contact with the earth; as such they are the prime site of entry of cold and damp. They may also "walk over" the less readily apparent threat of a buried charm emitting magical harm.

The heightened vulnerability of women in their childbearing years has already been mentioned. This is particularly so when vaginal bleeding is occurring for any reason, as at that time the uterus is seen as "open." If a woman is careless dangerous chills can "stop up" normal flow or, as Anna Perry admonished me, enable the deadly harm of sorcery to take advantage of her weakness. Other points of entry into the body seem to function in more symbolic terms, as body areas once open but now closed are seen as penetrable. These include the "mold" or "mole" of the head (fontanel) and the navel; a substance rubbed on the navel area, for example, is believed to enter the gastrointestinal tract and/or the female reproductive organs. Similarly, in infants the fontanel is seen as allowing access to the whole system; it represents the proximal end of a tube whose distal end is the rectum. Medicines are frequently rubbed on top of babies' heads, for example, in the belief that they will reach the whole body.[2] In adults, however, this area is mainly associated with access to the brain; hair from the very top of the head may be used in sorcery, for example, in order "to run a person crazy." It is also said that a person will "go crazy" if a bird picks up discarded hair and weaves it into its nest. Both nature and nature subverted can be dangerous when the body is vulnerable.

Once the body's external defenses have been breached the intrusive elements cause problems in two major ways. They may be dispersed to target organs or body parts via normal bodily processes and cause damage at their destination or, in contrast, they may cause illness by blocking normal processes and not allowing the body to function as it should. The body "appears to be viewed as a 'container' and to be constructed of containerlike organs and passage ways. Symptoms are sometimes perceived in terms of weaknesses in the structure of parts of the body and as breakdown in the container-like forms and/or functions of various organs" (Weidman et al. 1978:473). It is the blood that takes on an overriding significance in the internal workings of the body; it is so important that it will be discussed separately. For the moment it must suffice to say that most statements of body function will sooner or later be tied in with the state of the blood. When illness results from a natural or unnatural blockage of organs whose function is to rid the body of impurities (the skin; the gut; the kidneys; the uterus; the liver), for example, it is the blood that becomes "defiled." It is the blood that collects and distributes the cold, the damp, and the dirt. It is the blood that carries magical poison or animal invaders around the body.

The blood does not transport its load of wanted and unwanted substances in the manner probably familiar to most readers. Although the heart is viewed as an important organ and the site from which blood is pumped, the idea that blood circulates through the body and then returns to the heart is not emphasized. Instead it travels to various areas of the body in response to internal and external pressures. It flows *to* and *away from* organs and body areas with an emphasis on up-and-down movement; it is similar, in fact, to the movement of sap in nature. Should the body/blood contain unwanted or dangerous elements then movement from the top of the body downward seems to be favored so that these can be eliminated from the lower part of the body. The perceived workings of the gastrointestinal tract are an obvious example: the "good" in the form of food enters the mouth, is digested, and the remaining "impurities" eliminated via the kidneys and gut. A massage to remove pain from the body also demonstrates this theme: Stroking should go downward to allow pain "to go on out the feet"; massaging in the opposite direction would send the pain toward the heart or head and so is a dangerous practice. When impurities are contained in feces, urine, or menstrual blood they, of course, have form. But note that pain, too, is seen as something that can move around the body as if it has substance. The idea of substance may also be extended to such things as cold or fever; either may "accumulate" and travel to various locations in the body. A chest cold could be cured, Etheldean Mitchell learned from her elderly father in rural Alabama, by rubbing the marrow from a pork bone on the chest; after that was done rags were tied tightly around the chest so that it would not "spread to other parts of the body." (Lansing, Michigan; 1980)

The close tie between the natural world and the human organism that was discussed in the previous chapter is further illustrated by the fact that one of the most frequently mentioned causes of health problems is cold, damp air. The term "exposure" is often used in descriptions of cold-caused illnesses, describing both how the illness came about and the failure of the victim to take precautions. It is widely believed that upper respiratory infections associated with increased mucus production are caused by the intrusion of cold and/or damp air into the body. The presence of mucus or phlegm in the body is more than just a symptom that cold has entered the body, in fact; it is referred to as if it *is* the cold in the body. It is described as a tangible substance able to move about and "settle" in various places. Lillian Ashleigh never fully believed her physician's diagnosis of chronic cardiac disease, for example; instead she attributed her shortness of breath to the presence of "cold" in her body. She found this difficult to understand, she told me, as she was *always* careful to dress warmly before going outside. "Now, just like this cough I have, now I don't really feel that it's a cold. And yet I *know* it's *cold* in there, because the main reason of the coughing, I get that little lump of phlegm or mucus in my throat, and I have to cough until I can get it out. And of course I know that's cold in there." She died in congestive heart failure not long after she made these remarks. (Tucson, Arizona; 1970) Bernita Washington's cure for infantile pneumonia illustrates the same belief. "Rub him down with mineral oil and Vicks salve," she says, "and take a red cloth—it have to be a red cloth—and pin all around him. That'll stimulate him; then give mineral oil or cod liver oil to work it out." (Lansing, Michigan; 1989)

The usual route of entry for cold is through pores that have been opened by heat, leaving the body vulnerable to morning dew, chilly water, or sudden changes of temperature. A woman in rural Virginia described what happens then: "Cold gets into your body like when you haven't taken proper care of yourself—like in summer when you get wet swimming or get overheated. Then you sweat and your pores are open so the cold, dampness, air and germs can get in more easily and harbor there. Then in the winter it becomes a cold. In winter, it's the same problem. Maybe you're inside and get overheated and then go out in the cold air with your pores open and without wearing enough clothes" (Roberson 1983:147).

As the above remarks indicate it is believed that illness-causing entities can penetrate the body and not cause illness at once; the body can "harbor" that which entered while taking a swim in summer until it "becomes a cold" in the winter. The onset of symptoms may even be delayed for years: If the individual is young they may escape falling ill at once. But again the cold can "accumulate" in the blood, travel to the joints and lurk there; in later life as the body weakens the "old cold" will manifest itself as arthritis and rheumatism. In Bertha Alexander's words: "Well, in other words . . . it's *exposure,* that you get sometime when you're young in your body. Through your system as you get older, it take effect . . . dampness and not takin' proper care of yourself. Goin' out in bad weather and rainy weather, you expose yourself. Pores are open. You're subject to takin' a complaint, in through the blood. . . . [It] kind of grows into the system, and as you get older, it works with you." (Tucson, Arizona; 1971) (Snow 1977:41) The entry of cold and damp into the body is also responsible for problems associated with the adult female reproductive cycle; these will be discussed in a later chapter.

The health problems attributed to the imbalance of heat and cold are probably those seen as most easily preventable. Putting on warm clothes before going out in the cold and taking them off again upon coming in, avoiding swimming while overheated or going out in the cold with wet hair, these are simple measures that, if followed, would help the individual to avoid many health problems.[3] If someone *has* suffered colds or flu during the winter, Bernita Washington says, it is important to make sure that they are all out of the system at season's end. She believes that the body needs to be "changed over" in the springtime to prepare for the warm weather, just as winter clothes are put away and summer clothes put on. When she lived in rural Mississippi she used poke greens for this purpose, though recognizing that they are poisonous if improperly prepared:

> Now, the only thing that we used down there—we didn't buy any-thing when it become springtime—we go into the woods and get that poke salad. . . . Then you wash it; then you put it on and you *boil* it. Then you takes it out of that water, then you rinses it off real good. You puts it back into *another* water and you boil it again—you can even put meat in it, you can cook it just like you do any other green. But be sure that it's boiled and rinsed at least twicet; in other words that's to get the poison out, because it *is* poison. It's *one* thing they re-ally taught about it is to be *sure* that you boil it and be sure you got the poison out of it. Because it'll run you blind; that's what it does. Yeah, it'll run you blind if you don't fix it right. 'Cause it go right into the bloodstream and it'll run you blind.

> It just helps your body to come back in order for the comin' [summer]. In other words, like you change clothes. You got winter clothes and you got summer clothes, O.K.? So it's just to change your body over, you know. Maybe you had a lot of colds and flu and stuff all in the winter time; so now, you know, you tryin' to build your body back up so you won't have to go through all of this in the *summer*time. 'Cause see, lot of people have summer colds? Because they doesn't take any-thing to build the body back up from the winter that they went through.

The plant she is referring to is *Phytolacca americana* L.; it has a long history of medicinal use by Native Americans and European settlers as well as by African-Americans. And Bernita is right; it is quite toxic if not prepared properly or if it is picked when too mature (Morton 1974:109–110; S. Foster and Duke 1990:56). But her herbal remedy is not readily available in the city so in the late spring of 1988, when she had been suffering for two weeks from "that flu or pneumonia that's going around," she had to find something else. She was instead taking a laxative each morning which was, "workin' my body. I don't want this cold in my system for the summer."

Not everyone takes the precautions necessary to avoid or mini-mize the depredations caused by cold, of course, and older inform-ants frequently talk about the know-it-all attitude of young people who fail to listen to their advice. Arnella Lewis, known in the Tucson neighborhood where she lived for "telling it like it is," certainly had no sympathy for the teenagers whose attire she found unsuitable:

> *Now this here is wintertime, isn't it? If I go out here half-dressed, half-nekkid, catch a whole lotta cold, won't try to do nothin' about it, you know I'm gonna be sick! . . . I brought it on myself! . . . Lookit the girls today, walkin' around here with no clothes on. Their mini-skirts up to here. I saw some with shorts on yesterday. Shorts! Up to here! They don't feel it now! They young, blood's thick. But you wait until they get up 25, 30 years old, maybe 40. They gonna be crippin' along,*

got the rheumatism. "I'm hurtin."" They brings it all on theirselves! They exposin' theirself! They not takin' care of theirselves! They just goin' head on, just dressin', and you cain't tell 'em nothin'! More nekkid folks now than I ever seen in my life! Walkin' nekkid in the street. And when they get my age, mightn't get as old as I am, they gonna feel it. Sumpin' gonna happen to 'em! If they don't go into TB, they gonna have pneumonia; if they don't do that, they gonna have arthritis; they gonna have rheumatism. They gonna pay for it. All that cold is settlin' in their joints. . . . When they get older, they gonna feel it. They be to the place they be walkin' on crutches, sticks, and ever'thing else! (1970) (Snow 1977:43)

The temperature had been 82 degrees on the day in question; I elected not to tell Arnella that I had been wearing shorts myself.

Improper diet as a cause of illness is mentioned nearly as often as is cold. There is intense interest in the ingestion of food and the processes of digestion and elimination, an interest that begins in the newborn period and continues to the end of life. Unlike cold, which should never enter the body, what one eats obviously must do so. The theme of moderation and balance is again present; and so is the propensity for self-blame. High blood pressure results, according to Bertha Alexander, from "eatin' too much and gettin' too fat, the blood goes up to your head too fast. But you know you can help that yourself, just don't eat all that rich food." (Tucson, Arizona; 1971) It is not just overeating or eating the wrong sorts of foods that is considered dangerous; even good food can be a problem if it is eaten at the wrong time, in combination with various other foods, or at certain times in the life cycle. The female reproductive cycle is again involved, and diet must be carefully monitored anytime there is vaginal bleeding and during pregnancy or lactation. Food proper for adults may be "too strong" for children; for the elderly; for invalids. And the wrong food may, like cold, lurk in the system. Both were blamed by one of Camino's urban Virginia informants for "high blood": "They are just storing it up, their blood's gonna go bad if they go outside in skimpy clothes . . . or if they eat a lot of junk" (1986:75).

Some foods, fine if eaten alone or with most other foods, may be seen as poisonous if consumed in wrong combination. The old Southern belief that eating fish and drinking milk at the same meal is dangerous is still repeated (Cussler and DeGive 1952:59). Gloria Standish was told this by "the old folks" when she was growing up in Detroit. She doesn't really believe it, she says, but hasn't tried it. "It's just as well to be on the safe side." (Detroit, Michigan; 1984) Jimmie Lou Fox, who moved to Michigan from Alabama a few years ago, has also heard that there are fatal food/liquor combinations. One should never drink whiskey while eating either watermelon or bananas, for example. This "causes a chemical reaction and can kill you." She has never seen it happen but says her mother in Alabama has; like Gloria, she is not sure it is true but is not about to take a chance. (Saginaw, Michigan; 1981)

It is not only improper combinations of food that can poison the system, however. Adulturated food and drink is perhaps the most commonly mentioned vehicle for sorcery, adding an element of danger to every cup of coffee or plate of greens consumed.[4] One must be just as careful about *where* and *with whom* one eats as in what is eaten. If for any reason envy has been aroused in others it is wise to avoid eating in public, Anna Perry warned me by letter after I had moved to Michigan: "Witchcraft is real, it can be did; you can be hypnotized. You hafta be careful where you eat and drink. Parties is not good. You know some ladies is looking at that man of yours. You is new there, so don't be so fast in going to parties and eating and drinking, it isn't good." (Tucson, Arizona; 1972) (Snow 1974:86) She believed that magically doctored food can kill only the person for whom it was intended.[5] Over the years a number of informants have told me that as children they were admonished never to accept food in the homes of their playmates; those who are most worried about magical attack may refuse to eat food cooked by anyone other than themselves.

A connection between diet and physical well-being is perhaps found in most health belief systems; and it is not surprising to find beliefs about foods appropriate to age, gender, and state of health. Diet takes on great significance in this health culture in ways that will merit further discussion, however. As in many aspects of African-American health beliefs diet and its effect on the body can only be understood by looking at its effect on the blood—it is the blood that carries the constituents found in food, good or bad—throughout the system. An injudicious diet therefore affects all parts of the body: "We just eatin' our disease and drinkin' it," says Daisy Jackson. "Whatever goes *inside* of you, it goes all over you." (Lansing, Michigan; 1988) Certain foods have the added ability to change the quality of the blood, causing it to become "too high" or "too low", "too thick" or "too thin", "too sweet" or "too acid," and so forth. The direction and speed with which the blood moves through the body is also affected by certain foodstuffs, sometimes with fatal effect. The impact of diet on the blood is something that must be constantly monitored throughout the lifespan.

A dirty body is a sick body, people say, on the outside *or* the inside. A good deal of attention is therefore paid to keeping the body clean—and cleaned out. Again the connection between the ebb and flow of the life force with the changing seasons is shown, as an unclean body may be associated with seasonality. There is a direct connection made between the sap in trees and plants and the blood in the body, so that the blood is seen as sinking downward in the fall. As the sap rises in the spring the blood that has collected lower in the body will begin to rise as well. If the blood is in a proper state, well and good; if not, beware. In Anna Perry's words, "When spring comes birds start mating. Fishes in the water start mating. The sap is rising and impurities start rising too. If your system's defiled, why you're liable to come up with *anything!*" (Tucson, Arizona; 1971) The association of a body that needs to be purified and the spring of the year is made explicit in some farmers' almanacs. In June, according to one almanac, the diseases prevalent are "mostly of the stomach and liver, dyspepsia, indigestion, inflammations and eruptions. This is the month that cancers and tumors develop. Purify and enrich the blood and drive out all impurities with a good cathartic and you will avoid the diseases of June" (*MacDonald's Farmers Almanac* 1980:n.p.).

A "spring cleaning" is a common measure in both rural and urban areas, then, though the cleansing agent may differ depending on what is available. Bernita Washington's poke greens served this purpose when she lived in Mississippi, removing any residual impurities from colds suffered during the winter. Sulfur is another purifying agent, its bitter taste made palatable by mixing it with a sweetening agent such as molasses or honey; the sulfur is believed to open the pores to let impurities escape. Sassafras tea is also popular: Pleasant-tasting and red in color, it is obviously good for the blood. If the bark or roots are not available outdoors they can be obtained in tea bags at the health-food store. And laxatives, of course, are always available if sulfur or sassafras or poke greens are not to be had.

It is not just in the springtime that cleansing measures need to be taken, however. Many health problems are blamed on disordered excretory function, and the kidneys, the intestines, and the liver are all thought important in the processes of cleansing the body. Menstruation is also widely viewed as a means of ridding the body of dirty blood, and interference with usual menstrual patterns is frightening. Traditional ideas about venereal disease are tied in with dirt in the body as well; the resultant "bad blood" may be blamed on failing to bathe after a menstrual period, wearing dirty underclothing, living in a filthy house, or having sex with too many partners, none necessarily infected. A dirty system is reflected in the blood that becomes "defiled," in Anna Perry's term, by the substances (vaguely associated with "germs") which move through the body to cause symptoms. Just as the presence of mucus is associated with cold in the body, accumulated impurities are associated with heat: fever, inflammation and, above all, skin eruptions. The latter, ranging from acne to measles to a syphilitic chancre, represent "something in the body trying to come out" as the body attempts to clean itself.

Bodily impurity in early stages may merely produce a "sluggish" feeling; if addressed promptly more stringent measures may not need to be taken. Commercial laxative preparations may be used to "clean off" the liver, for example, just as they may be used to "work" accumulated cold out of the body. Bernita, showing me her collections of such items, indicated that cleaning off the liver takes less than a full "dose":

[It] also cleans your liver off. Lotta people wake up in the morning time and they feel so sluggish and feel sick on the stomach and stuff like that. Sometime your *liver* need cleanin' off, so that's very good to clean your liver off. Dependin' on how you feel, you take it 'til you feel better. You don't ever take a *dose;* a dose would be a teaspoonful. You don't ever take a dose. Say you would use about that much [poured out about 1/4 teaspoonful into her hand], I use about that much and no more than that. And you takes it until you feel better. (Lansing, Michigan; 1986)

A "dose" is used if more alarming symptoms develop.

A good deal of time and money is invested in measures aimed at keeping the body "cleaned out"; these are instituted shortly after the birth of an infant and last throughout the life cycle. "I don't worry about my grandbaby being constipated," Odelia Kurtz told me one afternoon at the pediatric clinic where I was working. "I puts a spoonful of that children's laxative in her bottle every night!" (Lansing, Michigan; 1982) Even Janine Jackson, who ordinarily disavows any sort of health measures outside of prayer, believes that the digestive process needs help:

Sometimes people say, "What you buy for medicine?" And I say, "Well, sometime I buy Feenamints and then ever' now and then I buy Ex-Lax." That's to get you all cleaned up. I had a sister, she'd laugh at me; I'd say, "Yeah, if you don't get all that *food* outa you, you know, it builds *up.* And then you could—I don't know what'd happen to you— but just keep yourself clean-runnin', just clean, and you'll feel much better!" And you really do. (Lansing, Michigan; 1986)

And if you don't? Again, whatever happens, you brought it on your own self.

Much of the time the various sources of threat outlined above— from cold, from dietary folly, from failure to keep the body clean— express themselves in natural ways. It must be stated again, however, that all of these may be implicated in unnatural health problems as well. Natural forces may be subverted by magical means; food or drink may be adulterated or unnaturally poisoned; normal bodily functions be blocked by ritual acts. Almost anything that goes wrong with ordinary body processes, that is, may in certain circumstances be seen as stemming from the deliberate actions of others.

The Mind

The healthy individual is in possession of an untroubled mind in addition to a well-cared-for body. It is much more difficult to achieve this happy state, however, than it is to keep the physical body well fed, clean, warm, and rested. The constant anxiety brought on by the trials and tribulations of everyday life, where everything that is valued seems to be in short supply, understandably takes its toll (Satcher and Creary 1984). When the living space is—rightly—perceived as dangerous it may contribute to "intolerable levels of social ambiguity (and therefore anxiety)" for many people:

> *Situations of ambiguity abound in the life circumstances of immigrants into inner-city areas. Uncertainty is an omnipresent condition of life for long-term inner-city dwellers who have become trapped in areas with many environmental deficiencies, overcrowding, high rates of crime, and who manage only marginally to subsist; certainly not to thrive. Given the precarious nature of survival in such settings, distinctions for both newcomers and oldtimers may become blurred between friend/foe; appropriate/inappropriate; acceptable/unacceptable; right/wrong, etc.* (Weidman 1979b:99)

In social terms, according to a 61-year old woman living in Harlem:

> *We are, by reason of the lives we have led, a suspicious people. We are the children of suspicious people, as were our grandparents and their grandparents. This has been so with us even back to those people most of us call foreparents. Now, if we were otherwise we would probably all be white or dead! Every reasonable black person thinks that most white people do not mean him well. Every reasonable black person knows that many other black people cannot afford to treat him fairly. Most black people believe that most other human beings will seek their own advantage at the expense of other people. We do not really think it has much to do with the justice of a situation. People will do what profits them. We think white people are the most unprincipled folks in the world, but everybody bears watching. I believe we are righter to think in this way than any other, considering our circumstances.* (Gwaltney 1980:7)

It is not surprising to find that the problems of daily life, particularly relationships with other people, are the source of "nervous troubles," and "nerves," and "worriation." These commonly heard terms refer to a broad range of symptoms ranging from inability to eat or sleep to "falling-out" spells to full-blown mental illness.[6] If a man or woman becomes *too* absorbed with their problems they may fall ill because, "'they study themselves so'" (Dougherty 1976). Certainly Mother Delphine, the Tucson healer, felt that such single-mindedness was a sure way to mental illness:

A person that's sick in mind, mentally sick, doctors can't find that. They X-ray, and they can't find it. They say, "Well, I don't see nothin'; there's nothin' wrong." And yet they sick! Mentally sick, sick in mind. It's a believing, you know. You can believe hard on something, it just come to you. I think that's the way people go crazy! They believe one thing too strong, and the next thing you know, they flipped their wig, and they in the insane asylum. But I get people with all kinds of feeling, like some of 'em says, "I can't sleep, I can't sleep. . . . Mother, why I can't sleep?" . . . They're sick, they're thinkin' too hard about somethin'. Their bills are worryin' them.

You know how times is. Things is changed 'n everything is high. Some people get such a small wage, don't make much money, they can't make ends meet. And then it come to them when they stop still, you know. Like they'll lie down, and they get to thinkin' and it get into the mind. They're so weak, they can't throw it off. Well, next thing you know, it's daylight! (1971) (Snow 1977:59)

Many of my Tucson informants commented that such "worries" and "nervousness" can make a person sick. Perhaps even *kill* you, said Sister Erma: "Peoples have lost their mind. Right, this'll kill you. You can worry yourself to death. Over your bills and over your money." (1971) Louis Winston, who lived alone in a small house a few blocks away from Sister Erma, knew that there were all sorts of causes for "trouble"—but he believed that "worry" over loved ones was infinitely worse:

Seems like worry is worse than trouble. Trouble is when you've killed a man, and you're shuckin' through the woods tryin' to keep away from the law. You know if the law catches you, you'll get the electric chair. That's trouble.

But—worry is when you're fussin' with somebody you love. Maybe it's your wife; maybe it's a brother or sister. But I'll tell you, dear, seems like you can't eat, and you can't sleep at night. No matter what you do, you can't forget about it. Can't get it off your mind. That's why I say that worry is worse than trouble. (1970) (Snow 1977:60)

Years later in a Virginia city one of Camino's informants echoed his words while explicitly linking health and happiness: "If you're happy and feel good, then you will be healthy. But if you are unhappy, well then you may as well forget about it, because worry can cause you to be sick, can take your mind. Some people worry themselves down to nothing, and one way worriation is sure to come out is in sickness. Why do you think people say 'he's *worried* hisself sick'?" (Camino 1986:65). Although problems were "omnipresent" in the neighborhood where Camino worked, she also found that "worriation" differed along gender lines. For men it clustered on (in descending order): wages, on-the-job discrimination, providing for wives and/or children, the emotional welfare of their families, and keeping extramarital liaisons discreet. Worriation for women, in contrast, was defined by their nurturing roles and centered around family life.

Such problems are commonplace in both rural and urban African-American communities (Rainwater 1970; Coles 1967, 1971a; Gwaltney 1980; Kotlowitz 1991; Lemann 1991). Weidman and her co-researchers used the questionnaires developed by the nationally based Health Interview Survey to gain some estimate of the morbidity of chronic conditions in inner-city Miami, for example, and found that "nervous trouble" ranked number one for their Southern Black respondents. It is interesting to note that the category "nervous trouble" contained most of the references to emotional and mental problems, that is, respondents did not talk about biomedically defined psychiatric conditions nor did they respond to the check list item, "mental illness." No Southern Blacks or Haitians gave any replies to this category: "There was a reluctance to acknowledge 'mental illness' but a great tendency to admit to 'nervous trouble' (Item #20) instead" (Weidman et al. 1978:361–362).

A widespread concern with nervous conditions is also reflected in a study of low-income African-American and White patients attending a rural clinic in Virginia (Nations, Camino, and Walker 1985). Nearly half of those interviewed divulged that they were suffering from one or more "ethnomedical" complaints; the most frequently mentioned three (composing 63 percent of the total) were "high blood," "weak 'n' dizzy," and "nerves." All three are problems that exhibit the respondents' perception that stressful events and strained social interactions affect mental and physical health.[7] The debilitating effect of such problems is graphically illustrated by one individual's description of weekly "weak 'n' dizzy" spells: "If I get excited and upset, I get nerves, then my blood flashes up to my head, it rises very fast and then I get weak 'n' dizzy. I can't motivate, can't do nothin'. I feel like everything done run out of me. I'm like an old apple, all dried and withered away, tired and worn out." Nervous troubles seem to be viewed as more alarming than symptoms that are more obviously physical. The ability to "keep on keepin' on" is highly valued and "nerves" interferes with day-to-day functioning. The mind that is not working properly affects all aspects of an individual's life, that is, in a way that pain in a single body part does not.

It is apparent that mental/nervous/emotional problems are common and are very troublesome. The underlying processes producing them is unclear, however, in no little fashion because the term "nerves" may be used to describe a physical entity, a state of mind, *or* the manner in which the problem occurs. Somehow the mind, the emotions, the nerves, and the blood all interact to produce disvalued states. And clearly the nerves must be strong to withstand the assaults of daily life. On one occasion Bernita's husband, Joseph, had been sitting silently listening as she told me what sorts of things could cause the blood (and the blood pressure) to go up. When I asked if she thought that high blood pressure caused symptoms, he interjected:

> I can answer *that* question! You see, when your *blood*, when your pressure runs *up* your eyes comes lookin' *dim* because your *blood* is goin' on up. [It's] gettin' too *high* on you. Nerves, your nerves is startin' to goin' weaker. Goin' down on you.

"Your nerves will start going down on you?"

> Uh-huh. In face of *buildin'*, you see, they goin' *back*. And then that'll make you have a nervous breakdown or anything. 'Cause see if I get angry I knows about it, if I get *too angry?* My blood'll [be] raised up and I just cain't *talk*, you know, explain myself. Looks like somethin' *dim* starts comin' over your eyes. (Lansing, Michigan; 1987)

When this happens, he said, he simply goes to his bedroom to lie down until he feels calm. He had been prescribed medication for hypertension but had recently stopped taking it as, "it went back on my body." He chose instead to eat large amounts of garlic while striving to maintain emotional balance; it was a few months after this discussion that he suffered a stroke.[8]

The statements of individuals cited above make clear that "nerves" produce physical, mental, and emotional changes. When the patients at a rural Virginia clinic were asked if they thought that "nerves" is a problem of the mind or of the body, they gave various answers: 60 percent asserted that it is a problem of both; 25.9 percent believed it to be "a mind thing"; and only 14.8 percent viewed it as purely physical (Nations, Camino, and Walker 1988; see also C. Hill and Mathews 1981). A view of nerves as somatic is expressed by African-American and White residents of a rural county in Florida when they talk about the "'coating on the nerves'," in which the "nervous system is apparently viewed as almost precisely duplicating an electrical system using insulated wires, the condition of the insulation being tied directly to the degree of illness or health" (Murphree 1976). Camino's urban Virginia informants similarly see nerves as "likened to 'strings' or 'wires' that 'hold you together'. . . " and outside forces—particularly social and emotional stressors—can cause them to "become 'broken,' 'frazzled,' 'torn,' 'shot,' 'wore out,' or 'wrung out'." Because women and children are seen as constitutionally weaker than men, their nerves are seen as thinner and weaker. Children may have "weak nerves" but these usually remain uninjured because they have had less time to be exposed to stressful events. Women, however, are further weakened by their physiology: "That's just women's nature, with women having kids and all. And monthlies. Wears out the nerves" (Camino 1989).

It is obvious that "the nerves," however they are perceived, are located in a way that allows stressful messages to flash all over the body, but it is unclear exactly how this occurs. People talk easily about how "cold" can intrude via pores left open by carelessness or filth can accumulate in a body with sluggish digestion, but there is no explicit parallel statement of how extraneous events produce worriation. By inference the sensory organs are involved, allowing in the disturbing messages that stimulate the nerves to react and overreact to outside events. Once inside, the unpleasant internal responses that people describe so clearly are set in motion. Even the unborn child is not free of risk from the outer world as it is mediated by the emotional state of the mother: *Any* excessive emotion can "mark" the fetus, though such marking may require the mother's touch on her own body to transmit the signal. Strong sensory input appears to weaken the internal self—or the child within the uterus—via the nerves.

Like most other problems, mental and emotional derangements may have an unnatural cause. Full-blown mental illness, in fact, in contrast to the more benign forms of "nerves" or "worriation" is very frequently blamed on sorcery (Marshall 1955; Wintrob 1973; Golden 1977; Hillard 1982; Pellegrini and Putman 1984; Brandon 1988). Inability to fulfill daily tasks or the compulsion to do something that one does not wish to do may signal that the individual is the victim of evil magic. Of special concern is the belief that the victim may not recognize the change in behavior that is so obvious to others, refusing to believe that help is needed. Or, if the individual *does* realize that something is terribly wrong, he or she may be unable to believe that the perpetrator was involved. Says Bernita (whose own mother was magically killed by Bernita's stepfather, according to family lore) about such things:

> It's one thing about it, most *time* with dealin' with stuff like that, like if somebody did somethin' to *me* like that, there's no way you could tell me. "Oh, somebody done fix you," you know. Say like if that girl in there [referring to her young daughter] *did* it and you say, "Probably that lady over there did it to you," there's no way I would believe that lady did it. I would believe anybody else do it before I would believe she did it; which she might would have did that, see. You won't *ever* come to the knowledge of believin' that's the one did somethin' to you, you would *never* believe *that* one did it. You would believe someone *else* did it.[9] (Lansing, Michigan; 1987)

The victim would then stay in the dangerous situation while fruitlessly blaming someone else. Although any sort of magical activity may result in mental changes, the ritual use of the victim's hair is frequently mentioned because of its proximity to the brain. Hair from the "mole" of the head is particularly effective because here "'the brain is more exposed'" (M. Bell 1980:162). Alternatively, magical charms may be placed over a doorway so that when the victim walks through, their emanations can enter the head. Then, "he is being held mentally or put into a frame of mind that sends him away or runs him crazy" (p. 409). Presumably the doorway charm—like the magical poison that is ingested—will harm only the intended victim. A disordered mind, whatever the source, is profoundly disquieting.

The prevention of problems caused by cold, dirt, or poor eating habits is simple when compared to trying to prevent those that end in damaged nerves. Unfortunately, the very definition of "worriation" reflects the difficulty with preventive measures. The sorts of things that keep people awake at night, that is their minds "tied up," are those that they are most powerless to change. "Just try not to do that," says Bernita, speaking of the effect of worry on the system—but that is much easier said than done. And since there is little that people can do to alleviate the anxiety that they feel, it is not surprising to find a magical and/or religious component in preventive measures taken to ward off life stressors. Prayer and scriptural passages are commonly incorporated into all manner of everyday activities, and religious/magical ritual is frequently used to transform an everyday household object or substance into something with the power to cleanse and to protect.

A variety of commercial products incorporating elements of religion and magic are also available to the individual who needs help in dealing with everyday life; these products have long been used for such a purpose (*Drums and Shadows* 1940:55–56; Mulira 1990). These, too, are designed to repel or attract—they may help keep the house and its environs free from gossipy neighbors, bill collectors, and those who do not wish one well—they may help to find a job, win a lawsuit, or hit the numbers. The purchase of candles, oils, incense, aerosol sprays, and amulets of all kinds promises whatever might be wanted or needed. Some establishments deal exclusively in such things and they are to be found in most large urban areas; most carry a variety of booklets describing ritual techniques as well as the paraphernalia necessary to carry them out. If such a store is not nearby then items for every possible use are available from mail order sources (Snow 1979). The manufacture and sale of such products is big business; according to one source there are more than 15 national clearing houses in the United States manufacturing and distributing such goods (Davis, Boles, and Tatro 1984).[10]

The Spirit

Just as the body must be maintained and the mind kept untroubled, so must the spirit of the individual be attended to if a state of health is to exist. Just as the intrusion of cold can weaken the body and an emotional shock weaken the mind, so may chronic stress and/or inappropriate behavior weaken the spirit. Again "worriation" is a contributory factor; Camino's Virginia informants used the phrase, "lost the use of self" to describe the effect on the spirit of constant stress:

> *In this disorder, the body and mind are rendered lethargic, yet the soul becomes agitated. Experienced people recognize the feelings of "heaviness, like you got a weight pressing on your chest," and unwillingness to get out of bed in the morning, "no get up and go," "sitting and staring like a zombie," "not wanting to do like you should," feeling puny, and "feeling your spirit moving around under your skin" as primary indications of "lost the use of self." "Worriation" or stress is viewed as an external force which presses in on the individual's body, especially in the area of the heart; if this continues, these forces "go way down inside, to the arms, legs and even get your soul." The soul is then viewed as impelled into a restive or frenzied state, which undergoes considerable frustration because an unpeaceful soul cannot work to operate the body and the mind as it should. That is, the body and mind on the one hand, and the soul on the other hand become engaged in an inverse relationship; the more torpid the body and mind become, the more excited the soul becomes. This produces a bizarre state of being, for the emotions and the soul work at cross-purposes, not harmoniously as they should. "Lost the use of self" usually emanates from the failure to adequately resolve psycho-social conflicts in one's life. . . . (Camino 1986:91–92)*

The spirit may also be weakened by failure to "nourish the spirit" just as much as by out-and-out sin.

The presence of an invisible spirit world filled with powerful beings both good and evil means that a constant vigilance must be maintained; the individual whose own spirit has become weakened is in grave danger. Some sorts of spirits seem to habitually lurk around humans and human habitations seeking to cause trouble. They may be described as "a bad spirit," "evil spirits," or simply as "evil influences"; they are frequently blamed for significant deviations from accepted behavior. According to Mother Delphine: "Then there's demons. A demon is a bad spirit. You know, don't have no desire to do right. Do wrong. We have some people in the world have *never* done right. Wrong doin', that's a demon tell you to do that, that's a demon is overpowerin' the *good!* Which the Devil did tell Christ on the last day he would do that, he'd be goin' to and from seekin' the children of God. That's what he meant." (Tucson, Arizona; 1971) (Snow 1977:45) In extreme cases they may actually enter the body and "take over," so that one is "demon-possessed."

Failure to maintain vigilance against such evil influences may even produce symptoms in individuals who are *not* misbehaving. Janine Jackson is a profoundly religious woman living an exemplary life, for example, but a moment of inattention on the job gave Satan that little edge he needed to cause her to have an accident. She and a sister were discussing whether God would "send" illness or misfortune as a means of getting a person's attention:

> I have a sister I was talkin' to about it. I said, "This is *Satan* work; people are so hard to understand that this is really *Satan!* They think [it's] God. [God] wouldn't do this to get your *attention!* No, He don't! No way. And He never have put no sickness on nobody. Just like my *knee,* that wasn't Him! That was my carelessness and Satan let it happen! Uh-huh. God didn't have *no* part of it; God didn't have no part of it. Just my carelessness, not hookin' the mixin' bowl *down* on the stand and then when I didn't hook it down, my leg, when I got up, *bang!* Because you know he's always out there ready; just that one little inch and mistake you make, Satan is [ready]. Yeah, he'll put somethin' on us." (Lansing, Michigan; 1986)

Janine's sister does not agree with her on this point; she, like many other people, *does* feel that God will punish the sinner who "goes away" from Him. And the things that happen are usually attention-getters: an accident; a paralyzing stroke; the birth of a deformed child; sudden death. Said Bertha Alexander, for example:

> *Seem like a lot of times things come through Him like that; lot of times people will be well. And then on down the line somethin' will happen to him, sometimes be crippled. And then be out workin' around machinery sometimes, somethin' will explode. Cause him to lose his sight, accidental things. So many different things, for sinnin' all the time. We here in the world sin. Things gonna come upon us, unless we serve Him more. I think if we go away from Him, He might suffer some of these things to happen.* (Tucson, Arizona; 1971) (Snow 1977:55–56)

Whatever form they take, the resultant problems are not viewed as responding to orthodox medical care. "Many, many people are in the State Mental Hospital who the doctors are unable to cure," I once heard an evangelist at a Baptist revival declare. This is because their sickness is "the sickness of sin," and "medicine will not reach the mind nor a sin-diseased heart." (Tucson, Arizona; 1971)

Exactly how such things happen is not made specific: One does not hear an explanation paralleling the entry of cold into open pores or even the flash of anger on nerves. Instead, a demon slips from the corner of the room into an unprotected body, or God strikes down a sinner with spiritual lightning. Here, as Glick (1967) suggested, the importance of the *why* is uppermost. Such happenings *do* call attention to the victim or the victim's family; people *do* wonder aloud why it happened; people *do* interpret them as somehow deserved, whether the sender is God or the Devil. And discussions of the "why" reveal what sorts of behavior are thought deserving of such punishment. These are frequently those that make the victim or his family stand out in some way: accumulation of too many material goods; failure to share good fortune; thinking you are better than other people; making fun of the less fortunate. Whether attack comes from an angry God or from Satan it is better to be spiritually safe than sorry. Preventive measures also have a moral tone: "If people do right," says one of Carole Hill's informants in rural Georgia, "they do better about sickness" (1988:127). "Doing right" means living the sort of life laid down in the Bible as pleasing to God; "doing right" means behaving in the sorts of ways seen as appropriate by members of the community.

If good spiritual entities can *send* sickness and pain to the sinner they can also provide special help, of course. One 68-year-old California woman who had undergone surgery for colon cancer astonished her caretakers by not requesting any postoperative pain medication, for example. When questioned, she revealed that she had not *needed* any (Heiligman, Lee, and Kramer 1983), "because angels were watching over her and taking care of her. She could see them gathered around her bed, but they did not talk to her. They had humanlike features and were surrounded by a bright glow. She claimed that their comforting presence had nearly eliminated any postoperative pain." The fact that religious belief is generally divorced from medical care is emphasized in this case by the fact that a psychological consultation was deemed necessary. Not everyone has a bright band of angels, of course, but it is believed that individuals may augment their spiritual strength by "feeding the spirit": This might mean "daily readings of Bible passages, attending church services, listening to gospel music, doing a favor for a friend, or 'just getting out of the house'" (Camino 1986:65). As in other aspects of health belief, it is important to be *doing*. Even medicinal plants may be associated with religion, and people frequently note that these are mentioned in the Bible. And if you don't know just which ones to use? "Report on Herbs & Plants of the Bible: How They Are Used Today," read an ad in the *Chicago Defender* (January 31, 1987, p. 36); a $3 money order to an Illinois address brought the information by return mail.[11]

The Bible is also of immense importance in maintaining spiritual health. In inner-city Miami it was found to be especially important for Bahamian and Southern Black respondents, especially the reading of the Psalms. One small group of individuals were asked to indicate which ones they used most frequently and to what end; 37 different Psalms were mentioned, 7 of which were reported as helpful in maintaining a sense of well-being. The underlying themes of these (Psalms 23; 27; 29; 37; 38; 40; and 51) revealed that they were being used "to increase 'control' and a sense of mastery. Such control, for the most part, depends upon bringing in 'good' and keeping out or preventing 'bad.' The psalms are used 'for' something and 'against' something else. They are used to 'bring in' or to 'prevent,' to 'ensure' something positive and/or to protect against something negative"

(Weidman et al. 1978:608; see also Baer 1984:133–134). Again, external forces are enlisted to augment personal power when people perceive themselves as weak.

Religion is also heavily represented in the various products available in the candle shop or by mail order. The catalog of such an establishment in inner-city Detroit advertises "7 Archangels," "7 Saints," and "Faith and Hope for Every Need" candles, for example, as well as "Water from [the] River Jordan (not for internal use)" and "7 Holy Spirit Bath Liquid." An entire shelf in the shop offers Bibles, books of the Psalms, and books in which the Psalms have been handily grouped according to topic and need. In the latter, that is, the Psalms appropriate to "Marital Harmony" or "Spiritual Love" or "Overcoming Sorrow" are collected in one section. Drug stores and grocery stores in areas with a large African-American population may also carry a selection of such merchandise. I bought a bottle of "High John the Conqueror Triple Fast Action Spiritual Bath and Floor Wash" in a drug store only a few blocks from Bernita Washington's home in Lansing, for example. It was on the same shelf as the peanut butter and the boxed macaroni and cheese. Only a few feet away, state of Michigan lottery tickets are available, offering hope of a more secular sort.

In summary, the idealized state that represents harmony and health is difficult to achieve and maintain in the best of circumstances. It means a constant monitoring of ever-shifting environmental factors that are capable of harming mind, body, and spirit. Staying well means paying attention to the natural environment; monitoring factors such as temperature, season, the signs of the zodiac, and so on. Staying well means paying attention to the supernatural environment; the Devil is everywhere and God keeps His eye on more than the sparrow. Staying well means paying attention to the social environment; relationships with others are fraught with opportunities for trouble. Staying well means being on guard.

Staying well also means moderation and the avoidance of excess. The body must be fed the proper foods, be rested, exercised, and kept clean inside and out or it will "break down on you" in a variety of ways. The mind must be kept active and engaged but not become preoccupied in "worriation" or your nerves, too, will "go down on you" and you will fall ill. The spirit needs to be constantly aware of God's love for His children lest sin or inattention result in divine punishment or Satan stepping in during a moment of spiritual weakness. Social relationships necessitate behaving in a fashion that will not arouse the envy or ire of others as revenge by magical means is merely a social misstep away.

A state of health and balance, then, is conceptualized in a very broad sense. Health promotion and the prevention of illness includes strategies beyond those found in orthodox medicine. Household medicine cabinets do contain aspirin and mouthwashes and laxatives to help ward off sickness. But the home may also contain holy books, religious pictures, and prayer cloths saturated with holy oils. Prayer and the reading of Scripture and the recitation of biblical verses is just as important—perhaps more important—a part of health behavior as eating right or taking the doctor's medicine. The wary householder might also sprinkle salt around the house to keep away unwanted visitors, add a dollop of pepper and a little urine to the mopwater to prohibit the entry of evil spirits, and put flowers in the kitchen window to warn of the malignant intentions of a jealous neighbor. Above all, "Let's just keep *prayerful*," as Bernita Washington puts it. "'Cause one thing about it, in the Bible [it] tell us that He said, 'I will not have you ignorant.'"

And that means taking action.

Notes

1. Menstrual paraphernalia had been the means by which Lila had been "poisoned," she told me. On the day of the anniversary party Lila's sister had walked into a bedroom to find one of the sisters-in-law sprinkling powder in a box of menstrual pads. It was only sachet, she said; something that would make them smell nice. Two weeks later Lila was dead. She had begun to behave strangely in the days before her death, gloomily staring out windows and talking of throwing herself out. On the day she died she had become violently ill; her face "was black, and she was foaming at the mouth and down over her clothes." Her husband drove her to a hospital emergency room though not, according to Anna, before obeying his mother's instructions to drive around the neighborhood for a long while. Anna saw the darkening of her daughter's face and the foaming at the mouth to be particularly sinister; they were obviously not natural occurrences. According to Hurston (1935:332), "If a person dies without speaking his mind about matters, he will purge (foam at the mouth after death). Hence the expression: 'I ain't goin' to purge when I die (I shall speak my mind).'"

2. The idea that the fontanel area is a pathway into the inside of the mouth and thus the gastrointestinal system is demonstrated by the treatment of a folk condition known as "fallen palate" or "fallen tongue palate." Descriptions of fallen tongue palate include pain, redness, and swelling, so I have always assumed it must be something like tonsillitis. In any case, one common treatment is to reverse the symptom—the hair of "the mole" is very tightly braided in the belief that it will pull up the swollen, "fallen" tissues (see Puckett 1926:368–369; Webb 1971; Waller and Killion 1972; Morson, Reuter, and Viitanen 1976; Dillard 1977:115; Roberson 1983:166; M. Bell and Clements n.d.).

3. Preventions and treatments for upper respiratory infections were the most commonly occurring items of health lore collected by my students from African-American informants. Nearly half of those interviewed (31/66; 47 percent) contributed 51 such beliefs. Sixty-year-old Minnie Lord, for example, drinks a mixture of codliver oil and orange juice during the winter months, "to keep away a cold." (East Lansing, Michigan; 1985) Should one dare to intrude, of course, it would quickly exit the body courtesy of the cod-liver oil. A magical component is introduced into the same preventive measure by one of Frankel's informants, who stated: "My mother used to line all eleven of us kids up the first Saturday of every October and give us each a tablespoon of castor oil with a glass of orange juice after it—to keep the cold out during the winter" (1977:73). Interestingly, of the dozens of self-treatment practices I have heard over the years—

including those collected by my students—not a single one of them involved the use of Vitamin C, the preventive measure so commonly heard in general American popular medicine. There was no mention of Vitamin C tablets, that is, or that it might be present in orange juice. The latter, in fact, is much more likely to be seen—along with lemon juice, vinegar, kerosene, turpentine, and whiskey—as "cutting" agents to prevent the buildup and/or eliminate the presence of mucus in the body. These same agents are also used to "cut" blood that is perceived to be "too thick" or "too high," as will be seen.

4. The term "poison" is frequently used as a synonym for sorcery, in fact, even if food or drink is not involved. According to Metraux, Haitian planters were deeply afraid of the dark powers of the slaves, especially *wanga*, "a term applied to any object or combination of objects which has received, as a result of magic procedure, a property that is harmful to one or more people. *Wanga* are also called 'poisons'" (1959:285); see also Hurston (1935:290–291).

5. Once when Anna and her family were living in Kansas she took one of her young sons to a church supper. The plates were handed out already filled with food to those in attendance, and the little boy, on a whim, decided to trade plates with his mother. The cook saw this exchange and rushed over, demanding to know why the switch had been made. Anna saw this as evidence that the plate intended for her had been poisoned—and the cook no doubt saw the exchange of plates as an accusation of sorcery. Anna stood up, took her child, and went home supperless. Anna's neighbor Sister Erma also believed that such poison would kill only the intended victim: Her maternal grandmother died after eating food cooked by a relative with whom she had been quarreling. And, said Sister Erma, "Whatever it was she ate, it didn't kill anybody else." Henry Jackson, the old man who lived in the alley behind Sister Erma, was often ill. The appropriate neighborly behavior toward invalids included taking gifts of food to them, but Henry was afraid that someone might try to make him even sicker by "cookin'." He solved his problem by having nothing at all to do with his neighbors—that way he was often lonely, he said—but at least he didn't have to worry about being poisoned. (Tucson, Arizona; 1970–1971) The idea that one must be careful where one eats also "prevails" in the Virginia neighborhood where Camino did her research; she was told by one woman: "You got to be careful of where you eat from. If you're not sure about somebody, better not eat their food, 'cause they can put anything at all in there. People at work bring me food sometimes like a piece of cake or a cookie, stuff like that and I smile and say 'thank you, I'm saving it for later,' and as soon as they're gone, I just go over to the next trash can and chuck it right in" (1986:193).

6. In biomedical terms "falling-out" is a fainting spell. In its chronic form it is a seizurelike disorder that some scholars feel qualifies as a culture-bound disorder. In Miami it is a significant problem for Southern Blacks, Bahamians (who refer to it as "blacking out"), and Haitians (who call it "indisposition"). See Weidman 1979c for a number of articles on the condition. The term appears again in the material on beliefs about the blood and its functions.

7. It is of special significance that *none* of these complaints found their way to the patients' charts; all were confided to staff anthropologist Linda Camino before the clinic visit. In a further study the researchers compared 47 patients suffering from "nerves" with 102 control subjects using the Holmes-Rahe Social Readjustment Rating Scale. Results indicated that the "nerves" patients suffered more recent life stresses than did the control subjects. The researchers consider the condition to be, in biomedical terms, "an emotional disorder that has associated serious medical problems and some relationship to anxiety and depression" (Nations, Camino, and Walker 1988).

8. It is true that certain compounds in garlic have a hypotensive effect but the amount that would have to be eaten for this to take place far exceeds that

usually used. And even if a therapeutic amount *is* consumed the problem remains that "high blood," unlike the biomedical "high blood pressure," is usually treated only when symptoms occur. The result—from the biomedical view—would be sporadic treatment at best (see Block 1986 for a history of the use of garlic as medicine).

9. This particular belief holds in those instances where the instigator of the problem is someone close to the victim—a family member, spouse, or lover. The hexed individual refuses to believe—or as a part of the hex *cannot* believe—that the loved one would do such a thing. There is seldom any problem in identifying the attacker if that person is already *seen* as the enemy, however; he or she may already be watched for signs of harmful intent.

10. It is against the law to suggest that products have any supernatural attributes and some sort of disclaimer of same is required. Phrases such as "sold as curio only" or "no claims of supernatural effects or powers of any kind are made" may appear in very small print. Items may also include qualifying terms such as, "so-called" or "spurious" in their descriptions. I purchased a small bottle of Goofer Dust (grave dirt) in a candleshop in the Watts area of Los Angeles, for example (owned by the "Seven Sisters of New Orleans and Algiers, Louisiana"); the label declares it is not just your *everyday* Goofer Dust but, "Highest Quality Alleged Goofer Dust." My favorite descriptor, however, remains the "So-called lucky attraction charm curio" in the form of a "Lucky helping hand simulated root replica" offered by a mail-order house in Gary, Indiana. There are other creative ways to bilk the customer: I have a mail-order Black Cat Bone in my collection that arrived tightly wrapped in foil. The instructions that accompanied it said that if I *ever* unwrapped it, it would lose its power. Some of these items are inexpensive but the cost of their frequent use adds up quickly: A "spell" may require a number of items, for example, or instructions may say that an ingredient must be replaced every few days. A woman I knew in Detroit a few years ago spent approximately $40/week from her very limited income for candles, incense, and oils "for protection."

11. The seven-page report lists 33 plants along with the biblical passage(s) where they are mentioned. "Suggestive Benefits" are listed for each plant; garlic, hyssop, and cucumber are mentioned as helpful for high blood pressure, for example. These "benefits and suggestive uses" were gathered by the author from articles and "testimonies of people who have had results, or know of people who have had results." The disclaimer that the plants are "not for therapeutic uses" is printed prominently on page one, however, along with the admonition that a physician should be consulted before using herbs. It is also noted that "what may be benefical [sic] to some may not be to another" (Taylor 1986).

5

To Be Healthy You Must Have Good Blood

Rannie Toomer's little baby boy Snooks was dying from double pneumonia and whooping cough. She sat away from him, gazing into the low fire, her long crusty bottom lip hanging. She was not married. Was not pretty. Was not anybody much. And he was all she had.

"Lawd, why don't that doctor come on here?" she moaned, tears sliding from her sticky eyes. She had not washed since Snooks took sick five days ago and a long row of whitish snail tracks laced her ashen face.

"What you ought to try is some of the old home remedies," Sarah urged. She was an old neighboring lady who wore magic leaves round her neck sewed up in possumskin next to a dried lizard's foot. She knew how magic came about, and could do magic herself, people said.

"We going to have us a doctor," Rannie Toomer said fiercely, walking over to shoo a fat winter fly from her child's forehead. "I don't believe in none of that swamp magic. All the old home remedies I took when I was a child come just short of killing me."
 —Alice Walker, "Strong Horse Tea," *In Love & Trouble*

One afternoon in 1984 John and Eva Thompson brought their infant daughter, Patty Ann, to the pediatrics clinic for her first immunizations. They were a new family to the clinic so Dr. Foster, the resident, began the interview by asking if there were any diseases in the families of the parents? "No," said Mrs. Thompson. "Diabetes in my family," her husband replied. The resident went on with the physical examination of the baby and indicated that although the infant was quite plump she was also long, so that she was within normal limits on the growth curve. She noted that the child was being fed cereal gruel from a bottle but, after commenting that she didn't really *need* anything but milk until she was a few months older, did not press the issue.[1] Did either of the parents have any questions? They did not. In that case the nurse would be in to give the infant her shots, and, if there were no problems, she would see them at the next regularly scheduled health maintenance visit. Dr. Foster then left the room.

She was scarcely gone before the mother asked me if I had ever heard of giving babies catnip tea "for the colic"? I replied that I knew it was a popular remedy in the neighborhood—but that I had always wondered how people knew how strong to make it. Her response was, "Why, it *says* right on the box!" She added that if you put a little honey in it it tasted better, and Patty Ann liked it. She then went on to say that what she would *really* like to have on hand for colic was "azefitty drops" (asafoetida), as that was what her own mother had used for her and her brothers and sisters in Mississippi. But she didn't know where to find it—or even if it was available "up here." I told her that both gum asafoetida and asafoetida drops were for sale in a pharmacy only two blocks from the hospital. Good, she said; she could buy some on the way home. But she had another question for me first: She had been with a friend in a doctor's waiting room the previous week, and heard someone say that "azefitty" was *also* good for high blood pressure. What did I think of *that?*

I asked if she had high blood pressure and she said that she did; she had been under treatment with medication (mentioning a popular beta-blocker) for the past three years. Her physician had told her to quit taking it while she was pregnant, however, and also not to take it while breastfeeding. She was still breastfeeding baby Patty Ann and did not want to stop just yet; but she was worried. Her blood pressure had been "very high" during the last months of her pregnancy; it had been measured at 170/100 on the day she had left the hospital after giving birth. She had not had it checked since, she said, but she continued to worry about it. She *knew* she was overweight and besides, her mother had high blood pressure and her aunt had died of it. Even her 11-year-old daughter had it but, "of course, she's real fat."

Here her husband chimed in and said that it was in *his* family, too: "My mother, she just falls out with it." "I can always tell when it's high," Mrs. Thompson went on, "and what I do when I get dizzy is I just eat a lot of garlic." Interjected Mr. Thompson, "They say that eating lots of green vegetables will bring the blood down, too, but it takes awhile." They both agreed that one shouldn't eat a lot of red meat, especially pork—"that'll *really* run it up!" During this exchange the nurse came into the room to give the baby her shot and, hearing some of this, went out to get the resident. Dr. Foster returned looking rather irate and said to the mother, "I thought you said there *weren't* any diseases in your family!" There was a pause before Mrs. Thompson replied in a surprised tone, "I didn't know high blood pressure was a *disease!*" A discussion followed about an antihypertensive medication that can be taken while breastfeeding, the mother was referred back to her physician, and the family left. The resident, still annoyed, said to me, "I don't know why these people always tell *you* everything!" (Lansing, Michigan; 1984)

In this case, neither did I, although I have the uneasy feeling that the abundance of gray in my hair led the mother to think that if there was *anyone* in the clinic who would know about old-timey home remedies it would be me. I had introduced myself as "Dr. Snow" but had not said that I am not a physician; only that I liked to meet new clinic families. During the resident's history-taking and physical examination of the child I had said nothing at all. It does seem obvious that the initial question about catnip tea was a test: Mrs. Thompson clearly knew about catnip tea for colic, exactly how to prepare it, and, in fact, was already using it. Had I responded in a negative fashion she probably would not have gone on with her questions about asafoetida; as I did not, the discussion about high blood pressure and its home treatment could take place.

The foregoing incident has been described in some detail because it illustrates a very important problem that occurs for the social scientist working in clinical settings: whether or not to intervene. The use of catnip tea for colic and the eating of garlic or green vegetables for high blood pressure are equally valid in the traditional system. They are based on ideas about the nature of colic and high blood pressure, their causes, symptomatology, course, and proper treatment. They are not seen as equally serious, of course; believers in both the biomedical and the traditional systems know that infantile colic is less of a problem than "high blood" or hypertension. Nevertheless, the health professional probably has no qualms about judging his/her treatment for the latter as superior to any sort of home remedy, irrespective of whether the patient agrees. To the social scientist, however, the two explanatory models are supposedly of equal value. And in fact "high blood" *is* a perfectly rational part of one system, just as "high blood pressure" is in the other. Eating greens *is* a perfectly rational part of one system, just as the use of an antihypertensive drug is in the other. But the social scientist who intellectually has a foot in both camps also has his or her own beliefs, and these may naggingly say that one way is better than the other. I believe that catnip tea, if properly prepared, probably works as well as anything else for a colicky baby; I do *not* believe, however, that avoiding pork and eating lots of greens is as safe a way to "bring down" elevated blood pressure as is the taking of medication. Should I say something? If I do not, am I contributing to serious health problems down the line for this young mother? It is a question that I have yet to satisfactorily resolve.

Contrasting ideas about the blood and its functions contribute importantly to misunderstandings between physicians and African-American patients in clinical settings. It has already been noted that blood, the shimmering red symbol of life itself, is of immense importance in African-American traditional medicine. The findings in the Miami Health Ecology Project, for example, led those researchers to consider blood to be the "health cultural focus" for all three of the groups of African descent studied. They also point out that the health profiles of these groups—Haitians, Bahamians, and Southern

Blacks— are very different from those of the Cubans and Puerto Ricans in the study. They suggest that "the similarity in Bahamian, Haitian, and Southern Black conceptualizations of blood and blood behavior may be explained by the tenacity of pan-African symbols in the most basic of behavioral realms—that concerned with health and well-being" (Weidman et al. 1978:572). More recently, Laguerre has noted that in the Caribbean—though there are differences in traditional medical beliefs from one country to another—there is "still a basic point of similarity. The similarity is the blood which plays a central role in the functioning of the body and in the maintenance of its well-being" (1987:66; see also Mitchell 1983).[2] Camino also found in the Virginia city where she worked that the blood "possesses enormous symbolic importance, having sensory as well as ideological significance" (1986:72–78).

The material in this and the following chapter are in no wise to be taken as a comprehensive statement of the meaning of blood in African-American traditional medicine—that is a book in itself— rather it is meant to demonstrate the range of beliefs and their remarkable similarity in rural and urban settings all over the United States. It is hoped that even this brief treatment will show the importance of fitting a single belief into its broader cognitive and cultural matrix. Knowledge of the whole system may seem to be excess baggage to the clinician or public health researcher interested only in beliefs with "real" clinical significance. The frequent misunderstandings that arise because of the orthodox "high blood pressure" and the traditional "high blood" beliefs, for example, obviously have a greater potential for serious health consequences than does a feeling that a "spring tonic" is necessary to properly ready the blood for the summer to come. "High blood," however, aside from its implications as a cause of "noncompliance" with clinical regimens or its possible role in use of dangerous or ineffective home remedies for hypertension, makes sense only as it fits into the total pattern of beliefs about the blood.

In the traditional system the blood is a substance in constant flux, responding to a variety of external and internal stimuli in a variety of ways. The consideration of what causes the blood to change includes external factors as diverse as the season of the year; the ambient temperature on a given day; occurrences triggering strong emotional states in the individual; failure to keep the body clean; and the position of the heavenly bodies. Internal factors are as varied as what one eats for breakfast, the normal physiological processes that digest that breakfast, failure to keep the body clean internally, the disruption of normal processes when one is ill, and the use of remedial measures to restore health. All of these factors may further vary according to the individual's age, gender, or special body state such as menstruation or pregnancy. As well, the foregoing events and processes may be changed or interfered with by the intervention of a supernatural being or the malignant deeds of a sorcerer. The blood, in short, responds to many things; some of these are in the power of the individual to control and some are not.

Singly or in combination these stimuli are responsible for a whole range of changes in the blood. The generation of new blood and the disposal of old blood may be affected. The blood may become over-heated or take on cold. Blood volume may rise or fall; it may thicken in consistency or thin down. Its motion (perhaps a better term than circulation) may speed up or slow down; indeed, seem to pause or even stop. The location of the blood may shift; again, not so much circulating as temporarily accumulating in various portions of the anatomy. Its state of cleanliness may be affected if it collects impurities, becoming "bad," "nasty," or "defiled." Its flavor may change so that it is said to be "bitter," or "sweet," or "acid." Finally, it may take on abnormal inclusions and become the habitat of magically sent animals.

The state of normality for some of these variables is based on the presence or absence of a factor: Blood is clean or it is not; animals are present or they are not. More commonly, however, the variables move along a continuum with normality (and health) in the middle range and anything above or below that spelling trouble. The blood may be "too high" or "too low" in volume, be "too thick" or "too thin" in consistency, shoot too high or fall too low in the body to maintain health. It can move with dangerous speed or be sluggish; become too sweet, too bitter, too acid, and so on. The picture is further complicated by the fact that the forces acting on the blood and the end results are not single cause-and-effect propositions. The thick blood/thin blood continuum, for example, may be affected by climate, temperature, by diet, relative age, gender, food eaten, or by the use of various home remedies. The diet alone contributes to variations in the blood's consistency, movement, volume, location, flavor, and amount of heat or cold present in the body. No surprise that the prescriptive and proscriptive measures whose aim is keeping the blood just right require constant attention. Their aim is maintaining a delicate balance between the factors impinging on the state of the blood and their presumed effect.

The Thick/Thin Continuum

The change of blood from a thinner to a thicker state and back is a normal process that may take place without an individual knowing that it is going on; this shift in consistency is expected to take place in response to changes in environmental temperature. Only if it moves too far on either end of the continuum—becomes so thick that it clogs up in the body, for example, or so thin that it is perceived as "watery"—does this process become perceived as abnormal. In rural North Carolina, for example, it is believed that the blood can "vary in thickness or volume. If it is too thick or heavy, it moves slowly and causes circulatory problems. The solution is to thin the blood by letting it or by taking blood tonics to dilute the viscosity. Alternatively, blood that is too thin makes one susceptible to attacks from cold air, leading to ailments of the lungs. The solution is to take foods and herbs that are 'hot' and thicken the blood or to apply 'hot' herbal poultices to prevent 'cold' attacks" (Mathews 1987). The blood is believed to be relatively thicker or thinner according to: the age of the individual; the special life stages such as puberty or the climacteric; the experience of a body state such as menstruation; and the foods or remedies that are consumed. All of these factors—disparate though they may seem—are linked conceptually by their association with heat and cold. (It is this association, which may be external to the body or an internal state, that is most reminiscent of the old principles of humoralism.) There is also some overlap with ideas about blood purity and volume; blood that is too thick, that is, may be high in volume and/or relatively impure; blood that is too thin may be equated with low volume.

As mentioned above, certain life stages may predispose the individual to problems with environmental cold. Infants and prepubescent children have blood that is relatively thin, and they have a special need to be kept warm. The blood should automatically thicken at puberty, however, and remain so during the years that the adult man or woman is sexually active. It was teenaged girls— "They young. Blood's thick."—who Arnella Lewis saw as endangering their future health by wearing shorts. For her elderly self, however, "poor me, I couldn't stay warm with what I had on." She subscribed to the view, as did most of my Arizona informants, that after the climacteric the blood automatically begins to thin down, rendering the individual more susceptible to cold. Roberson's informants in rural Virginia also reported that older people "stay cold much of the time" because they have less blood or thinner blood (1983:123).

Gender is also implicated in relative vulnerability to cold and cold-related health problems. Because of normal blood loss and the idea that the body is "open" at certain times in the female reproductive cycle—during the menses, after a miscarriage or abortion, or during the postpartum period— women have fewer defenses against the cold at these times. This vulnerability is based both on the loss of a protective substance and on the fear of interference with a normal bodily process: Should the vaginal bleeding, whatever its cause, be impeded because of cold any one of a number of serious problems might result. Cold in the form of air, winds, water, dew, and even foodstuffs is seen as a potential killer for women in their childbearing years.

Climate and season are particularly important in ideas about the relative thickness of the blood; again there is an association with heat and cold. No matter what the cause, thin blood is associated with constitutional weakness and enhanced vulnerability to illnesses associated with low ambient temperature. These illnesses are primarily those acute upper respiratory ailments with increased mucus production (phlegm, the "cold" humor) and chronic disorders of old age such as arthritis and rheumatism. It is believed that the blood will automatically thicken at the onset of colder weather, and people who live in warmer climates are thought to have thinner blood than do those who live where winters are more severe. Arizona informants often mentioned that they thought their years there had thinned down their blood.[3] Other studies have confirmed the link between cold-thickened blood, sluggish circulation, increased blood volume, and the accumulation of impurities in the body. Southern Black informants in the Miami sample, for example, associate thick blood with cold winter weather. They further indicate that the concomitant buildup of impurities necessitates a cleansing ritual before the return of hot weather (Weidman et al. 1978:546). I do not recall ever hearing of a measure being needed to help the blood thicken for winter but apparently the body needs a little help in the spring of the year. The use of "spring tonics" in the form of blood thinners/purifiers is common.

Camino's informants in a Virginia city also point to environmental conditions, especially cold wind, as causing the blood to thicken. The theme of balance between too thick and too thin is clear in their ideas about the process. Blood that is too thick, they say, can be dangerous because "'it's harder to go through the vessels'" and, as well, might be the first stage of "'high blood'" (Camino 1986:74). A few individuals even went so far as to say that a "no-fail" way of keeping the blood from becoming dangerously thick is to donate blood regularly; such a practice "'will thin it down, lower it, loosen it up, and make you feel pure'" (p. 76). As such draconian measures might cause the blood to become too thin, bringing on "low blood," more salt should be added to the diet to keep this from occurring. The importance of keeping the blood in balance is illustrated here by the fact that too *much* salt is also dangerous. It can cause the blood to become *too* thick, I was told by Reverend Hastings, the Grand Rapids healer. He saw a direct connection between the blood volume, thick blood, the diet, and emotional upset:

Salt. Salt is a dangerous thing. Well, this is your blood that is the cause of that. Anytime your brain is got *too* much on it—too much blood and it's too thick—you notice you're easily upset. That's why we're on about lose weight; the more you lose weight the less blood you have. And if you can get your weight down, you got less blood. But anytime your blood is high it is *thick;* it is thick. And when it is thick you are quick-tempered, or you don't quite think right. And you can't—and like you're talkin' to me—you can't quite understand what I'm talkin' about. It just don't work right. Now, *high blood,* you can bring it down with *apple* juice. Apple juice will bring it down; carrot juice will bring it down. But it don't bring it down over*night.* But just a glassful

a day will bring it down quicker'n any medicine. You take pills for
years and years. (1987)

Many of the individuals who had "spun out" at the doctor relied on
advice from Reverend Hastings in the treatment of their high blood
pressure.

As mentioned, Arizona informants frequently spoke of the presumed thin state of their blood because of their years in a hot
climate. The topic of "too thin" blood is much less of an item of
conversation among African-American friends and informants in
Michigan (not a hot climate by any stretch of the imagination). It is
the balance between thick and thin that is important to maintain,
according to Bernita Washington—if it is too thick, you treat it, and
if it is too thin, you treat it. On the day that the following conversation took place Bernita's husband, Joseph, was a silent listener
although—as usual—he jumped in when there was something he
wanted me to know. Although the discussion started out with a
thick/thin reference it is clear that "thin" and "low" and "anemic"
are conceptually intertwined for the couple. Said Bernita:

> O.K., I never knew the reason why that it was too thick and neither
> why it was too thin, but I know that peoples have always, sometime
> peoples have always at a certain time had blood that was *too thick*.
> O.K., when I was a kid I had real thick blood, O.K.? When I was a kid.
> Like if I cut my finger or sliced my feet or something, blood'd come
> out of there and it would just lump up, you know. 'Stead of just run-
> nin' it'd become lumps. You know, it'd just cake up as it come out.
> O.K., so *that* blood is too thick, O.K.? So that's how you can tell thick
> blood from thin blood—thin blood would just really continue to run,
> run, run, run.

> O.K., what we did, what we was taught to do was [when] we was
> comin' up, that a kid, a grown person, whatever, had blood and it was
> too thick—and the parents would *notice* kids more than they do now—
> so if they notice that kid *had* blood that was too thick, they would put
> just a little epsom salt in some warm water and let 'em have that. Not
> too regular, say just about twice a month. You could use that and that
> would thin it down. You can use a fourth-teaspoonful of *vinegar* in
> some water and that will thin it down. But you don't use it regular
> enough to just really thin it too thin, too fast or too slow, whatever.
> You just do it and let it take its own time of doin' it, like it is sup-
> posed to.

Epsom salts and vinegar may also be used to "bring down" blood
that is too high in volume, as will be seen.

I then asked her if she thought that blood could also be too thin?
In her reply she made a connection between blood thickness, cold,
and low blood volume ("anemia"):

It could become too *thin* by not even takin' anything or not even usin' anything. But you can tell when a person have real thin blood; he stays *cold* all the time. Yeah, he stays cold all the time. And a person that have quite a bit of blood, thick blood, you know; they doesn't get *cold* as the rest of people. Say like anemia, person that anemic; they usually stay cooler all the time. Well, if it was me, if it was me and I felt that mine was thin—like I have a daughter that is anemic, right. So she's like that; she stays cool all the time because she's anemic.

It doesn't mean that she don't *have* blood; but it just mean that it runnin' over on the low *side,* the reason why that it's anemic. But that is thin blood. So what we did, you can go to the store and just buy some beets, you can now even get 'em in a can that's already fixed. O.K., then you put 'em on the stove and you put just a little sugar in 'em and let 'em cook just a little bit, right? And just let 'em eat that. The best thing it is the *juice* that's inside of it; now that is really good, and it will bring it right up to the level where it's supposed to be.

At this point Joseph, who had been sitting in the other room watching TV, joined the conversation:

I'll tell you another thing for the blood, [to] build blood, is *wine.* Wine is good; any kind of wine is good for the blood because it build blood. You go in any doctor's office right now, bet they'd give you a glass of wine if you got low blood or if your blood ain't *red;* they gonna give you some wine. And they say that's a temporary, to make your blood *back,* to build blood. Every doctor give me, 'fore I walk out of the office, they give me a glass of wine. And if they give you an operation they'll give you wine; that's in the place of drawin' the blood out of somebody else to give you.

"So they might give you wine instead of a blood transfusion?" "Uh huh." Bernita was not particularly pleased at the interruption; and in particular not pleased about the description of wine as a medicine. In her opinion her husband drinks far too much of it already. And not for its utility as a blood builder. (Lansing, Michigan; 1986)

Purity/Impurity

The purity of the blood is a matter of great concern *all* of the time—though it, too, may be particularly problematic after a long cold winter—and any occurrence that is seen as signaling the presence of impurities in the body is a call to action. After she had been in the city for some time, for example, Jacie Burnes brought her teenaged daughter and the youngest of her sons to the pediatrics clinic one day. It was Jacie's first trip to the facility since Dr. Sally Dye, the resident she had come to know and trust, had finished her training program and moved away. But Jacie had called that morning and said it was important that the boy and girl be seen. And what was the purpose of the visit, a nurse asked? Both of the children had broken out in "bumps," said Jacie, and she was concerned about their overall health. Jacie volunteered that she believed the skin eruptions were due to the children's failure to drink enough water for their "kidneys to act proper." This had never been a problem in South Carolina, she said—there it was so hot that all of her children automatically drank enough water to "flush out" their systems. Since she had moved her family to Michigan, however, she had had difficulty getting her brood to drink what she thought was the amount of water needed to do the job. The nurse entered into the chart the notation, "Mrs. Burnes believes that her children do not drink enough water."

The new resident looked at this entry without response, however. She had different diagnoses, suggesting that 14-year-old Wanda was suffering a mild case of teenage acne and that 3-year-old Tyrone had impetigo. Her treatment plans also differed for the two: She discussed the importance of keeping the skin clean "at this time in your life" with the teenager; for Tyrone she wrote out a prescription for an antibiotic. She stressed to Jacie the importance of the little boy being given all of the medication and told her to bring him back in when it was gone. Were there any questions? Jacie again mentioned her fear that her children did not drink enough water. "*All of us* should drink a lot of water," responded the resident as she left the room. After a moment Jacie commented that she could not understand why one child had been given medication and the other had not—did the doctor think one child was less important than the other? In her mind the terms "acne" and "impetigo" only confirmed her belief that the systems of her children were dangerously unclean. She wished that Dr. Dye were still with the clinic; *she* would have understood! She did not return with Tyrone for the follow-up appointment.

The belief that the body needs to be kept clean inside and out to avoid illness is a common theme in African-American traditional medicine (though by no means restricted to this population, as the most cursory examination of laxative ads clearly shows). Above all, the blood must be kept clean: "Bad" or "impure" or "poisoned" blood can carry filth to all parts of the body. Whereas the blood can move from a thinner to a thicker state and back without being perceived as abnormal, it can never change from a pure to an impure state without being seen as unhealthy. Such a state may result from the body's response to environmental factors such as climate and season; the entrance into the body of some outside disease-bearing agent; some disorder in the body's own normal cleansing abilities; or a lack of balance in sexual functioning. A number of bodily processes have as an important part of their function the release of potentially toxic substances from the body. Regular sexual activity is important for health, preventing a deadly "buildup" of sexual secretions. The primary function of the intestinal tract and the kidneys is the elimination of impurities in the feces and the urine. Sweating is believed to release other impurities via heat-opened pores and, for women, menstruation and postpartum bleeding serve the purpose of discharging blood seen as dirty or tainted.[4] Some of these processes are obviously important throughout the life cycle; others are dependent on age, life stage, and gender.

In traditional belief—as the anecdote about Jacie Burnes and her son and daughter illustrates—the single cause of bodily impurity may be blamed for a number of disorders that in biomedical terms would be attributed to different causes. Impurities in the system are represented by two major manifestations: an increase in body heat and/or skin eruptions. The latter are often described as "something in the body trying to come out." Just as mucus in the body is seen as "cold," a rash may be seen as the physical form of bodily heat. As a Bahamian woman in Miami who was suffering from a bad rash put it, "'I always have it. I believe it is heat in the blood. The doctors believe it is a skin rash caused from acid in the blood'" (Weidman et al., 1978:462). The "heat rash" common to children in Florida is also interpreted as heat actually entering the blood. In a magical extension of the association between heat and rash, in fact, Murphree and Barrow reported the belief that disposable diapers should not be burned as this would "'cause the baby to develop a diaper rash'" (1970).

Ideas about the state of cleanliness of the blood prove once again the close relationship of the human organism with other natural phenomena. The connection between winter-thickened blood and impure blood has already been alluded to, as has the belief that measures are needed to help thin and purify the blood at winter's end. The belief that the pores have closed in response to cold logically leads to the idea that this has blocked one of the body's ways of ridding itself of impurities; in concert with the thickened blood these then build up in a kind of sludge. Roberson's rural Virginia informants, for example, viewed the buildup of impurities in the blood over the winter as something akin to a car engine getting dirty (1983:123–124).

A further connection between natural forces and the body is evident in the belief that this now-tainted blood will fall lower in the body for the duration of winter. It mimics the sap falling in the trees and, as well, is influenced by the signs of the zodiac. In the winter months "the signs" are linked with the lower portion of the body and, in the spring, the cycle of renewal begins anew. Pisces, associated with the feet, gives way to Aries, which "rules" the head. The sap is rising in the trees and the impurity-ridden blood rises in the body and causes problems if something is not done. As recently as 1980 a popular almanac made such connections explicit: April was described as a month to "begin to 'clean up.' Malaria, boils, bilious attacks, blood diseases, catarrh and skin eruptions begin to show; neuralgia and nervous troubles generally will add to the pangs of other disorders" (*MacDonald's Farmers Almanac* 1980, n.p.).

As was noted in the section on winter-thickened blood, additional measures are often instituted in the spring that serve to cleanse the blood as well as thin it. Such regimens may be tacked on to an already stringent pattern of bodily purification. A weekly "dose" of laxative was standard in the household of Anna and Tom Perry for child and adult alike, for example, with the children given an extra dollop of Syrup of Black Draught (a popular over-the-counter laxative preparation) every Friday afternoon to "get them ready for school on Monday." Each spring Anna also instituted a nine-day course of sulfur and molasses and, if available, a supper of poke greens to help clear the blood and "clean off the liver." Castor oil was also taken to "lubricate the joints" stiffened by the colder weather. Such heroic measures were to be implemented only once a year, Anna said; "You can't take a blood tonic all the time; it would work in the blood too forcible, strip things out that you didn't want out" (Snow 1977:45). Her husband, Tom, refused to participate in these cleansing rituals, however, so that each spring she hid "liver pills" in his hot cereal every morning for nine days. She was pleased that she was able to fool him into doing what was good for him. However, Tom confided to me later that he could *see* the little white pills in the cereal, and he had always managed to remove them when Anna was not looking. (Tucson, Arizona; 1971)

Some of the items currently used as spring tonics have been taken as such for centuries by African-Americans, Whites, and Native Americans alike. The same remedies that are used to thin the blood in the spring usually also serve to purify it; catnip tea, sassafras tea, poke greens, sulfur and molasses, cream of tartar, castor oil, and epsom salts are frequently mentioned as being effective. In rural Virginia most of Roberson's informants reported having been given sassafras tea as a spring tonic as children; many were continuing to use it for themselves and *their* children: "The primary purpose in imbibing this tea is to purify the blood and thereby enhance health status. Several persons explained that the tea is good for cleaning anything out of the body or 'cleaning out your system.' Part of the belief stems from the associated belief that over the winter many impurities build up in the blood, perhaps through being indoors more and having more colds than at other times of the year. A rash, according to some informants, indicates that the impurities are coming out and the tea is accomplishing its purpose" (1983:113).

In the city a trip to the drug store may provide an alternative to going to the woods to dig a blood-cleansing root; the owner of a pharmacy serving a largely African-American clientele in Lansing told me that his sales of sulfur increase dramatically in the spring. (Will Upshaw, Lansing, Michigan; 1986) When I mentioned this popu-

lar remedy to Bernita Washington she indicated that it should not
be indiscriminately used. She enjoys her status as a woman having
a wide knowledge of home treatments, their preparation, and correct
use and is rather jealous of it. She frequently mentions the danger
of sharing her knowledge with those who might be careless, for
example; she would not like anyone else to "get in trouble" by
improperly using something. When I asked if—since her favorite
poke greens were not available—she considered the use of sulfur and
molasses from Mr. Upshaw's nearby pharmacy as a substitute spring
tonic, she replied,

> If you're not aware how much you should take it's not good for you.
> Because you're only supposed to pick up just no more than you can get
> on the small end of a knifeblade; that's *all* you're supposed to have.
> You get any more than that, then you're in trouble. So that's all you're
> supposed to have.

But it is effective, she went on to say, if you know how much
to take, and it is valuable for more than simply cleaning up the
blood. As is true for many substances—for example, salt—something
with a physiological effect when used internally may also have a
broader symbolic action when used externally. It is not just the
human *body* that needs a spring cleanup, and if sulfur will remove
impurities from the system it will also remove them from the environment as well:

> Like in the springtime of the year we'd go out and we'd get every-
> thing that need to be burned and stuff. We would burn it on the out-
> side, we would burn it in the house to get the germs and stuff out of
> the house. That's the most important thing we used sulfur for; we just
> used it mostly for the *health* of the house! Sometime you can move
> into these old houses—like you move into a house, something like
> that—and the house is old and been there for a long time. Lotta people
> done livin' in it, whatever, you know. So, the best thing in the world
> to do before you get in there is just to smoke it out; take your sulfur,
> make you a sulfur smoke in every room before you move in there.
> That kills all the germs and everything that's *in* there. You can do it in
> your own *home*, every so often. (1987)

Burning sulfur is also good to remove the residual evil of a hex
from a household. But she did not tell me that until later.

Efforts to maintain clean blood and a clean system begin at birth
and continue throughout the life cycle. One of the first health-main-
tenance procedures that an infant will undergo, in fact, has as its
end the assurance that the child will break out in "the little red
hives" in the first weeks of life. The little red hives represent the
expulsion from the infantile system of the dirt accumulated during
the long months in the uterus. When Janine Jackson's daughter-in-

law called to say that her baby was fussy, Janine knew that the little
red hives were trying to come out:

> Well, Annie kept cryin'. Long as they is on the *in*side, look like wants
> to get out, I guess it be irritatin' 'em or sumpin'. Then you gives them
> somethin' *hot*. Now *we* would use *ca*tnip, they call it. 'Cause that's
> what my mom used to give us. I know nowadays they *do* buy it in
> the store, I think. But she would break it off the bush green, wash it
> real good, and then she *steam* it. And put just a *little* bit of Karo
> syrup or sumpin' in it, just a little [to] kill that bitterness out of it.
> And you give 'em that and put 'em in bed; [they] wake up and they's
> all broken out with those red hives. Well, Annie started hers about
> three months old, two months old. Important for 'em to come out, uh-
> huh. It's something that I guess they *hurt* or something; upset 'em,
> they keep irritatin' 'em. Until when they once break out real good, like
> I say, you see 'em all over the place. Those little red hives. And you
> can see the difference in the way they actin'. (Lansing, Michigan; 1986)

The fact that doctors never seem to know what the little red hives
are, not to mention the importance of them "coming out," does little
to convince neighborhood women of their competence in giving
medical advice.

It is not just infants who need help in ridding the body of
unwanted dirt. Although several bodily processes are seen as cleansing the body these alone do not seem to do the job; to be on the
safe side various maneuvers are employed to make sure that the
body is clean. Cleansing agents/tactics are those that open the pores;
"bring on" or "bring down" a menstrual period; promote kidney
function; or are cathartic. Laxative use ranked very high (#4 of 28
categories) in the list of responses of Southern Blacks in the Miami
study to the question, "What are the most important things that you
and your family do in order to keep good health?" (Weidman et al.,
1978:309–310). Bowel activity is a matter of intense interest and is
closely monitored; even small infants may routinely be given laxatives to make sure that they produce frequent bowel movements. In
rural Georgia both White and African-American respondents believe
that the body can become "polluted" from taking too much medicine
and overeating, the latter generally occurring "at social occasions
such as Christmas, Thanksgiving, and birthdays and at recurrent
gatherings such as homecomings and campmeetings; the remedy is
taking a laxative to rid the body of impurities" (C. Hill 1988:123).
The importance of the blood being purified is even more forcefully
brought out by the suggestion of some of Roberson's informants
that blood transfusions may be necessary when other purificatory
methods fail (1983:124). To repeat Janine Jackson's admonition to her
sister, why even take a chance? "Just keep yourself clean-runnin',
just clean, and you'll feel much better."

The processes of ingestion, digestion, and elimination are, of
course, a normal part of life so that the function of the kidneys, the

gut, and to a lesser extent the liver are of importance irrespective of the age or gender of the individual—the danger here health-wise is when the body's cleansing mechanisms are sluggish or abnormally slowed. Another natural state associated with vulnerability in body functioning is puberty; here the problem is not the process that is slowed but the unruly onset of the body's preparations for adult sexuality. Until the system has settled down into its adult functioning the young adult—male or female—is at risk. For Haitians in Miami, for example, "puberty is one period when the individual's body is 'hot' or 'heating up'. Elaborate precautions must be taken at this time to avoid 'cold' foods which not only affect the condition of the blood (with sometimes serious consequences) but also the appearance of the skin" (Weidman et al. 1978:376). After the system is regulated women will have a body-cleansing advantage over their male peers in the process of menstruation, an advantage that will be lost after the menopause. Incomplete or impeded menses, however, render a woman vulnerable due to the retention in the body of dirty blood.

The onset of adult sexuality is problematic in its unsettled advent, then, and thereafter a balance must be maintained between too little and too much sexual activity. For both men and women its total lack may be seen as dangerous if semen or normal vaginal secretions accumulate in the body. In the following passage the "blockage" of these secretions from lack of sexual intercourse in a Bahamian woman results in mental problems. She perceived that her "first mental condition came after the separation of her and her husband. She told of how lonesome she was by not having sex. The stuff which is called the false discharge was backing up to her head and causing a lot of problems such as nervous pain in her head and body, dizziness and pains in her stomach and other problems. She believes if she had been having sex these things would not have happened to her" (Weidman et al. 1978:475). The male counterpart of such a problem is accumulated semen; it may either back up into the head or simply cause acne. If the latter is the case either sexual intercourse or masturbation may be suggested as a cure (Jordan 1975).

It is unbridled sexual activity, however, that seems to be more dangerous. Like so much in African-American traditional health culture, excess is dangerous and sexual excess—especially if too many partners are involved—can result in serious problems. And sexual activity is very directly aligned with dirt and impurities; in rural North Carolina, for example, if blood impurities "increase because of poor hygiene or excessive sexual activity, they will erupt or 'boil out' of the body causing skin sores, rashes, and escaping heat in the form of fevers" (Mathews 1987; see also Murphree 1968). Traditional ideas about the etiology of venereal diseases are strongly associated with the view that the blood can be defiled. "The mother and father got to have good blood and good health to bring a fine child," said Anna Perry, going on to comment that if the mother is with "a lot of different men" her blood would not be pure. "All their stuff's in her system," from whence, she noted, it would go from there straight to the blood of her infant. A woman might try to cleanse her own blood with Beef Iron Tonic (an over-the-counter preparation) before getting pregnant. But it would be better yet to take a blood test before getting married: "Then you know your blood is clean." (1971)

Bernita Washington also became concerned with the health of her sons and daughters as they reached puberty. Although she was never able to talk to her children about sexual matters she had no compunction over "dosing" them for any real or imagined ailments; she made up her "teas" and her children took them, no questions asked. One preventive treatment for the disease she calls "the clap" illustrates both her belief that the blood can become "impure" due to sexual intercourse and the early age that she believes it likely to begin. As soon as her three sons were old enough to begin seeing girls, she says, she routinely dosed them with a tea of turpentine and water for nine mornings in a row. "All of those teas you take for nine days." The dosage given depended on the age of the boy, one drop per year: "If he's 12, or 13 or 14 then you use that many drops, 12 or 13 or 14. It'll kill it if it hasn't gone too far." For "the whites," a problem that she sees as equivalent in girls and women, her treatment consisted of a tea made from boiling rusty nails in water. (1991)

"Bad blood" is a term often used to describe venereal infections although it is not restricted to such problems. It not only refers to the fact that the blood has become contaminated in some way but, usually, that some sort of disvalued behavior has taken place. For both Southern Black and Bahamian informants in Miami, for example, "bad blood" is used to describe syphilis as well as a variety of other conditions and behavioral aberrations. Haitian respondents use the term *sang gate* to refer to blood spoiled "by improper foods, by emotions, sexual contact with 'bad people,' or malign magic." Again, syphilis is one form of such "spoiled blood" (Weidman et al. 1978:461, 514). Roberson's informants, while using the term to refer to venereal and other diseases, also broadened the "bad blood" category to refer to blood become dirty from harmful behaviors such as smoking, drinking, and taking drugs (p. 124). This differential understanding about the etiology of sexually transmitted diseases is of particular concern in light of the recent and alarming increase in the incidence of syphilis in the United States. Data show that in 1989 incidence rates for syphilis were the highest that they had been for 40 years, with African-American men and women particularly at risk (Rolfs and Nakashima 1990).[5] And though the incidence of gonorrhea has decreased since 1975, there is an increase in infections caused by bacteria resistant to treatment (Schwarcz et al. 1990). I will step again out of my observer role to comment that turpentine-and-water teas will not solve such problems.

One marker of the viability of a traditional health system is whether it is able to incorporate new disease entities as well as explaining the old. In African-American traditional medicine there is growing evidence that exactly this is happening with AIDS, which joins syphilis as a new and particularly dangerous form of "bad blood." Traditional explanations of increased vulnerability for poor health—dirt and poor diet and cold—are being added to more orthodox ideas of nosology. In one study, for example, though respondents were generally aware that AIDS is acquired from sexual intercourse and/or sharing needles with an infected individual, most also thought it might be due to lowered resistance to impurities, poor health habits, exposure to cold, improper nutrition, or a body weakened by menstruation (Flaskerud and Rush 1989).

Interviews with caretakers of HIV seropositive infants in Newark also demonstrate that the problem is identified with lack of cleanliness (Meltzer and Kantor 1990). As one individual put it, "I think that what it really comes down to is filth, and people's hygiene habits, and what they do sexually and intravenously wise. That's what I think." The fact that the blood is affected increases the seriousness of the problem: "They haven't really learned that much about how to fight it cause it's in your blood. And your blood is your lifeline. . . . You keep stuff out of your blood, any disease you have—you're not attacked so much." And the fact that it is linked with other blood disorders is clear in the following passage: "This is something that I'm new at. That's the reason Dr. _____ had to explain to me, about what was happening in the body. With the red cells, and the white cells. . . . Ah, if I can remember. I think the white cells, or corpuscles, or red corpuscles, they eat up the white, or the red eat up—the white eat up the red. And it makes—makes you have more—less strength, and—I can't remember now, all what—he told me so many things about it." Bernita Washington put it in almost exactly the same words; when she first spoke to me about AIDS in 1987 it was in terms of a new and frightening disease that no one can cure (though God can protect the individual from contracting it). Four years later, while noting that it is still incurable, she speaks of it as "a problem with the blood, like something goes wrong with your red cells or your white cells. So many things can go wrong with your blood; like AIDS, a lot of things will give you impure blood." And "to be healthy you must have good blood." (Lansing, Michigan; 1987)

The fact that any health problem that does not respond to ordinary treatment may come to be seen as unnatural in origin is also exemplified in some of the explanations for AIDS. Farmer, for example, provides a fascinating description of Haitian villagers' attempts to fit AIDS into their model of pathology; in 1985–86 their views of *sida,* their term for the problem, had to do with some disorder of the blood:

> Fully 18 of 20 informants interviewed during this period referred directly to *"blood"* in our discussions of sida, and for many other residents of Do Kay as well, sida was a sickness of the blood. Perhaps the most commonly heard observation was that sida *"dirties your blood"* (li sal san ou). There was frequent allusion to *"poor blood,"* usually a gloss for anemia, as a prodrome of sida, and some referred to the dangers of blood transfusion. For example, when in the course of an obstetrical intervention Ti Malou Joseph needed a unit of blood, several of her covillagers observed that, given the *"sickness going around"* (maladi devo a), a transfusion was tempting fate. For some, it was a question of exposing the transfusion recipient to a microbe (mikwob); for others, one of *"mixing bloods that don't go together,"* causing reactions that eventually *"degenerate into* sida." Several informants began to speak of sida *as a slow but irreversible process that was invariably fatal.* (Farmer 1990:10)

By 1988, when it became clear that the traditional model of the blood was not enough to explain the disease and its sequelae, the explanation began to shift from a natural to an unnatural etiology. *Sida* began to be talked of as a "sent" disease, one caused by the malignant intent of others.

Notes

1. The practice of mixing cereal—usually oatmeal—with formula or milk is common among African-American mothers in the community; nipple holes are enlarged with an ice pick or similar object to allow the gruel through. Despite the admonition of nurses and physicians that milk alone is all babies need for the first few months of life, many women feel that it is not enough to satisfy the hunger of their infants. Babies fed cereal from the bottle are not as fussy and "sleep more," they say; some also believe that too much milk in the diet gives babies thrush (oral moniliasis).

2. Twenty years ago when I analyzed the beliefs about health and illness collected from African-American informants living in southern Arizona, I felt that many of those having to do with "natural" illness were probably of European origin. The concern with the balance of heat and cold, the association of the former with the blood and the latter with phlegm, and so forth, were so reminiscent of the old ideas of humoralism that an independent origin seemed unlikely to me (1974; 1977:34). I am no longer quite so convinced; the similarities of the beliefs in the Miami groups (and the differences between those of African descent with those of Cubans and Puerto Ricans) and the more recent findings of other scholars is quite compelling (Mitchell 1983; Roberson 1983; Camino 1986; Laguerre 1987; Farmer 1988, 1990). Still, it must also be noted that many ideas about the blood are shared by African-American and Southern White individuals (Murphree 1968; C. Hill 1976; Nations, Camino, and Walker 1985). Whatever the beliefs about the blood and its functions brought by the slaves from West Africa might have been, it is probably safe to say that some of them meshed nicely with the then-current humoral beliefs of Europeans.

3. My announced intention to go home to western Kansas for Christmas in 1970 caused Sister Erma to predict darkly that I was sure to get sick if I went, as my blood was now "too thin for that kind of weather." Sure enough, in my absence I developed a severe upper respiratory infection and returned to Arizona coughing, sneezing, and generally miserable. Sister Erma was too polite to say, "I told you so," but it was clear that she felt vindicated. I, of course, blamed my infection on a virus that I had probably picked up at Denver's holiday-crowded Stapleton airport.

4. The interplay between gender, strong emotional states, and bodily function is underscored in Farmer's description of the traditional illness known as *move san* ("bad blood"), a disorder common among rural Haitian women. It is brought on by emotional upsets and pregnant or lactating women are seen as particularly vulnerable; when this occurs it may result in *let gate,* or spoiled breastmilk. The *move san/let gate* complex is "an illness caused by malignant emotions—anger born of interpersonal strife, shock, grief, chronic worry, and other affects perceived as potentially harmful." As it is a frequently cited reason for early weaning it often results in "disastrous effects" on infant health (Farmer 1988).

5. Rates of infection for both African-American men and women decreased between 1982 and 1985 but began to increase dramatically in 1986. Between 1985 and 1989, for example, there was an increase in incidence rates of 106 percent for men and *176 percent* for women. The authors of the study cited suggest that "adverse changes in sexual behavior" may play a part, quoting studies linking illegal drug use and associated high-risk behaviors such as prostitution with the increase (Rolfs and Nakashima 1990). However, Handsfield suggests that race and ethnicity should be seen as "epidemiologic markers," not risk factors for sexually transmitted disease, and that while drug use (particularly "crack" cocaine) may have a specific influence it is important to remember that "the underlying problems are unemployment, poverty, poor education, prejudice, and inadequate health care, which in turn lead to crime, prostitution, substance abuse, family disruption, and despair. All these factors combine to create an atmosphere conducive to the spread of STDs [sexually transmitted diseases], a situation with ample historical precedence. The message is clear: although we may limit the spread of syphilis, human immunodeficiency virus (HIV) infection, and other STDs, true control will not come until the nation and governments at all levels develop the will and means to solve the interactive problems of the inner city" (1990:1452).

6

So Many Different Types of Things Will Run Your Blood Up

A storm out of the Gulf hammered Memphis. Poncho snapping in the wing, Tucept took the soul of the Tribe in hand and, centering himself, he conjured up the Board of Destiny. He sent his futuresight along it into the eons and traced the path of power. Soon he would be ready. Strange shadowed figures, dark brooding haints stalked the woods with him, relishing the storm, spirits of much power, this one in the top hat, and that one in the ragged cloth of a slave with a jackleg preacher's Bible, here a cripple and this one a basket weaver. Their presence drew the storm to him and spurred its intensity. Tucept threw his hood back and let the storm wash his face. Thunder drummed. Lightning wreathed him and he drew power in surging singing waves.

On the Drive, red embers of a lit pipe glowing in her palm, an old gingerheaded woman rocked and waited.

—A. R. Flowers, *De Mojo Blues*

One bright Arizona morning 64-year-old Arnella Lewis woke up unable to see and unable to use her right arm. As she had no phone she felt her way to the front porch and simply screamed until a neighbor came running. An ambulance was called and she was taken to the hospital serving the indigent of the city. Here, she later reported, an ambulance attendant asked her for 15 dollars as a "fee" for taking her into the emergency room. She did not have 15 dollars, she said, and couldn't see to find it if she *did!* If money was required before treatment they could just take her right back home. She was then taken into the hospital emergency room where she was examined by "one of them student doctors." She was told that her blood pressure was very high and that she had suffered a "light stroke." The hospital was full, however, and so it was determined that she could be cared for at home. She was given a bottle full of pills and told that she could "never let them run out"; she would have to take them the rest of her life. She was then sent back home in the company of her brother, who had been called to come to the hospital to get her. By nightfall she was at home in bed surrounded by relatives, neighbors, and members of her church. The medication had been discarded without a single dose being taken. Arnella's response to the admonition to take the pills for life was, "Now that don't make no sense," an opinion that she did not mention to the physician who had examined her. It was an opinion shared by her friends and neighbors, however; the only disagreement seemed to be just which home remedy would best serve to "bring down" her blood.

The day after this episode I happened to be walking down the alley in front of Arnella's home and saw a number of women gathered on her porch, an overflow of those crowding her small home. "Miss Arnella's done had a stroke," said one when I asked what had happened. I was invited in and found her sitting up in bed, dressed in an old-fashioned lacy gown and peignoir still smelling faintly of moth balls. The room was filled with people and she was most definitely holding court. The dramatic story of the previous day's happenings was related one more time: how she woke up unable to see; the call for help; the trip to the hospital; the greed of the ambulance attendant; the perceived poor care from the young doctor. She spoke of how worried her brother had been when he heard the news and how he rushed to the emergency room to bring her home to a concerned neighborhood. Now the main problem was what to do about her "high blood."

She confessed that the condition was her own fault as she had always liked "good eating." The result was "blood on the brains" which had "boiled up" as a result of eating too much rich food. A home remedy had not yet been selected, and in the tiny kitchen a lively discussion as to what would be best was taking place among the gathered women. The choice had been narrowed to honey-and-vinegar in hot water for nine days (the treatment which she finally selected), or a pinch of epsom salts every day for a similar period of time.[1] Treatment of another sort had already begun, however. Arnella was not only sitting propped up in bed but *sleeping* in that position; this practice she believed would help to "bring down" the blood to its proper level. As I left she was putting in her order for that night's dinner, a meal that would be cooked and brought in by a neighbor. "How about some fried chicken," said the woman who had volunteered to cook. "No," said Arnella, "I had fried chicken last night!" Instead, she had a taste for "some of that good old Creole gumbo."

Some days later I returned to find Arnella up and around and "cured" by her postural treatment, her home remedy, and, especially, the visit of "the saints" of her Pentecostal church along with her minister. He had laid his hand on her head as they all prayed, she said, and she "felt the stroke leave" her body. She had been cured by "spiritual healing," said Arnella's niece Ella; "they pray for you and then God do the work. It did; I know she can use herself, and she couldn't use herself. And they prayed for her; they just went there and they prayed for her. And she got up out of bed, and she walked that same evening. That child was so sick, and her blood pressure went down. . . . " Arnella had also begun using a preventive suggested by an aunt in Oklahoma who had advised (Snow 1977:35), "Well, honey, your sight will come back, it will eventually come back. But you drink you a teaspoon of vinegar in some water and that will prevent another stroke. And keep your hand rubbed in it, in white vinegar. Take a teaspoonful of that vinegar in water, that'll thin your blood, too, that'll prevent your havin' another stroke." The young physician who surely would have labeled Arnella as "non-compliant" did not get a chance to do so; she did not return for follow-up care. In this clash of explanatory models it is unlikely that he knew of "high blood" or that his patient might take "high blood pressure" to be the same thing; certainly Arnella did not know that they differed. Both parties thought that they had communicated; they had not. (Tucson, Arizona; 1971)

High Blood

When an African-American man or woman is told, "Your blood pressure is a little high," what does that mean to him or to her? Obviously to some individuals it means the same thing that it does in biomedical terms; a measurement of systolic/diastolic blood pressure higher than the recognized limits of normal. Many others understand it in terms of a condition quite different from what is meant by the health worker, however—one that contrasts in causal factors, in the presence and nature of symptoms, in duration of the problem, and in proper treatment for it. They believe that the blood itself has for some reason moved higher than the safe middle level in volume and/or location in a continuum where *both* extremes are seen as abnormal. The important thing, says Bernita, is *balance:* The blood "should stay where it's not up too high and not down too low. It should stay like that." Getting it "to stay like that," of course, is the problem. It requires maneuvers aimed at controlling physiological processes, emotional states, and interpersonal relationships. And as Arnella's experience indicates, the individual who fails to do so may be faulted if the blood is out of balance; he or she should have paid more attention.

The condition known as "high blood" seems to be more frequently mentioned in informants' discussions of ill health than is the other extreme, "low blood." This may perhaps be explained by the high incidence of hypertension and its related morbidity in the African-American population—it is certainly not uncommon for African-American individuals to be told that their blood pressure is high. This is not one of those instances when a condition such as the little red hives or a hex-related illness exists only in the traditional system. Instead, parties from both sides agree that the disorder is a problem, irrespective of the fact that they may view it quite differently. When asked, "What is your one most serious health problem or health worry in your family right now?" "high blood" was ranked first by

Bahamian families in Miami; it also ranked first for Southern Black families, although they were more likely to use the orthodox term, "high blood pressure" (Weidman et al. 1978:315ff). Among the ethnomedical complaints presented by both African-American and White patients attending an ambulatory clinic in the Appalachian foothills of Virginia the one most commonly mentioned was "high blood"; several of the other problems mentioned ("nerves," "weak 'n' dizzy," and "fallin' out") relate to it as well (Nations, Camino, and Walker 1985). Carole Hill's comparative study of the health beliefs and practices of Whites and African-Americans in a Georgia community reveals similar concern: 70 percent of the African-American sample reported problems with their heart or blood, most describing these with the term "high blood" (C. Hill 1988:63).

It must be abundantly clear that terminology can be a confusing issue, and the fact that there is overlapping terminology and differential meaning of "high blood" and "high blood pressure" is an important contributor to problems between clinicians and African-American patients over the treatment of the latter disorder (Satcher and Ashley 1974; Z. Payne and Hall 1978; Z. Payne 1980; Powers 1982; Weidman 1982; Satcher and Creary 1984: Bailey 1988, 1991). Many people see "high blood" and "high blood pressure" as equivalent terms and use them interchangeably: A query about high blood *pressure* may be answered in terms of high blood; a discussion of high blood include statements about the pressure. Introduction of the term "hypertension" may muddle things even further: It may be seen as equivalent to high blood and/or high blood pressure or it may be viewed as an entirely separate entity. One afternoon I listened as a pediatrics resident questioned a new father very thoroughly about medical problems in his family history. He emphatically denied any, including "any history of hypertension." Somewhat later in the interview, however, as the resident remarked that it was unusual for there to be absolutely *no* medical problems, past or present, the young father said, "Well, I *do* have high *blood,* but I take medicine for that!" (Lansing, Michigan; 1987)

All of Roberson's rural Virginia informants were familiar with the conditions known as "high blood" and "low blood," and most reported that family members suffered with one or both. Some individuals said they did not use the term "high blood," but instead used "high blood pressure" or "hypertension." Irrespective of terminology used, however, those who offered explanations "stipulated that they were not very confident of their knowledge in this area" (1983:150). Camino's informants in an urban Virginia neighborhood use "high blood" and "high blood pressure" interchangeably, sometimes saying "regular high blood pressure" to distinguish that condition from "hypertension," reserving the latter term for the presence of increased tension or stress in one's life combined with increased blood volume (1986:78). In a large sample of African-Americans and Whites in metropolitan Detroit just over half of respondents (52.2

percent) referred to the problem as "high blood pressure," and those "who answered 'other' used the folk term 'high blood'" (Bailey 1988). And in New Orleans, research among a sample of hypertensive women discovered that

> participants described their illness in terms of *"pressure"* or *"pressure trouble."* When asked for more specific terms, the response was usually *"high blood pressure," "high blood,"* or *"hypertension."* Many informants discriminated between *"high blood"* (or *"high blood pressure"*) and hypertension. They considered *"high blood"* simply a shorthand version of the term *"high blood pressure"* (*"I just say 'high blood'"*), but hypertension was considered *"something else again."* Over half said that these two illnesses were different but related. Fifty-three percent differentiated between high blood and hypertension, 37 percent said there was no difference, and 10 percent said they did not know or were uncertain of the distinction. . . . (Heurtin-Roberts and Reisin 1990)

In Los Angeles the term "hypertension" has also been reported as a source of confusion, with many people understanding it to refer to feelings of nervousness and/or as equivalent to hyperactivity in children (Satcher and Ashley 1974).

High blood/pressure in traditional belief differs from the biomedical model in a number of ways. If asked to define "high blood" or "high blood pressure," someone subscribing to the traditional view might suggest that it means (a) having too much blood, (b) having blood located high in the body, and/or (c) having blood that is too sweet. In the latter case blood pressure is intimately connected with qualities of sweet and bitter taste. Daniel Moerman has described this dichotomy as the basic concept of health on St. Helena Island, South Carolina (Moerman 1975, 1979, and 1981), with the healthy individual one whose blood is neither too sweet nor too bitter. His analysis suggests that "under most conditions the blood tends to become sweet, and the pressure, consequently, tends to rise. Flavor is the independent and pressure the dependent variable. One informant explained this tendency by saying 'a person, he wouldn't want to eat so much bitter stuff.' This suggests at least indirectly that the sweetness/high pressure is associated with the diet. At other times, however, "the blood seems naturally to tend toward excess bitterness, reducing pressure, and causing weakness, lassitude, and perhaps constipation" (1981). Moerman does not mention the blood varying along any other dimension but only makes a passing comment that most people he spoke with felt that epsom salts taken as a laxative must be used in moderation because of its tendency to "thin out" the blood (1975).

Kathryn Heyer has also done research on St. Helena with a focus on rootwork and malignant magic. Her dissertation includes a brief description of the herbal healing tradition and it parallels Moerman's findings—blood that is sweet if high and bitter if low (1981:56–58).

African-American traditional healers in rural North Carolina also say that health requires a balance in the blood; here again it can become "unbalanced by being either too sweet (a condition know as 'high blood') or too bitter (a condition known as 'low blood')" (C. Hill and Mathews 1981; Mathews 1987). So far as I know these are the only reports tying qualities of sweetness and bitterness with increase or decrease in pressure in a systematic way. It is difficult to know the reasons for this apparent regional variation, although it is tempting to speculate that it represents an older and perhaps "purer" African tradition. This is particularly true for the Sea Islands of South Carolina where the emphasis on African-born slaves, their high number relative to Whites, and the islands' isolation resulted in "a geographical, social and cultural basis for the retention of many elements of African culture in the Sea Islands and the development of a distinctive African-American culture" (J. Jackson, Slaughter, and Blake 1974).

The fact that the areas where the bitter/sweet and high/low contrasts are found are also those where there is still a viable herbal tradition in healing suggests that this is part of an older system.[2] Only a single informant of mine—Bernita Washington—has ever linked sweetness and high blood. She says that "too much sweetening" will cause the blood to rise: "Say if you know that you are eating too much *sweetening;* you know you can't have a lot of sweetening, that'll run your blood pressure up, a lot of it. So many different types of things *will* run your blood *up.*" When I asked her if this meant that the blood then *became* sweet, however, she said no. (1986) It is reported in other studies that the blood can become "too sweet," to be sure, but this sweetness is not necessarily tied in with a high/low continuum. Instead it is usually linked to the condition know as "sugar," akin to diabetes but with traditional elements included (Snow 1977:38; Weidman et al. 1978:462–463; Roberson 1983:154; Nations, Camino, and Walker 1985; Camino 1986:67–68; C. Hill 1988:63; Mathews 1988).[3]

The processes believed to result in high blood (the traditional term will be used from now on to lessen confusion) include a belief that the blood can expand and contract in volume and/or can move higher or lower in the body. My impression is that most believers in the traditional system think that both of these are possible. It is felt that there is a normal or usual amount of blood in the body but that this can rather quickly increase so that one has more than the system can deal with effectively. It can then "back up" into the upper part of the body—particularly the head—literally squeezed up because it has nowhere else to go. It is also recognized that the blood moves about in the body and the term "high blood" may represent a *shift* of the blood—whether a normal or an increased amount— higher in the body. This view usually incorporates an element of suddenness and turbulence so that the blood "rushes up" to the head; it is seen quite literally as boiling over.

Various reasons were given for the expansion in volume or shift in location that denotes high blood. Environmental conditions are sometimes implicated: Blood thickened by cold air was seen as a first stage of high blood by Camino's Virginia informants (1986:74). A similar idea was expressed by a 56-year-old man in Detroit: "My blood is probably high today because it's a little chilly outside and I'm gettin' older" (Bailey 1988). In contrast, according to a Southern Black informant in Miami (Weidman et al. 1978:553), "I have high blood. If I get hot, and I don't make it some place to lay down or sit down, I fall-out" [i.e., suffer a fainting spell]. The hot days of summer may heat the body both externally and internally, then, causing the blood to rise to the head more quickly (Brunson 1962:65; Nations, Camino, and Walker 1985; Heurtin-Roberts and Reisin 1990).

Diet and emotional upheaval, however, are most frequently implicated in the production of high blood: Either or both can cause a change in blood volume and consistency or send the blood shooting high in the body.[4] Dietary folly may include both overeating and the eating of the wrong kinds of foods. These are sometimes categorized in general terms as "greasy foods," "fattening foods," or "too much rich food." If people are asked to name a dietary item that can cause high blood, however, it would be red meat. Pork—one of the cornerstones of a soul food diet—is especially problematic. A elderly woman interviewed by Gwaltney suggested that the fault lies with the eaters, not the food. She called pork a "strong food" eaten by the slaves—"you know they had to be healthy"—and attributed the fact that it now causes health problems to a weakening of the blood from racial mixing:

> Now, you know all this mixin' and doin' is not good for our people. Our fo'parents loved pork and all that strong food. Now, they didn't have no high blood pressure nor no diabetis nor no stomach trouble, neither. But they was almost all black and that is why they was not mean like a lot of these nigguhs you see now! Strong people need strong food. Them strong black people ate pig and yam and goat, and it help them. Now! All that strong food is too much for they children. They systems just won't take it! When I was a chile, my mother fed me yam from her own mouth and I was strong! So now I can't eat the food of my fo'arents because I just ain't the woman they was! (Gwaltney 1980:219–220)

Strong food or no, it is implicated as a culprit in high blood in virtually every study in which traditional beliefs about high blood are described. In Miami a Southern Black informant said, for example, "I have high or low blood. The doctor said I have a blood trouble of some kind. I don't know whether it's high or low. He said not to eat pork. Any time I eat that pork my head goes to spinning; so I don't bother" (Weidman et al. 1978:440). Note how closely this statement compares to the words of this Bahamian woman: "Mrs. H.

said, "You can tell if your blood is high, because your head bothers you. You have a headache or swimming; you can't keep your head up. . . . I can eat a piece of pork and I have to run to the doctor, because my blood goes up. You can feel it. It goes right up in the head, and you can get a stroke" (p. 427).

In New Orleans (Heurtin-Roberts and Reisin 1990), "respondents made such statements as 'I know if I eat a little piece of pork it'll go up and stay up for weeks' and 'I knew if I ate that gumbo it would run my blood up but I did it anyway.'" And the Reverend Barrett, the minister of the small Baptist church attended by Bernita Washington and her family, even managed to work it into a sermon one morning: "Man cannot live by bread alone," he said, "nor pork chops neither. *They'll* run your blood up for sure!" (Lansing, Michigan; 1991)

The mechanism for this reaction may or may not be stated. Bertha Alexander commented one day that she had changed doctors and mentioned that her first physician had given her medicine for high blood pressure. I asked her what she considered high blood pressure to be and she replied, "The blood goes up to your head too fast, I guess, when you get excited or nervous it goes up. Sometime can cause it to bust a vein, they say; have a stroke. I don't know exactly whether it's missin' some veins or not goin' in a correct spot or what. [It's from] eatin' too much and gettin' too fat; starts your heart to gettin' heart trouble." Like her nearby neighbor Arnella, she had thrown away her medication when she changed doctors as, "You know you can help that yourself, just don't eat all that rich food." (Tucson, Arizona; 1971) Individuals living in the urban Virginia neighborhood studied by Camino told her that high blood results when an individual eats too much salt or rich food (identified as fatty, greasy foods, or red meat). The rich foods release fat into the blood and salt "settles" there causing it to thicken. The "rising blood" is then forced or "squished" to the head where the blood vessels are thought to be weak (1986:74). In the Appalachian foothills similar ideas were revealed by African-American and White patients attending a primary care clinic; all of those who reported that they suffered from high blood felt that diet was the most important etiological factor, citing too much pork, rich or red meat, fattening food and salt; salt was said to act by "drying up" the blood and meat by thickening it (Nations, Camino, and Walker 1985). And as so many other threats to health in this traditional system, present-day folly will have to be paid for sooner or later. Young people like "fast food" but, predicted the Reverend Moses Hastings, this will someday take its toll:

People love to eat french fries, but that's gonna be your number one killer after while because of the grease. And potato increase more *blood,* potatoes do; they increase your *blood* sometimes. 'Course the doctor don't *say* it, they don't tell you about it—but you watch a year or so from now, all the young folks. They just like fast *food,* now; they go for the *hamburger* and the *french* fries. They gonna turn out with, as the years go, they come out with bad *stomach,* high blood pressure. And young peoples gonna be havin' *heart* attack more than old people. [That's] potatoes that's fried, now . . . you fry 'em with that grease in it, it never settles too good in your stomach although you may go [and] eat 'em and keep goin'. (Grand Rapids, Michigan; 1987)

Wrong diet and emotional upset together produce a deadly combination; said one Virginia patient: "I try to stay calm. If I get mad, I can feel the blood raisin' up, I feel like the blood is going to pop out of my head. I try to stay away from any pork meat, that'll send it (blood) up high for sure. It (pork) makes your blood thicker. The blood get thicker and then it puts pressure on the vessels in your head" (Nations, Camino, and Walker 1985).

There is danger both in the sudden emotional upheavals that might result from an angry scene and the more chronic sort of "nerves" or "worriation" brought on by continuing life stresses. In Bailey's survey of beliefs about high blood pressure among White and African-Americans in Detroit, for example, more than 90 percent of both groups reported that it is caused by "emotional worry" (1988). Emotionally caused high blood is almost always associated with a change in blood movement rather than a change in volume— movement that is swift, sudden, and directed toward the head. Family problems are frequently cited as a primary cause of such problems; here is a 53-year-old Virginia homemaker: "When I get to worryin' about the kids, what kinda' trouble they's in, ya know. When I get bogged down with worriation, I get the awfullest attack of the nerves. That sends my blood up right high, then I get just so weak 'n' dizzy and every now and again it (the blood) gets so high on the brain it causes me to fall right out. . . . They tell me high blood can even cause hemorrage [sic] on the brain" (Nations, Camino, and Walker 1985). It has already been mentioned that *all* of the patients in this Virginia clinic who reported suffering from high blood felt that diet was a cause of the disorder; two-thirds of them also cited "excitement, anger, upset, 'worriation,' nervousness and stress" as triggers for the problem. "I ain't doin' well," said a 39-year-old woman in another study who was concerned over her invalid mother, problems with her children, and the loss of her long-time male companion. "Even I can tell you that. There's too much pressure and it's makin' *my pressure* bad. And I been feelin' real sad for myself" (A. Kleinman 1988:134).[5]

In New Orleans similar factors—including concern over children— can cause the blood to "accelerate" so that in one woman's memorable phrase, it "shoots up to my head and rings like a bell" (Heurtin-Roberts and Reisin 1990; see also Blumhagen 1980). Bernita Washington agreed:

Nerves will play tricks upon you, it will run your blood pressure up. And I don't know; well, just quite a few things could run your blood pressure up. Say you and your husband having misunderstandings all the time. That's another problem that run your blood pressure up, you know that. Try not to *do* that! And the *worst* high blood pressure that you could have is *nerves,* nerves. Worriation and stuff being followed by different things. "The kids are bothering me," you know. And then, "I've *got* this problem with my daughter," and whatever. And then when you do any thinkin', all that tied up there and that will really tie your blood pressure up *quick.* (Lansing, Michigan; 1986)

When I asked Bernita's neighbor Janine Jackson (who had recently seen a physician for the first time in her life) what she thought about high blood pressure, she answered that she knew little about the subject. She went on to muse aloud, however, and expressed herself in traditional terms:

I guess I kinda know what they mean; your blood is up high. What make it run up I don't really [know]; I guess it's from too much meat. Somebody used to tell me about your blood, but like I said, since I didn't go to the doctor much I didn't go *through* that! [A pause] And then to me, you rush your blood up by, you can do that by *worry* and rushin' yourself. What you doin' I don't even know. Just like this woman passed away the other day. And I do think you go through somethin' and you bring that on, you know; like rushin', you can bring the high blood on. And unless you not take your rest you can have *low* blood. That is what I think about it; I don't know.

"What did she die of?"

Somebody said high blood rushed up, and then somebody said heart attack. But she had worked Thursday and had come home and made the dinner. They say she's gonna take a rest and lay down, and when she went to lay down, they heard somethin' fall. And they went in there and when they got her to the hospital she were gone. But you never know; she could've had a heart attack. Wasn't hardly a stroke. I guess a stroke can [kill you], but not that fast I don't think. (Lansing, Michigan; 1986)

Many people who believe in the traditional system think that the condition known as high blood is associated with symptoms. Some even say that one can actually *feel* the blood rising up into the head so it is not surprising that the symptoms are often felt in that part of the body. On St. Helena Island, symptoms differ according to age, with a rise in pressure causing "fevers in children, colds in adults, and a nonspecific condition called 'high blood' (characterized by nausea, dizziness, short memory, and headache) among the aged" (Moerman 1975). Both age and gender are reported by North Carolina root doctors to play parts in the kinds of symptoms suffered in high blood, said to occur most frequently in obese middle-aged women and young men. Headache is a "key symptom" for both groups, while dizziness, insomnia, and disordered interpersonal relationships is a particularly female manifestation. These healers claim that dizziness is never reported by males, but that males are more likely to report blackouts from heavy drinking, indicating high blood (C. Hill and Mathews 1981). According to Bailey (1988), a "majority of the sampled Detroit Afro-Americans (63 percent) perceived such symptoms as headaches, dizziness, tenseness, dry lips, seeing spots, and ringing in ears as associated with their elevated blood pressure."

In New Orleans more than 70 percent of the women interviewed reported experiencing symptoms, including "headaches, weakness and dizziness, blurred vision, seeing sports or glitter, nosebleeds, 'glarey' eyes, the 'blind staggers,' blacking out and 'falling out,' chest pains, drowsiness, red eyes, smelling fresh blood in the nose, tasting fresh blood, and having one's breath smell like blood. The sensation of having blood in one's mouth and nose, along with reddened eyes, was said to indicate the presence of blood at a dangerously high level in the body; one's blood has 'gone up'" (Heurtin-Roberts and Reisin 1990). If one looks at all the reports of symptoms associated with high blood, headache is the most commonly mentioned, followed by dizziness, vision problems, and "falling out," a term used to describe a sudden collapse when the individual, though usually able to see and hear, is unable to move. Unlike hypertension, then, high blood is *not* "the silent killer." In the traditional view, in fact, if symptoms are *not* present, the blood may be seen to be in its proper balance so that medication and/or home remedies are not taken (Satcher and Ashley 1974; Dougherty 1976; Powers 1982; A. Kleinman 1988:132). In Miami, for example, "several Black hypertensive patients included statements such as the following: 'I don't need medicine if I stay calm'; or 'I use other things to cool the blood and bring it down'; or 'If I don't have a headache, I know my blood pressure isn't high enough to need medicine'" (Weidman 1982:219). This is, of course, a major problem from the view of the health professional.

The differences between the traditional "high blood" and orthodox "high blood pressure" are brought sharply into focus when ideas of prevention and treatment are considered. Because in traditional terms the blood is seen as constantly in flux—in this case moving between higher or lower volume or location in response to known stimuli—it is logical to see high blood as preventable and treatable. As the main culprits in causing the blood to rise are dietary folly and strong emotional states these are the focus of most preventive techniques. The ingestion of items seen as interfering with the blood's ability to thicken or "go up" may be tried. An individual whose blood has a tendency to rise, that is, may attempt to prevent this by occasionally taking a pinch of epsom salts or a small amount of vinegar—substances that in larger doses are used to treat high blood. Increasing the intake of foods such as garlic or pickles—believed able to thin or bring down the blood—may be tried as well.

The most frequently heard preventive measure is one of avoidance, however. The individual who wishes to minimize the probability of developing high blood might avoid food and drink thought to increase blood volume or cause it to rise in the body and might stay away from too much salt, rich or greasy foods, red meat (especially pork), and sweet things. Such avoidance may be easier said than done, however. Both culture and income are important determinants in eating habits and many of the items in a "soul food" diet are high in salt and fat content (Satcher and Ashley 1974). In the Atlanta Municipal Market the "rows of cured and fresh cuts of virtually every part of the hog, displays of collard greens and crackling, and the dominance of lower-priced high-carbohydrate foods provide an immediate and dramatic insight into the dietary practice which dominates low-income black food habits and which by cultural heritage also pervades the menus of black middle class families" (Z. Payne 1980). "Fatback" or "fatmeat" (salt pork) is both cheap and highly salted, and regional cooking styles may also add salt and grease to the basic diet. Roberson reported that fried foods are preferred by her rural Virginia informants who—even when they bake chicken or fish instead of frying it—frequently add bacon or fatmeat as flavoring. Vegetables are similarly seasoned and fresh fish and pork are cured in brine (1983:109). Carole Hill's Georgia informants also prepare vegetables "Southern style": cooked until mushy with a good deal of salt, and with pork or fatback frequently added. She also comments on the importance of the latter as the cheapest meat available in local grocery stores and often the only meat eaten by the poor (1988:95). As well, dietary instructions/prohibitions suggested by physicians may not be clearly understood.[6]

The other major cause of high blood, emotional upset, is even less avoidable. Individuals living in poverty in deteriorating neighborhoods, both rural and urban, have virtually no chance to avoid a stressful lifestyle (Harburg et al. 1973; Harburg et al. 1978; C. Taylor 1990; Kotlowitz 1991; Lemann 1991; Klag et al. 1991). The inner city is an environment where "overcrowding, inadequate housing, high crime rates, juvenile delinquency, alcoholism, drug abuse, unemployment, and cultural friction constitute some of the social ills," and where health problems are caused and exacerbated by "violence, homicides, and accidents, stress-related diseases, and infections" (Satcher and Creary 1984; see also Weidman 1979b).[7]

Rural poverty has its own set of problems (James and Kleinbaum 1976; Wagner et al. 1984; James et al. 1984; C. Williams et al. 1985). Robert Coles, for example, has described sharecropping as "a mean, terrible, brutish way of life become flesh, become infections and injuries and wasting away and 'bad blood' and 'weak blood' and 'tired blood' and running noses and running sores and draining ears and draining wounds and 'poor bones' and 'poor teeth' and 'poor eyes'—all of which, again, amount to the objective side of being poor, the objective side of what we call 'poverty,' in this case the extreme rural kind" (Coles 1967:145). I once asked Bernita Washington if she missed living in rural Mississippi and she replied:

You could *raise* more down there; you could raise more [garden]. The only thing it is about it, you didn't hardly have enough *food* for kids, you couldn't get doctors, stuff like that. So that's one reason I like it better up here. You *can* get a doctor if you have to, you know. That's why so many people *died,* you know; they used their little home remedies and stuff and sometimes the home remedies really wasn't *working!* You needed something else, you know. You just couldn't get it 'cause you couldn't afford it. So, up here you can get better medical attention; you can get a little more *food* and stuff like that. It's much better up here.

And what had sharecropping been like?

Well, like you didn't have to pay house rent or anything like that. But then you'se half-cold catchin' *pneumonia* because you didn't have the facilities to keep warm and stuff with. So, really I don't miss too much. And sometime not a *roof!* 'Cause down South, I have been layin' in the bed [and] you can tell when the sun rises, 'cause it peek right through the hole. If you had a baby, if you ain't careful you had to move your bed from right here 'cause when it snow, it snow right down on top of his head! Oh, it was terrible; it was terrible. (Lansing, Michigan; 1987)

Life in the city has brought new problems to her and her family, however; some of the younger members family were involved with drugs and caught up in the violence associated with their use. And how does she recommend that one *avoid* the running up of the blood due to arguments with a spouse, worries about money, or concern over the children? All she can say is, "try not to *do* that!"

But "trying not to do that" requires the iron will—or denial—of a woman such as her neighbor Janine Jackson. Janine had first disclaimed knowledge of the causes of high blood pressure but went on to suggest that "worry and rushin' yourself" must have contributed to the recent death of another neighbor. She then went on to relate that her husband had died when some of her children were still quite small and that she had had to raise them alone. She had frequently been asked if she was not worried about trying to do so, but said she had always replied:

No, there's no point in it; I have *taught* 'em the *Way!* Worry don't help none. Bible tells us worry isn't a sin, but I know one thing, it don't *help* you! So why worry? And so that's what I think happens to a lotsa people; they go through this worry and they run the blood up, you know, and whatever. And brings on a heart attack or whatever. They're rushin' theirself *away!* But I tell 'em, "I'm gonna get my time out; I don't have time to worry about these kids." I love 'em and tell 'em what's right and I *hep'* 'em any way I can hep' 'em. But worry? And that's what I'm sayin'; by not worryin' and kinda takin' care of yourself or whatnot, you can stand somethin' that a person much younger than you can't take it. That's why I say it don't pay to worry. (Lansing, Michigan; 1986)

It may not pay to worry but it is very very hard for most people not to do so.

Once the blood has increased in sweetness or viscosity, expanded in volume, or sped up into the head, preventive measures are of no avail—it is the abnormal condition itself that must be dealt with. Traditional treatments are quite logical if the underlying premises (that is, the abnormal changes in the blood or its location) are accepted. The length of treatment seen as proper is also logical, though quite different from the orthodox system. Traditional remedies are ordinarily short term, used as they are only until symptoms abate or for a designated number of days, often nine. A physician's directive that antihypertensive medication must be taken for life often makes no sense, then, and in fact may be seen as downright dangerous. Treatments for high blood (whether prescription medication or a pinch of epsom salts) if taken *too* long are believed by many to bring the blood down too much; the result will be the opposing problem, "low blood." This explains Arnella's response: "Now that don't make no sense" and her discarding of the medication given to her in the emergency room; far simpler and less dangerous to simply take her honey-and-vinegar for nine days and then watch her diet. Taking too much "blood medicine" may even cause cancer, according to Reverend Hastings: "Right, it can do it; it can do it. You can take it so long and that's where a lotta times it turn into what they call blood *cancer;* cancer, yeah. Blood start, and then the white cells start eatin' up the little red cells. That's right; that's right." (1987) Taking prescription medication only when one "feels bad" makes sense in the traditional system even if it does not to the physician or nurse.

The constant monitoring of the blood to keep it in that safe middle ground—neither too high nor too low—means that people try to avoid known causal factors, treat symptoms by a variety of internal and external measures, and initiate habits to prevent recurrence. Any and all of these may be augmented by religious and magical means. And any and all of these may be taking place while the individual is also being treated for hypertension in a formal health-care setting. In a study of self-treatment among elderly Michigan African-Americans, for example, 82 percent of the 50 participating individuals said that they used home remedies; 78 percent had used such remedies in the past six months. When asked if their doctors knew of their practices, however, 80 percent said that they did not (Institute of Gerontology 1978). One out of six stated that they would continue to use home remedies "after seeing a doctor if the physician did not give or prescribe a medicine for their complaint" (Boyd, Shimp, and Hackney 1984:v). The very different ideas about what should be done about the problem of high blood/pressure makes this a prime arena for misunderstanding between physician and patient; this can only be exacerbated if practitioners are not aware of these differences. In the New Orleans sample of hypertensive women, for example, only 3 of the 15 resident physicians treating them "knew something about the recognition of different illnesses by the patients they treated" (Heurtin-Roberts and Reisin 1990).

Nor is "doctors' medicine" necessarily seen as superior. A survey conducted among patients attending a hypertension clinic at Atlanta's Grady Memorial Hospital resulted in a list of 29 different home remedies, including herbs available at a municipal market only a block from the hospital (Z. Payne 1980). Similarly, some patients in a hypertension clinic in the Watts section of Los Angeles reportedly used herbs instead of their medication and returned to the clinic only to see if the problem was under control (Satcher and Creary 1984). In rural Florida, DiCanio observed: "Some individuals who had had a previously diagnosed and treated illness were, upon its recurrence, less likely to return to the doctor on the grounds that they already knew what the illness was. A frequent question and answer pattern was something like this: 'Would you go to a doctor if you had _____?' 'If I never had it before, I would.' This sounded reasonable until a respondent said this in connection with her 'high blood.' She had a prescription for her hypertension which had been depleted two years previously and never renewed" (1976:127–128).

In Detroit, African-American men were six times more likely to use a "folk care regimen" than White men (26.5 vs. 4.2 percent); African-American women were three times more likely to do so than White women (41 vs. 14 percent). Further, "regardless of the type of home remedy or patent medicine used by the informant, self-prescribed home medications were generally taken prior to medical consultations and were continued after consultation, along with prescribed medications, even though the informant did not tell the physician of this fact." One man reported using sassafras and leaf teas in treating his slightly elevated blood pressure; although he was simultaneously being treated by a physician he "continued his folk treatment regimen in conjunction with his physician's prescribed medication because, he stated, 'If I tell him that I am using herbs, he would think that I was silly'" (Bailey 1988). Telling others of personal experiences serves to transmit traditional health beliefs and, on occasion, provides insight as to why physicians are often kept in the dark about them. As an elderly individual in Rhode Island confided:

> *My Godfather . . . told my mother about garlic water for high blood pressure. She would take five buds, . . . peel them and put them in a quart jar. Recently I started taking it myself in the morning and when I go home at night. When I went to my doctor for my check up last week he was surprised that my pressure was so good for my age and he said, "What are you doing?" I said I was drinking garlic water and I went on to tell him the story I'm telling you now. He said, "The only thing I can see that garlic water would do for you is give you a bad breath." I said, "Well, doctor, I'd rather have a bad breath than no breath."* (Bell and Clements, n.d.)

The patient had ended the conversation with the physician on a humorous note. However, it was the medication that was discarded and the traditional remedy that was continued: "But my pressure has gone down considerably and I don't take water pills or anything now. I still take it, and none of my friends have complained about my garlic breath. So, I think I swear by it."

Only a small proportion of treatments do not involve the ingestion of substances although their rationale is the same as that for oral remedies: getting the blood back to its normal state. Most of these nonoral regimens are associated with the presumed presence of blood in the head—Arnella was sleeping propped up on pillows, for example, to help the blood to drain back into her body. Massage may be tried to get the blood to moving again in a proper direction—a Bahamian man in Miami "sees a 'white ball flying around' just before blacking-out. . . . He blacks out when he is worried or upset. Sometimes the black-outs last 10–15 minutes, sometimes 30 minutes. Nothing helps bring him out; he must come out by himself. When he feels a 'seizure' coming on, he rubs his neck, because blood clots in this area as though it's running to his head. By rubbing his neck he gets the blood circulating again, and it comes down" (Weidman et al. 1978:427).

Just as people often say that they can "feel" the blood rise to the head, they may report feeling it leave again. In Miami a Bahamian woman with arthritis, back pain, high blood, and "sugar" went to a spiritual healer; this individual made a "reading" through leaves and psalms and prayed for the patient who "felt the blood run down her neck and back from her head, and her head stopped paining" (Weidman et al. 1978:465). And Arnella "felt the stroke leave" her body after prayer and her minister's healing touch.

Occasionally substances are used externally on the afflicted part of the body; these are usually simple and readily available. It was white vinegar, for example, that Arnella's aunt suggested be rubbed on the right hand weakened by the stroke. Calene Price also suggested:

When blood pressure is up and you have swimming in the head, get some vinegar or lemon juice or both and put [it] on your face—it will bring pressure down fast. (Flint, Michigan; 1981)

Plain old tap water will do with the help of a spiritual agent, said Reverend Hastings:

High blood is just what you call about will bring about strokes; bring about strokes. In other words it will bring about upset mind, you know; you can't think right, you quick-tempered. You just can't *think* right. So you can take sometime just a glass of water, just a glass of water; you can take a glass of water. Just let it run sometime [and] the Spirit will take over. Take that water and just wash your face with it; just wash your face. (Grand Rapids, Michigan; 1987)

The headache associated with high blood may be treated in a similar fashion. The head may be rubbed or bathed with substances that will draw out the pain (and presumably the excess blood); poultices may also be bound around the head to achieve a similar effect. Again, these are usually products available in any grocery store or pharmacy; plant remedies vary according to where they will grow. When Bernita lived in Mississippi she tied peach leaves around the head for such headaches; in Michigan, with no peach tree available, she either rubs her head with aloe sap from the plants grown on her windowsill or ties a browned cornmeal-and-salt poultice around her head with a cloth. In South Carolina, high blood pressure is treated by bathing the head with a decoction of boiled pokeweed root, and the associated headache treated by binding Spanish moss around the head. The moss may also be worn in the shoes where it will presumably draw down the pain from the head (Morton 1974:109, 153; Heyer 1981:58; Deas-Moore 1987). Blake (1984) told of the elderly woman in the Sea Islands who refused to take pills for high blood pressure as she thought wearing moss in the shoes a better remedy. At his suggestion that she do *both,* her retort was, "You don't know no more than that fool doctor."

Most home treatments for high blood are taken internally, however; their aim is also to bring the blood back to a healthier state. Their action depends on whether the blood is perceived to be too sweet, too thick, overheated, too high in the body, or abnormally increased in volume. In those areas where the blood is considered to be too sweet when the pressure is high most treatments consist of teas made from herbs "to bitter the blood" (Moerman 1975, 1979, 1981; C. Hill and Mathews 1981; Heyer 1981; Mathews 1987).[8] Such a plant is yellow root, commonly used to treat high blood in both rural and urban areas in Georgia. It is the most popular of the folk remedies reported by patients attending the hypertension clinic of Atlanta's Grady Memorial Hospital, for example, and is available at the large municipal market only a block away (Z. Payne 1980). It is sold in small grocery stores throughout the city and used in the treatment of diabetes as well as hypertension, alone or along with orthodox medical treatment (J. Parsons 1981).[9] Hill reported its use along with the antihypertensive drug Inderal; "Yellow root powder" is also available over the counter in the area (1988:116–121). The use of wild plant remedies in their fresh state obviously depends on the locale. The recent increased interest in "natural" foods and remedies, however, has made various plant products in the form of teas widely available in health-food stores or by mail order.

The most widespread treatments for high blood seem to be those available wherever anyone can grow a garden and/or has access to a grocery store or a pharmacy. A few items such as epsom salts or aspirin may be seen as purely medicinal; many others, however, are used as food as well. Sage, says Daisy Johnson, "will take the poison from fresh pork" so it will not affect the blood. (Lansing, Michigan; 1987) Kitchen remedies such as baking soda or cream of tartar and the ever-popular garlic are frequently mentioned as efficacious by individuals in widely separated geographical locales, rural *and* urban. Vinegar and lemon juice are also widely consumed, often with honey added to improve the taste. Pickles or pickle juice may be selected for a similar reason; it is the vinegar that is seen as the active ingredient and it tastes better in this form. Various vegetables may also be eaten in the belief that they change the blood in a positive fashion: they may be specifically named (for example, cucumbers, onions, wild leeks, poke greens, dandelion greens, or celery leaf tea) or lumped as "green vegetables." Other foods, such as rice, skim milk, and white potatoes or potato water, are occasionally reported as well.

The processes by which these treatments are thought to work, if mentioned at all, may be vague. In the Southeast, as mentioned, some substances are said to "bitter" the blood (C. Hill and Mathews 1981; Mathews 1987). My informants in Arizona stated that vinegar, pickle juice, and epsom salts "cut" the blood and opened the pores so that it could be sweated out. Bailey's Detroit respondents consumed "epsom salts, sassafras tea, garlic tablets, vinegar, lemon juice, aspirin, and cream of tartar," indicating that these substances, "not only lowered their blood pressure but also flushed the body of all impurities" (1988). New Orleans women reported using "garlic, vinegar or lemon juice in various combinations to 'thin' and 'cool' the blood and 'draw it away from the head'" as supplements to orthodox medical care (Heurtin-Roberts and Reisin 1990). Often, process is not mentioned at all and a remedy is simply said to be "good for that."

Irrespective of the physiologically active properties thought to be present in any of these remedies most share a magical attribute: their color. With a few exceptions such as yellow root the treatments—whether external or internal—for high blood use substances that are colorless, white, or green. Things used to treat too *much* blood, utilize the symbolic power of opposition to its red color. It is often "too much red meat" that triggers the condition and it is logical to reverse the course by employing nonred substances. This view is further supported by the fact that most treatments for low blood—items seen as blood *builders*—are nearly always red. Symbolism may also be employed in the length of treatment. As has been mentioned, a course of treatment often lasts for nine days. The numbers three and its multiple nine, so important in European and American folk medicine, are heard over and over as people discuss how much of something to take or how long it should be taken; this use of numbers is true for all home remedies, not just those for high blood. In such instances treatment is augmented with the power attached to a ritual number.

Of course, the belief in the efficacy of prayer or the healing touch of a minister of God adds yet another dimension to the restoration of balance. Bernita Washington suffers from high blood pressure but seldom takes the medication prescribed by her physician. "I'm supposed to; he told me to, but I don't. I was takin' little bitty little pills, high blood pressure pills which you take I think one a day. Last year." And why had she quit taking them, I asked?

Well, *I* felt that—I always the type of person that I know that God can *heal*—and I gives Him a chance to *do* that; I don't *take* that chance from *Him*. I give *Him* that chanct. Because I know that He can *do* it. Sometime you can take too much medicine. Sometime you can take the *wrong* medicine. I've know peoples to get medicine too *strong* for them! I've know people to get medicine for *one* thing and it wasn't what was wrong; something *else* was wrong with them. So in *that* case, what you do is *pray* about it. Then if you find yourself that God said you need to go to a doctor. He'll give you—He doesn't have you ignorant—if He says, "You need to go to a doctor," then you *go!* And He gonna di*rect* the doctor that you go to; He gonna direct the doctor what to *do!* If you have to go. But it's good to always give God a chance to fulfill with you what to do. (Lansing, Michigan; 1987)

Two years later (summer of 1989) Bernita invited me to go shopping with her as she prepared to take a trip to Mississippi and Georgia to visit relatives. I was heartened when she said that she needed to stop by the nearby pharmacy to get her blood pressure medication renewed; I needn't have been. Although the prescription had been filled only two months before, she felt that she wanted "fresh" pills to make sure that they would work.[10] Was she going to begin taking the medication as her physician had directed? No, she meant only to take them for one week in preparation for the coming trip, "to make sure I don't have any problems while I'm down there." Off we went to the pharmacy where she also purchased a package of Black Draught granules (an over-the-counter laxative preparation); she didn't mean to take a full dose, however. "Just a pinch" was all she needed, she said; it would "tone" her system for the time that she would be gone from home.

Both the causes and treatment of high blood, then, must be seen in more than purely physiological terms. It *is* in physiological/pharmacological terms, however, that traditional treatments tend to be viewed by outsiders. The first question posed by even the most open-minded individual when hearing of a folk treatment is usually, "Does it really work?" The question, "In whose terms?," generally does not get asked. As Hufford pointed out, however, "a simple comparison of what 'they' do with what medicine does, often accomplishes nothing more than to translate some part of what the tradition does into medical language" (1984). He noted that features of ritual and context that would be seen as crucial by an alternative practioner might be simply ignored by the scientifically trained researcher as irrelevant. The result is that "when the investigator has finished eliminating what was taken to be 'cultural baggage' there is nothing left to investigate)."[11]

Low Blood

The medical staff of a church-sponsored community clinic were surprised one afternoon when the blood pressure of Marvin Newton, 62, was found to be significantly elevated. He had been attending the clinic for three years, and his blood pressure had thus far been well controlled with diuretic medication. The staff were further surprised to learn that he had not taken his medication in the month since his last visit. When asked why he had discontinued its use, he reminded them of the blood test that he had been given on his previous visit. A review of the chart revealed that he had had a routine blood count and that the white blood cells were slightly lower in number than normal; this finding was explained by the physician as "your blood count is a little low." He was told that it was probably nothing to worry about, but that it should be checked periodically. Mr. Newton interpreted this to mean that he now had "low blood" instead of "high blood," and he feared that continuing the medication would further endanger his health. He was told that it was the cellular elements of the blood that had decreased abnormally, not the pressure, and he promised to begin taking the pills again. (Lansing, Michigan; 1984)

As noted earlier low blood seems to be less frequently mentioned in the context of illness by informants than is high blood—70 percent of Hill's African-American sample reported experiencing problems with their blood or heart that they labeled "high blood," for example, while "very few" experienced problems with low blood pressure or "low blood" (1988:63). Several women, however, confided that their blood had been low after suffering miscarriages or after having the "woman's operation." When references to the condition do occur they also reflect ideas which differ from the biomedical model in a number of ways. As Marvin Newton's experience shows, overlapping terminology is again a problem. It is rendered even more complex because *two* biomedical categories—lowered blood pressure and anemia—are incorporated in the traditional condition of low blood. It too must be considered in cultural terms.

> *"Low blood"* is a condition in which blood volume is not as great as it should be for normal functioning. *"Low blood"* can produce anything from slight symptoms of listlessness or fatigue to states of semi-consciousness or unconsciousness lasting from a few minutes to hours or days. The circumstance of extremely low blood or *"no blood"* can result in death. When *"low blood"* is given as the reason for *"blacking-out"* . . . it tends to be perceived as lacking in sufficient volume to nourish the body properly or to reach the brain. It is the element of *"nourishment"* or lack thereof, which seems to account for the identification of the medical term, *"anemia"* with the traditional term, *"low blood."* The two, in fact, are not synonymous, but the equation is similar enough for the syncretism of meaning to have occurred. . . . (Weidman et al. 1978:425–426)

A question about low blood pressure may also be translated into "low blood" and understood to be the same as anemia; when one young woman at a prenatal clinic in Lansing was asked if she could define low blood pressure, for example, she replied that it is "sort of like when you're anemic; your blood is low from not eating the right food" (Snow and Johnson 1978). This terminological confusion was also demonstrated in the Miami project when interviewers used standard condition categories in an attempt to establish levels of morbidity. When asked if anyone in the household had high or low blood pressure, for example, answers such as the following were collected from Southern Black households:

> *Q: High or low blood pressure?*
> A. Now that is what they told me in the hospital, low blood. . . . He said your blood is a little low and gave me pills to take. After I take the pills, I take Geritol. That's blood-building too.
> A. Yes, S. She had low blood. They gave her blood and iron pills.

And from a Bahamian household:

> *Q: High or low blood pressure?*
> A: Well, low blood. We are anemic. J. and I. (Weidman et al. 1978:369)

Low blood is the other end of the continuum from high blood and is seen as no less dangerous; indeed, some say it is even *more* dangerous. If asked to define "low blood" or "low blood pressure," an individual subscribing to the traditional view might suggest that it means, (1) not having enough blood, (2) having blood that is too thin, (3) having blood located low in the body, or (4) having blood that is too bitter. The latter is the view in the Sea Islands and environs where qualities of sweetness or bitterness are attached to high or low blood pressure. In most instances, however, low blood refers to lack—not having sufficient blood or having blood that is deficient in substance or nutrients. Said Lillian Ashleigh in Tucson:

> They say you can have *high* blood or *low* blood, and I know the low blood is not *enough* blood and they say it can make you just as sick as the high blood. (1970)

Sister Erma Allen, the neighborhood evangelist and healer, had a similar belief: "Darlin', low blood pressure is not enough blood to go through. They have to give you iron, they give you iron pills, iron tonic to build the blood. Then they give you food to eat, tell you to eat beets or liver, somethin' like that. Then some of 'em, they'll tell to drink wine. But I wouldn't drink wine, I wouldn't prefer wine. I used to be a wino myself, [and now] I don't prefer no drinks." (1971) (Snow 1977:36)

Arnella Lewis, whose own blood had recently "gone high," felt that blood pressure might get so low that the heart would have a difficult time pumping blood through the body. The fact that she aligned pressure and volume together was made clear by her surefire answer to the problem: having a blood transfusion. Camino's informants would agree with her explanation in their conception of "watery blood": blood so thin and low in volume that there is not enough "to supply energy or enough to 'make the cycle' of circulation" (1986:76). And they would no doubt all agree with this Southern Black informant in Miami: "Low blood may be causing my tiredness. I may also need iron. Low blood is when you don't have enough. [Your blood] can turn into low blood if you need iron" (Weidman et al. 1978:543).

The blood can move into an abnormally low state for a number of reasons. Janine Jackson was once told that she had low blood, she says. And what she sees as the cause—a lack of rest leading to a tired feeling—would in the orthodox system be seen as a symptom:

> I remember once that they said *I* had low blood, and I don't know where it came from. But it *was* a tiresome feeling; it'll make you tired, you know. I had just a little low place to walk up, and by the time I'd get to the top of this little hill I would be so *tired*. And they said my blood needed buildin' up. And somebody told me to take Mogen David wine to drink and somebody buy me some; Mogen David wine, it's a cookin' wine. And I bought some and I drank some about twice, and I said, "No, that's a beverage I'm not takin'." But they tell me it's not strong. They said that'll build your blood up. I took two swallows of it twice and I didn't take no more. So I don't know much about the blood.

"Did you get over it?"

> Yeah, it just disappeared. I think it come from a lack of rest; lotsa people say that [they] have a low blood. (Lansing, Michigan; 1986)

When I asked the Reverend Hastings about the condition he implicated advancing age in the development of low blood pressure, seeing it as a problem of blood consistency and location:

> See, high blood pressure works with your brains; sometimes it's high in a spot and low in another spot. And each time you get lower in spots and that little part of your brain can't function, then it will function the other way. You ever woke up in the morning and you feel like your head is light? You got to shake your head a little bit? Then it seems like you can't get your *eyes* open; then you gotta [be] thinkin', "What I suppose to do?" You got to shake your head, you know, [to] have enough blood out.

"So what you are saying is your blood is too low. . . ."

> Too low, drained out. But *low* blood pressure in a person, that's about the worst that you can *tangle* with; because if it gets *too* low, then that's why we come about with this stuff at night. And also, have to mind with a woman carrying a baby and she has low *blood,* and that's how you come up with ill-formed baby; like children, you know. Ill-formed. 'Cause the blood is too low to function and *water* takes over.

"So then if the blood is out of your head it's too low, and it's drained out of your head so that your brain doesn't work right?"

> Doesn't work right. Once your brain gets half-dry without blood it does not work right. That's the reason when a person is past 50 years of age he always should sleep on kind of an elevated pillow, you know. Always say when a person is past 50 you subject to stroke, you subject to heart attacks; you should sleep on a level pillow. That's when you shift [to a level pillow]. Kind of elevated like; not too high, not too low, just kind of a slantin' pillow. Level off with your neck. Draining. (Grand Rapids, Michigan; 1987)

Anything that is seen as "thinning" the blood may also be associated with the development of low blood. The close tie between cold/thick/high blood is paralleled in heat/thin/low blood, for example, so that summer's heat may be a contributory factor for the condition. Alcohol consumption may also be blamed for dangerously thinning the blood; Camino's informants saw its consumption as a prominent cause of thin and low blood (1986:76). A young man in Tucson once told me, in fact, that the *real* reason the police do not like people to drink and drive is that alcohol thins the blood; if there were to be an accident the drinker would be more likely to bleed to death.[12] In most cases, however, it is improper diet that is blamed for the development of low blood. Dietary folly includes not eating *enough* of some sorts of foods and/or eating too *much* of others. What is required is a balance in the diet of foods that are blood-builders and foods that are blood-thinners. Too much of the former can result in high blood; too much of the latter in low blood. And, as the experience of Mr. Newton reveals, taking remedies for high blood— traditional *or* prescription—must also be monitored to make sure that the balance has not shifted from "high" through "just right" to "low."

As the foregoing examples demonstrate, low blood also produces symptoms. These usually reflect the fact that the body now lacks what it takes to feel energetic, lively, and able to get on with the tasks of the day. The sufferer complains of tiredness, lassitude, decreased energy, and feeling worn out. Janine Jackson could barely muster the energy to walk up the little hill by her home, for example. Where low blood is associated with bitter blood, constipation is also reported to be a symptom. The elderly person whose blood has "drained" overnight may experience feelings of lightheadedness in the morning. Some symptoms of low blood are in fact the same as those of high blood, particularly dizziness and fainting spells, so that symptoms alone are not enough to differentiate the two conditions. As a Bahamian woman in Miami described it: "Something's happening to me. I am having a lot of dizzy spells. Why, I don't know. I have made an appointment to see the doctors next week. I started to go to the hospital last week and got dizzy and fell out in the street. I did not hurt myself much. I believe my blood is low" (Weidman et al. 1978:460).

Problems of living may also exacerbate an already existing condition. Mathews quoted a 45-year-old woman who had been referred to an obstetrics-gynecology (Ob-Gyn) clinic. She was "feeling poorly," she reported, and had "never been the same" after losing blood in a miscarriage five years previously. "It's just time like these when things are getting next to me that it brings on the spells and my blood gets lower" (1982). Exactly what is believed to produce the symptoms is unclear—they may reflect the undue pressure that not having "enough blood to go through" puts on the system to send it where it needs to go—and, of course, not having enough to fuel the running of the important organs of the body.

Virtually all of the regimens suggested to avoid or treat low blood are oral, reflecting the fact that the causal factors are primarily dietary. The prudent person avoids overindulgence in foods or beverages seen as blood thinners: alcohol, garlic, lemon juice, vinegar, pickle or olive brine, and so on. Anna Perry loved pickles, for example, but was afraid to eat them very often lest they "cut" her blood. The use of substances such as epsom salts, baking soda, and cream of tartar—ingredients in a number of home remedies, not just those for high blood—must also be monitored. And oral treatments for high blood, of course—whether these are traditional or prescription preparations—may be seen as bringing the blood dangerously low if taken for too long.

Once the blood is perceived as being *too* low, of course, just the opposite course is taken; foods and beverages identified as blood builders are consumed. In locales where the low blood is also seen as too bitter, remedies are identified as "sweet medicines." Moerman reported the use of plant products such as sassafras, mullein, and carrot seed in its treatment, along with food and drink such as beets, sugar, and wine (1981); Heyer, also working on St. Helena Island, listed sassafras, beets, and sugar as treatments for low/bitter blood (1981: 56). Similar items are recommended by North Carolina root doctors: beet leaves, carrots, sassafras, aloe, coffee, wine, sugar, and salt (C. Hill and Mathews 1981). In a later work Mathews listed many of these same items and adds red meat, strawberry leaves, blackberries, molasses, and honey (1987). In most of these instances the active principle is the use of a sweet remedy to reverse the bitterness associated with low pressure.

A number of the items listed above also appear as treatments for low blood when the association of bitterness is not made, however. The principle of reversal may still be in play by including sugar and other sweet foods in the category of "rich" or "fattening" substances. If high blood is caused by eating too much rich food, that is, low blood should be treatable by increasing its intake. Similarly salt, known to cause high blood, may be added to the diet to help prevent low blood or raise it if it is already low. If eating too much red meat is a prime cause of high blood, then eating more of it is a useful treatment for low blood; this is especially true, it is said, if it is eaten rare. When Arnella heard that a physician had told Freda Thomas that her blood pressure was low, for example, she made a special trip to Freda's home to advise her to eat rare liver, beef broth, and beets to build up her blood again. And when Cassie Seales' 16-year-old daughter Ruthie became pregnant the doctor told the girl that she needed iron for "low blood pressure"; she took the pills provided by the prenatal clinic and also ate the liver, beets, and beef suggested by her mother, a licensed practical nurse. (Lansing, Michian; 1973).

The fact that items used in the traditional system might, because of high iron content, also be seen as useful in the orthodox system helps to blur the differences that exist. This blurring is exacerbated by the fact that informants *also* commonly list "iron" or "iron pills" or "iron tonic" as useful treatments for low blood, just as might a physician treating iron-deficiency anemia. The presumed efficacy of such ingredients is also reflected in the names of over-the-counter preparations such as, "Beef, Iron, and Wine Appetite Stimulant," available in the pharmacy a few blocks from Bernita and Joseph's home. Its label states that it is used "to help build energy-rich red blood." The fact that such treatments are also used traditionally for the treatment of low blood *pressure,* however, makes clear that the explanatory models differ.

Irrespective of iron content many treatments for low blood also invoke the principle of imitative magic. The "sweet" beets, sassafras, and wine that are used to raise low/bitter blood in the Sea Islands are also used where the high/sweet and low/bitter dichotomy is not reported; in these instances it is their red color that is probably seen as efficacious. If green, white, or colorless treatments are useful to bring down or cut high blood, then it is logical that the remedies for low blood be red or at least dark in color. And, in fact, many of the items informants in widely scattered geographical areas class-ify as "blood builders" fit this bill; the direct replacement of blood is most obvious in the suggestion of meat as medicine, of course, and more obvious if the meat is served rare. "The doctors say I should eat lots of red meat and rare liver because my blood is low," said one of the new mothers in Frankel's study; however, she was unable to bring herself to eat "meat with the blood all running out of it" (Frankel 1977:36).

Bernita Washington, who herself suffers from high blood, makes clear in the following comments that her ideas on low blood/low blood pressure and anemia are intertwined:

> *Low* blood, when you doesn't eat the right kind of foods, your blood doesn't circulate and it doesn't be like it should. 'Stead of runnin' *normal,* it'll run a different way, be on the *lower* side; *lower* part of your body more so. That causes *low* blood. *High* blood goes up, *low* blood runs down.

And how would she treat it?

> Well, if you had low blood pressure and you *know* you have low blood pressure, O.K., what you do then is eat the things that you know that you is really supposed to eat. In other words—I'll have to go all the way back to high blood pressure—*high* blood pressure is something that will give you a stroke. *Low* blood pressure will *also* give you a stroke! *Low* blood pressure will give you a stroke quicker than it would if you had *high* blood pressures! Now, if you *know* you've got low blood pressure, you's a anemic person [and] you eat the food that anemic people should eat.

> You *drink* plenty juice; you *drink* plenty milk; you eat plenty vita-mins—when I say vitamins [I mean] the food with vitamins in it. You also eat a lot vitamins that have the main important cereals in it, with all kind of vitamins. Say if you was gonna eat the raisin cereals, stuff like that; you eat a lot of that. O.K., you also could eat *beets.* You also could drink what you would call a little glass of *wine* every morning, which we would call Mogen David's wine. You could also use that;

that is good. [And] many other things, too. That brings your blood pressure *up;* to stop you from being anemic.

"It sounds like you need to keep your blood balanced," I said.

Well, it should stay where it's not up too high and not down too low. It should stay like that. (Lansing, Michigan; 1986)

Our last formal conversation on the topic of the blood was a few months later; high blood and low blood came into the conversation in a tangential way. I had asked about blood becoming thicker or thinner according to the weather, prompting her remarks about her anemic daughter who "stays cool" all the time. I knew that one of her daughters was pregnant at that time, and asked if she was the one suffering from the anemia. No, she said, and another daughter was mentioned whom she had treated for the problem:

I got one, Marlene; Marlene was anemic. But then you know I kept on her a lot of stuff to keep her blood pressure right; keep her blood right. You know, it's go up and it's come down; go up and come down. *I* used to be like that when I was younger; I used to be anemic when I was younger. You couldn't even get blood out of my finger. But I would always [do], you know, like the older peoples that I would always be *with* [would tell me]. They'd always let me know the things that I should *have* to build it up; and so I just took care of it.

Her final comment on the high blood/low blood continuum underscores her belief that the blood can move from high to low—or low to high—and produce similar symptoms. The measurement of pressure simply tells the individual exactly where the blood is at a given time:

It's one thing that I *do* know [and] that's like *high* blood, *low* blood, you really can't tell the difference unless it's checked because it all works alike. *High* blood will make you a nervous condition; *low* blood will make you a nervous condition. *High* blood will give you a stroke; *low* blood will give you a stroke. You know what I'm sayin'? So, it really can't hardly be divided.

"So you really have to have it checked?"

You should, yeah.

As usual I took this opportunity to suggest that it would be a good idea if she *did* so; as usual, she suggested that God is a better healer than the elderly physician whose office is only blocks away:

Within *my* family I *teaches* my kids about healing because *I* does it a lot, for myself and also for *them.* We have never gone to doctors a whole lot 'cause we never could *afford* it. And so, my little baby girl [her youngest child, the then 17-year-old Jonell] she, *I* could get sick like when I used to have those headaches and she would come in. I have *taught* them that when I am sick, *come* to me! Pray and *heal* me, pray with me, whatever. And so, this is how we go about doin' things like that. But now, let me tell you, there's still a lotta people that things be botherin' 'em so bad, "I just *gotta* go to a doctor!" And sometimes you can just go to a doctor, go to a doctor, go to a doctor. And when they get through goin' to a doctor, doctor *still* didn't do anything for 'em. So, it's good to pray and do things for yourself. (Lansing, Michigan; 1986)

She promised that she would take a pill the following morning, however, because she knew I wanted her to do so.

Notes

1. Anna Perry, who was there that afternoon, later told me that Arnella would have been *much* better off choosing the epsom salts. But then no one was surprised that she had chosen the better tasting remedy; everybody knew how she liked to eat.

2. I do not mean to imply that herbal treatments for ailments are restricted to the southeastern part of the United States. The fact that many plants used in traditional remedies do not grow in the North does not mean that people do not prefer these "more natural" treatments or that they are completely unavailable. In the spring of 1988 I spent a day at the office/home of a popular healer in a Detroit suburb; in the hours spent in the waiting room a number of the waiting clients confided that they had chosen him because of his use of herbs. A sizable collection of dried herbs was stored in a basement room; these had been purchased from a wholesale distributor in Indiana. In the summer of the same year I visited a candle shop in inner-city Detroit that had jars of dried herbs for sale; on the shelf above these were a number of books on the medicinal use of herbs. Herbal products are also available by mail order, of course.

3. Weidman provided an excellent example of the importance of knowing patients' explanatory models of a disease such as diabetes: "For example, some black Americans in Miami distinguish between 'sugar' levels in the blood and in the urine. When aloe is taken to 'bitter' blood that is too 'sweet,' then, conceptually, it is impossible for the blood to remain sweet. Consequently, when urine testing indicates high levels of 'sugar,' the conclusion is drawn that there are high levels in the urine but not in the blood. 'Water pills,' therefore, may sometimes be seen as being able to 'draw' the sugar out" (1988).

4. Heurtin-Roberts and Reisin (1990) suggested that there should be recognition of two separate folk conditions: "high blood," linked with heredity and diet, and "high-pertension," linked with stress and strong emotional states. In this discussion I use "high blood" to include both causal categories; this reflects what I (and others) have heard from informants and is less confusing to the reader.

5. See Kleinman (1988:133) for a particularly egregious example of a woman trying desperately to tell her physician of some multiple problems in her life only to have them turned away as he reduces her to her disease.

6. Olive Parsons, my oldest Arizona informant, had seen a physician for the first time at the age of 82. This followed a bout of gall bladder trouble that had resisted every home remedy for "gas" she could think of to try. The gall bladder was removed and she was told never to eat pork again, a proscription that she

found to be a real hardship. Ham was frequently served in the homes of relatives and friends, and it had always been her favorite food. Still, she was carefully avoiding it. However, she clearly did not extend the term "pork" to include the fat that it contains (which, of course, was what her physician wanted her to avoid), and I once watched her add a full cup of bacon grease to a pot of greens she was cooking. Lunch consisted of the greens—which were quite literally swimming in grease—and cornbread, which had received its own liberal dollop of bacon grease before it was baked. Dessert was fried donuts from a nearby bakery. As she cooked she complained of having been "taken off the pork," and as we ate the greens and cornbread—*cum* bacon grease—she talked about how much she missed eating ham. But she intended to follow the doctor's orders, even though she thought he was too young to know much. (1971)

7. Stress-related elevations in blood pressure are not restricted to those African-Americans who live in poverty, of course. A number of studies reveal the correlation between feelings of anger and hostility (and often the felt need to suppress these emotions) and higher blood pressure; see Durel et al. (1989) for recent research in Miami. See also Armstead et al. (1989) for a study demonstrating that the blood pressure of African-American college students "significantly increased during the presentation of racist stimuli but not of anger-provoking or neutral stimuli."

8. All of these studies list several of the same plants by their common names, but only Moerman provides the scientific names as well. This is an important point if one is attempting to document plants used as remedies in different areas: A single species may have a number of common names and/or one common name may refer to several different plants (Croom 1983). The most common variety of the popular plant remedy *Xanthorrhiza simplicissima* or "yellow root," for example, may also be called "parsley-leaved yellow root," "Southern yellow root," "yellow wart," or "shrub yellow root." A different species, *Hydrastis canadensis,* may also be called "yellow root" although it is usually referred to by another common name, "golden seal" (J. Parsons 1981).

9. See J. Parsons for the case history of a 54-year-old Georgia man who developed chronic arsenic poisoning after "he had prepared and consumed between 32 ounces to 48 ounces of an herbal tea made of 'yellow root' per day for two years" (1981). Samples of the root purchased at the municipal market (presumably the Atlanta market) contained arsenic; arsenic is a contaminant, not a natural constituent of the plant. Although the author notes that it is difficult to identify the exact species from specimens of roots alone, the most common variety of the plant used is *Xanthorrhiza simplicissima.* It is a plant often mentioned in the treatment of high blood (see also Boyd and Tjolsen 1986 for a discussion of the safety of herbal teas and remedies).

10. She showed me the bottle of pills she kept in her purse and allowed me to count them; she had taken less than half the amount that she should have according to the instructions on the label.

11. Moerman (1981), in contrast, goes to the opposite extreme in discussing the traditional medicine of the Sea Islands, viewing it as one with "ample pharmacological power. At least eleven of the plants used on St. Helena have been at one time or another official drugs in the U.S. Pharmacopeia, four of them (*Chenopodium, Aristolochia, Sassafras,* and *Zanthoxylum*) for more than a century. Given that one of the primary public health problems in this community is hypertension, not only is it particularly apt that the system is phased in terms of 'pressure,' but it is also notable that a number of these bitter medicines are effective diuretics. Several plants may have more directly hypotensive actions, notably coral bean; over a dozen curare-mimetic alkaloids, undoubtedly hypotensive, have been isolated from species of the genus *Erythrina.*

"Taken together with the undoubted effectiveness of the several anthelmintics in use (*Chenopodium ambrosiodes* and *Melia azedarach*), the weight of evidence indicates that this system is an effective one against at least two of the major health problems on the island today. . . ."

While his position of taking this treatment system seriously is entirely laudable I believe that assessing it as effective against hypertension does not take into consideration that two different systems of explanation are involved. Contrasting therapies can only be compared, that is, when there is agreement about what is *being* treated. Moerman's example of the use of *Chenopodium* as an anthelmintic does fulfill this requirement: It is used *as* an anthelmintic and is *effective* as one. The same thing cannot be said when comparing treatments for high blood in the traditional model and high blood pressure in the orthodox medical model, however. The fact that users of the system have very different ideas of what the disorder is makes it difficult to judge how well herbal treatments are working—an individual may have blood that is perceived to be high in pressure and sweet in flavor in the traditional system, for example, and not have hypertension in the orthodox sense. And if a man or woman *does* have hypertension in the orthodox sense herbal medicines—irrespective of their pharmacological effectiveness—can only be evaluated alongside orthodox treatments if they are used in the same way as such treatments. Herbal remedies (or any others) must necessarily be limited in action if they are used only for short-term regimens and/or when the afflicted individual is suffering symptoms. Other problems may arise when such remedies are used along with antihypertensive drugs; the frequent use of epsom salts as a cathartic may reduce the potassium level if diuretic agents are taken simultaneously, for example.

12. Substances may be implicated in blood changes but with entirely opposite effects, however. As noted, North Carolina root doctors associate the ingestion of alcohol by young males with the "blacking out" of *high* blood (C. Hill and Mathews 1981). As in so many other things in African-American traditional medicine, it is balanced use that is important. A substance that in excess can cause some sorts of problems may, in moderation, be used to prevent others. My anthropologist friend Margaret Boone (personal communication, 1986) has told me of overhearing two young African-American women discussing the use of alcoholic beverages to thin the blood of menstruating women; this practice they thought would "help pass clots."

7

There's Somethin' About
a Girl Gets a Disease
Quicker than a Boy

Rae Ann swept through her head again for other possible remedies to
her situation. For a nosebleed, you put your head way back and stuffed
tissue up your nostrils. Once she'd seen her brother Horace plaster his
whole set of keys on the back of the neck. The time he had the fight
with Joe Lee and his nose bled. Well, she'd tried ice cubes on the neck,
on the stomach, on the thighs. Had stuffed herself with tissue. Had put
her hips atop a pile of sofa cushions. And still she was bleeding. And
what was she going to do about M'Dear's towels? No one would miss
the panties and skirt she'd bundled up in the bottom of the garbage.
But she couldn't just disappear a towel, certainly not two. M'Dear
always counted up the stacks of laundry before the Saturday put-away.
> —Toni Cade Bambara, "A Girl's Story,"
> *The Seabirds Are Alive*

A woman who is "on her period" should always wear shoes,
Etheldean Mitchell was told by her mother when she was a girl in
Alabama. If you are foolish enough to go barefoot at such a time
"your veins will open up and allow poisons to enter the body." She
was also warned that she should *never* "leave a sanitary pad around
so that people can see it, because they might use it to put a hex on
you." She has told her daughters these things but believes that they
do not take them seriously. But she does; she recalls the story she
once heard of a woman driven crazy because "someone found some
of her menstrual blood." It is difficult for her to burn used sanitary
pads now that she is living in the city, however, and she continues
to be uncomfortable about leaving them in the trash. (Lansing, Michigan; 1980)

The menstruating woman should also avoid sexual intercourse,
according to 74-year-old Frances McNair. "The menstrual period opens
up oceans of blood and that's very dangerous." Sexual activity at
such a time might increase the flow so that, "if you get yourself
punched in certain ways it's just pouring forth. And that's why it
is dangerous and an ignorant, bad thing to do. Even the Bible says
this!" Still, she recognizes that some women will do so anyway.

Prostitutes cannot always follow this rule, for example. Because of their trade they "don't have time to wait 'til the period is over, so [they] put sponges into the vagina to soak up the blood." No doubt they are jeopardizing their health but she understands their position; after all, everyone has to make a living. (East Lansing, Michigan; 1983)

LaNeel Brooks, 28, is a college student interested in the health lore that has been handed down in her family over the years. She, too, was warned of the difficulties that can occur should a woman not take good care of herself at such times. But she was taught that many of these can be prevented if certain rules are followed. She is proud that she and her sisters are the fourth generation of family women to follow the special dietary practices that prevent headaches and fatigue during the menses. These were taught long ago to her grandmother in Alabama by *her* mother, LaNeel says. And they still work. All the woman needs to do is eat banana pudding one week before the expected menstrual period and, as well, eat sweet potatoes in the week following its cessation. No headaches, no fatigue.[1] (Saginaw, Michigan; 1983)

Hallie Wilmot is another college student who is also familiar with many of the old tales. Some of these have been told to her by relatives and friends and others she has read in books. Like LaNeel—and unlike the daughters of Etheldean—she has a good deal of curiosity about the beliefs passed on "in my tradition." Her interest is more than academic, in fact, and when some practice particularly strikes her fancy she often tries it out. On two occasions she has tested the belief that a man will be "very loving and faithful" if a woman mixes some of her menstrual blood in his food, for example. She doesn't remember where she first heard this, as "it's pretty much common knowledge." And did it do the trick? Well, "once it worked; the other time it didn't." She has also experimented with a Jamaican recipe for "Mannish water"—said to be an effective love potion—which she learned of from a friend in Detroit. It worked pretty well, she reports, "although the guy I tried it on didn't need much help in that direction anyway."[2] (Detroit, Michigan; 1984)

Blood used to excite and hold a lover. The warm feelings engendered at the thought of a remedy passed down from one generation of women to the next. But also headaches. And fatigue. And poisons entering the body. And oceans of blood flowing. Or her own blood used against a woman in a hex. These are stories heard from Michigan women, young and old, over the last few years. They are not new beliefs, of course, they repeat themes that I have heard over and over in the past 20 years. Nothing in my fieldwork in southern Arizona was so striking to me, in fact, as the deeply ambivalent feelings that women held about the reproductive cycle. What I saw as merely a normal part of the adult life of women was viewed by virtually every woman I talked with—from 36-year-old Wilma Jordan

to her 84-year-old grandmother Olive Parsons—as potentially dangerous. They spoke of problems ranging from "hard periods" to a greatly
feared entity known as "quick TB." Menstruation, failed attempts at
birth control, miscarriages and abortions, pregnancy and birth, the
postpartum period—all were cause for unease. The women's concern
was not necessarily misplaced: Many women had suffered miscarriages and/or the death of newborn infants. And all could relate
stories of what had happened to girls and women who flouted the
rules of safe behavior that they had been taught. My last night in
Arizona, as was noted earlier, was largely spent listening to Anna
Perry's warning of the dire results that I might expect if I did not
become more careful in disposing of menstrual paraphernalia.[3]

As there were few young people living in the Tucson neighborhood where I had worked, however, I wondered if the things that
I had heard were only "old wives' tales," stories of little import to
a younger generation of women. This led to subsequent research
with a colleague in Michigan to ascertain the beliefs and attitudes
that women here have about the reproductive cycle.[4] Our data, gathered from women attending prenatal clinics in Lansing and Detroit,
demonstrated that these are "young wives' tales" as well. The same
stories and the same fears were repeated by these younger women,
many of whom were just beginning their childbearing careers (Snow
and Johnson 1977; Snow, Johnson, and Mayhew 1978; S. Johnson and
Snow 1979, 1982). Other studies on the beliefs of African-American
girls and women—from Michigan, Maryland, Florida, and the Dis-
trict of Columbia—concerning the reproductive cycle mirror these
findings (Scott 1975; Frankel 1977; Weidman et al. 1978; Poland and
Beane 1980; Boone 1982). Again the stated fears and concerns of these
women are not misplaced; many of them are at high risk for their
pregnancies, and this situation has unfortunately worsened in recent
years. The focus of this chapter and the next will be the disparity
between traditional and biomedical explanations for women's reproductive life. In this instance it is probably safe to say that cultural
beliefs are contributing to poor fertility control—and thus to poorer
health—for many women.

It has already been mentioned that in this health belief system
(as in many others) women are seen as constitutionally weak. Prior
to adolescence there seems to be little or no difference in threats
to health associated with gender, though boys and girls are often
seen as differing in temperament even before birth. It is after
puberty that women's relatively weaker bodies—compounded by
the aggravations of daily life imposed by their roles as caretakers
of others—puts them at a distinct disadvantage health-wise (Dougherty 1978:95; Roberson 1983:122; Camino 1986:105–153; Nations,
Camino, and Walker 1988). The fact that, relatively speaking, "men
have it good" is often verbalized when women speak of such things.
Men suffer less from "nerves," for example, both because of their

superior anatomy and their social roles. As one woman told Camino (1989), "Men get by in life so easy, honey—they just don't seem to worry that much about life. They don't have to look after as many people. They just go about their life, always having some woman doing for them—cooking, cleaning, fussing about them." In the words of a 21-year-old mother of four in Florida: "Women have all the luck, you know. We got these nasty bodies . . . [and] everything happen to women. She have to take time out to bleed for a little while. You know? And then, when she does, she crampin' if she got her period . . . and guys, all they do is stick you and go do somebody else" (Dunn 1988).

It is menstruation, pregnancy, and childbirth that renders women so "weak-nerved," made vulnerable by the bodily openings specifically associated with sexuality and reproduction (Camino 1989). As Sister Erma Allen put it: "There's somethin' about a girl gets a disease quicker than a boy. On account of her different sex. She's easy to catch, or she's eager to catch ever'thing. Because she'll get it in her breast. Different things come through the breast, through your vagina too, you know. These are two things you have a man don't have, that make you easily get sick" (Tucson, Arizona; 1971) (Snow 1977:32).

These "different things" that can cause her to fall ill reflect the common problem sources outlined in the previous chapters: the cold in air and water; failure to keep the body clean inside and out; eating the wrong foods at the wrong times; the ever-present danger of sorcery by means of bodily fluids. And, of course, the added dangers of pregnancy and birth. Menarche, then, signals only the opening chapter of many many years of watchful caretaking if the girl/woman is to remain in good health. There was and is an almost Victorian prudery in discussing the known risks attendant upon a young girl's reaching puberty, however. Bertha Alexander recalled that in her girlhood—if you heard anything from a friend about something like menstruation and came home and asked your mother—she would "run you out of the house" and say not to pay attention to things heard from children who were "half-raised." *Then* when you found out that your friends were right after all, you no longer trusted or wanted to confide in her. Better not to lie: "Your child is gonna believe what you say better'n what she would anybody else if you start in time and tell her—and tell her the truth." Still, she said, she was glad that her only child had been a boy—she had let her husband tell *him* the facts of life! (Tucson, Arizona; 1971)

Bernita Washington is more than a quarter-century younger than Bertha but she, too, had been kept in ignorance about what to expect at puberty. It was not because her mother had refused to tell her what she needed to know, however, but because she had not lived to do so. She had died when Bernita was about ten years old, whispered to have been killed by sorcery by her husband, Bernita's stepfather. After that, Bernita and her younger brother were sent to live with their grandfather, "a very mean man," who provided her with no information prior to her first menstrual period:

Well, I was between 12 and 13. [I learned about it] only by my other girl-friends and stuff, not by my parents. At that time parents didn't teach their *children* that; they taught 'em the things that they just really wanted them to know. Things like that I guess they just didn't want 'em to *know!* Because they told 'em, like children, the midwife brought 'em in *bags* and they told 'em they found 'em in stumpholes, you know. And all that kind of type of stuff. So we wasn't *taught* nothin' like that very much. [I heard about it] from little girls, but really, knowin' how it work and what about it, I didn't know. Sometime peoples just *tell* you things and until it happen to you, you really don't know.

And did she tell her grandfather after it happened?

No, no, no, I did not tell him! I did not tell him. I told the older people, you know, like other womens. And they would teach me how to survive and take care of myself. Well, they would tell you how to protect yourself from the blood bein' on your clothes and stuff like that. At that time we would tear up white sheets, like you know you had an old white sheet or something that has worn out. She show us how to tear up those things and how we would fold 'em and put them on for protection.

I asked her what she thought the purpose of menstruation might be:

You mean *why* do [we] have menstruation? It's the *life* of you; it is the life of you. It's something you *really have to do* as far as I could say; it's something you really have to do. But it's really the *life* of a woman that she would *do* that; that she would have her period. That is her life. Just like a baby when it's born; the cord is his life. So that's the same that it is with a woman. Not sayin' that she won't *live* if she doesn't have [a] period, you know. Nothin' like that; that's not the case. But it is sayin' that it is very important in your life that a woman do that, because that is what she is *supposed* to do.

When Bernita was 15 she ran off to be married and she gave birth to Marya, the first of her seven daughters and three sons, at sixteen. Had she been able to talk to Marya about such matters when the time came? No, she had not—*could* not. She was far too embarrassed to do so until after the fact:

My oldest daughter, no, I didn't tell [her]. I was too embarrassed to tell her, because *I* wasn't taught that way and *I* didn't think she should have been taught. 'Cause I didn't know *to* tell her that! So, when she *did* have her first period she just screamed; she had a fit. She didn't know anything about it and she didn't know what was *happening* to her. She didn't know what *reason* she was bleeding! Because she hadn't been taught that.

So I was a kid 16 years old along *with* her, you know what I'm saying? I was 16 years old when she was born, and so that made me really a kid along with *her*. So I was too embarrassed to really tell her. I know that I *should* have told her, because after I began to get older and started havin' kids I come under the knowledge *more* what to do and how to do, [and] what to say.

And the next daughter, did she tell *her?* No, she let Marya tell Dalila, two years younger. "The *next* one *told* the next one; I didn't have to do it." She had been pregnant again for the ninth time when Marya, then 16, gave birth to *her* first child, Josie. And 16 years later Josie gave birth to a son, Mikey. Bernita was thus a mother at 16, a grandmother at 32, and at 48 a great-grandmother. (Lansing, Michigan; 1987)

Just *what* "the next one told the next one" in three generations of women in this family fits nicely into a core of traditional ideas about the nature of femaleness that is widely shared among African-American women. If menstruation is the "life" of women it is important that it proceed normally: it should "come on" in a timely fashion and end when it should; all of the blood should be expelled from the body in a flow that is neither too heavy nor too light. And anything used to catch it should be disposed of as quickly and quietly as possible. Women's explicit correlation of a normal menstrual cycle with feelings of health and well-being is one that has been noted by a number of authors (Scott 1975; Carrington 1978; MacCormack 1985; Weidman et al. 1978:396–405). For the women from all of the ethnic groups—Cuban, Haitian, Bahamian, Puerto Rican, and Southern Black—in the Miami Health Ecology Project, in fact, the following ideas were true:

1. The menstrual period is used as a diagnostic measure. It serves as an indication of well-being; of being normal physically and normal in one's sex role as this relates to reproductivity and heterosexual activity.

2. The menstrual period is the means by which one's health is maintained. The monthly out-flowing of blood from the body provides a cleansing action and/or removes unnecessary blood that might rise and cause headaches or strokes.

3. The frequent statement that "it is natural" seems to indicate a sense of being in harmony with nature and the natural rhythm of life (Scott 1975).

Anything interfering with this natural process is therefore dangerous. If the flow is impeded the blood will be retained; if the flow does not stop the body will be weakened. A menstrual period perceived by a woman as different from the usual is a reason for concern, then, and a cause for this dysfunction is sought. Possible risk factors are sorted through until an explanation is found—whether it be cold or wrong diet or allowing an enemy to get hold of used menstrual pads—or the methods of contraception suggested by health care professionals. The very means of preventing pregnancy heralded as safe and effective by clinicians, that is, may be seen as potential killers by the women expected to use them.

Menstruation may be something that women are "supposed to do," in Bernita's words, but it remains something that is frequently viewed in very negative terms. And its association with sexuality in a group where there is a good deal of puritanism about discussing such things makes it very difficult for many girls and women to talk about (Liebow 1967:143, 149, 151; Schulz 1969:156; E. Martin and Martin 1978:53; Boone 1989:99). In general, sexual activity is seen as normal, natural, and expected behavior between men and women, and it may begin at an early age. It is *talking about* sexual matters, not acting them out, that is the problem, particularly between the sexes. Men and women frequently do not discuss contraception or contraceptive methods, for example. And there is a real tension between the feeling that sexual expression is normal, natural, and good, on the one hand, and the view of some religious groups linking sexuality with sin and temptation (see M. Williams 1974:124ff for a discussion of the symbolism of the body in a Pentecostal church; see also Weidman 1979b and Lefley 1979 for a discussion of sexual conflict and episodes of "falling out" in women in Miami). In her sensitive account of the socialization of young women in a housing project in St. Louis, for example, Ladner noted that "many mothers find themselves unable to discuss this topic freely and often fail to provide the necessary information about the meaning of menstruation until the girl asks for it." In some instances the information provided could only mystify the listener; one 17-year old, for example, recounted: "Mother told me that the monkey was going to 'split his tongue' one of these days and he was going to bleed. That is how she used to explain it to us [her sister included], so I started looking for my monkey . . . I was about fifteen. At first I was kind of scared because I thought she was talking about a real monkey that had cut his tongue out. I didn't really know what she was talking about at first . . . That is the way old people explain it. My grandmother told me the same thing when I was fourteen" (Ladner 1971:178–179). Small wonder that many girls in Ladner's study "considered the onset of menstruation as a traumatic event, where they expressed fright and a general uncomfortable feeling of not knowing precisely what was happening to their bodies" (p. 179). This can only be compounded when/if young girls have no information at all before this event; 63 percent of the women interviewed in one Lansing prenatal clinic reported that they had had no knowledge of menstruation prior to menarche (Snow and Johnson 1977).[5]

Some of the reluctance to talk about menstruation is perhaps due to the fact that menstrual blood is so often seen as "dirty," "unclean" or "nasty." Many women, in fact, believe that the main purpose of the menstrual period is to rid the body of this disgusting substance (Scott 1975; Snow and Johnson 1977; Poland and Beane 1980; S. Johnson and Snow 1982). Jamaican women sometimes augment this cleansing process "by the use of a laxative at the end of the menstrual period for 'a good washout'" (MacCormack 1985). The girl-child who is nearing menarche is in danger of retaining dirty and therefore dangerous blood, then, and if an older woman believes the first period should have "come on" by now steps might be taken to hurry up the process. These usually involve heat (hot towels on the abdomen; hot baths; hot teas) which will "open the pores" and allow nature to take its course. The association of menstrual blood with bodily impurities is explicit in Bernita's linking it with measles and pimples; they all need to be "brought out." The very best thing to "stimulate the system" of a young girl to help initiate her periods is a tea made from horseradish leaves, she says, but, failing that, almost any sort of tea will do. It is the *heat*, not the content, that does the trick:

> Mostly you can give 'em any kind of tea, you know. You can give 'em little *coffee*, tea, or whatever. It really doesn't matter what *kind* of tea. That will—I don't know *what* it does but—it just an old *sign*. It's like kids when they used to have measle and stuff like that, and they'd always give 'em warm water and [corn]shuck tea. And it does just bring it right on out, whatever on the inside, brings it out.

> Like a lot of people right now, I guess, probably it *does!* If they was havin' maybe like pimples on their face and sumpin' like that. Different little things that every once in a while you look in the glass and say, "Oh, there's a pimple." Tomorrow morning, look, "Oh, there's [another] one right there!" Why, then whatever it is, you get you some kind of tea or something and drink it, and it will just bring it right on out and then you're through with it! (Lansing, Michigan; 1987)

Once brought on, however, menstrual periods are associated with almost totally negative feelings. In some ways menstruation seems to be a metaphor for death and blight: The menstruating woman may have the *potential* for fertility, that is, but for these few days she is shedding life. She is powerful in a very negative sense, and as her presence pollutes everything in her immediate environment she is subject to numerous behavioral restrictions. She is particularly damaging to other living things—whether animals or plants or people—and there is a good deal of sexual symbolism in the proscriptions on her behavior. Women from rural backgrounds, for example, say that farm animals will immediately sense her state and "come after" her. The male animals will have a sexual interest in her; the female animals will be jealous and try "to run her." She should also stay out of the fields, where snakes attracted by the smell of menstrual blood will crawl up the vagina if she squats to urinate. And in the South the fabled "whip snake" may trip her up and then "whip her to death," said one aide at the Lansing clinic. Whip snakes just can't stand menstruating women.

The fact that she represents nonlife is also shown by the destructive effect that she has on plants: Seeds that she sows will never come up and flowers will wilt if she picks them. She should stay out of the garden lest the tender new seedlings die. Sexual symbolism is also found in her killing effect on garden produce: Although in most instances women are seen as weaker than men this principle is reversed when a woman is displaying this aspect of her reproductive powers. If she *must* go into the garden to gather produce, it is said, she should at all costs avoid stepping over the cucumbers lest she kill the vines. Nor is she seen as her normal self in her own house: If she attempts to can food, the jars (especially tomatoes) might explode. She may not be allowed to cook for fear the milk will curdle, a cake fall, the bread fail to rise. Who would want to eat her cooking anyway, tainted as her touch would be? "They had to be done with that," Marya Smith says. "Not right after a baby, [or] havin' a period, they couldn't cook. Nobody'd want to eat that *food*." And a man, of course, must be wary of the blood that she might have put into his dinner to control him: "Take some of your monthly period and cook it in his food. It'll run him crazy—make him stone crazy 'bout you. When I'm on my period, my boyfriend don't never let me cook nothin' for him" (Dance 1978:310). One young woman at a Lansing prenatal clinic told me that her husband refuses to eat *her* cooking—particularly spaghetti sauce—when she is menstruating. He is fearful that she will put menstrual blood in his food to "control" him. And how did she feel about that, I asked? She shrugged, "Well, at least it's five days out of the month when I don't have to cook."[6] (1975)

Usually powerful males are not the only people to feel the pernicious effect of the menstruating woman; she may also harm individuals who are especially vulnerable and weak. Newborn infants are particularly prone to damage from her touch, and the belief that a menstruating woman should not pick up a newborn baby is very widespread. Following the principle of imitative magic the woman may cause the infant to "cramp," "strain," or develop an umbilical hernia. I was told this by the older women in Arizona; I have heard it from teenagers in Michigan. Women in Louisiana say that if a menstruating woman picks up a newborn infant she will cause it "to strain," but the danger may be averted if a piece of the woman's clothing is pinned to that of the infant (Webb 1971).[7] Informants in California and Washington also report dangerous and sometimes long-lasting effects on the infant: It might "grow up to be very nervous," have "a bad case of the colic," develop "terrible cramps," or be seen to have the "stretches" (stretch abnormally). However, tying a string from a sanitary napkin around the baby's waist allows the mother who is menstruating to care for her infant. The "stretches" may also be cured by passing the afflicted infant through the collar of a horse (University of California at Berkeley Folklore Archives).[8]

Most behavioral proscriptions, however, are aimed at protecting the health of the woman herself. Many of these have to do with the proper disposal of used menstrual pads or tampons, which must be kept away from those who might wish her harm. The use of menstrual blood in sorcery has been mentioned a number of times; there is no better way to attack a woman at the very core of her being (for a selection of several dozen of these uses of blood during conjuration from "Her Private Time" see Hyatt 1973, Vol. 3, pp. 2513–2540). Cassie Seales was raised in rural Arkansas and says that her mother always made her burn menstrual rags and pads. "Yes, when I was a girl comin' up I heard that—that they could take your period and do all sorts of things, you know, if they didn't like you. They could turn you into a snake, have you barkin' like a dog. Oh, anything that they wanted to." She herself has never been the victim of such activity, she says, though one of her sisters once had a snake put into her arm by a woman who disliked her. Cassie saw this "thing [that] was just runnin' up her arm" and has never been able to forget it. (Lansing, Michigan; 1973)

As a girl in Mississippi Bernita Washington was also taught to burn menstrual cloths, both to be sanitary and to avoid their use in what she calls "hoodoo" or "underground":

> Well, we burned 'em because that was the sanitary, that's the way we was taught for *sanitary* [reasons], you know. To keep everything clean. The lady that taught me, we was always particular, you know, about puttin' stuff *down* like that. Because like long about then older womens would *teach* the younger womens to not to use those cloths and put them *down*. Because [someone] could get ahold of those cloths and they could *do* things to you, you know, and type stuff like that.

The fact that so many women view a normal menstrual period as an important indicator of their health and well-being has already been noted. Exactly *how* this important process is thought to occur, while agreed upon by many women of African-American ancestry, is very different from the orthodox view. Many of the women in the Lansing prenatal clinic "seemed to view the uterus as a hollow organ that is tightly closed between menstrual periods while it slowly fills with the tainted blood and then opens up to allow the blood to escape during the menses" (Snow and Johnson 1977). Similarly, Weidman and her co-researchers reported that (1978:560) there is "evidence in this group that menstruation is perceived to occur in faucetlike fashion. It 'comes on'; there is 'flowing' or 'bleeding'; then it 'goes off.' Both conceptualizations are appropriate in view of the likeness a body may have to a blood-filled container with a continuing supply of new blood. A certain amount of 'overflow' must [be] released periodically . . . " (Weidman et al. 1978:560). Should this overflow be impeded by "blockage," says Bernita, the result may be:

> a *blood* tumor or something. It's when the blood does blockage and doesn't really come out like it should. And that will leave what you would call a *lump* of blood there. It lumps, O.K., in your body and then it will cause what you call a blood *tumor*. When your period doesn't come up and you *did* have something to block it; that it didn't come out freely like it should. (1987)

Among the things that can cause such a blockage is the woman's diet: Should she eat too many "acid" or "drying" foods such as lemons, vinegar, pickles, or olives the flow may stop altogether.

If normally the uterus is "open" to allow the blood to drain out, it is logical to consider it possible for unwanted entities from the outside world to enter a woman's body. It is this presumed openness that makes the avoidance of any sort of cold or damp so important; they might clot the blood and cause the flow to slow down or even stop. As one of Frankel's informants related, "I missed my period a few times, but I didn't know I was pregnant. I thought I had taken cold or something. When you take cold it can make you miss your period" (1977:37). And it can make you sick (Carrington 1978); at the very least the woman may expect a "hard period" with cramps or clots. In extreme cases the body will react exactly like a stopped-up sink so that the blood "backs up" high in the body. It may thus move into the head to cause headaches or a stroke; it may kill a woman on the spot. The death of a girlfriend made an indelible impression on Cassie Seales: "No, I don't think you should bathe. When I was growin' up my girlfriend she died from bathin' during her menstruating period. They say it stops you, stops your womb up or somethin' up there, the water does. She was taking a bath during her menstruating period and she died in the tub. Another reason I don't think you should be in too much water is you'll catch cold. You'll catch cold because your veins are open" (1973) (Snow 1974:91).

Menstruating women are particularly vulnerable to the upper respiratory infections caused by the entry of cold air. But it is a woman's own fault if she does not use common sense, says Bernita. Of *course* she will get sick if she is not careful:

> That's depend upon how you take *care* of yourself, too! O.K., if it's winter time and stuff like that, the pores of your skin is open. In other

words, it's just like [when] you wash your hair, right? Say if I wash
my hair in the winter time and I go outdoors [then] I catch cold, O.K.
So the pores of your skin is open, right? So when a woman period
comes on, *all* of her, well, I should say the pores of her skin is open,
O.K.? So if she *don't* take care of herself, sure. I believe she would
catch *pneumonia!* (Lansing, Michigan; 1987)

Such ideas may be reinforced by readily available booklets used in
self-treatment practices. The 1980 version of *MacDonald's Farmers
Almanac,* for example, warned: "In the North, February is the coldest
month of the Winter. It offers new opportunities for catching cold
and starting pneumonia and consumption. Rheumatism, sleeplessness,
constipation and female troubles begin this month." And in 1987 I
purchased the most recent edition of *Humphreys' Manual,* designed
to accompany a popular brand of homeopathic remedies; it suggested:
"Sometimes, in regularly menstruating women, during the flow or
just as it is about to commence, the flow stops or becomes suppressed
from exposure to cold, especially damp cold" (1967:n.p.).

It is the effect of cold and damp on the body that is also responsible for the dreaded "quick TB," when the onset of symptoms is
rapidly followed by oral hemorrhage and death. It is greatly feared
by both White and African-American women in the rural South;
supposedly the menstrual flow suppressed by cold can be expelled
from the mouth in a fatal hemorrhage (Stekert 1971).[9]

As one young woman who had been reared in the hills of West
Virginia put it:

This TB thing was really a rage. Old people . . . really worry about it,
quick TB. And they just worry a young girl to death. They keep tellin'
her, "Lordy, look at that young'un runnin' around here barefooted;
she's gonna have that quick TB before she's in her late twenties." And
it really worries you; they really frighten you with it. . . .

See, if you skip a period, like cold in your female organs, it could lead
into worse conditions. Like TB—anything wrong with her female organs could make her have TB. Cold settlin' in the body especially gives
the possibility of quick TB, pneumonia. Pneumonia, that's scar tissue on
your lungs; and TB, right away that's a place for it to fly. (Arlene
Bauer, Haslett, Michigan; 1975)

She also reported that a woman could expect a "rough period" if
this coincided with the signs of the zodiac ruling "the privates."
Quaint though such a belief may sound, it should be pointed out
that these women are talking about empirically observed menstrual
changes in tandem with tuberculosis. Amenorrhea may occur in the
later stages of untreated tuberculosis and, as well, when antituber-
culous drugs are used along with oral contraceptives (Altshuler and
Valenteen 1974). It should also be noted that "quick TB" is not the
only unwanted entity that can "fly" into the unprotected body: The

continued relevance of the traditional system is underscored by the belief of some African-American women in California that AIDS may also afflict a woman whose body is already weakened by menstruation (Flaskerud and Rush 1989).

As cold is blamed for so many menstrual symptoms it is not surprising to find that heat is used to treat them. A plain old hot bath can "bring on" a late period, alleviate cramps, help dissolve clots. Hot teas are frequently consumed as well, and if there is still a viable herbal tradition, teas made of plants may be used (de Albuquerque 1979; C. Hill 1988:116) But kitchen remedies can also help and these are readily available to all. Sage or nutmeg or ginger tea all work equally well, it is said, and have done so for a long time. "When the flowers is clogged I give them hot ginger tea" (C. Johnson 1934:201). In a more modern version warmed ginger ale "helps thin out the blood clots," says Elma Martin; it has been used to good effect by three generations of women in her family. (Detroit, Michigan; 1985) The symbolism of color occasionally enhances treatment as in Mary Harkness's reported cure for menstrual cramps: the sufferer lies on her stomach on a hot water bottle for exactly one hour—but it only works if she has a red ribbon tied around her neck. (Detroit, Michigan; 1980) The power of numbers may also be utilized, as in the Louisiana practice of wearing a string with nine knots in it tied around the waist (Webb 1971). And if a period is too heavy and too much blood is being lost? Just drink flour and water; it will thicken the blood just as it does gravy (Weidman et al. 1978:540).

The idea that the body "opens" to allow the expulsion of menstrual blood has already been noted; this is a process that is believed to occur over a number of days. The uterus is just beginning to open a few days before the onset of the menses, is completely open throughout, and will take a few days after to close completely. The idea that the internal organs of reproduction are open to the outside world at this time means that the body is also receptive to the entry of sperm, and these days are seen as those when a woman is most fertile. There is a very powerful proscription against intercourse during the menses itself, however. On the one hand it is seen as potentially injurious to the woman; on the other, just downright vile. It is said to produce symptoms ranging from heavier-than-normal flow and severe cramping to cancer of the uterus or an albino infant. And because menstrual blood is seen as so filthy, this, combined with any ambivalence about the sexual act itself, results in very strong feelings about such activity. As one woman put it, "You're supposed to be cleaning yourself *out,* not getting dirty!" (Lansing, Michigan; 1975) Only a man who was "a dog" would even *suggest* it, according to one college student; her mother said that it would certainly be grounds for divorce. (East Lansing, Michigan; 1984) It was among the most important things that she was told as a young girl, says Bernita:

We was always taught that when you get old enough to have relationship with your boyfriend or whatever, you might say, we was taught that a man shouldn't *touch* a woman like that. Or girl, whatever. They wasn't supposed to touch 'em. So then we would ask why, you know. And they said, "Well, it's easy for you to get pregnant like that. And then it's really a *sin*, it's really *wrong* to do that." So we was taught that a man was not supposed to touch a woman *period* when her period's *on*.

Her strong feelings against sexual activity during the menses were shared by the girls and women in the two Michigan prenatal clinics. Nearly 63 percent of the respondents in the Lansing study felt that sexual activity should be avoided, for example, and expressed themselves in very strong terms. "Even an animal won't do that!" said one (Snow and Johnson 1977). The percentage of women in the second study who thought it wrong was even higher; 81 percent of the total sample and 91 percent of the teenagers in the sample agreed (S. Johnson and Snow 1982) that it should not take place. Nor is the disgust at the thought of intercourse during the menses only an attitude of women—Marya Smith was horrified to learn that men can "tell" when a woman is in this state: "There's a different way that your eyes [look]; your eyes look gloomy. O.K., mens can look at a lady and tell when her period on her." "By looking at her," I asked? "How could you tell by looking at her?" "Well," she said:

I haven't been able to find that out. A man told me one time, he said, "Ummmmh, I was thinkin' about sayin' sumpin' *to* you, but I can see you ain't in no shape!" I says, "What you mean?," you know. He was raised up down South and he meant that my period was on. He said, "I meant that you ain't in no shape! Ain't your period on? 'Cause your eyes gloomy; I *know* it is!" I was so embarrassed. I didn't know people could tell it like that, you know. I been goin' through this world, you know, and people been goin' around knowin' it. And I didn't know nobody knew it. Well, mens can tell. (1983)

The husbands and boyfriends of many of the patients seen at Detroit's Hutzel Hospital also "express incredulity at the idea of having intercourse with a menstruating woman, believing that only a 'pervert' would do such a thing" (Poland and Beane 1980).

Such a view of menstruation falls into the well-developed idea of "dirt"—outside or inside the body—as a prominent cause of health problems in the traditional system. It is closely allied with the linkage of sexuality, venereal disease, and just plain dirtiness that was briefly mentioned earlier. Although the majority of women attending a prenatal clinic in Lansing, Michigan, believed that sexual contact was a possible mode of contracting venereal disease, it was by no means the only one mentioned. More than one-third also thought that it could develop if a woman was dirty, did not bathe frequently enough, failed to bathe after a menstrual period, or wore dirty underclothing; one of six women also thought you can "pick it up" by using public toilets. The "dirt" of germs, toilets, menstrual blood, and vaginal secretions was seen as equivalent. The idea that the uterus opens and closes to "let out" dirty menstrual blood was also revealed by the fact that one in six women did not know that venereal disease poses any risk to the developing fetus; after all, said one, during pregnancy "the uterus is closed and germs cannot enter" (Snow, Johnson, and Mayhew 1978). There was a general reluctance to discuss the topic of venereal disease, and a few women refused to do so; after all, "nice women" do not know about such things!

The women attending a prenatal clinic in Detroit revealed similar beliefs: In their responses to a question regarding the development of venereal disease 83 percent checked the answer, "Intercourse with infected person." However, other positive responses included: "From toilet seats," 16.5 percent; "Dirty personal habits," 20.5 percent; and "Too many sex partners," 26 percent (S. Johnson and Snow 1982). A number of women in both the Lansing and Detroit groups also believed that the pap smear is a test for venereal disease and, if they were neither dirty nor promiscuous, saw no reason to have it done. As noted earlier the increased risks to health now posed by the spread of AIDS may also be included in the area of sexuality and dirt; one Newark respondent described this as due to "filth, and people's hygiene habits, and what they do sexually and intravenously wise" (Meltzer and Kantor 1990). And though there was a "general reluctance" to talk about AIDS, limited discussions with mothers in a welfare hotel in New York reveal some of the same vague ideas about causality that are attached to other sexually transmitted diseases. They were aware of the role of sexual contact and "dirty needles" but did not have accurate information on the details of sexual transmission, and "were concerned about 'kissing,' 'touching,' 'toilets,' 'mosquitos,' and so on. There was a belief expressed that there are two kinds of AIDS, the carriers—they never die—and the one who has the virus and dies" (Shedlin 1989).

As noted, it is the perceived "openness" of the body via the reproductive organs that makes women so vulnerable to the entry of unwanted entities—whether cold air, germs, dirt, or semen—just prior to, during, and immediately after the menses. The corollary to this idea, of course, is that it is "closed" at midcycle. "Is that *true?*," whispered Cassie Seales' 18-year-old daughter, Ruthie, on one occasion, leaning over to poke me in the ribs. I nodded that yes, it was true. "No wonder," she said, sitting back to listen to the rest of the talk. My friend Dr. Shirley Johnson was speaking on the female reproductive cycle at a lunchtime "brown-bag" session for clerical staff at the medical school. It was her description of the time of ovulation that provoked the question from Ruthie, who was working as a secretary in a clinical department. Ruthie's two-year-old daughter had been born when she was a junior in high school. "It seemed like every one of my girlfriends had a baby that year!" she told me later. They had all talked about "being careful," but they had believed they were "safe" eight days after menstruation. Would they be surprised when she told them! (East Lansing, Michigan; 1973)

When Bernita Washington spoke of menstruation as "the life" of a woman she was also referring to the connection between the menses and sexuality, a topic which she is distinctly uncomfortable in discussing:

> Only thing I really know is good about it, like I say, it's the *life* [of a woman]. Only thing I really know is good about it when a woman, O.K., say like she is, uh—oh, how would I say this? Let me make it plain, O.K.; let me say it plain. O.K., say as long as a woman have her periods, during the time of her periods she's, she's, she's, uh, she's more [long pause] *ready* for sex more, O.K.? And after her period, she's more ready for sex more. O.K., that's why I said it's a *life* to her. And before, too, right before. After, too.

"Right before, during, and right after her period?"

> Right. And this is what would cause them to get *pregnant* faster, you know; this is why I said this is a *life* to them. You know, it makes them more [pause], I don't know how you'd explain that.

"More interested in having sex?"

> Yeah, that's the way I would use it. (Lansing, Michigan; 1987)

The idea that this time of the month was safe for unprotected intercourse also made sense to some women interviewed in the Lansing prenatal clinic; if the body was "closed," they reasoned, sperm could not enter the body to cause a pregnancy (Snow and Johnson 1977). Their belief was, of course, exactly the opposite of that of the clinic staff, who were frequently puzzled at their clients' failure to control their fertility. An attempt to assess women's knowledge of the time of ovulation was also included in the self-administered questionnaire used in the Detroit study (Johnson and Snow 1982). The question was asked in two ways: "When is it possible to become pregnant?," and, "Is there a 'safe time' to have intercourse without becoming pregnant?" Of those who responded, 63.5 percent were unable to answer the first question correctly and 79 percent were not able to answer the second.[10] Women who believe themselves "safe" at midcycle, then, may be timing their presumed "safe" intercourse towards the time of ovulation. This practice may be made even more likely because of the previously mentioned powerful cultural sanction against sexual activity during the menses.

Their negative feelings about this practice spilled over into their willingness to accept the intrauterine device (IUD) as a birth control method. Since many clinics make a practice of inserting the device during a woman's menstrual period we asked, "Some physicians prefer to insert the IUD while a woman is having her menstrual period—would you be willing to have it done at that time?" Seventy-two percent of those who said they were *otherwise willing* to consider the IUD answered that in such a case they were unsure or would not do so. It was revulsion at such a thought that indirectly resulted in the third pregnancy of Marya Smith's oldest daughter, Josie. She had run out of her birth control pills and was ambivalent about having the prescription refilled; she was not sure they were "good for" her body. She thought she might like to try an IUD, but when she found out that her physician wanted to insert it during her period she quickly changed her mind—"No way I'm gonna do that!" Before she got around to getting more birth control pills she found herself pregnant again. (1984)

Poland and Beane's (1980) data about women attending family planning and prenatal clinics in the same setting also suggest that such a practice "occurs at a time when the patient is severely embarrassed by exposure of her genitalia and her menstrual blood. Both our patients and their consorts are extremely uneasy about the idea that a woman should expose her genitalia to a doctor while she is menstruating." Poland and Beane also looked at beliefs about menstruation, clean versus dirty body parts, and IUD use among a subgroup of adolescents in these clinics. The girls were disgusted at the thought of checking the body for an IUD string and/or looking at a bowel movement to make sure the device had not been expelled:

> *[They] had strong feelings about looking at bowel movements and touching their genitalia. In one of the family planning classes taught at the clinic under study, a nurse urges the patients to take their fingers and feel the cervix and vagina in preparation for the IUD string check. The response is one of horror and disgust accompanied by disbelief that a nurse, someone who is clean, would suggest such a thing. The likelihood that many of these patients will, indeed, explore their vaginas and locate their cervices is very low. Not only would they be touching a dirty area, but any behaviour of this sort is suggestive of masturbation, a heavily sanctioned activity.* (Poland and Beane 1980:33)

Women who are concerned that the *right amount* of blood be expelled from the body each month are also concerned when they are told of—or experience—the heavier flow that often results when the device is in place. They believe that it can only weaken the body. Traditional ideas about just how the female body is actually formed also have a negative impact on attitudes about and use of the intrauterine device. A view of the internal organs as comprising hollow tubes or containers leads some women to fear that the device will somehow wander out of the position it should be in. It might then damage them, their sexual partner, or in the case of contraceptive failure, their unborn child. Some of the women that we interviewed in Lansing believed that an IUD somehow "plugged up" the cervix to prevent sperm from getting "up there," for example. In Miami a Bahamian woman said: "I have had a coil in my 'stomach' for five years. It hurts badly when I have my monthly. I suffer from cramps and pains everywhere. Maybe it needs to come out. When I have sex, too, it hurts me; my back hurts a lot" (Weidman et al. 1978:397).

A Southern Black informant, eight months pregnant, had "tried the pill and the IUD and neither one worked. She still has the IUD in the side of her 'abdomen.' She is so afraid it will hurt the baby" (p. 398). And MacCormack (1985) noted that many Jamaican women fear using the intrauterine device because of the fear that it will get lost in the body; they believe that the vagina and uterus "are a single tube. The tube may be open at both ends. Thus women tie a binder below the breasts in late pregnancy and perhaps in birth 'to keep the baby from coming up and choking me,' or 'to keep the placenta from coming up.' To insert a coil in this tube is to risk it drifting upward, becoming lost in the body."[11] Another complaint was that it might cause pain to the woman and her sexual partner as it worked as a "blocking device" to keep sperm from entering the womb. Profound dissatisfaction with the method may be expressed in religious terms: One woman living in a New York welfare hotel who had retained the device for only one day explained this by saying, "God don't want me to have this" (Shedlin 1989).

The strong feeling that there is a "normal" amount of blood that must be expelled each month also contributes to feelings of unease if the flow is lessened. The lighter menstrual flow, occasional spotting of blood and/or actual cessation of the menses that can occur with oral contraceptives means that this method of birth control is seen as dangerous as well. Failure of "all" the blood to come out can only mean that this filthy substance is building up in the body. In Miami, women were asked by Scott: "If there is less bleeding than usual/normal, how does this affect your body/health?" Responses included statements "such as 'you are nervous and depressed,' 'your blood rises,' 'your blood pressure will go up,' 'mental illness,' 'it means something is wrong' and 'it means you need nourishment.' . . . " One Southern Black mother described her feelings about the possibility as, "I guess I get nervous because I wonder where the flow is going . . . " (Scott 1975).

The use of the oral (or injectable) contraceptive Depo-Provera in Jamaica similarly caused women to worry because it produced long periods of no menstrual flow. According to MacCormack (1985), this "was interpreted as a sign that Depo-Provera had 'blocked up their tubes.' Women were also concerned about developing high blood pressure and believed thay would have too much blood accumulating in the body if they did not menstruate a satisfactory amount every month."

Despite such misgivings many women try to use oral contraceptives but—in many instances—give up on them after a trial. Oral contraceptives were the most popular choice of birth control in the inner-city clinic in Detroit; nearly 83 percent of the women who had ever used any method (135/163; 37 had never used contraception) said that they had tried them. One out of five said that they had become pregnant while taking them; this was not surprising because 65 percent had (in our assessment) used them incorrectly. A further 76 percent had discontinued their use because of feelings of dissatisfaction (S. Johnson and Snow 1982). The contraceptive experiences of the women interviewed by Shedlin were similarly "at best, uninformed, unsupervised, and sporadic." Most reported a "brief period of pill use after a first abortion or birth at 15 or 16," then cessation because of unpleasant experiences. These were reflected in such comments as "One time I used pills . . . my blood pressure went high," and "I planned on birth control but changed my mind. . . . I don't like taking medicine. . . . If I take something, I feel like I will be addicted. . . . " (1989).

If methods of fertility control that are recommended by physicians are perceived as not working well or having a dangerous effect on the body it is not surprising when women fall back on traditional methods. Lansing women spoke of trying ice water–and–vinegar douches (ice water to "slow down" the sperm and vinegar to kill them); holding the breath during orgasm (to keep sperm from reaching their destination); standing up right after sex, holding the nose and then blowing forcefully out the mouth (to help expel the semen from the vagina). And, of course, intercourse only during the middle of the month when it was "safe."

In Miami a Southern Black woman "said she had used all [the birth control methods] except the pills, and not one of them helped. She used the coil and got pregnant; . . . the diaphragm and got pregnant; the foam and she got pregnant. She hasn't tried the pill, because she has high blood pressure. . . . She takes quinine tablets after her period . . . for about three days" (Weidman et al. 1978:402). And if the doctors cannot help, perhaps an older woman with much experience can. Said one Bahamian woman: "I used to use the pills, but they made me bleed a lot (too much). I have high blood. These pills made my head hurt. My stomach cramped me. I was so sick the doctor took me off of them. They wanted me to take the diaphragm. I said the hell with all that. Now I use red vinegar and cold water for douching. . . . An old woman told me about this. It works fine" (p. 400).

Many traditional methods do *not* "work fine," unfortunately. And the timing of "safe" intercourse at midcycle, fear of some contraceptive methods, and/or use of ineffective methods, can only contribute to unwanted pregnancies. Sixty percent of the women sampled in the Detroit clinic indicated that they had been pregnant at least once when they did not wish to be. Of these women, "58 percent were not using contraception at the time or thought they were 'safe,' almost 25 percent said they had either used a method incorrectly or the method failed, and more than 25 percent did not know why they became pregnant or said it 'just happened'" (S. Johnson and Snow 1982). Chances are that many of these women have had more unwanted pregnancies in the years since.

And what happens to the woman when the menstrual periods cease altogether in midlife? There is a rather surprising disjunction between African-American women's views of the menstrual cycle and what happens when menstruation finally ends—they have very *strong* opinions about the former, that is, and seem to have almost none about the latter. The women who were interviewed or who filled out questionnaires in the Lansing and Detroit, Michigan, pre- natal clinics were quite vague about health issues in the menopausal years, for example. As noted above, their view of the menstrual cycle was quite different from that of the medical staff and they perhaps could not be expected to have similar beliefs about the menopause; certainly they did not share the concerns of the health professionals. Most of the women had had difficulty controlling their fertility and, in many cases, had poor reproductive histories. It is probable that many would/will also continue childbearing rather late in life so their lack of knowledge in this area is troubling. Half of the women in the Lansing study did not know that it is possible for a woman to become pregnant during the climacteric; of those who did, many did not know there were any additional maternal risks with a meno- pausal pregnancy. Eighty-seven percent were unaware of any addi- tional risks to the fetus in a pregnancy at that time (Snow, Johnson, and Mayhew 1978; S. Johnson and Snow 1979). Thirty-seven percent of the women in the Detroit study also did not know if pregnancy can occur at this period of a woman's life (S. Johnson and Snow 1982).

One might expect that these women who exhibit so much fear and ambivalence about menstruation would be greatly relieved to see it end—and perhaps they are—but if so there is little talk about it. Whereas there are dozens of home remedies for menstrual prob- lems there are almost none for menopausal disorders, though Jordan cited the eating of a salad of pussy willow leaves or clover, said to have female hormonal action (1975). Although most of the Arizona women I knew were deeply concerned about menstruation I do not believe any one of them ever mentioned the menopause. And I have only one spontaneous mention of it in my notes from my Michigan years, when 65-year-old Lucile Patterson told me that too much calcium in the diet is dangerous for women. The proper amount of calcium hardens bones, she said, but *too* much calcium will "harden your arteries and cause tumors in the change of life." (Lansing, Michigan; 1985)

It might be surmised that women who have in part seen menstruation as a means of ridding the body of excess blood would become concerned about high blood/pressure because the periods have stopped. Surgical menopause was in fact blamed for this condition by one Southern Black woman in Miami, who "had a hysterectomy in April. . . . The operation was done at JMH. She said she didn't get high blood pressure until after the surgery [when she no longer had her 'monthly']" (Weidman et al. 1978:543). Both hysterectomy and menopause were also reported troublesome for some New Orleans women: "According to patients, when the menstrual flow is stopped, excess blood goes up to the head, aggravating one's 'pressure troubles.' As one woman phrased it 'There's no place for all that waste blood to go so it backs up into your head'" (Heurtin-Roberts and Reisin 1990). Still, reports such as these are rare. It is almost as if the intense focus on a woman's health dissipates right along with this aspect of her sexuality.

More often, when the health of older women is mentioned the emphasis is on the weakening of the body in general, just as it is for older men. In old age the blood might "thin down" and offer little protection against chilly air, people say. And of course one can only expect to pay for failure to take care of the body when young with rheumatism, creaking joints, and the like. Perhaps men and women are seen to merge healthwise at the end of their lives, just as small boys and girls are not seen to differ much before puberty.

Certainly the emphasis on the end of sexuality at menopause is paramount for Bernita Washington. If nothing is going to come of it why on earth even bother? She also spent a good deal of time ridiculing women who "pretend" that they are still interested in such things as a way of seeming young:

> Menopause is when a woman has reached the age of her flowers, reached the age of not having her periods anymore. Flowers, that's the period. They use that word; that was the proper word, yeah. So when a woman had reached the age of *not* havin' her periods anymore, then this is when [she] be coming into what you call *menopause*. So then when she gets in that state, then *she* not *supposed* to have no relationship with a man after that.
>
> I don't guess it would *do* anything, but then, what are you doin'? *Nothing!* You don't have anymore *nature*, O.K. Because your period's your nature. And when *that's* gone, you know—that's not sayin' that won't come into your mind and stuff like that. But it's *best* to not, when you *reach* that stage it's best to not to have no relationship with a man again.

"Do women talk about the menopause?"

> Not *too much*, not too much! They don't like to talk about that, you know; when they get a certain age most of 'em don't want to talk

about it. Because you know they don't wanta say, they wanta say, "Hey, I ain't no menopause, I still got a boyfriend," and all *this* type of stuff, you know. They still want to be a *girl!* That's why. They still wanta say—get 60 and 65 years old—and say, "Hey, I still gotta boyfriend, I still makes love" and all this kind of type of stuff.

But that's not necessarily true, you know. They may be *there,* but what are they doing? And just like sit at a table with a big bowl of *food* and not *hungry!* It's in they *mind* and so they just *feel* that they're really doin' somethin' that they're not doing, that's all! You really *feel* that you're doin' something that you're not doing!

I haven't gotten quite that *far* yet. . . . Now I'm like, you know, maybe like this month, next month I might not even see it. For about two years [now]. *Womens* like, say, between *my* age and yours, O.K., maybe women like that will sit up and talk about some things like that maybe to certain *people,* O.K. But there are *some* peoples come along, and *this* lady probably want *that* lady to feel like *she* is a little more *active.* "I can do a little bit more than *you,*" you know, at these type of things. Those type of things are being sex.

Just like an older man. Older man, say if he get 65 or 70 years old, but he *still* wants to look at a young girl! He *still* wants to put his money out there and say, "Hey," you know, "you can have this." Or, "I'll buy you this." Or, "I'll do this." But what is he doin'? Nothing! Do you know what I'm sayin'? He's just gettin' rid of his money!

"'Cause he really can't do anything?"

Well, I don't think so! [We both laugh.] I don't think it's too much, and I'm serious. I really don't think it's too much, and I'm serious." (Lansing, Michigan; 1987)

Boone pointed out that in traditional societies puberty rituals are dramatic events signaling the young person's readiness for an adult sexual role, but that there is ordinarily no public ritual marking the menopause. Instead, it is the occurrence that "usually" occurs at about the same time, becoming a grandmother, that is "widely heralded as a proud event." She went on to note, however, that the positive changes that can accrue to attaining the status of older woman depends in part on the *discontinuity* of her life stages:

Throughout the world's cultures older women teach younger women how to be good mothers, wives, and workers by imparting knowledge of religious, sexual, and subsistence skills. They also frequently embody a man's or a family's wealth and prestige. They can symbolize freedom because they are no longer equally subject to the constraints of the sex and marriage "market." These changes rely at least partly on the discontinuity between early responsibilities and later ones. Where a woman's life stages overlap a great deal, she can be placed under enormous stress to fulfill multiple roles. (Boone 1989:118)

Certainly the reproductive patterns of many African-American women mean that they do continue to fulfill multiple roles—their first grandchildren may be born to their young daughters while they are still having children of their own, for example, so that childrearing responsibilities are blurred. Because Bernita's childbearing years were extended, for example (her first child at 16 and her last child at 40), she was still having babies when her oldest children had begun having children of their own. This lack of discontinuity in roles perhaps contributes to the fact that there is so little in the ethnographic literature about the African-American menopausal woman.

On the day that Bernita and I talked about the menopause the conversation reverted to the fact that she had been raised "without a mother or a father." "I had to raise myself!" she often says. And she said so once again on this day to explain her own discomfort in discussing topics of an intimate nature. She had been more at ease talking to her three sons; all she had to do was "dose" them with her turpentine tea to prevent "the clap" and admonish them to "be careful" when with their girlfriends:

> Well, the boys I didn't have too much to tell them, more than about just being careful, you know. "Hey, if you go out there and be with this girl and [you might] get her pregnant. You shouldn't do it because the parents have the responsibility and you won't have it." Stuff like that. "You are *young,* and you can't take care of it and *I* can't *either!*"

She had seven daughters, however, and with daughters it is not possible to gloss over the biological reality of menstrual blood. It has already been mentioned that Bernita was only 16 when her oldest daughter, Marya, was born, and that she had been "too embarrassed" to tell Marya anything about menstruation before the girl had her first period. And when it did happen and she had no choice but to talk to her daughter, of course, Bernita passed on the information that *she* had been given by "the older womens." She allowed Marya to pass it along to the next sister and so, presumably, right on down the line.

Marya was visiting her mother that afternoon and filled me in on the newest births in her own family. Her oldest daughter, Josie, who was born when Marya was 16, had had her first child when *she* was sixteen. Now 24, Josie had been pregnant four times: one pregnancy had ended in a miscarriage, she had three living children, and had been surgically sterilized. Marya's second daughter, Dodie, had also given birth at 16, had already had a second child and was now pregnant again. "I don't know *why* those girls of mine are always getting pregnant," Marya said to me in a puzzled tone. "I done *told* them when to be careful!" And what had she told them? Exactly what her mother had told *her:* "If you're going to do those things," then five days before your period and five days after are "safe." (Lansing, Michigan; 1987)

Notes

1. If LaNeel was aware of any sexual symbolism in the consumption of bananas and sweet potatoes she did not mention it; although I have heard dozens of menstrual prescriptions and proscriptions over the years this is the only one of this nature I have encountered. It is much more common to hear about foods that should be avoided "when your period is on."

2. The "Mannish water" is used by a woman "to make her man more virile and potent," says Hallie. It is prepared by the woman squatting "over the pot in which food (traditionally rice) is cooking. The steam from the pot wafts up into her vagina and back down into the pot. A man who eats this will be very 'cockstrong.'"

3. Anna Perry knew all about the dangers associated with being a woman. Her daughter Lila was killed, so she believed, by means of poisoned powder sprinkled on a sanitary napkin.

4. I acknowledge the collaboration of my longtime friend and colleague, Dr. Shirley M. Johnson, in this research. Our very different backgrounds—hers in endocrine physiology and mine in cultural anthropology—has allowed us to approach issues of women's health in a complementary fashion.

5. See Henton (1961) for an early study comparing the attitudes of African-American and White girls concerning menarche; African-American girls were twice as likely (73 percent vs. 36 percent) to say that they had been "upset," "unhappy," "unclean," "worried," or "ashamed" at its occurrence. Recently Scott et al. (1989) compared the attitudes toward menarche of middle-class African-American adolescents with those found in previous studies on White adolescents. Although the mean scores on positive feelings about the event were slightly positive, African-American adolescents had slightly greater negative feelings about it. When their results were compared with other studies among African-American adolescents the authors concluded that they perceive menarche "overall, as a relatively negative event, although one that raises some positive feelings as well."

6. Although I have attempted to focus on beliefs that are current, it should be noted that these not only have a long history, but in many instances have shown little change. Under a section entitled *Special Feminine Taboos,* for example, Puckett (1926:423–424) stated: "During certain physiological periods there are special taboos applying to women. Should a woman step over melon vines during menstruation they will bear no fruit. The Negro women of Pulaski County, Virginia, refuse to handle food at this time, under the assumption that they would spoil the cooking. If they assisted in making cucumber pickle the pickles would get soft; likewise cake filling would refuse to harden. Wine would never become clear if handled at this time, no matter how often it was 'wracked off.' Cider would not change into vinegar because the 'mother of vinegar' is killed. The same general idea is found in Europe, although among the Timne people of Africa a menstrous woman is forced to observe certain taboos, among which are cooking for her husband or planting anything."

7. Although attempts to link African-American traditional beliefs with African counterparts is often problematic it is nonetheless tempting to do so on occasion. Dr. Debra Rothenberg—a physician who is also a graduate student in anthropology at Michigan State University—described a traditional malady known as *dauda* among the Hausa of Niger. *Dauda* is an entity in which a new infant is seen as "going backwards" in development, that is, is malnourished and failing to thrive.

One of the causes is said to be that a menstruating woman has picked up the child before his/her naming ceremony, which takes place seven days after birth. The midwife can prevent it from occurring by tearing off a bit of the cloth on which the woman in labor is lying, dipping it in oil, and rubbing it on the head of the newborn infant (personal communication, 1990).

8. The "magical divestment" of a variety of ailments by "passing through" has a long history in European and American folk healing; the victim may be passed through or under the bellies of animals, under table legs, through chair or ladder rungs, horse collars, and so forth, symbolically stripping him or her of the symptoms (Hand 1980:163–165, 170).

9. The association of cold or damp, femaleness, and tuberculosis is a very old one (Chase 1865:198–199, 201; Gunn 1867:546; Pierce 1895:691–692; Waring 1967, footnote). "Quick TB" seems to be a condition that afflicts only women; I have heard of only one man succumbing to it. Ella Thomas's first husband reportedly died of it after he lost "too much blood"; this apparently weakened his system in the same fashion that menstruation weakens women. And again, cold and damp were implicated: "He died of tuberculosis. He give his sister a blood transfusion, and they took too much blood from him. He only weighed 125 pounds, and they took 300 cc's of blood from him, and that's too much blood. And you couldn't tell him nothin'. And you see, it's damp out in California, and instead of him wearin' them heavy clothes, he'd pull off them heavy drawers and go on his shirt sleeves. When he give his sister that blood transfusion, instead of wearin' them warm clothes and things, he didn't do it. Then he took that quick kind of TB. He must not have been very strong or sumpin'. And see, he's supposed to drink wine to run that blood back, and he didn't" (Snow 1977:44). Until rather recently tuberculosis was virtually eliminated as a public health problem in the United States and "quick TB" might have disappeared as an entity in the traditional system. Now, however, the number of cases of tuberculosis is rising due to the lowered resistance to infectious diseases of individuals infected with the AIDS virus; "quick TB" may be around awhile after all.

10. These data must be seen as only suggestive; because the answers were provided on the questionnaire some of the "correct" answers were no doubt only guesses. The lack of knowledge of time of ovulation was therefore probably even higher than the numbers recorded.

11. The idea that something can be lost in the mysterious interior reaches of the female body had also precluded Bernita Washington from the use of the birth control method she calls "condos"; she knew of them but would not let her husband use them. After intercourse, she says, if a man is "sleepy or just wants to rest awhile," then the condom "will come off inside you and it ain't goin' to come out unless you go to a doctor." The idea of going to the doctor to retrieve a lost condom was apparently more threatening to her than the fear of another pregnancy—she continued, laughing, "No wonder I was pregnant so often!" (1991) Her 11 pregnancies—spread over 24 years—produced ten living children and one neonatal death following a traumatic accident.

8

Some Slip Up, Some Plan, and Some Have 'Em to Have 'Em

Little monkey came here in a shopping bag.

Samantha teased Brother about the caul, the gauzy web clinging to Junebug's see-through skin. Old Miss Julia Strothers, Old Mother Strothers, nurse and midwife and baby-sitter and fortune-teller, had gathered every scrap of web and wrapped them in a handkerchief and stuck them deep into her bosom.

Got to be mighty careful. This some powerful stuff, child, Ima take this veil home with me and do what have to be done. Don't you pay no mind to what I'm doing, you just keep your eye on this little one. He got the sign. Child born with the sign. Sign writ all over this child plain as day. Watch him. Watch him real good.
—John Edgar Wideman, *Sent For You Yesterday*

Alice Jones was 17 and pregnant for the third time. Her first baby had been born prematurely when Alice was only 14, and he spent the first few weeks of his life in a pediatric intensive-care unit; now a healthy three-year-old, he shared a small apartment with his mother and grandmother. The following year Alice again gave birth prematurely but this infant lived only a few hours. And now the doctors and nurses had told her that this new baby might *also* come early. Alice had told *them* something, too—she wanted this one to be the last one. So could she have her tubes tied? But there was concern about sterilizing someone so young and it was decided that she must have parental permission. Her father was in prison and he could not sign the requisite papers, and her mother refused to sign, believing that it was morally wrong to interfere with God's plan. Alice would just have to learn to be more careful. Shortly thereafter she gave birth prematurely to a daughter, who spent a number of weeks in intensive care before she was brought home to join the family. And *was* Alice careful? That depends on whose view one takes: From the standpoint of the clinic staff she was not. She was already pregnant again when she returned for her postpartum checkup. And no, she had not been using birth control. From her vantage point, however, she thought that she *had* been careful: She believed that she could not get pregnant before the return of normal menstrual periods. And why *do* women have children? "Well," she said rather wistfully, because "some slip up, some plan, and some have 'em to have 'em." She had slipped up four times in as many years. (Lansing, Michigan; 1975)

Pregnancy Risks

Today most people—health professionals and laypersons alike—would agree that there are growing difficulties for young women in their reproductive years. And one does not need to be a physician to know that too many babies born to African-American mothers are not healthy. These babies, in fact, have a two-fold or more risk of dying in their first year than do White babies (Shiono et al. 1986; Infant Mortality Among Black Americans 1987; Lieberman et al. 1987; J. Kleinman and Kessel 1987; Joyce 1987). A comparison of infant mortality rates in the years 1978–1985 in the metropolitan San Diego area, in fact, revealed that the rates for the infants of Indochinese refugee women were "below that for non-Hispanic Whites and substantially below that for Blacks" (Weeks and Rumbaut 1991). In my own state of Michigan the 1988 mortality rate for African-American infants was 21.9/1,000 live births, for example, in contrast to a rate of 8.6/1,000 for White infants (Bouknight 1990); in 1989 the rate for White infants decreased slightly—to 8.3/1,000—while the rate for African-American infants remained at 21.9/1,000 (Chargot 1990b). Considerations of space make it possible to mention only briefly some of the social, behavioral, and biomedical factors that coalesce to contribute to this problem. Social risks have been identified as: low income, single marital status, non-White race, and less than a high school education on the part of the mother.[1] Stressful life situations also increase the likelihood of complications of pregnancy in the absence of a strong system of social support.

Conventional biomedical risks have included unfavorable combinations of age and parity; birth interval of less than two years; a history of miscarriage or neonatal death; and other medical conditions that complicate pregnancy. Some of the latter conditions that are particularly problematic include diabetes, hypertension, and certain sexually transmitted diseases. Maternal/fetal health may also be adversely affected by use of alcohol, tobacco, and illicit drugs. As well, drugs that are helpful for the nonpregnant woman may not be so in pregnancy; methadone, for example, may cause fetal malformations. All of these risk factors are presently exacerbated by the deadly interplay of newer problems: AIDS as well as syphilis and gonorrhea; cocaine (especially in the form known as "crack") as well as heroin and methadone; an upswing in violence; increasing rates of homelessness.[2]

Infant mortality rates are closely tied to prematurity and there has recently been a dramatic increase in the numbers of these early births (Joyce 1990). In many parts of the country a disturbingly common scenario is that of a low birthweight infant born to an unmarried young mother who has dropped out of school, is living in poverty, and who has received inadequate prenatal care.[3] Most health professionals would probably agree that a pregnancy is not a good idea for someone who is young, poor, undereducated, and single—her health and that of her infant may be compromised—and almost certainly her life choices will be restricted even further. Some might even go so far as to say that childbearing should be put off indefinitely unless these factors change for the better. For very many African-American girls and women, however, the only factor that can be guaranteed to progress is that of youth; they will, in fact, grow older.[4] But very many will also *remain* poor, will *not* see schooling as leading toward a better life, and will find themselves in sexual partnerships in which marriage is *not* a viable option. To deny themselves parenthood would be too much to ask. This does not mean that many women do not attempt to prevent pregnancies; they do. The studies already cited show that a variety of contraceptive methods are tried even when they are seen as dangerous to the health. But too frequently these methods are used sporadically and/or incorrectly and then they fail. And these failures are indeed often to the detriment of both mother and child.

Much media attention has been focused on the escalating numbers of infants born to teenage (or younger!) mothers; like their older counterparts some of these might also prefer to delay pregnancy.[5] But it is also an undeniable fact that many of the African-American adolescents who have so little control of their fertility do not seem to place a high premium on doing so. Sexual activity is seen as normal and natural—indeed, the term "nature" is a synonym for libido for both sexes—and the relationship between males and females who are not related by blood is almost *expected* to be of a sexual nature. The early expression of sexuality by adolescents—who are by definition "high-natured"—is not seen as surprising, then. The pregnancies that are the tangible results of such activity may be cause for dismay (Schulz 1969:154; Rainwater 1970:58; Ladner 1971:199) or accepted with little concern (Young 1970; Stack 1974:46–47; Dougherty 1978:52, 76–82). They are a familiar occurrence in any case, so that "people know how to think about the problems and how to work toward the best solutions, given the limited alternatives that are available to them" (Rainwater, p. 59).

And these alternatives may not include marriage as a realistic option. This is especially true when societal barriers make middle-class mainstream values—with their emphasis on education leading to well-paying jobs, which in turn allow stable marriages and family life—seem like empty dreams. Premarital sexual relationships and out-of-wedlock births are not cultural values so much as a response to those societal factors that continue to militate against successful marriages. For a lower-class family that has adapted to difficult life

© Barbara Brandon distributed by Universal Press Syndicate

© Barbara Brandon distributed by Universal Press Syndicate

© Barbara Brandon distributed by Universal Press Syndicate

circumstances by dependence on the members of an extended kin network, in fact, a marriage might be seen as deleterious to the group. There may be pressure on a family member *not* to marry if this would mean withdrawal of the individual's resources from the kin network. Marriage, in this instance, "implies the willingness of an individual to remove himself from the daily obligations of his kin network. People in the Flats recognize that one cannot simultaneously meet kin expectations and the expectations of a spouse. While cooperating kinsmen continually attempt to draw new people into their personal networks, they fear the loss of a central, resourceful member in the network. . . " (Stack 1974:113–114). There was a good deal of pressure on the part of her kin to keep Ruby Banks from marrying, for example, and she said in part: "They look for trouble to tell me every single day. If I ever marry, I ain't listening to what nobody say. I just listen to what he say. You have to get along the best way you know how, and forget about your people. If I got married they would talk, like they are doing now, saying, 'He ain't no good, he's been creeping on you. I told you once not to marry him. You'll end up right back on ADC.' If I ever get married I'm leaving town" (Stack 1974:115).

Women may see no advantage to marriage, "especially if they cannot count on economic or emotional support from their men and would have to rely on public assistance anyway" (Carrington 1978). And men who cannot find work cannot adequately support wives and children. There is a long history of high rates of unemployment and underemployment for African-American males and this is a worsening trend; the numbers of these men not in the work force has nearly tripled since 1960 (Joe 1987). The number of African-American families headed by women has *also* tripled since 1960; nearly 60 percent of these families are poor.

Some authors have suggested that the birth of the first child becomes a symbol of attaining manhood or womanhood when the usual avenues for mainstream success are absent or truncated (Schulz 1969:41, 155; Ladner 128; Aschenbrenner 1975:56; Frankel 1977:43; E. Martin and Martin 1978:63; Kennedy 1980:37). This assumption was not borne out by Boone's data, however, where women strongly disagreed with the proposition that "a girl becomes a woman by having a baby." Although children were valued by both men and women in the community there were "indications that these women make conceptual distinctions between the realms of male/female relations, pregnancy and child-rearing. This is expressed in the dissociation of marriage and childbearing, and in the isolated importance accorded to pregnancy as separate from motherhood. The 'gestator' role is valued by itself, and pregnancy is an important stage in the life cycle in the late teens and early twenties, which need not coincide with either marriage, family formation, or assumption of the role of 'mother'" (Boone 1985:1008). And hoping for a wedding might mean putting off indefinitely a very valuable part of life. One unmarried woman in our Detroit sample responded to the question, Why did you become pregnant? by writing in, "After all, I *am* 21!!!!" She was already rather elderly to be having a first child in comparison with the rest of the population using that facility—what would be gained by waiting longer? (S. Johnson and Snow 1982). The dissociation of marriage and parenthood makes issues of legitimacy seem less compelling, and descriptions of illegitimate children as "unnatural and unwanted" (Schulz 1969:154) are rare. More commonly, as Charles Johnson long ago wrote of rural Alabama (1934:49), "There is, in a sense, no such thing as illegitimacy in this community." The very fact of it's *existence,* according to Stack (1974:50), "seems to legitimize the child in the eyes of the community." And in Aschenbrenner's words (p. 56), legitimacy "applies to parents, not to children." The babies, certainly, are innocent of the actions of their parents (Young 1970; E. Martin and Martin 1978:46; Boone 1982). Some parents may even put pressure on unmarried sons and daughters to produce a child; grandparenthood is valued, too (Stack 1974:120–121; Dunn 1988).

The factors that lead to the separation of marriage from childbearing also contribute to a deep division between men and women. "There ain't more than two kinds of people," said a streetcorner man in Washington, D.C. "And it ain't white people and black people, color don't make no difference. It's men and women" (Hannerz 1969:70). Romantic love is greatly idealized but it is also recognized that it may not last—or be found with the steady sort of person on whom one can depend in daily life. Even when a man and woman are together the relationship may be perceived as a fragile one: In a study of the household/family networks of 140 pregnant African-American women in Cleveland, for example, the subjects were asked to list the persons living in their household and also to name the ones they considered to be family. The relative importance of blood kin was demonstrated rather dramatically by the fact that 37 percent of the women living in a household with their male partner did not mention him as a family member (Reeb et al. 1986). If "conditions prevent the ideal combination of lover and provider, a common solution is to keep the two matters separate, and to simultaneously maintain two types of relationships" (Aschenbrenner 1975:43).

At best, men and women lead very separate lives; at worst, they share a fundamental distrust of the nature of the opposite sex (Liebow 1967:103–160; Hannerz 1969:70–104; Schulz 1969:177–180; Rainwater 1970:61–64; Frankel 1977:103; Dougherty 1978:17–18; Boone 1982, 1985, 1989:99). Women often say that men are "dogs" who move from one sexual conquest to another; men often complain that women are interested only in the money and gifts that they provide. Although Shedlin found that the most frequent answer to the question, "Who gives you support?" was a woman's husband or boyfriend, this was more likely to be couched in economic than social or emotional terms. An important aspect of having a male partner, in fact, was being able to tap into the additional help of his network of female kin (1989:13). Personal relationships between the sexes may be marked by a cynicism that is then played out in a self-fulfilling prophecy: Little is expected of them so little effort is expended on them. To repeat the quote from 21-year-old Diane, a high school dropout with four children who is separated from her husband: "Guys, all they do is stick you and go do somebody else" (Dunn 1988). As another woman from rural Mississippi put it, in marriage "there was no death do you part" (Lemann 1991:33).

Such low expectations of the behavior of the opposite sex may be present at a very early age: In Ladner's study 10-year-old Kim had already decided that "men are no good" and 6-year-old Rachel, when asked if she wanted to have a baby when she grew up replied, "No, because boys are no good. When the baby comes they go with another girl" (1971:66, 129). In his ethnographic account of a neighborhood in Pittsburgh, Melvin Williams recounts this interaction among a group of young (12 to 14 years) girls who are sharing a quart of wine; it captures their blend of sexual sophistication and naiveté already touched with ambivalence about the opposite sex:

Twelve-year-old girl: I can't let a boy get over on me because I don't have any hair, just a little bit.

Fourteen-year-old girl: That doesn't matter, girl, most of them can't find the hole anyway. You put it in, and if he has hair he'll think it's your hair. You'll be in the dark anyway.

Thirteen-year-old girl: I got a little bit (exposes repeatedly and rubs).

Fourteen-year-old girl: I got some too (exposes).

Thirteen-year-old girl: *(laughs) Mine is straight (repeats several times), yours is all curled up.*

Fourteen-year-old girl: *When I wash it, it's long and straight. (To twelve-year old): Let me coach you, honey; see, when he is grinding, there is a hard bone down there and it is cushioned with hair.*

Twelve-year-old girl, interrupting: *But I don't have any hair.*

Fourteen-year-old girl: *That's all right.*

Thirteen-year-old girl breaks in conversation: *How do you know when he's come off in you?*

Fourteen-year-old girl: *You can feel it, it's warm.*

Thirteen-year-old girl: *I had some last night.*

Fourteen-year-old girl: *I know, you wouldn't give me a chance.*

Thirteen-year-old girl: *If I am pregnant, I want you to come to the hospital with me, hear? I been missing two weeks.*

Fourteen-year-old girl: *Now, girl, if you're pregnant, you have a long talk with him. Tell him you know he's got a lot of girls but as long as you're the ace girl.*

Thirteen-year-old girl: *That's what my mother told me, as long as I am the ace.*

Fourteen-year-old girl: *Tell him you want him to marry you to give the baby a father. Ask him about the baby's name.*

Thirteen-year-old girl: *Do you think he loves me?*

Fourteen-year-old girl: *Yeah, girl. (Continues to drink).*
(1981:127)

The middle-class dream is a joke to most of the members of youth gangs in Detroit. Eighteen-year-old Hank has learned that his girlfriend is pregnant and he wonders if maybe they *could* marry (C. Taylor 1990:49-50): "I could get a real job maybe, getting married to Debbie would be OK, she gets a word-processing job when she graduates from business academy next month. This crew shit ain't paying much. . . . Deb's cool people, we could get a apartment and just chill for awhile. Anyway, Lee, what do you know about getting married or babies?" Lee, at 14, knows all he needs to know: "Sucker. I know that marriage is for suckers, later for that bitch, let her have the baby. You ain't got to marry nobody 'cause they going to have a baby. . . . How you going to get a job, you ain't finish school, you can't do nothing but steal and sell dope, fool." And 17-year-old Marvin chimes in; no one *he* knows will have the kind of life depicted in a popular television show:

Babies ain't no big thing. I got four kids by different babes. Lee is right, you ain't got to marry no babe just because she's having your baby. Me, I don't do nothing for mine. I figure like this, didn't nobody give a damn bout me and I made it so they'll be OK, just like me. One of the babes I got fat had her brother and mother talking that marriage stuff, I just looked at them and laughed. . . . Right, get married and be like my man Bill Cosby with the def kids [laughing]. I'm a terrorist, a gangster. I don't want no family, the fellas, they my family. . . . I don't want no babe and I ain't got no time for no marriage life. What you going to get married for? I see all the players and they ain't married. If you know a bitch, why marry her? You already got her. . . . Marriage is for fools, you can shack up, but who needs marriage? When you tired of a bitch fuck her and kick her ass to the curb. . . . That is what my old man did to my momma. . . .

No ambivalence there.

The fact that pregnancies are unplanned does not mean that they are always unwanted, of course—but what if they *are?* The "limited alternatives" to these that Rainwater (1970) speaks of—whether the options of abortion or adoption or keeping the child—have all shown distinctive patterns among low-income African-American families. There has been a good deal written about the African-American extended family with its emphasis on cooperating networks of consanguineal kin (C. Johnson 1934; Schulz 1969; Ladner 1971; Ward 1971; Stack 1974; Aschenbrenner 1975; R. Hill 1977; E. Martin and Martin 1978; Kennedy 1980). A new mother—especially a very young one—is at less of a disadvantage if she can count on help from her own mother (Felice et al. 1987; Giblin, Poland, and Sachs 1987; Norbeck and Anderson 1989). Even a woman living by herself is not necessarily socially isolated if she is a member of such a network; in one study of 140 pregnant African-American women living in Cleveland nearly 80 percent of women living alone said that they considered themselves to be members of intergenerational families (Reeb et al. 1986). If family members live in separate households these "often operate almost as one unit and movement of personnel between houses is without formality. . . . It is sometimes ambiguous where one household unit ends and another begins in terms of the functions and personnel of the household" (Dougherty 1978:17).

Any family member in need may therefore be rather easily incorporated into these households, including newborn members. These tiniest of kinsmen are not lost to the kin group, then, even if—for whatever reasons—marriage and the setting up of an independent household is not an option for the parents. In some instances a pattern of informal adoption within the network of cooperating kin—often referred as the "giving away" of children—helps insure that babies and children are looked after. This practice will be discussed in greater detail in the next chapter.

The importance of blood kin and the fact that there are culturally approved ways of caring for the babies born into extended families is also reflected in attitudes toward abortion. Traditionally, African-Americans have rather strongly equated abortions with murder of the innocent so that there is a consequent disapproval of the practice on moral grounds. "I know one thing. You couldn't pay me to destroy a baby"—said one elderly midwife—"They'll never get in my way from goin to heaven when I die" (Logan 1989:116).

In a survey in the Pruitt-Igoe housing project in St. Louis 90 percent of male and 94 percent of female respondents said that they disapproved of abortion as an alternative in a hypothetical teen-age pregnancy, though some said that abortions might be allowed "for health reasons" (Ladner 1971:257). The women interviewed by Frankel in a Philadelphia maternity ward had very negative views of abortion; it was "morally disapproved, and in addition greatly feared, and no woman interviewed ever admitted to having attempted to produce an abortion in herself or anyone else." Many women, however, were "quite ready to discuss the various methods they had heard of, their relative efficacy, and their possible consequences" (1977:64). "My mother wouldn't let my cousin even come to the house, the first time I was pregnant," said one. "She didn't tell me then, but later I found out it was because she was afraid she'd tell me about getting an abortion, 'cause she'd had a whole bunch of them. And my mother told me not to let *anybody* take me to anyone who said they could get rid of the baby" (p. 66). Carrington suggested that women are "divided" in their opinions about the matter and that teenagers are most vocal in their opposition to abortion (1978). And although nearly half of the African-American women interviewed by Shedlin in a New York City welfare hotel reported having had a previous abortion, they expressed much stronger feelings against it than did the Hispanic women in the sample. Said one, "No abortions . . . that's why I got them kids. I can't kill no kids. . . . " (1989:16).

Despite these strong feelings it is also a fact that some girls and women have not elected/do not elect to continue a pregnancy—and their abortion choices may be part of the orthodox *or* the traditional medical systems. The availability of legal medical abortions is very much a part of shifting public policy, of course, and these policy changes may have a very direct impact on maternal and child health (Joyce 1987; Boone 1989:29–31, 34, 187–188).[6] But there have always been traditional methods of ridding the body of an unwanted fetus as well, and these methods do *not* depend on political issues. They are part and parcel of the traditional lore of pregnancy and will no doubt continue to be tried by some girls/women who see no other way out of a difficult situation; some of these methods are innocuous and some are life-threatening. They include trauma, for example, jumping off high places; the introduction of objects into the uterus; sitting in a tub of very hot water; soaking the feet in a tub of water containing some substance; douching with various products; inhaling the fumes of/or squatting over a pot of some boiling substance; and rubbing the area around the navel with some substance; and the ingestion of substances (Puckett 1926:332; Cameron 1930:25–26; Hand

1961:6–7; Murphree 1968; Ladner 1971:258; Harrison 1975/1976; Frankel 1977:63–65).

Some of these methods are based on ideas about how the body works—heat "opens" the pores and the veins, for example, so perhaps it will "open" the uterus. Some products are used because they are believed to have a "penetrating" and "cutting" effect: The same mustard or turpentine that may be placed on the chest to "cut" a cold may also be swallowed or rubbed on the belly to "cut" the embryo, for example, or paint fumes inhaled with similar effect. Substances such as quinine, nutmeg, and various herbal products are swallowed because they are known to promote uterine contractions. And some other products used seem to have a strongly symbolic appeal: red pepper, gunpowder, and buckshot, for example, to expel the unwanted fetus. Number magic is often employed as well: Directions may call for nine buckshot to be swallowed or some other method be tried for nine days. The following story was told to me by Arlene Bauer; it is illustrative both of method and perceived effect:

> Well, Nonie got pregnant [and] she didn't want to be pregnant. She used turpentine on her navel; I don't know if she took any internally. But in the early months of pregnancy she took two bottles of castor oil, but she was too far along to induce any abortion and all it did was just about shit her to death. If you're early enough, in the early stages of pregnancy, it will kill the embryo and release it. You can use castor oil in early, early stages; turpentine has to be used in the later stages. I don't think she took the turpentine; she used it on her navel. But that castor oil just about killed her! I fed her peanut butter and cheese until it was running out her eyeballs. (Haslett, Michigan; 1975)

More recently Hallie Wilmot—who likes to try out various home remedies that she hears of—recounted two methods of abortion that she had heard about. The first she learned from a coworker and involved swallowing a mixture of turpentine, quinine, and 100-proof whiskey: "She said that she had used it once [and] it worked but she almost bled to death. Probably wouldn't use it myself." The second method was espoused by a local physician who had "lost her license after being railroaded by the medical establishment." It consisted of a cup or two/day of a tea made of tansy, squaw vine, and pennyroyal, brewed "medium strength" and taken for a week. Hallie had "never had the opportunity to try this, but am assured that it works and is safe." (Detroit, Michigan; 1984) The belief that herbal products are more natural and therefore safer may lead to the ingestion of potentially toxic substances such as pennyroyal and nutmeg (Payne 1963; Fatality and Illness Associated with Consumption of Pennyroyal Oil—Colorado 1978; Tyler 1987:178–179).

When Marya Smith became pregnant for the first time as a teenager she was afraid to tell Bernita, her mother. If she aborted the baby, she thought, her mother would never need to know. She first

tried jumping off of the house and when this did not do the trick
she enlisted the help of her younger brothers and sisters. If they
jumped up and down on her stomach surely she would lose the
baby:

> I was sorry that I had did what I did and got pregnant. And Mama
> don't believe in killin', y'know. Doin' away with babies. But I got on
> top the house and jumped down. [And] I had the kids jump up and
> down on my stomach; stand up on my stomach and jump up and
> down. I was pretendin' I was doin' some exercise. And you know no-
> body exercise nobody's stomach, but that's what I was doin'. And my
> Mama found out. They was tellin' her, "Mama, Marya's got a soft stom-
> ach, we like to bounce up and down!" And she says, "What you got
> those kids doin'?" And I couldn't lie; I had to tell her. And then she
> said, "Don't you ever do that again!" 'Cause she knew what I was
> tryin' to do. So she said she wouldn't let me do that and told me not
> to do that again. (Lansing, Michigan; 1982)

Both mother and daughter were pregnant at the same time, in fact,
and ironically it was Bernita whose unborn baby died in an episode
of domestic violence. Marya continued her pregnancy and gave birth
to her first daughter, Josie. Seventeen years later when Josie discovered that she was pregnant for the third time in two years she
thought about having an abortion; this time it was Marya who
denounced it as "murder." Josie later miscarried—and when she became pregnant for the fourth time the following year she had the
child.

When pregnancies are maintained, ideas about what must be done
to insure the birth of a healthy child vary widely; so do explanations
for why things sometimes go wrong. In the traditional view, pregnancy—though a time of potential danger—may be seen as a normal
and natural part of a woman's life requiring careful behavior but
little expert intervention. Women, after all, have had babies since
time immemorial. In the view of health professionals, in contrast,
pregnancy is viewed as a medical event requiring constant monitoring and the probable use of increasingly high-technology interven-
tions. There may be considerable disagreement between health
professionals and many of their patients on the importance of prenatal care and when it should commence. Health professionals see
early entry into the health care system as essential in helping to
prevent poor pregnancy outcomes. Margaret Boone describes the
devastating problems in perinatal health among disadvantaged African-American women in Washington, D.C., and concludes that to
solve them prenatal care must be the first priority:

> *Whatever program innovations of a social, psychological, or culturally*
> *tailored nature are introduced, they should eventually contribute toward*
> *an increased use of prenatal services for minority women. The importance*
> *and effectiveness of prenatal care for inner-city Black women are clear,*

*and their necessity is an inescapable conclusion of the detailed analysis
in this book [Capital Crime]. When women are compared along important
demographic, social structural, and lifestyle dimensions, they are
repeatedly differentiated according to prenatal care. . . . (1989:21–22)*

For a variety of reasons many of these women do not receive adequate prenatal care even when it is available, however, and these
findings are mirrored in other studies. More than half of a group of
adolescents followed through their pregnancy and the first postpartum year in Detroit were first examined at 20 weeks' gestation or
later (Poland and Beane 1980). Shedlin noted that for their last
pregnancy many of the poor African-American and Hispanic women
in a New York welfare hotel either received no care at all or had
waited until between their fourth and sixth months to seek it
(1989:17). Similarly, less than one-third (30.8 percent) of low-income
African-American, White, and American Indian women who had
recently given birth in a midwestern city were judged to have had
adequate care during their pregnancies (Lia-Hoagberg et al. 1990).
Lack of prenatal care is not limited to metropolitan areas: In rural
Georgia only 5 percent of African-American women were reported
to visit a doctor regularly during pregnancy, compared to over 60
percent of White women in the same area (C. Hill 1988:88).

Such statistics do not necessarily mean that women do not know
of the importance of prenatal care, however; certainly many of them
are aware of the fact that *health professionals* feel that it is important. Virtually every woman interviewed in the Lansing prenatal
clinic said that a woman should seek such care early in a pregnancy,
for example—but if they believed this their actions did not match
their words. A later review of their medical charts revealed that, in
fact, only one out of four of them had initiated prenatal care in the
first trimester of pregnancy; their average first prenatal appointment
was in the 21st week of gestation. This tendency on the part of the
patients to tell interviewers what they wanted to hear occurred
around a number of issues; it seemed to take place most often when
the women felt that they would be scolded for their own beliefs
and practices (Snow, Johnson, and Mayhew 1978). In another study
"almost all" women acknowledged that prenatal care was important,
yet again this did not always encourage them to seek it out: Forty-
four percent of those who were assessed as having received inadequate care "remained unmotivated to obtain adequate care" (Lia-
Hoagberg et al. 1990).

Why do women say one thing but do another? There is no single
answer to this question. Illicit drug use is highly correlated with
inadequate and/or no care for some women (Poland, Ager, and Olson
1987; Boone 1989; Shedlin 1989) but certainly not for all. Some
women find that their experiences in clinical settings are so unpleasant that it is not worth the effort to continue. Still others are
unimpressed by what occurs during the prenatal visit: "Some young

women have said to me," reported Carrington (1978), "'When I come to the clinic, 'they' never do anything but feel my stomach and then that's it.'" It may be felt that care is more important for some mothers-to-be than for others: Many Detroit women in one study indicated that prenatal care was most important in a first pregnancy, "whereas women who had a baby felt that they already knew how to take care of themselves and needed less care" (Poland, Ager, and Olson 1987). And some women may in fact *agree* that early and continued prenatal care is important but be unable to take advantage of it.

It is clear that women already burdened by poverty and a host of personal and emotional stressors face numerous problems in seeking prenatal care: need for child care; lack of transportation; the almost certain knowledge that they face long periods of waiting in crowded clinics (Snow, Johnson, and Mayhew 1978; Poland and Beane 1980; Boone 1982, 1985, 1989; Lazarus 1988; Shedlin 1989; Lia-Hoagberg et al. 1990). Poor women in Detroit have begun to use emergency walk-in centers for care, even when they feel the physicians there are less competent (Poland, Ager, and Olson 1987) than those in other settings.

Irrespective of the time when prenatal care is initiated it is obvious that the providers and many of the potential users of that care have divergent views of its importance. It can be disconcerting to learn that what one thinks is best can be viewed so differently by another, however, and I must admit that I was shocked when Marya Smith told me of her one and only hospital birth in rural Mississippi. Her first four babies had been born at home, with a midwife in attendance and her mother there to hold her hand when the pains were bad. It was only because she began to hemorrhage that an ambulance was called to take her to a hospital when Sonny, her last baby, was born. *That* must have been a great relief, I said. But no, it was just the opposite: She was so fearful of what would happen to her at the hospital that she prayed that she would die on the way! Marya feared what she had not experienced and I do not know what sorts of stories she might have heard about what happens in a hospital—certainly her mother is deeply afraid of them to this day—but it is a particularly disturbing fact that many poor women hold very bad memories about what they *have* experienced in health care settings. They sometimes find the very people who are charged with helping them to be uncaring, hostile, or even frightening (Boone 1985, 1989:195–196; Giblin and Poland 1985; Poland, Ager, and Olson 1987; C. Hill 1988:136–138; Lazarus 1988; Lia-Hoagberg et al. 1990). Most of a group of 200 poor women who had just delivered an infant at Detroit's Hutzel Hospital

> complained that physicians, nurses, social workers, and clerks were rude, uncommunicative, confusing, nasty, and frightening. Discontinuity of care in large public health or hospital-based clinics was a disincentive

> *to keeping appointments, and the brief contact with a physician was not sufficient reward for the long (often 3-4 hours) waiting times. Women attending walk-in clinics, on the other hand, often saw the same doctor and described the staff as friendly and less hurried and the doctors as less frightening. The hurried, often rude atmosphere of prenatal clinics communicates a lack of interest and concern. If we want poor women to receive quality prenatal care, we must communicate its importance by the manner in which that care is provided.* (Poland et al. 1990:611)

When women have such negative experiences it is perhaps less surprising that they do not seek prenatal care early than that most of them do so at all.[7]

As unfortunate as it is that so many women apparently perceive the staff in health care settings as unhelpful and hateful it would be unfair to label all such individuals in that way. It must also be recognized there are many professionals who continue to struggle to deliver quality care—in settings that are underfunded and under-staffed—to patients who often appear uninterested in their own health. These professionals may find it difficult to understand why a woman with multiple health problems and a poor pregnancy history does not come in the moment she suspects she is pregnant again, for example. And time is such an important commodity to busy middle-class professionals that it is difficult for them not to be annoyed at patients who fail to appear for scheduled appointments. In a clinic that has many such "no-shows," appointments may then be deliberately overbooked to compensate for those patients who fail to appear. This means, of course, that those who do keep their appointments may be penalized by long periods in a crowded waiting room despite the real efforts that they have made to be there. The examination, when it does come, must scarcely seem worth it to the pregnant woman—and it must be necessarily rushed even by a professional who truly wishes to be helpful.

In the Lansing prenatal clinic one-third to one-half of the patients were "no-shows" on any given day so that overbooking was deemed necessary. A woman who had had a long ride on public transportation—often with small children in tow—therefore faced long periods of time in a waiting room crowded with other pregnant women and their small children. This was also frustrating to the staff who sometimes wondered aloud why a woman did not simply call and *say* that she was unable to keep an appointment? This was a very unusual occurrence, however, even for those few women who did have telephones in their homes. Many of the women did not, though most were able to provide a number where they could be reached in case of emergency. The telephone numbers provided might be those of family members, friends or neighbors, a nearby church, a neighborhood corner grocery or bar—anywhere where someone was willing to take a message. The women were aware that they were dependent on the goodwill of others and sometimes commented that they tried not to abuse the privilege. They clearly did not see a telephone as something to simplify their lives, as I believe middle-class people do—instead they truly were something to be used in emergencies.

On one occasion I was able to glimpse more directly the difficulties in getting—and giving—good health care in this publicly funded clinic. Arlene Bauer had been suffering for many months with painful lumps in her breast, and I finally convinced her to see a physician. I pulled some strings so that she could be seen by a particular doctor in the general medical clinic, and the appointment was made. On the scheduled day she arrived promptly only to find the waiting room full; it was one of those times when more than the usual number of patients had come in. Still, she sat patiently for several hours. But as the time neared when she knew her children would be arriving on the schoolbus she became quite anxious; she needed to be home. So did she tell the receptionist her problem? No, she simply stood up and walked out. The next day I had an irate call from the physician to see why my friend had not stayed to be seen—I had asked him to see her and he had tried. And *I* had tried. And *she* had tried. And why had she simply left without explanation? Well, she said, "I was afraid they would be mad."

If you multiply this one small story by 10 or 20 or 50 times—day after day after day—it is easy to see why parties on both sides become frustrated and angry. It will take a good deal of time and attention on the part of health professionals to break this negative cycle—but two recent studies in North Carolina and Florida demonstrate that when extra efforts *are* made to provide and/or coordinate health care to pregnant women their health and that of their infants is greatly improved (Buescher et al. 1991; Nguyen, O'Sullivan, and Fournier 1991).

Pregnancy and Traditional Belief

Pregnant women have multiple sources of information guiding their behavior, of course, and only some of these are "professional." It is a fact that in the United States today most girls/women receive at least some prenatal care in the orthodox setting. It is also a fact that most of their babies are born in hospitals. Even "adequate" prenatal care is measured in mere hours over the course of a pregnancy, however, so that much of the advice, counsel, and support that a woman receives is found outside of the orthodox health care system (Hahn and Muecke 1987). The presence of an extended family network of cooperating relatives is often extremely important to the low-income pregnant woman: If the advice that she receives in a health setting is unwelcome she can always fall back on those upon whose caring she can depend. One woman in rural Georgia found her supportive family and her belief in a loving God much more helpful than a public health nurse, for example: "She went to the public health clinic once to see what they had to say about pregnancy but was 'lectured' by the nurse, so she decided not to go again. 'Anyway, Mama knows more and all they talked about was eating habits. Not to eat this and that and not to gain weight. I believe that doesn't matter. God gave me the baby and He wants it to be healthy, not starved to death. My family knows best'" (Hill 1988:137).

If the counsel offered pregnant girls and women outside the professional system is *also* sometimes unwelcome it is at least balanced by the promise of other sorts of help. The women who are the recipients of unsolicited advice may

> *feel annoyed by the freedom with which such advice is offered, and complain of the "nosiness" of other women at this time in their lives. These are the women, as a rule, who (at least verbally) place their main faith in the advice of doctors, and scoff at most other advice. There are some, however, who seem to enjoy the protectiveness expressed toward them in this manner by older women—especially their mothers. Also, in a very realistic sense, the help of neighbors, friends and relatives can be indispensible among the poor during pregnancy, because they function so close to the margins of existence much of the time. This is especially true when a woman goes into labor and must be taken to the hospital, and her other children looked after for several days. It is worth taking unasked-for advice for a few months to assure that someone will be on call when needed.* (Frankel 1977:65)

And she, of course, may someday be on call for help herself.

The advice that the pregnant woman receives goes beyond being merely a set of do's and don'ts intended to promote physical health; the spiritual and social well-being of both mother and child are involved as well. Traditional pregnancy beliefs address a variety of factors that are seen as advantageous—or dangerous—for the pregnant woman and for her unborn infant. And they describe the strategies that can be invoked to keep both from harm. They demonstrate once again the intimate connection of the individual—in this instance the woman *and* the unborn child that both is and is not part of her body—with the natural, the supernatural, and the social realms of experience. The previous chapter detailed how one aspect of femininity—menstruation—puts a woman at risk while simultaneously allowing her to radiate a power that can negatively affect her immediate environment. The woman who can lay waste an entire garden, that is, may drop dead if she takes a bath. Pregnancy—that time when in Newman's words a woman is in a state of being "supremely female" (1969)—similarly exhibits both risk and the simultaneous radiation of a power which can affect the immediate environment. When this power moves from the woman to the outside world it is usually positive, however, associated with increase instead of devastation. A pregnant woman may be asked to plant a garden or bake, for example, in the hope that her obvious fertility will magically assure that seeds will sprout or bread rise. But the mother-to-be is also the link between her child and the outside world, and the attendant risks are not so much for herself as for her unborn child. I do not mean to imply that pregnancy is not seen as potentially dangerous for the woman, of course; but traditional beliefs about danger to her tend to be connected with the specific process of labor and birth. Beliefs about dangers *during* pregnancy, in contrast, are generally focused on the potential of harm to the developing fetus. The woman who may be asked to plant a garden in the belief that it will bear more fruitfully, that is, may also permanently damage her child by a single careless act.

It was mentioned in the previous chapter that Bernita Washington was profoundly uncomfortable discussing sexual matters; she had been given little information about such matters in her own girl-hood. Today she knows that some of the things that she had been taught are not true—some of these "-isms," as she calls them, she attributes to ignorance—people just did not know any better then, she says. And some were just stories concocted to avoid dealing directly with the topic:

> When we was kids comin' up I was about 11 or 12 years old before I knew that a kid wasn't dig up out of a stumphole! That's what we was always taught. We wasn't taught that women have babies. We was taught that they was dug up out of a stumphole, so we'd always try to go and dig for one. That's what we thought. 'Cause you know how kids is, "If this is what Mom say, I wanta see can I get me one?" You know, "It that easy, I'll get me one!" It ain't like now, sayin', "I can get pregnant; I can have a baby like my Mama had!" It wasn't like that.

> Now kids know that if they get pregnant where the baby comes from. At that time kids didn't know. They didn't know if they was dug out from under a stump. One time they said that the midwife brought them in the *bag!* That's what they taught the kid. "Oh, you'll have a baby tomorrow!" you know—that's what the midwife come to the door and said—"You'll have a baby tomorrow!" The midwife's gonna bring one in the bag! So that's all we knew! We didn't know any better.

At the time (1987) when we had that particular discussion only the two youngest of her seven daughters were childless and, along with a granddaughter, still living in her home. Was she finally able to tell these girls what they needed to know, I asked? No, she said, she did not *have* to tell them—and she was greatly relieved that the school system was providing the information that was so difficult for her to talk about:

> Even the little girl that I got here now [13-year old granddaughter Toni], they will write you a letter or call you from school. "Do you want your kid to look at this sex movie? Do you want your kid to

look at how they have periods, how to take care of themselves?" And they do that at clinics [too]. I say, "Hey, yeah, let mine know." There a lot of time, you know, me, it's [up] to me, I don't know why, but I always felt embarrassed doin' it. But I would do it if I had to. But after they started to showin' it and these kinds of things, I felt more released. Because that way, [there was] a way that they would get over and I didn't have to tell 'em.

Two years later, however, both of the daughters had infants. Bernita then began to keep an even closer eye on 15-year-old Toni. She closely monitored the girl's comings and goings, complained about the style of her clothing, constantly lectured her on the importance of staying in school, and so on. When Toni became pregnant she waited as long as possible before confiding in her grandmother as she—rightly—feared that Bernita would be extremely upset at the news. Of these last three pregnancies not all were in fact unplanned— Toni and one of the daughters had both been "caught"—the other daughter, however, wishing to be married and tired of waiting for the right man, chose to become pregnant. If she was not going to be a wife, she said, at least she could be a mother.

All three of these young women—one a high school sophomore, one a high school graduate, and one with a degree from a local community college—received prenatal care in an orthodox setting. And all three also depended on Bernita's advice during their pregnancies. She may not have *approved* of the pregnancies but, once they were a fact, she did not waste time in scolding her daughters and granddaughter. These babies, after all, would be the newest members of the family, and she saw it as part of her role to assure that they would arrive in this world safe and sound. And Bernita has not relegated *all* of the things that she knows to the category of "-isms." Some of the beliefs that she transmits to the younger generation are unchanged from those that one might find in a century-old collection of folklore; others have been modified to include some of the information that might be passed on at a prenatal clinic. She continues to believe in the possibility of "marking" the child, for example. "I've got ten kids [and] just about all of 'em is *marked* with something!" she says. But she now thinks—without invoking the term "first trimester"—that this is most likely to occur in the first three months of pregnancy.

Signs of Pregnancy

The fact of a pregnancy is revealed in physiological terms, of course, so a question about how a woman knows she is pregnant usually brings mention of the cessation of menstruation, weight gain, breast tenderness and so on. But these are not the only sorts of things mentioned: "Signs" of pregnancy in the traditional system include factors not present in biomedicine, and these may be present in the mother-to-be *or* others in her immediate social network. They can take the form of physical changes, premonitory dreams, and/or behavioral shifts in interpersonal relationships. The importance of the impending addition of a new family member—and the invisible tie among kin—is revealed by the fact that a pregnancy may be known to others even before it is known to the mother-to-be. "My father knew I was pregnant before I even knew," for example. "He could tell by the vein in my neck. He said he could see a double heartbeat in my neck and that was a sign I was pregnant" (Frankel, p. 38). And, of course, older women who suspect that young girls are sexually active are on the lookout for any indication of a pregnancy.

Cassie Seales knew that Ruthie, her daughter, was pregnant before Ruthie knew herself. The older woman was alerted to this fact when she noticed that the girl's skin was "lighter and brighter" than usual. This phenomenon in association with pregnancy has been noted by others (Dougherty 1978:89); Frankel (1977:38) has suggested that a chronic anemia intensified by a pregnancy might indeed cause a woman to look paler. Nor is this "brightening" the only cutaneous manifestation of a pregnancy; Marya Smith says that the skin color changes in pregnancy are the opposite of what is normal for the individual woman. If the skin is light it will darken; if dark it will lighten:

> They get lighter and they get the pinkest cheek! And if you was real light you'd begin to get real dark; real dark. I got a sister like that now! Right, real dark; real, real dark. Like sumpin' is bad wrong with you. Oh, she gets so black and gets bumps all over her face, and her nose get real, real big. Yeah, every time. Real big nose. She is pretty afterward.

> But I was always cuter while I was pregnant; I'd rather be pregnant than to have the baby! When my oldest was born, I thought I was the prettiest thing in the world. Look like my legs got *so* big and pretty; I *love* pretty legs. I tell you, I remember I had some little pink and blue earrings—the little inside was pink, and around it was blue, and it was like a hollyhock flower. And make my face look so round and pretty; [and] look like any way I styled my *hair* was pretty. I lay down and go to sleep at night, not turn it up or anything, or roll it, and it was *just* so pretty. I thought I was the prettiest thing in the world. I wished I had had a picture of that! [I was] Sixteen. (Lansing, Michigan; 1982)

Obviously she had a change of heart during her pregnancy; at some moment the frightened young girl who had begged her brothers and sisters to jump up and down on her stomach became "the prettiest thing in the world"!

The message that someone is pregnant is often delivered via a dream and the pregnancy may be that of oneself, a family member, or friend. Fish are a common theme of these dream-messages (Frankel

1977:38); it is frequently talked of in prenatal clinics in Detroit (Marilyn Poland, personal communication, 1989). Thirty-nine-year old Jackie Forde laughed as she reported that her mother had called from Mississippi to see if she was pregnant again. "At my age!" In fact her mother had called *all* of her grown daughters with the same question. The older woman had been dreaming of sitting on her front porch and fishing in a small puddle in the yard. Her mother would no doubt continue to check with all of the female members of the clan until she located a pregnant woman, said Jackie. And that would "prove" the old belief once again. (East Lansing, Michigan; 1987)

Hallie Wilmot's grandmother was not put off one spring by Hallie's plea of midterm exams at the university; she was to come home to Detroit for the weekend, no excuses. Once there, says Hallie, the old lady "dragged me to the doctor for a pregnancy test because she dreamed about fish for several nights." In this instance it did not take the grandmother long to discover that *someone* in the family was pregnant; it just wasn't Hallie. (Detroit, Michigan; 1984) And in the spring of 1987 a second-year medical student confided to me that she was expecting a baby; she had dreamed of pregnancy three nights in a row and knew that *someone* must be expecting, she said. Still, she was surprised to learn it was herself; she had thought that it was probably her cousin. (Andrea Swan, East Lansing, Michigan)

Behavioral changes are also frequently mentioned as indicators of pregnancy; again, these may occur either in the mother-to-be or in others. Men have a special ability to detect pregnancies, according to Dougherty: "It is sometimes a girl's sexual partner who tells her that she is pregnant. Because women 'be more quarrelish' from the onset of pregnancy, some men know from a woman's attitude that she is pregnant" (Dougherty 1978:89). If a young person is pregnant she may "fade away" from an older person even if they had previously been close, according to one of Frankel's informants. Another woman's behavior was just the opposite, however; "Now, my aunt always knows I'm pregnant before I shows or anything. She says it's because the only time I ever comes to visit her is when I'm pregnant—and that's true, too. I never do visit my aunt except right after I gets pregnant—sometimes before I know it myself" (1977:38).

Precocious behavior in an infant or small child may also alert others that his or her mother is pregnant again. The toddler son of 19-year-old Tina Rowland "sensed" that she was pregnant again even before she knew herself, the new mother reported, expertly disrobing the infant Tiffany for her first well-baby checkup. As a single mother with no relatives in the city, she depended a good deal on the advice about childrearing that is proffered by the elderly woman who lives in the apartment upstairs. It was this old lady who had first commented on little Rashid's precocious behavior, in fact. After observing that the baby boy had crawled up the stairs at two months of age and then began walking at seven months, she had said to Tina, "Girl, you're fixin' to have another baby! He's doing things too fast!" The little boy instinctively knew that he would have to "grow up sooner," she said. His time of being "the baby" was about to be curtailed by the arrival of a new brother or sister. (Lansing, Michigan; 1986)

Selection of Gender

How the gender of a child is determined is also very differently viewed in biomedical and traditional terms. Some believe that a mother and father can deliberately create a boy or girl by their actions. Occasionally the principle of opposition is invoked; if your first-born is a boy and you want a girl, for example, simply turn the marital bed around (Hand 1961:28). Or, should the father carry a leather string in his pocket during intercourse, "It will bring a boy" (Murphree 1968). Another method depends on the association of left and right with gender. The idea that femaleness is connected to the left and maleness with the right is a centuries-old belief that is still encountered today (Murphree 1968; Emrich 1972; Meigs 1982). The belief that eggs of one gender only are produced by each ovary— girls by the left and boys by the right—was stated by several women in the Lansing prenatal clinic. A woman who wishes to choose the sex of her child need only turn and lie on the requisite side immediately after intercourse to send the sperm to the correct ovary. One young woman was even *more* specific: "Just have your husband point in the right direction at the last minute," she said. "If you know what I mean." (1975)

Prenatal Determination of Gender

Once a pregnancy is established the interesting matter of the gender of the coming child becomes a topic of discussion. Newman (1969) encountered a large number of such beliefs among pregnant White women but found that they appeared "hardly at all" among her African-American respondents. Frankel (1977), in contrast, discovered a wide range of such beliefs among the women she interviewed in Philadelphia. My experience mirrors Frankel's; though I do not believe I have ever heard one mention a *deliberate* attempt to determine gender of the unborn, the African-American women I have spoken with often read "signs" that indicate whether a coming child will be a boy or a girl. Some of these signs are probably familiar to most readers: The child is carried high/low and is therefore a boy (or girl); the abdomen is round/pointed and the child is therefore a girl (or boy); the child is positioned in the front/back and is therefore a boy (or girl), and so on. Some of the more interesting of the gender predictors are those containing some statement of what boys and girls (or men and women) are like—or should be like. The unborn child is very active (or lazy) and is therefore a boy (or girl), for example. Or a pregnant woman who becomes prettier is carrying a boy—if she "loses her looks" she is "donating" them to her unborn daughter; it is important for girls to be pretty. If the pregnant woman cannot stand the smell of perfume her baby must be a boy; everyone knows that girls like to smell nice. And Bernita Washington heard from "the old folks" that if a woman's hair grows rapidly during pregnancy the child will be a girl and if it breaks off or falls out, a boy. But, "That's just another of those old -isms," she says. She lost hair during *all* of her pregnancies and seven of those produced baby girls!

Particular sorts of behavioral patterns are also associated with determining the sex of the unborn child. Again these may invoke the principle of opposition—as in the belief that if a child's first word is "Mama" the next child will be a boy (Hand 1961:28). And just as a toddler can "sense" that the mother is pregnant again, he or she may also be able to tell if the newcomer will be a sister or a brother. This prescience may sometimes be extended to include more distant family members as well: Marya Smith knew that a coming grandchild would be a girl months before the birth, for example. She has heard some of the younger women in her family speak of ultrasound and amniocentesis and such, and she presumes that these are good "new" ways of predetermining gender. Her own knowledge, however, came from her observations of her little grandson, Mikey. Mikey began behaving in a "babyish" manner soon after Josie, his mother, brought home a new brother; he refused to look at the new infant and ignored Josie. Instead he began to follow his young aunt around the house—holding on to her skirts and hanging around her knees—though previously he had wanted to have little to do with the teenaged Dodie. It was all made clear a few days later when Dodie announced that *she* was pregnant: Mikey had not only "known" this, says Marya, but he knew the new baby would be a girl. If it were a boy Mikey would not have had anything to *do* with Dodie: "You know how mens is, and womens," said Marya. But, she went on, "He loves her—Mikey just loves her. It's an old sign, but a good one." Sure enough, some months later Dodie gave birth to a daughter. In this instance what Marya took to be the little boy's knowledge of a coming girl-cousin *I* took to be jealousy of his new baby brother, a view which I kept to myself. (Lansing, Michigan; 1983)

The Doctrine of Maternal Impressions

The fact that many African-American women do not receive the amount of prenatal care deemed necessary by health care professionals has already been discussed, as well as some of the reasons why this might be so. It must also be recognized that for many of these women traditional beliefs about what affects a fetus provide culturally appropriate explanations for pregnancy outcomes.

A wide range of seemingly disparate ideas about pregnancy are understandable if they are viewed as an ongoing exchange of communications between the unborn child and the outer world. "I am here!" and "I am a girl!"—even the tiniest of fetuses is able to alert the mother or father, grandmothers, small cousins, or siblings. But the messages go in both directions and the unborn child is also affected by the outside world in a second-hand way via the mother's behavior. The age-old Doctrine of Maternal Impressions, usually referred to as "marking the child," is still very much a part of the lore of childbirth. It was the most commonly mentioned area of concern by the African-American women seen by Newman in California (1969); such beliefs were more widespread than any others among Frankel's sample of Philadelphia women (1977:51); and the possibility was subscribed to by 77 percent of the women we spoke with in Michigan (Snow, Johnson, and Mayhew 1978).[8] Traditional beliefs about childbirth were also commonly encountered by Roberson in rural Virginia, where they "did not vary with demographic characteristics. Male and female, young and old, educated and uneducated informants were all knowledgeable . . ." (1983:130).

The underlying premise of prenatal marking is that whatever happens to the mother also happens to the unborn child. She experiences the outside world by means of her senses and her emotional responses are transmitted inward; they may be further intensified by her touch. Because the child is in such a tender and fragile state it is sensitive to every nuance of the mother-to-be's behavior: Any sort of excess on her part—whether in physical work, patterns of eating and sleeping, emotional responses to day-to-day occurrences, or interactions with others—can overwhelm it. The womb is not so much a safe haven for this smallest and most vulnerable of persons, then, as it is a dark trap where he or she is at the mercy of the mother's every thought and deed.

The theme of moderation and avoidance of excess that so often appears in African-American traditional medicine is nowhere more emphasized than during pregnancy. Unfortunately this is more easily accomplished in word than in deed. No woman is able to control everything that happens throughout her pregnancy, of course, and she may spend weeks or months worrying about something that she was unable to prevent happening. And if she has previously suffered a miscarriage, stillbirth, or neonatal death she may already be carrying a burden of guilt: She may not understand a doctor's explanation of why things went so wrong, but she will certainly understand the words of her mother or her pastor. If her child is stillborn, sickly, or deformed she may be blamed by others—and blame herself as well.

Imprudent Physical Activity

The results of maternal behavior may be expressed in the child's emotional and/or bodily makeup. Some sorts of activities have a general weakening effect; many women, for example believe that working too hard can cause a miscarriage. "I quit work right away, as soon as I knew I was pregnant," said one of Frankel's informants, "after them two miscarriages I had." Other women may review their own experience, however, and note that it did not hurt *them* (1977:43, 51). Bernita Washington believes that the younger women of today are both weak *and* lazy; she had no choice but to work hard during her pregnancies:

> Some women say, "I can't do this; I can't do that." But you can do your housework; you can do all of your housework! Such as your cookin' and your washin' and ironin'—you can do all of that. You know what I'm sayin'? Such as your factory work; if you got to go into the factory and work, you can work as long as you can. Do you know what I'm sayin'? It's not anything but an excuse because they don't want to do anything. But some peoples are sick, some peoples get sick more than others—but still, the more you do the better you feel. I used to be like that; I used to be so sick 'til it look like I couldn't hold my head up.

> But I still went to work. I still chopped cotton seven days a week. Yeah, I chopped cotton seven days a week. I would be pregnant; I would be pregnant and I would go to the field and I would pick 2- and 300 pounds of cotton a day. Carry it on my back, 100, at least 105 pounds, on my back. Carry it maybe a half a mile, maybe two miles. My cotton gotta come back to the trailer; you have to carry it and get it back there yourself, they didn't come to you. And go back home the next day or the next night, have my baby. But like I say, people was *then, womens* wasn't as weak as they are now, *then.*

Virtually all of the women in the Lansing clinic, however (87 percent), expressed the fear (Snow, Johnson, and Mayhew 1978) that hard physical labor might cause them to miscarry.[9]

The sorts of work that a pregnant woman should not do are also discussed; heavy lifting is nearly always mentioned as potentially dangerous, for example. Nor should a pregnant woman do any painting; the paint fumes have a "cutting" effect and may cause her to miscarry. (For this reason breathing paint fumes is sometimes mentioned as a means of abortion.) The most commonly proscribed behavior, however—and one that is found in a variety of cultural settings—involves any activity that would require her to lift her arms over her head (Kay 1982:12). Hanging up clothes, reaching up to put something away in a kitchen cupboard, and so forth, may cause the umbilical cord to wrap around the neck of the baby and strangle it (Cameron 1930:21; Snow, Johnson, and Mayhew 1978). This was the most common belief elicited by Newman from both her White and African-American respondents (1969).

Again, an individual woman's own experiences color her own beliefs: One woman in Frankel's study said that it was nothing but an "old superstition," for example, noting that "as hard as I done worked with all of my pregnancies I never had that happen to a one of my (eight) children." Another woman, however, had given birth to a child born with the cord wrapped around its neck: The doctor "told me it must have strangled because I reached up too much while I was pregnant. . . . He said it must have been something like that, because he didn't see how the cord would have gotten extended like that otherwise" (p. 59). Jimmie Lee Fox has always heard it but does not believe it—she has seven healthy children "and did plenty of hard work even when pregnant," including hanging out clothes. (Saginaw, Michigan; 1981) Two women in Roberson's study also discounted the possibility as it had not happened to them; another woman, however, "had a baby with the cord wrapped around its neck, and did not 'reach up' in subsequent pregnancies" (1983:128). It is occasionally said that the baby, too, reaches out its arms when the mother lifts hers, thus entangling itself in the cord.

Imprudent Diet: Food Cravings

The dangerous practices described above—working too hard or doing certain sorts of work—are relatively straightforward. Either the mother has weakened her own system (and thereby weakened the infant) or by stretching her arms has allowed the umbilical cord to elongate and wind around the infant's head. If the child *also* stretches out its arms, of course, there is a component of imitative magic. Such a magical component is very much part of some beliefs about the marking of children, in fact. The mark, that is, may exactly duplicate whatever it was that the mother experienced—and if she touches herself at the same time it may be located on the infant in precisely the same spot. This is particularly true in the stories of strong emotional states marking children; these describe everything from the pregnant woman's dietary habits to her interpersonal relationships. In some instances the negative effects of emotional arousal cannot be stopped; in others quick intervention can preclude harm.

One warm Arizona afternoon I was sitting with Anna Perry in her living room when a young girl came up on the porch and knocked on the screen door; Anna went to the door and I heard the girl ask for something. "All right," said Anna, "I got that." She did not let the girl in but instead disappeared into the kitchen and returned a few moments later with a handful of saltine crackers. She unhooked the screen and handed these to the girl, who thanked her and then disappeared down the steps. It seemed rather odd and I asked Anna who the girl was; she replied that she didn't know. This seemed even odder as Anna was usually very wary of strangers in the neighborhood. Well, then why had she given her the crackers, I asked? "Because she was pregnant," was the answer. If she *didn't* get what she craved, she went on—especially if she touched her body—she would mark that child for sure. And since a pregnant woman never knew when "a craving" might come on it was all right for her to approach anyone at all to ask for that food. The usual rules of social intercourse were suspended, then, in the interest of the unborn child. (1971)

Such ideas may contribute to the failure of some pregnant women to heed the nutritional advice that they are given in medical settings. Should a pregnant woman change her diet? we asked the women in the Lansing prenatal clinic. And if so, what changes should she make? Virtually every woman responded that she should indeed change her diet—a pregnant woman, they said, should eliminate all "junk food," drink lots of milk, eat plenty of fresh fruits and vegetables, and so on. But as in the case of our question about their entry into prenatal care, what they said was not necessarily what they did. Not a one volunteered that they were consuming starch, clay, the heads of matches, and other such nonfood items, for example. And not a one said that it was imperative that a woman indulge in any food she craved lest she mark her child, although nearly all of them believed it to be true. Had we asked only the questions on diet per se we would have been told nothing about these other practices. (One set of alternative dietary practices emerged in answer to the question, Is it possible to mark a child during pregnancy? The other responses were to direct questions about clay and/or starch consumption.)

The diet plays an important role in African-American beliefs about health, as has already been noted, so it is not surprising that it figures largely in pregnancy beliefs as well. The *reasons* that a pregnant woman must be careful of what she eats may be vastly different in the orthodox and traditional views, however. In the former instance these are based on the contribution of the chemical components of food to the physiological needs of the developing fetus—the required amounts of protein, carbohydrates, trace elements, and so on—and these are generalized to *all* developing fetuses. In traditional belief there is much less talk of such matters; just *what* is in the pregnant woman's diet is less dependent on what is "good" for developing fetuses than it is on personalizing it for this particular child. There is less emphasis on generalized nutritional requirements, then, than on the recognition that this tiny human already has likes and dislike. "I *want* that," he or she signals the mother via a craving for sausage or pizza or sweet potato pie. And because unsatisfied cravings can mark the child physically or emotionally it is important to consume the item even if it is something the doctor says is not good for you.

The theme of moderation that is so important during pregnancy affects both how much and what a woman eats. Those who were raised in rural areas and had their babies at home often heard frightening stories of heedless women who were "greedy" and paid for it with their lives. When Marya Smith was pregnant for the first time she was terribly afraid that she would have such an "overweight" child:

Oh, yes, there's lotsa womens hemorrhaged to death; there's a many a womens at that time died in childbirth. There's womens that had babies overweighted and they couldn't afford to bring them into the world! The baby was too large! They was younger womens and they didn't have nobody to teach 'em that you should eat this and you shouldn't eat that, and you shouldn't eat so much. But they just, whatever they want to eat! And whenever they got ready to eat! And you know when you're pregnant you're kinda greedy, you know? And I guess you more greedy then. So now we don't get as greedy 'cause we don't want all that big baby, you know. So they just ate and ate. This one girl, I guess she was 13 years old and the baby weighed 13 pounds. She did not die but she had conversion [convulsions] and five midwives and they had to rush her to the hospital.

Where would a woman get prenatal instruction about such things, I asked? At a clinic?

The mother or some older lady had to tell her. There was no place to take her for to get no special instruction; the midwife didn't come 'til time for her to have the baby. Only thing we had was a clinic [where] they would use the back of the church on certain days of the week. And I don't care where you lived, you had to meet that clinic day or you wouldn't know how you gettin' along. Well, as I grew up I went to the clinic, always. But my mother sometimes never saw nobody but the midwife after nine months! 'Cause some places they was too far to go and they didn't have a ride. And you had to work. You couldn't say, "Well, I go to the clinic for a half a day and another half I work." You was a whole day and part of the night goin' and gettin' back! So if she's already pregnant, it's a little too far for her to walk most of the time.

I went to this clinic and there'd be a nurse there once a month. And I went and they would give you a little thing about pregnancy, not very much. How to prop your feet up when they swell, what to put on it when they swell—and they don't have to tell you [that] in the first place! And they would examine you. But they didn't give you instructions really in how to take care of yourself because you wasn't seein' 'em but once a month. So you only get to see 'em six or seven times because you don't *see* 'em in the first three months after you're pregnant. You gotta be sure you're pregnant before you go to the clinic. Or even go to the hospital if you ain't sure, [if] you think it's some other kinda *problem* because the clinic couldn't take *care* of that. So you had to be absolutely sure that you're pregnant and then you go to the clinic. And then you get to see 'em about six times.

Was she given any instructions about what to eat or not eat? Yes, but from her mother, not the nurse:

My mother knew because older peoples told her. My mother did tell me that fat food—rice, spaghettis, stuff like that—would make you have overweight baby, you know. And a lotta bread. So I eat a lotta greens and a lot of buttermilk which didn't have very much fat. I ate quite a bit of it with my first kid. And that helped make my kid healthy, too, by eatin' milk and bread and greens. Green peas, tomatoes, stuff like that. And that's what I ate. Now that's all I ate with my first child, because I was afraid I'd have a overweight child and I wouldn't be able to . . . because I seen my mother go through so much. And I was really nervous bein' pregnant; and I was so scared that my child was gonna be stillborn. She were pregnant and I were pregnant.

No doubt her fear of a stillbirth was intensified by the fact that her mother's parallel pregnancy had ended so violently.

The belief that a child can be marked by the mother's failure to consume a craved food—particularly if she touches herself at the same time—is found in virtually every description of birthlore (Cameron 1930:22; Hand 1961:18–19; Murphree 1968; Newman 1969; Frankel 1977; Snow and Johnson 1978; Carrington 1978; Dance 1978:309; Kay 1982:11; Roberson 1983:125). The importance of moderation is again underscored by the fact that the mother-to-be may also mark a child by eating *too much* of a desired food. The marks are not always physical: A child may always crave the food he/she did not get *in utero* or, in contrast, may always have a loathing for a food if the mother ate too much of it. More commonly, though, the child will bear a mark of the particular food on his or her body exactly where the mother touched herself. Such birthmarks are usually seen as fairly innocuous unless, of course, they are disfiguring. One young woman in the Lansing prenatal clinic, for example, said that if a pregnant woman craves chicken and does not get it the baby might "come looking like a chicken" or have chicken skin on its body. Another thought that unsatisfied cravings could produce mental retardation in a child, causing it to "go around with its mouth hanging open all the time" (Snow, Johnson, and Mayhew 1978).

As mentioned, Bernita Washington marked all ten of her children in one way or another—and when her older daughters began their own youthful childbearing they were able to observe the marks "put on" one another by their mother's behavior and so were careful to heed her advice. One of these marks is particularly interesting because it again underscores the closeness of the tie between human beings and the natural world—and the importance of the coming child to the kin group and the community as a whole. I had asked Marya if she agreed with her mother that it was important that a pregnant woman have a food she craved and she answered:

That was very important; it was just some old way of thinkin' that they should have it or it would make the baby greedy, or come here hungry or be hungry, or whatever. They would make sure she have it: If she wanted grapes, "You get up and go get that girl grapes," you know. That's what the mother would say to the son-in-law or the daddy or whoever, somebody else. "You go get those grapes!" She wanted watermelon, "Go pull her a watermelon." You go to some other peoples' house [and] somethin' you see that you want, they would give it to you. You got to give it to her. I don't care how mean they was, how much they didn't like to divide, how stingy they was—they would give it to you if you was pregnant. They would feed you, I guess, whatever you wanted.

What would happen if she did *not* get the food, I asked? She told me of the possibility of a birthmark—said she did not believe in it—then went on to give an example anyway:

A birth mark. Yeah, make a birth mark. My sister have a big cabbage on her shoulder [laughs]. I don't believe this stuff, but I'm tellin' you anyway. My Ma say she see this big old green cabbage in this lady's garden and she aksed for it. And the lady didn't give it. And she say, "Oooh, you could give me that!" And the baby came with a green cabbage. And time to plant the cabbage, that spot turn real real green and you can see it real good! It's so pretty, it looks like someone made it on her; it is pretty. It get green, oh, it get beautiful. You oughta see it when she was a little fat baby; it sits up there on her shoulder. That was a prettiest little thing you ever wanted to see.

This is the only example of such a connection that I have encountered; Roberson, however, also reported the belief that a birthmark will "deepen in color during the season of a food. A strawberry mark will grow redder, a blackberry mark, blacker."

Imprudent Diet: Pica

The propensity for pregnant women to consume items not usually considered to be food—most commonly clay, starch, or ice—is well known and often viewed as abnormal behavior. According to one dictionary, pica, as it is called, is defined as "a craving for unnatural food, as seen in hysteria and pregnancy" (*The American Heritage Dictionary of the English Language*" 1969:990). Nor does the practice fare much better in medical books: It is listed under "Eating Disorders" in the *Diagnostic and Statistical Manual of Mental Disorders* (1987), where it is defined as "the persistent eating of a nonnutritive substance." It is said to be "rare in normal adults, but is occasionally seen in young children, in persons with Mental Retardation, and in pregnant females" (1987:69).

Still, even professionals do not always agree as to whether the practice of clay-eating is to be deplored or recognized as a method of introducing minerals into the diet of the pregnant woman (for a review of the literature see Prince 1989); certainly it has a long history both in Africa and the New World (Hunter 1973, 1984; Hunter and De Kleine 1984). Women who chewed ice or ate starch during pregnancy in Boone's (1982) study, in fact, were more likely to have given birth to a normal weight infant than those who did not. Other items consumed by pregnant women—gleaned from just three studies—include baking soda, baking powder, ashes, dirt, sand, lemon peel soaked in koolade, the heads of matches, matchboxes, undissolved Alka Seltzer tablets, milk of magnesia in cake form, mortar, and the dust from soft red bricks (Frankel 1977; Snow, Johnson, and Mayhew 1978; Roberson 1983).

Disorder or no, the consumption of nonfoods may also be culturally patterned and seen as perfectly normal and expected behavior for pregnant women. Some feel that starch- or clay-eating should be instituted in pregnancy in much the same way that a physician might prescribe prenatal vitamin and mineral supplements. First-year medical student Carl Montgomery recalled how upset his newly pregnant wife had been when he bought her a box of laundry starch to eat; she had been reared in Puerto Rico and had never heard of such a thing. *His* mother, however, was from rural Mississippi and had raised nine healthy children—and she had eaten starch during every pregnancy. (East Lansing, Michigan; 1980) Eating starch and/or clay will bring a fat and therefore healthy baby according to some women (Carrington 1978); others believe that eating starch will make delivery easier. Starch is "slick" to the touch, after all, so a starch-covered baby will just "slide out." Still other women simply say such things as, "All the women in my family do it." One Lansing prenatal patient actually said that she did *not* think it was a good idea, in fact, but ate both clay and starch anyway as it was in her tradition (Snow and Johnson 1978).

Women who are ambivalent about the practice are able to devise reasons for their behavior—they may remark that they crave the taste of starch or clay or other things that they ordinarily would not eat—and everyone knows that cravings must be satisfied. One woman in Frankel's study developed a craving for cigarette ashes, for example—a habit that her husband and family deplored—and presented her own rationalization. "My first two babies were born in the eighth month," she said, "but the last two were full term. I figure the cigarette ashes made me carry the last two longer, so maybe it was a good thing to do" (p. 51). And one of the women in our Lansing sample was quite insistent that it was her *physician* who had instructed her to go into the back yard and eat dirt with a spoon; she needed minerals, he said (Snow, Johnson, and Mayhew 1978).

When women do speak against such consumption it is likely to be how *much* was eaten, not what was eaten. Again, excess is dangerous; the woman who eats too much starch might find the excess layered on the outside of the child at birth (the vernix in the biomedical view). "If you eats a whole lot of starch while you're pregnant, the baby will be born with a whole lot of white stuff all over its skin," said a woman whose previous baby had been born that way after she consumed three or four boxes of starch a day during pregnancy (Frankel, p. 59). Roberson also found that some individuals ate large amounts, "such as two or three boxes of starch per day. In the case of both soda and starch, it was reported that a baby whose mother ate these would be born covered with a white material resembling wet powder" (p. 127). Worse yet, too much starch or clay might cause the child to "stick" to the uterus and make the labor difficult. One woman told Frankel of her sister-in-law, who "ate a whole box a day for three months, and when it came time for the baby to be born they had to cut her open to get it out, because it was stuck up inside her" (p. 55).

For yet one more example of the fact that folk belief is not necessarily eliminated by education—even medical education—here is what Donald Liston had to say about starch-eating during pregnancy. A small group of medical students was discussing traditional practices in pregnancy when the topic of pica arose; the idea that too much starch might provide only empty calories for a pregnant woman was broached. "Not only that," said Donald, a second-year student—silencing the other students *and* the physician/anthropologist preceptors—"My cousin ate too much starch when she was pregnant, and when the baby was born it had lumps of undigested starch all around its neck, just like a string of pearls!" (East Lansing, Michigan; 1973)

Most pregnant women know very well that the doctors and nurses do not approve of their eating clay, starch, and the like during their pregnancies. It is difficult to say just how many women do so, then, because they are not always willing to admit it. Morton cites a survey by public health workers in South Carolina in which 40 of 200 expectant mothers reported consuming from one tablespoonful to a pound of starch per day (1974:165). About a third of Frankel's informants also admitted the practice but, "several more spoke of relatives who had the habit, and I sometimes suspected that this was a blind for their own indulgence" (1977:49). Like Frankel, we felt that more than the number who admitted to it actually did so. We tried to find out about it in a nonthreatening manner: Have you ever heard of anyone eating clay (or starch) during pregnancy, we asked? If a woman said that she had, we then asked what she thought about it. Fifty-eight percent of the sample said that they were aware of the practice and about one-third of these volunteered that they ate such substances during their pregnancies. Others, who did not directly admit that they ate such things, went on to make statements about friends or relatives who did so without harm (Snow and Johnson 1978).

Women can become quite proficient at not letting judgmental health professionals know what they *really* do, of course. Marilyn Poland reported the following experience from a Detroit prenatal clinic (personal communication, 1986):

I have worked in prenatal clinics serving low income black women in Baltimore, Augusta, Georgia, and Boston. I was used to seeing them sitting in the waiting room eating potato chips out of a bag and Argo Starch out of the box. When I came to Detroit, I saw the same [sorts of] women—many were born in the South and all have relatives living in the South—but no one ate Argo Starch. I was struck by this. When I asked women if they ate starch or clay or knew anyone who did, all denied that they ate these things, but most had heard of others who did.

I was curious about this and had the opportunity to test these assertions when a graduate student in anthropology who was black signed up for a directed study in reproductive anthropology under my direction. I placed her in the prenatal clinic waiting room one morning with a box of Argo Starch. I directed her to hold the box in her lap in clear view and to finger the contents. She was not to actually eat any. No sooner had she opened the box when an older black woman who was seated across from her approached and sat next to her. She leaned over to the student and said, "Look honey, if you want to eat that stuff eat it at home. If you eat it here they'll start giving us lectures again about how bad it is for you!"

Imprudent Behavior:
Strong Emotional States

The mother-to-be must monitor all of her feelings during pregnancy, not just her strong desires for certain foods or nonfoods; if strong emotional states are dangerous even for healthy adults it is not surprising that they can be devastating to those who are small and weak. Her responses to the ups and downs of daily life are transmitted directly to her unborn child and if these responses are uninhibited they may do irreparable damage. Shana Allen was worried about her three-week-old baby, for example, and had ostensibly brought her to the clinic on a November afternoon because she had "a cold." A resident examined the infant and said that the runny nose was good; it showed that her tiny body was "cleaning itself." He did not want to give any medicine to dry up the mucus, he went on, lest the viruses "stay inside" to produce more problems. After he left the room the mother continued to look far more concerned than the situation seemed to warrant, however, and a question brought out her underlying concern. She was deeply afraid that the new baby would not be "normal" because she had been "hooked up to all those machines" in the pediatric intensive-care unit. And she was afraid that she had somehow contributed to the baby's premature birth. She had gone to visit relatives in Flint on Halloween, she said, so that her eight-year old daughter could go trick-or-treating with her little cousins. Shana had thought that the trip would be all right; after all, the new baby was not due for several weeks. But on the following morning she had had to be taken to a hospital where she underwent an emergency Caesarean section. She was told that she had been bleeding internally but the doctors could not tell her why; it had "just happened." But things *don't* "just happen" in her belief and she had been reflecting on her behavior during the pregnancy. She had *thought* that she had taken good care of herself: "I don't do drugs!" But she had also been musing about how upset she had been the week before the birth when she had learned of the death of a beloved aunt in North Carolina—"She was just like a mother to me!"—and had been unable to attend the funeral. "I *should* have gone, but I just couldn't." And now her baby was damaged; there must be some connection, she thought. (Lansing, Michigan; 1986)

In traditional belief, in fact, Shana's baby might not have been spared if she *had* gone to the funeral; one of the commonest proscriptions on maternal behavior during pregnancy has to do with looking at the dead (Cameron 1930:21; Hand 1961:22; Snow 1977:33). "I guess you feel sorry and this will affect the child," according to Cassie Seales. "And it will be born—I haven't ever experienced it, but they say the child will come lookin' just like a dead person or maybe its eyes would look the same." And she did not believe in taking chances; she did not allow her daughter Ruthie to attend the funeral of her grandmother during Ruthie's pregnancy lest the baby "look funny." (1973) Any heightened emotion has the possibility of doing harm, in fact. It may be feelings which are usually seen as "good"—sorrow, pity, or sympathy—or disvalued states such as anger, hate, or ridicule of others. Sometimes they can be avoided; sometimes not. And if they are disvalued *and* deliberate they may bring on added unnatural or supernatural sanctions; the Almighty and the conjure man are equally interested in proper behavior on the part of the pregnant woman.

Whatever the emotion that is experienced at a dangerous level the resultant mark on the child may, as in the case of food cravings, be manifest in a behavioral or a physical manner. Etheldean Mitchell was careful not to be scared of anything during *her* pregnancies because that would mean the children would be frightened of the same thing; she was raised in the South and had seen too many children who had been marked in that way. (Lansing, Michigan; 1980) And in rural Virginia a woman "whose mother was scared, while carrying her, by a dog, is herself afraid of dogs. Moreover, this informant repeated the process with her own child when she was frightened by a dog during *that* pregnancy. A more dramatic instance of marking involved a pregnant woman who saw a man fall and become paralyzed. The birth produced an invalid son who could not walk" (Roberson 1983:125). Fright, in fact, is probably the most commonly mentioned emotion when women discuss the topic of prenatal marking. The resultant mark may be something that in biomedical terms would have an obvious genetic link: One woman in our Michigan study, for example, attributed the blue eyes of her first child to a horror movie in which she had seen a murder victim's "blue eyes opened wide" (Snow, Johnson, and Mayhew 1978). One can choose not to go to a horror movie, of course, and some women deliberately avoid doing so because of the inherent dangers. Lizzie Landon said that she did *not* believe such a thing was a problem; she had gone to horror movies during her pregnancies and none of her nine children was affected. Still, she commented, perhaps God knew she was ignorant and simply spared her babies. (Tucson, Arizona; 1971) *He* knew that she had been raised in a Catholic orphanage and did not hear all the old-time stories! Not all frightening experiences are avoidable, of course, and if a woman who believes in prenatal marking is frightened by something she may worry during the rest of her pregnancy. Frankel, for example, reported that one woman "who had seen several sights which violently revolted and frightened her while she was pregnant was in terror that her child would be born deformed in some hideous way. Since she was confined to bed and didn't see the baby for several days, she became quite agitated about it—even though everyone who had seen the baby, including her own eldest daughter, told her it was fine. Another who had had several horrible dreams shortly before delivery was in the same state until she had a chance to reassure herself by being taken to the nursery window to see her child" (1977:52).

Although Bernita admits to having marked all of her children by some behavior or other during her pregnancies she also sees limits to such occurrences. On one occasion she was involved in a discussion of marking in which the other women apparently suggested that anger at another might mark a child; this she pooh-poohed. She was angry at "the boss" plenty of times, she said, but never once was one of her children born White:

> Once in a clinic we was doin' a lot of talkin'. That was down South. And we was talkin' and so I asked the question, "My boss, he and I got into a big argument and he really upset me, and my baby wasn't born White!" And they said, "Wouldn't hardly be!" And I said, "What's the difference? What's the difference?" I said, "Angry's nothin' but angry." I said, "Whatever it is, if that was the case I'da had a White baby!"

Sometimes, she says, you have to use a little Mother Wit.

Prenatal Marking as Social Control: Supernatural/Unnatural Sanctions

The belief in prenatal marking also functions as a powerful mode of social control. It is commonly stated that a woman may be punished for disapproved actions towards others, and such punishment—minor or catastrophic—acts to suppress certain ways of behaving in the social context. The girl or woman who mocks or ridicules others puts herself and/or her child at risk. The "dire results" of such activity was the most frequently occurring motif among Newman's African-American informants when contrasted to the White women in her study. The "elaboration of forms of mocking behavior and of ensuing bad results . . . appears to be an extension of the subcultural recognition of humor as a form of aggressive expression" (1969). The girl who laughs at another who is pregnant, for example, will soon be pregnant herself, "and that's what happened to me, this time!" said one of Frankel's informants. "I laughed at my girlfriend, and a month later, there I was" (1977:46).

A more serious matter is the child born with some serious chronic health problem— mental retardation or a seizure disorder, for example—or with some deformity. The mother may have caused this because she saw someone with such a problem and made fun of them; the same thing was then "put on" her baby to teach her a lesson. "My grandmother told me not never to laugh at anybody, or say anything about them, because if I poked fun at somebody my baby might be born the same way they are." Adding, "But I don't like to laugh at people anyways. If somebody has something wrong with them I just feel sorry" (Frankel, p. 71). A woman in Roberson's study was less kind; she "laughed at a one-armed man during her pregnancy. The child from this birth holds her arm 'exactly like that man'" (1983:126). The idea that a child would be marked by a pregnant woman's mockery of a crippled or retarded person was a frequently expressed theme in our Lansing study as well (Snow, Johnson, and Mayhew 1978).

Such beliefs are frequently strengthened by supernatural sanctions (Hand 1961:23, 1980:57--67; Murphree 1968; B. Wilson 1985). It is often *God* who is said to be angry at a woman's transgressions—or those of some other family member—and He lets his displeasure be known to all. A child who is permanently marked in some major way acts as a continuing example to everyone in the community. And particularly to those who must care for it from now on. In a poor neighborhood the individual who behaves as if he or she is better than others is at risk; pride, said Sister Erma Allen, goeth before a fall:

> You should say thank God for a normal healthy baby. Because truly many many people don't have healthy children, they have abnormal children. There's a man out here had three children, and all of 'ems was deformed. 'Cause the Devil tries to afflict you with this; I disremember where you find it in the Bible. Sometimes people are raised up with pride so much that sometimes the Lord takes this to bring you down. When you're proud or not livin' for the Lord, [if] you get too proud, then God steps out of the way and let the Devil take over. The Devil causes these things. Then God can fix 'em. See, the Devil has never got dominion over you. He have dominion over you providin' God let him have dominion. God have to let him have dominion. (1971) (Snow 1977:57)

Mathews also provides an example in which a failure of communication in a clinical setting coupled with disapproved behavior came to be understood as divine punishment. There was:

a 26-year-old woman who suffered a miscarriage in the fourth month of her pregnancy. She went to the Emergency room of a local hospital where she was attended and released with a follow-up appointment in the OB-GYN clinic the next week. The patient never showed up for her appointment, and the medical personnel lost track of her case. The woman reported dissatisfaction with her visit to the emergency room indicating that the hospital personnel never told her "what was going on." She returned home and continued over the next two weeks to suffer some intermittent bleeding and reported an overall feeling of listlessness and depression. Her aunt prepared some herbal teas and gave her massages to relieve the cramps and bleeding. The woman reported some relief but continued to feel listless and depressed for the next few weeks.

The aunt decided that the woman's problem stemmed from the circumstances of the pregnancy. She reported that the woman had been seeing a married man and had conceived a child. Because the man refused to leave his wife, the aunt concluded that her niece had wished subconsciously to abort the child—a sin in her eyes. She persuaded her niece to seek the help of a minister. The niece saw the minister who urged her to confess and pray to God to be forgiven for the sin. After this session, the woman reported feeling instantly relieved of a burden and suffered no further symptoms. (1982:18–19)

The state of pregnancy does not make the woman and her unborn child immune to the practice of evil magic. The effects of unnatural activity—from pseudocyesis to the killing of both mother and child—are reported in collections of folklore and the staidest of medical journals (Dorson 1967:192–193; Clinicopathologic Conference Case Presentation 1967; Kimball 1970; Rocereto 1973; Cappannari et al. 1975). An infant's abnormal behavioral/physical attribute may be ascribed to sorcery if it seems to bear resemblance to some animal; to be nonhuman is obviously unnatural. In one instance, for example, "this woman got angry with another woman who was pregnant and decided to put a root on her. She went to South Carolina and had a root doctor to put a root on the pregnant lady. When the woman had the baby, it had skin like a frog or a lizard" (Cooley 1974:29).

"Down South," one woman told Frankel (p. 70), "they still believe people can curse the mother, and it will affect the baby she's carrying, if she's pregnant" (1977:70). Her own aunt had been so cursed, in fact, and "subsequently bore a child with a nervous ailment which caused him to 'bark like a dog all the time, so people wouldn't have anything to do with him.'" A health aide at the Lansing prenatal clinic, reared in rural Arkansas, was sure that a child can be "marked for death" before birth. This had happened to a woman in her community who was told that her child would die before its seventh birthday; sure enough, the infant was born with a defective heart and died not long before he turned seven (see also Clinicopathologic Conference Case Presentation 1967, for a similar account of unborn children cursed to die at a certain age).

In a discussion of deformity in infants Marya Smith went through the usual causes of such occurrences—laughing at cripples and so on—and then mentioned that "witchcraft" might cause a baby "to come looking like a demon." When asked to elaborate she provided examples from her own family that would—in biomedical terms— include spontaneous abortion, hydrocephaly, and Sudden Infant Death Syndrome. Why would someone *do* such a thing, I asked? In this instance the direct answer is a man's failure to pay a "hoodoo man" what he was owed—and, indirectly, the wrongness of attempts to control the behavior of others. The father of the afflicted children believed that his wife wished to leave him and so he sought out a "hoodoo man" to purchase a charm that would make her stay. The charm would do its work for only so long, however, and then she would get restless again. He was forced to go back and get yet another several times; such items can be very expensive, however, and he ran out of money. In desperation he asked for one more charm and said that he would pay later. The magic-worker agreed— with the warning that failure to pay would be severely treated. And his failure to pay *was* severely treated; it caused

> the baby to have a waterhead. I know my children's grandmother, she had a son with a big head; at that time they called 'em waterheads. He had this very small body. He lived to get six years old and never eaten anything harder than oatmeal. It was real soupy with milk in it; he nursed a bottle and then he [got] put on oatmeal. He had this great big head, all that ever grew, and he never moved the arm, feet or leg. And he still had the baby body and the only thing that grew was his head. [lowers voice] And they say that her husband knew the hoodoo and he wouldn't pay the peoples. And that one died at six years old.

> The hoodoo folks, they will bring stripes up on your family. So after *that* child died, then many more died. At four months, two months; she'd have miscarriage, like nine-months miscarriage. It was awful things was happening. My oldest son, they had a son the same year; [they were] four months apart. And they was hoodoo behind that baby; that baby died in six months without any *cause!* Listen, these babies was dyin' without anything *wrong* with 'em! They'd go to sleep happy babies! And they'd die overnight! You know, anytime you knocked on our door at night I knew that somebody was dead. (Lansing, Michigan; 1982)

Such beliefs also function, of course, as a warning to avoid such powerful people.

Labor

Pregnancies—those that proceed smoothly and those that fill a mother-to-be with anxiety about what she might have done to her unborn child—do finally end. Traditional beliefs concerning labor are divided into ideas about its onset and subsequent strategies to manage pain. The former may be associated with events in the natural world; the idea that changes in phases of the moon (especially the full moon) triggers labor is widespread, for example. In the Sea Islands it is tidal patterns that determine that the time has come:

> *A woman who had served for many years as a midwife, told us how she had been trained to time the contractions of a woman about to deliver and gave us a list of unequivocal signs of impending delivery of a baby. Yet, in spite of her training, she said there was only one infallible source of knowing when a child was to be born. It was the tides. In over thirty years of service, she asserted, and in spite of the more accepted signs of impending birth, babies were only born on the flood tide. Regardless of the statements of the pregnant woman, she would make no attempts to deliver the child if the tide was not in a flood stage. She also objected to all of the various instruments the doctors used to deliver children. In relationship to her service, she stated, "Woman get her baby by nature, I let the baby come by nature." Part of that attention to nature, obviously, utilized tides as a timing device.* (Blake 1979:25–26)

Deliberate attempts to start labor are known, however, and these often duplicate actions that earlier in pregnancy might be used to cause an abortion: taking a ride over a bumpy road; jumping from high places; sniffing paint fumes; ingesting castor oil or quinine. Some substances have both a physiological and a magical component in their action; the woman may be given gunpowder in sweet milk to drink, "to make her fight" (Cameron 1930:24), or, more commonly, black pepper tea (Murphree 1968; Holmes 1984) to drink. "If a woman has trouble delivering a baby, pepper or either snuff is blown into her face," according to the elderly Dr. Will Benton of Detroit. "This causes her to sneeze and the baby is pushed out. This is called 'peppering' or 'snuffing' the patient." (1985) The magical component is more obvious in the old Southern prescription for the drinking of dirt dauber tea (Van Blarcom 1930; Cameron, p. 24; C. Johnson 1934:200; Holmes 1984); the dirt dauber is a kind of wasp and the tea is made from the mud of its nest. Murphree (1968) suggested that the emergence of the creature from the tubular nest imitates the emergence of the infant from the birth canal.

A heavy meal—or a meal with certain components—may also cause labor to begin. "The night I started in to labor I ate two sour pickles and a dish of collard greens, and that did it," said one of Frankel's informants (1977:51). "My neighbor next door, she warned me that eating all that would start me in to labor." And Dr. Marilyn Poland has inadvertently started a new bit of birth lore at a prenatal clinic in Detroit (personal communication, 1986):

> *I was conducting a prospective study of pre-eclampsia in the prenatal clinic at Hutzel Hospital in Detroit. In the course of the study, I saw about 70 primiparous women over their pregnancies as I recorded their*

blood pressure, drew blood, and administered questionnaires at each prenatal visit. I got to know many of the women very well and enjoyed chatting with them about their pregnancies. One hot, humid August morning, a one week post-due 18-year-old woman complained to me about how poorly she was feeling and how her mother had tried enemas and driving her over bumpy roads to "bring on" labor. I explained that those things really did not work and that it was not uncommon for women to go a week or two past their due date, especially with a first pregnancy.

This did not seem to help her discomfort or her bad mood. She asked me if I ever felt like she did and I replied that I was ten days post-due with my first pregnancy and, living in Georgia, I knew what it felt like to be hot and uncomfortable. She asked me what I did to bring on labor. Without thinking, I told her I had a wonderful bowl of chili the night before our son was born. She asked me for the recipe. I immediately checked my knowledge of nutrition to make sure that the information I was about to give her represented good nutrition and a safe practice. She wrote down my recipe for chili and thanked me. Six weeks later she returned for her post-partum examination. That morning, five other women who were participating in my study asked for my recipe for chili.

The waiting-room network of small talk clearly works.

Only three or four short years went by between the time that Bernita Washington discovered that new babies were not dug out of stumpholes and the birth of Marya, her first child. Bernita had run off to be married at 15 and was soon pregnant—and when that first baby came she was alone. Her husband, Joseph, had gone for the midwife when the pains got bad but the hours passed and it became obvious that they would not return in time; she would have to deliver the child herself. She must have been absolutely terrified, I said. But no—she waved her hand dismissively at the thought—it was nothing to make a fuss about. After all, she explained, her sister-in-law had told her what to do in such an eventuality. You do what you have to do:

[You have] . . . the abdominal pains in your stomach. And there are other different types of pains that you would have that you doesn't usually have. O.K., so then you call in for the midwife either late night or the next day, 'cause they are trained. They are just like doctors, you know. Really, when Marya was born wasn't anybody there! They was on their way after the midwife. All by myself, 16 years old. That was Marya. So the baby was born. I was taught by my husband's sister; my husband's sister would tell me how to do and what to do if I was there by myself. So they just tell you [to] go ahead on in, just lay the baby at the end of the bed.

Right after the birth if he's not cryin'—if *you* there [alone] you have to be taught already what to do. So if the baby come [and] he's not cryin' you would have to spank him. See, the life would *come* from the after-birth out of the cord and into the baby. The baby's life is in the cord, is in the cord. And when he *cries* it come *out* of the cord into the *baby!* If the baby doesn't cry the life is still *in* the cord. And the baby will not live unless he cry first. And so after he cries, then that life goes through the cord into the baby and start the baby to breathing. And there's three notches below the cord, from the labor down the cord, that you cut the labor-cord. And you tie it and you put the bandage and stuff on it. And the next 20 minutes the afterbirth comes. (Lansing, Michigan; 1987)

The newborn Marya was crying so did not have to be spanked, says her mother. So the youthful Bernita had just laid her new daughter down, cut the cord and tied it, and waited for the afterbirth to be delivered. By the time her husband returned with the midwife, Bernita and little Marya—umbilical stump already dressed with a belly band—were both asleep. The new mother of 16 would be a grandmother at 32—and a great-grandmother at 48.

　　Marya had been old enough to help with some of her mother's later babies and four of her own five children had been born at home as well. What had the midwife done for pain, I asked Marya? She was very vehement in her reply: better to do nothing at all:

No! The pains was result in the births; they wouldn't want to cut those off, they wouldn't want to slow 'em down. Because I guess in their way of thinkin' if they go stop the pain, slowin' the pain down, then [it would] slow the baby up. At that time they didn't have the proficient things [they] do now, and the baby continue to come on.

It was mentioned earlier that Marya had been terrified when taken to the hospital for an emergency delivery; her last child, Sonny, was 13 years old when she gave this account in 1982:

I don't like the hospital; I'm afraid of hospitals. I wouldn't have went with Sonny but I had to, down South. I had to because I had a hemorrhage before the baby was born. So I saw this man in the back of my field; he was workin' all night cultivatin', gettin' the land ready for to start plantin'. So, I eased to the door and crawled out on the porch, and I hollered for him when he got around to my house to go and get somebody 'cause I was sick! So he knew I was pregnant so he assumed that it was time for me to have the baby. So he rushed; anybody that you told that you needed help they would rush and get somebody. So I was bleedin' so bad we didn't even wait for a midwife. We didn't try to get the midwife, they rushed me straight to the hospital.

But I'm afraid of the hospital; I think I like the midwife better. *Only* one thing; I just prayed that if something went wrong that I could die before I got to the hospital, that was the only thing. But I think that other than that I'd rather be at home. I feel more safe. Because I always *been* at home, so you see I was raised havin' the babies at home and my *mother* did, so I felt more *safe* that way.

Who was there when she delivered at home, I asked, just the midwife? Yes, the midwife:

And my Mom. Mom was always there; Mom would hold my hand. A woman, somethin' about havin' a baby, [if] she had a close friend while she was carryin' the baby, pregnant, or either she had a mother close—and those peoples the one that gonna be there when she's have the baby. They gonna go get her and the midwife. And they would hold the hand and they would grip this friend or mother hand. And talk about tight! I hold my Mama tight the hand lotta times, so that help.

Even [if] the pain was there, but seem like somethin' like, O.K., *pain* is actually in your mind, right? If you say, "This is not too bad," then it ain't that *bad!* So, it's just your *mind!* I would deal with these pain. And I did it before, I know what I *gotta* do. See, this was a *must* thing; you *must* let this baby come forth! You know, you got all this time *waitin'* on it, and you *must* bring this baby to the world, you know. And you just go on *through* with it! And forget about the pains; you in a hurry to get the baby here, you ain't really worryin' about the pains that much. So I think it's more like, you know, [you] wanta go on and get it here.

And what *was* it about a home delivery that she liked better? She has been with two of her unmarried daughters five times as they gave birth (1982 to 1986) since moving from Mississippi to Michigan, so has had an opportunity to view "modern" ways. And it is clear that she sees modern obstetrical procedure as interfering with nature and—in the case of surgical deliveries—downright terrifying. But times change, she knows, and people must change as well:

Like doctors, they put you on a slow base. And waitin' on the minutes and hours, [seem] like the time will never come. Like you gotta breathe so many times and you get so tired and exhausted. You can have all that, you know, all these new way of doin' it, and, "Huh, ain't no baby bein' come." You know we did that: it's near that time it ain't gonna be very long you start breathin' in person for the baby. But here they have you to do that soon as you get in the hospital! Then they come to find out you got to wait 'til tomorrow 'fore you have the baby! And it's a lot different, you know; something you're not used to.

And then they *have* you to have the baby and—[pause]—it's just different, I don't know. Maybe it's the needles and *knifes* and things that gonna get you kinda scared or somethin'. That it may have to go in and operate right away, you know. You kinda feel like, now, if sumpin' happen at *home* I'm probably gonna end up dyin' before I have that operation—lotta people *rather* die than have an operation, you know. But, as you get more modern in life and get more up in the styles to do this and do that, you begin to kinda relax with it, you know. Ain't nothin' I'm really crazy about, but, this is the way it goes. No more midwives; that's dead. Actually dead, even in the South—there ain't no more midwives.

It is much easier to do things one's own way in the home setting, of course. Still, some of the traditional ideas about the sorts of things that should and should not be done in the postpartum period have survived the modernization of childbirth; these will be discussed in the next chapter along with ideas about care of the newborn infant. And some of the old ideas may be instituted *in* the hospital setting as well, unbeknownst to health care personnel. A number of traditional practices for dealing with the pains of afterbirth employed the symbolism of cutting the pain, for example; a ploughshare might be hung over the bed or an axe, scissors, or knife be placed in or under the bed (Cameron 1930:24; Van Blarcom 1930; C. Johnson 1934:199; Murphree 1968). "When a woman is having afterbirth pains, to stop them put a case knife under the mattress," 65-year old Olouise Carter was told by her mother. Olouise had experienced it herself and knew that it worked; the midwife never made her go through very many of these pains before she placed the knife under the mattress. (Flint, Michigan; 1981) And the staff of a Lansing hospital maternity ward never suspected that Arlene Bauer's grandmother had a hatchet in her knitting bag when she came to visit her granddaughter and great-grandson. The old lady had brought it all the way from her home in West Virginia and merely slipped it under Arlene's mattress when no one else was around. And did it work, I asked? Yes, it did. "It cut those pains right in half." (1975)

The Incorporation of Modern Problems into Old Explanations

It is impossible to say to what degree the sorts of things that health professionals see as increasingly exacerbating the number of poor pregnancy outcomes—violence, alcohol/drug use, smoking, AIDS, and so on—are incorporated into the traditional belief system. There are indications, however, that such incorporation does take place—including some of the magical explanation inherent in marking the child. The magical danger of touch may be of great concern to women who have been physically abused during pregnancy, for example. One young woman in the Lansing study had been beaten up by her boyfriend a week or so before the interview and she was worried about her baby. It was not direct damage to the child that she feared, however— she had been struck only in the face—but that the baby might be born with permanently blackened eyes.

Women in the same clinical setting also offered different explanations about the dangers of tobacco, street drugs, and alcohol use during pregnancy. All participants agreed that the use of street drugs was wrong during pregnancy; if any of them used them they did not volunteer it. The majority (71 percent) also agreed that a pregnant woman should not smoke though only two women mentioned a correlation between smoking and low birthweight. Instead, "one woman stated that it would turn the baby black and several others feared that smoke could enter the baby's lungs to cause emphysema or bronchitis, . . . 'the baby may inhale some smoke down there'" (Snow, Johnson, and Mayhew 1978). This may be another example of telling the professionals what it is believed they want to hear, however. Tobacco is *not* always seen as noxious, in fact, and is widely used—topically, smoked, and chewed—in a variety of traditional treatments. Wilbur Watson cited a case in which a brand of chewing tobacco containing licorice as an antidote for morning sickness contributed to a pregnant woman's low serum potassium, for example (1984). In any case, high rates of tobacco use continue to be a problem for African-American women (Shiono et al. 1986; Boone 1989:22).

The women in the Lansing sample seemed less concerned about alcohol use in pregnancy, and 58 percent said that it was all right in moderation. One woman, in fact, said that drinking is good for the pregnant woman since it acts "to flush the kidneys" and also helps to bring a fat baby. Nor were injunctions against its use always of a physiological nature: Another woman suggested that a drunk woman might fall asleep on her stomach and thereby deform the infant's head. And Ruthie Seales told me that her little girl "walks sort of wobbly" because Ruthie and her boyfriend were "both kinda drunk" when she was conceived. The child was 15 months old at the time.

The problems of "crack" cocaine use and the appearance and spread of AIDS were unknown at the time most of the studies cited in this chapter were made. Again, however, there is some evidence that understanding of their effects is a mixture of biomedical and traditional knowledge. The women "sheltered" in the New York welfare hotel studied by Shedlin (1989) were deeply involved in drug use (estimated by the women themselves as upwards of 90 percent). Some of their comments—whether true belief or wishful thinking— certainly add risk to already uncertain lives. "Coke takes dope (heroin) out of the system . . . they work well together . . . they are not habit forming when together . . . like sugar with coffee . . . ," for example, and, "Crack is not addictive . . . it's boredom. . . it's all in your head" (p. 23). They also discussed drug use during pregnancy and birth: "Two weeks ago I had a miscarriage because of cocaine . . . ," said one. And, "Crack makes the baby come out fast . . . no pain . . . whoom!" And, "I had to smoke what was left to get the baby out . . . two hours later I almost bled to death . . . they put the baby in foster care . . . they found crack in her system . . . I never thought they would take her . . ." (p. 25).

A recent study of low-income African-American women's beliefs about AIDS demonstrates a similar mixture of the old and the new; whereas all participants agreed that it can be contracted through sexual intercourse or contaminated needles only three (of 22) women believed that these were the only ways to do so. Other explanations are fully in the traditional context, woven in with the known dangers of cold, dirt, wrong diet, and vulnerability during certain times in the life cycle (Flaskerud and Rush 1989): For example, "When you're weak, like when you're pregnant because of all the changes, it's dormant and that activates it. Babies are also weak and so they get it, and so are old people. . . . People live in unsanitary conditions. There are impurities in the air from factories. People are smoking; they're drinking; they're sick all the time; they don't take care of themselves when they're pregnant. Their system is low. When these things happen, it triggers AIDS." The authors also note that the younger women they spoke with were just as knowledgeable about traditional beliefs as were the older women. Those beliefs are obviously still passed on.

Notes

1. Some recent studies suggest that adverse changes in these factors account for much of the increasing disparity between racial groups in rates of premature births. In a hospital-based cohort of 8,903 women, Lieberman et al. (1987) examined four nonmedical risk factors (age less than 20 years, single marital status, not having graduated from high school, and receiving welfare) and found: "In whites, 89 percent of the women had none of the four socioeconomic risk factors, whereas only 32 percent of the black women had none. . . ." The latter group were also more likely to have multiple risk factors, and "about 77 percent of the increased risk of prematurity associated with black race was explained by the economic-demographic-behavioral factor or other variables related to it." Kleinman and Kessel (1987) examined 1983 national data for the effects of age, parity, marital status, and education on rates of very low or moderately low birth-weight infants. They also looked at secular trends in birth-weight data and found that between 1973 and 1983 births of very low birth-weight infants "increased among blacks and decreased among whites. . . ," and that for "blacks, adverse changes in maternal characteristics (primarily an increase in births to unmarried women) accounted for 35 percent of the increase in the rate of very low birth weight."

In contrast, Margaret Boone (1982) has looked at intragroup data in which "a sample of all Black women delivering single, low-birthweight infants (2,500g and less) in 1977 and 1978 was compared to a random, stratified sample of Black women with normal weight infants (2,501g and more). . . " in Washington, D.C. A subsample of women delivering *very* low birth-weight infants (1,500g and below) was also compared to a group of women delivering normal weight infants. Her results suggest: "Where illegitimacy rates are very high, marital status fails to separate high- and lower-risk women. Where reproductive age is young, and fertility levels high, young age also ceases to distinguish them. If the delivering group is young, unmarried, and poorly educated relative to the population of the United States, then greater age, married status, and more education may not imply differential keys to security for the pregnant woman. To be older (or younger), legally married, and a high-school graduate in a disadvantaged population may not mean that the woman is healthier, better supported, under less stress, or has better access to medical services (if broadly defined to include her own fears of health care providers). These factors do not confer a reproductive advantage, as in the general population, and their lack of significance sets apart as qualitatively different the context of pregnancy in the ghetto."

Similar conclusions were reached by Collins and David in an analysis of 103,072 births to African-American and White mothers in Chicago in 1982 and 1983. Although the risk of delivering a low birth-weight infant rose for women from both groups as income fell, the risk remained twice as high for African-American women irrespective of income, education, and age. The authors observed that generations of poverty are reflected in these findings: "Residing in a very low-income urban neighborhood is such a strong proxy of low-birthweight for Blacks that traditional indicators of favorable outcome (education, age, marital status) fail to identify clearly a low risk subgroup. The intense concentration of extreme poverty combined with the related issues of disintegrating social networks, substance abuse, poor nutrition, smoking, and inadequate prenatal care may produce such a powerful negative force that isolated changes in the classical risk factors do not dramatically reduce the high percentage of low birthweight infants" (1990:680).

The editor of the *American Journal of Public Health* commented in a recent editorial that despite technologic advances in neonatal care in recent years social change, "as reflected in infant mortality rate ratios, has remained static or retrogressed" (Yankauer 1990).

2. *Re: AIDS.* National statistics on mortality associated with the human immunodeficiency virus (HIV) among U.S. women between 15 and 44 years of age are terrifying. Between 1985 and 1988 the death rate for HIV/AIDS quadrupled in this population, and by 1987 it had become one of the ten leading causes of death. African-American women are significantly more at risk; in 1988 their death rate was nine times that for White women. The majority of deaths in both groups were among women in their childbearing years (25 to 34 years old), and if "current mortality trends continue, HIV/AIDS can be expected to become one of the five leading causes of death by 1991 in women of reproductive age. Because women infected with HIV are the major source of infection for infants, these trends in AIDS mortality in women forecast the impact of HIV on mortality in children as well" (Chu, Buehler, and Berkelman 1990).

Michigan statistics also reveal that African-Americans have higher rates of AIDS morbidity and mortality. By December 1989, 49 percent of adults with AIDS in the state were African-American, though they make up only 13 percent of the state's population. When these numbers were broken down according to age and gender 44 percent of adult males, 81 percent of adult females and 64 percent of the children with AIDS in Michigan were African-American; these rates appear to be related to a disproportionate amount of IV drug use (Bouknight 1990). In the first half of 1990 a survey of HIV seroprevalence among childbearing women revealed an overall infection rate of 5.9/10,000: African-American women accounted for 79.5 percent of the seropositive cases though constituting only 19.6 percent of the women tested; their overall rate of HIV seropositivity was 23.8/10,000 compared to 1.3/10,000 for White women (Michigan HIV/AIDS Report 6:1, January 1991).

Trends in the financing of medical care for AIDS patients indicate a shift away from private insurance and a move toward Medicaid payment, thus increasing the burden of care on public hospitals/emergency rooms (Green and Arno 1990).

Re: Drug Use. The association of drug use by pregnant women and rising rates of low birth-weight infants/infant mortality is also made (Collins and David 1990; Petitti and Coleman 1990; Joyce 1990; Bouknight 1990; Handler et al. 1991; Spence et al. 1991). Health officials have suggested that Michigan's 1989 rise in infant mortality rate is in part due to increased drug use by pregnant women *cum* a rising birth rate in the state. A random testing of infants born in Detroit's Hutzel Hospital in 1989, for example, showed that nearly *43 percent* of them had been exposed to cocaine, marijuana, and/or heroin *in utero* (Boyle 1990). The amount of these drugs (often in combination) in the meconium of the infants indicated drug use on the part of the mother for the final two trimesters of pregnancy (Marilyn Poland, personal communication, 1990). In another ongoing study it was demonstrated that 6 percent of infants and young children treated at another Detroit hospital had cocaine in their systems: As none had been breastfed and any of the drug from exposure during pregnancy would have dissipated it was suggested that they were inhaling secondhand drug smoke (*Detroit Free Press*, November 24, 1990, p. 2a).

Re: Violence. Increasing rates of violence are similarly associated with escalating social problems: deteriorating living environments; substance abuse; poverty; feelings of hopelessness and despair and on and on in a sorry litany. In a study of injuries over a one-year period in a low-income African-American community in Philadelphia, for example, those that were violence-related surpassed any other type in the age group 15 through 49 years (Wishner et al. 1991). It is worth noting that the reversal of positive trends in infant mortality rates and homicide rates in the last five or six years coincides with the introduction of the deadly form of cocaine known as "crack." In 1987, for example, the homicide rate for African-American males was 85.6/100,000, or 34 percent higher than the 1984 rate (Fingerhut and Kleinman 1990). And intragroup statistics show that African-American males are again disproportionately at risk: They are seven times more likely to be murdered than are their White counterparts (rates of 85.6/100,000 compared to 11.2/100,000 for White males). There are also significant *inter*group differences per state, however, and my home state of Michigan has the sorry distinction of ranking first in this category. In 1987 the homicide rate for African-American males in Michigan was 231.6/100,000—3 times the national rate for African-American males and nearly *21* times the national rate for White males!

Sometimes, of course, this violence is directed against women. In her disturbing book about infant mortality in Washington, D.C., Boone noted that violence is a significant risk in the pregnancies of disadvantaged women, especially if they themselves drink or live with those who abuse alcohol. She also found an association with very low birth weight infants: "The best evidence for the role of alcohol, violence, street crime, and domestic disputes in poor pregnancy outcome is the fact that notations about these kinds of events occurred *only* in the medical records of women with very low-birthweight infants. The medical records of women with normal-weight infants are remarkably devoid of notations about violence, scars, alcoholism, and family disruption. The medical histories of inner-city women with the smallest infants show that violence is both domestic and broadly environmental, and can be a frightening, integral, negative aspect of inner-city life" (1989:137–138). For a recent study of the effect of traumatic injuries—including domestic violence—against women see Grisso (1991).

Re: Homelessness. All of the above—disease, drugs, and violence—come together in one package for the homeless. In her pilot study of a group of Hispanic and African-American mothers living with their children in a welfare hotel in New York City, Shedlin describes the once-elegant building as a "decaying shell with foul smelling and filthy public spaces" (1989:8). The part-time pediatric clinic located in the building, for example, once had to be closed for two weeks while two six-pound rat carcasses were removed from the walls. It is virtually impossible, she wrote, to separate life in the hotel from substance abuse and a drug subculture (p. 23); it is a place where "teenagers with beepers deal crack outside the front door, drug paraphernalia lie discarded in hallways, and women with dilated pupils give birth prematurely in their rooms, hallways, or the lobby. . . . The women themselves, not the least reluctant to discuss drug use in the hotel in great detail, gave estimates of use of upwards of 90 percent. . . ." Not only is the hotel not a haven, then, but is *itself* perhaps "the greatest environmental obstacle to care and health" for these mothers and their infants and children (p. 45).

3. The preponderance of public attention has been on the teenaged mother at risk, and most programs are geared towards these younger women. Older women are also at reproductive risk, however, and again there is a disparity according to race. Examination of maternal mortality in women over 35 years of age, for example, reveals that African-American women have higher mortality rates than do White women with or without abortive outcomes (Buehler et al. 1986). Boone rightly calls these women "The Hidden Group at Reproductive Risk": "Inner-city Black women at the two extremes of the reproductive age spectrum have one characteristic in common: They both contribute disproportionately to the statistics on poor pregnancy outcome in inner-city neighborhoods—both for natural, bio-logical reasons and for reasons related to substance abuse. For older women afflicted with alcoholism, or who have partners who are alcoholic, a late pregnancy can be very high risk, indeed . . . " (1989:113). As previously mentioned, our data indicated that women in Michigan prenatal clinics did not seem aware that pregnancy in later years was a problem for either the mother or her child (Snow, Johnson, and Mayhew 1978; S. Johnson and Snow 1982).

4. Actually, "guarantee" is the wrong word here, too. The problem of increasing violence among young people is dramatically illustrated by a Detroit physician's study revealing that homicides—usually by gunshot—are the leading cause of death among Detroit African-American children over the age of nine years (Watson and Anstett 1990:1A, 8A): "Among boys ages 10–14, the homicide rate rose from 10 per 100,000 in 1980 to 28 per 100,000 in 1988. Among boys 15–18, the rate increased from 44 per 100,000 in 1980 to 145 per 100,000 in 1988. Girls were not immune. Among girls 10–14, the rate went from three per 100,000 in 1980 to 13 per 100,000 in 1988. Among girls 15–18 in Detroit, the rate rose from 5 per 100,000 in 1980 to 21 per 100,000 in 1988."

In 1989 194 Michigan children were homicide victims—most of these deaths (131/191, 68 percent) occurred in Detroit and most of the victims (147/194, 76 percent) were African-American (*Lansing State Journal,* January 16, 1991, p. 3B). An ongoing tally of police records kept by the *Detroit Free Press* also revealed that from January 1 to October 24, 1990, 204 young people 16 years old and under had been shot in Detroit; 27 of these children died (*Detroit Free Press* October 24, 1990, p. 2B).

5. Although there has been an emphasis in the media on the "epidemic" of pregnancies among teenagers this does not mean that young people do not wish information on reproductive issues; many of them do. When asked, high school students in Detroit expressed a need for information on "high risk areas of birth control, substance abuse, and venereal disease" (Giblin and Poland 1985). Most of them also indicated that they would prefer to receive this information in a private session with a doctor, not by written material or by a presentation to a group. Unfortunately, many of these same students admitted that they had *not* visited a doctor in the previous year—even when needed—because they were afraid of them. There is also evidence that educational materials on sexual issues may need to be designed in a "culturally appropriate" manner to reach specific subgroups: Data collected from Hispanic and African-American adolescents in inner-city Miami, for example, revealed significant differences in their beliefs and knowledge concerning sexuality and contraception. Many of these young people held conflicting beliefs simultaneously: Contraception is "good" because it prevents pregnancy, but "bad" because the various methods are hazardous to the health of users (Scott et al. 1988). Their misconceptions about genital anatomy and concerns about the dangers inherent in contraceptive techniques were similar to those that have already been described. Dunn's (1988) research with young Florida mothers also reveals that they are not a homogeneous group when it comes to

fertility decision-making but exhibit a variety of strategies in attempting to prevent new pregnancies.

6. It has already been mentioned that the infant mortality rate in Michigan rose in 1989. Health officials believe that this can be attributed to increasing drug use by pregnant women and a rising birth rate. The latter is at least partially due to the fact that poor women no longer have access to Medicaid-funded abortions; this voter-approved law went into effect on December 12, 1988. A preliminary report by the Department of Public Health indicated that abortions declined by 23 percent in the first nine months of 1989; this decrease (and an increase in births) occurred primarily among urban women under 29 years of age. The most significant drop in abortions (nearly 40 percent), however, was among those 15 years of age and younger (Boyle 1990).

Some months after these figures appeared it was reported that a loan fund set up for women who could not afford an abortion had been "swamped" with requests, and three out of four women who asked for such help had to be turned away. Additional statistics that state officials suggested were tied in with the "huge increase" in unwanted babies of all races being born included: (a) the 23 percent drop in abortions cited above; (2) a 7.2 percent increase in births in the same period; (3) a 31 percent rise in the number of children enrolled for welfare before birth by mothers on Medicaid; (4) a 22 percent rise in the number of children under age three in the welfare system; and (5) an 8 percent increase in the number of children served by the state program supporting children with complex health problems, costing an additional $15 million (Chargot 1990a).

In February 1991 "Antoinette," a 28-year-old crack addict in Detroit, gave birth prematurely to a tiny infant who exhibited symptoms of severe crack withdrawal. His mother had wanted an abortion but did not have the means to procure one; the money she had went for drugs. "I see such women every week," according to a Detroit gynecologist, going on to say that "I'm seeing for the first time in my life the frequent experience of delivering a baby to a woman only to have her show disinterest." Antoinette, in fact, said that several times in her pregnancy the baby had stopped moving but that she had not sought medical care because she wished it to die; after her baby was born she did not go to see him for four days and did not want to take him home. A day or so later, however, she had changed her mind and said that she was going to try and be a good mother (Chargot 1991).

7. Women may be poor but they are not entirely powerless, of course. In her description of the experiences of White and Puerto Rican prenatal patients in a large inner-city hospital Lazarus (1988) noted that women resisted some medical judgments and procedures in a variety of ways: by failing to return for appointments, telling doctors what they wanted to hear, and, in the case of one Puerto Rican woman, pretending to not understand English.

8. It is worth noting that the women in all three of these studies were using orthodox health care at the time they were interviewed.

9. In contrast, one occasionally hears that it is problematic for a woman to be physically inactive: One woman who developed pneumonia during a pregnancy was "prescribed medication which made her very sleepy. Her father told her she 'better stop taking that medicine or the baby will stick to you'" (Roberson 1983:127–128; see also Kay 1982:12). The idea that the child may "stick to the uterus" of a woman who is lazy or who sleeps too much during her pregnancy is also found in Latin-American traditional medicine. It was mentioned by several of the Hispanic women in the Lansing clinic and was said to contribute to the need for Caesarean sections. One young woman was caught between the advice of the doctor, who suggested that she get more rest, and that of her mother-in-law, who admonished her that she should "keep moving." It was the advice of the mother-in-law that was followed, of course. "I have to *live* with *her!*"

9

God Doesn't Want Us
to Misuse a Child—
But He Wants Us to Be Firm

Her new baby doll. They placed the soft plastic and pink flannel in the
little girl's lap, and she turned her moon-shaped eyes toward them in
awed gratitude. It was so perfect and so small. She trailed her
fingertips along the smooth brown forehead and down into the bottom
curve of the upturned nose. She gently lifted the dimpled arms and
legs and then reverently placed them back. Slowly kissing the set
painted mouth, she inhaled its new aroma while stroking the silken
curled head and full cheeks. She circled her arms around the motionless
body and squeezed, while with tightly closed eyes she waited
breathlessly for the first trembling vibrations of its low, gravelly
"Mama" to radiate through her breast. Her parents surrounded this
annual ritual with full heavy laughter, patted the girl on the head, and
returned to the other business of Christmas.

— Gloria Naylor, *The Women of Brewster Place*

Bernita Washington was home alone when her first baby came and
she had no other alternative than to deliver the child herself. Nor
did she have any help in the next few days after the birth:

I didn't have anybody, no bigger kids and no family or nothin' like
that to help me with my kid, or to see after the house and everything.
O.K., the next three days I did whatever I always did. You didn't have
any problems as long as you don't *lift* anything heavy, eat something
that might run your blood pressures up, or sumpin' like that. Now *we,*
after our babies born, we used to drink a teacup of castor oil—a teacup
of castor oil, a whole teacupful. That is to keep your bowels enacted.

Now a lot of womens, they have babies and it'll be, sometime they
come *home* and they bowels still don't be done *moved!* Because they haven't took anything for relax [them]. *Then* they would give 'em a teacup of castor oil [and] the next day they would make 'em eat *turnip*
greens! And that opens your stomach up, tight bowels. The turnip
greens will keep you with good open bowels. The castor oil was medicine for your insides that'll heal you back *up!*

But, as she says when recalling carrying 100 or so pounds of cotton
on her back the day before delivering a child, "*Womens* wasn't as

weak as they are now, *then.*" Now, she says, women even refuse to put up with the pains of labor without medication! And that, she feels, poses its own problems: In the summer of 1990 when her 15-year-old granddaughter, Toni, gave birth, the girl had to remain hospitalized a few extra days because of a slight fever. *"Probably,"* sniffed Bernita, "they gave her too much anesthetic." When Toni came home from the hospital her grandmother urged her to drink a cupful of castor oil to "heal up her stomach," but Toni had refused. "I told *all* of 'em but they wouldn't do it," Bernita reported, referring to her daughters and granddaughters who have borne children. "That's why their bodies is weak." (Lansing, Michigan; 1990)

Postpartum Restrictions

Despite Bernita's protestations that a woman who has just given birth should be able to carry on all of her usual activities, she herself had followed many of the rules of behavior for new mothers once she had enough children to help out after the birth of a new sibling. It is only in retrospect that she labels a number of these practices "nothing but a bunch of old -isms!" In the traditional system these "-isms"—her word for superstitions—reflect the conventional wisdom characterizing a woman who has just given birth as particularly vulnerable. At delivery there is a shift in emphasis from the protection of the unborn child—which was primary throughout the months of pregnancy—to the protection of the new mother. It is she, not her infant, who is in the weaker state. In the next weeks her behavior will by hedged round by a variety of maneuvers designed to keep her from harm. Some of these—the proper disposal of the placenta, for example—are specific to the postpartum period. Others reflect again the familiar risks of cold, dirt, or improper diet.

Many of the traditional beliefs associated with this liminal period (in which the infant and mother are newly separated after their nine months as one) symbolically illustrate the safety of family, hearth, and home. There are restrictions on the new mother, for example, aimed at protecting her from the outside world. Some of these practices, tied as they are to home births, are disrupted when childbirth takes place in a medical setting and may be largely memories. Others, not so dependent on physical setting, continue to shape behavior in the old ways. One of the first changes brought on by the removal of birth to the hospital is the weakening of the idea of a needed period of confinement for the new mother. Traditionally this period (often incorporating the ritual numbers three and nine) was thought necessary to allow a woman's body to recuperate from the trauma of birth. "My mother and grandmother always told me 'Stay in the bed nine days, rest three days, then *feed* that baby,'" said one of Frankel's informants (1977:68), going on to confess that when forced to follow this restriction after giving birth in South

Carolina she "used to sneak out of the bed when nobody wasn't looking. . . . " Many of Roberson's rural Virginia informants suggested that a woman's "system is down" following childbirth, with some recommending the new mother remain in bed for three days and at home for nine. The period of confinement should actually last even longer according to some of the older women interviewed: "They shouldn't do for a month. Nowadays they do, but they shouldn't or when six comes around they be half-sick again. See, they do, because they thinks they feels all right, but see, they haven't given their system a chance to build up. See, your system is down. That's the way I feel" (1983:129).

The fact that "nowadays they do" still leaves individuals brought up with conflicting beliefs uneasy, and when possible they sometimes make compromises. "I don't think she should go out too quick," said Cassie Seales, "I don't think her body is strong enough. I never went out 'til my babies were at least three or four weeks old." And though Cassie had no control over the fact that her teen-aged daughter Ruthie gave birth in a hospital, she did not allow Ruthie out of the house for several weeks after she came home with her new baby. Ruthie chafed at this restriction but, she said simply, "I did what my mother told me." (Lansing, Michigan; 1973)

The failure of the new mother to take care of herself at this vital juncture may result in a variety of unpleasant outcomes. "I lost my zip by stirring around too soon after the baby came," one woman said to Murphree, referring to a loss of libido (1968). Roberson was told of the woman who—ignoring the advice to stay at home the requisite number of days—hemorrhaged and had to be hospitalized (1983:129). And an elderly Alabama midwife graphically described the possible consequences of "stirrin too soon":

> *Mrs. Patterson did that once. Like to died. They had them five boys. I said, "Mrs. Patterson, don't you be too fast." I said, "Honey, you get them female organs outa shape you talkin bout crawlin. You gonna have to crawl outa the bed to the bathroom on yo' knees. You ain't gonna be able to walk just cause it hurts you so bad down there." Sometimes they have to stay on the bed a couple of days so they can kinda gradually get back in shape. Her female organs got to get set back in place. The baby was born there at night and I went there the next mornin and Mrs. Patterson had done got outa bed with all her clothes. She messed around there. When I went back there the next mornin she couldn't get outa bed. I had to rub her up. I sho did. Put a tight band on her. Real tight band on her. They lay down flat and I rub em up and put a tight band around 'em. Make em take a deep breath while I put a tight band around em. My mother taught me how to do this. As I was growin my mother taught me. (Logan 1989:117–118)*

Marya Smith agreed that the process of childbirth leaves a woman's body in such a fragile state that for some time after giving birth any sort of physical activity—lifting, climbing stairs, or too much walking—might "take the body down." The delicate balance of her internal organs could even be damaged by the footsteps of someone walking *around* her, she said, especially if they were the steps of a stranger.

> Even when I had *my* babies, because of the stairs. I learned that a woman's body is not adjusted after the baby is born. You have to prop the feet up so high to get your stomach back in place. A woman could easy damage her body right after the baby is born; all that pressure and then walking is like *takin'* your body down. And they tell me that it's so hard for the doctor to get your body back in shape once you *do* that to it.

> But you can't stand peoples to walk *around* you, even on the floor; it'll kill you. Or peoples even walkin' in the house, you know, after you done [had a baby]; they calls it to "knock your body down." I don't know what the real word for it [is]. No stranger wasn't *allowed* in; they just wasn't allowed in. That was an *old* condition, they just didn't allow 'em in.

"Do you mean if a stranger came in and walked around her it would be bad?" "Oh, that's *kill* 'em," was the reply. "That's what they tell me." The outside was not allowed *in,* that is, and for a prescribed number of days the new mother was not allowed to go out. (Lansing, Michigan; 1983)

Postpartum bleeding further weakens a system already "down" from pregnancy and the delivery. And just as in vaginal bleeding from any other cause, the body is seen as "open" and vulnerable to anything that might act to obstruct the flow. The same rules about bathing, shampooing the hair, or heedlessly going out in the rain apply alike to the menstruating woman, one who has just had an abortion, or the new mother. Said Sister Erma Allen: "You can be exposed before your baby gets old enough. After you have your baby. See, some people have a baby and three or four days, just up and go like that. This is exposure. This is exposure to TB. And many times people go and take abortions, keep from bein' pregnant, take abortions. This goes into TB" (Snow 1977:43). (Tucson, Arizona; 1971)

Nor does the fact that such behavior may not immediately cause problems mean that the careless girl or woman will not have to pay for it sooner or later: Getting your feet wet after having a baby, reported Stella Bird, "will bother your health later in life." (Saginaw, Michigan; 1978) Or, "I'm all right now; I might feel it when I'm older, but right now I'm O.K.," according to a woman in rural Virginia who had gone out in the wind and rain shortly after giving birth (Roberson 1983:145). Cassie Seales precluded any such problems for her daughter Ruthie by having the young girl take a shower and wash her hair when she first went into labor. Ruthie did not have a full tub bath nor wash her hair again for a full 40 days after her baby was born. Again, "I just did what my mother told me." Marya

Smith has less control over her daughters, however. She asked me to ride along to the hospital on the day that she was to bring her daughter Josie and Josie's second baby home. "Boy, I can't wait to get home and wash my hair," Josie observed as she settled herself in the back seat with little Marcus. Marya immediately reminded her of the dangers involved in such a practice only to hear, "Oh Ma, that's just more of your old slavery medicine!" "Lou, *you* tell her, she'll *listen* to you!," said Marya. Caught in the middle, I mumbled something about it being a warm day and so perhaps it would be all right. (Lansing, Michigan; 1983)

The fact that the postpartum blood—like menstrual blood—is seen as filthy is another reason that it must all be released from the body. Indeed, it is perhaps even *more* important that it be shed, representing as it does nine full months of accumulated dirt. "A woman should stay in for a month after the birth of a baby," according to Stella Bird. "Women are not clean enough to be in public, and it can ruin health later in life." (Saginaw, Michigan; 1978)

The old idea that a new mother should do no cooking is also based in part on the polluting attributes of such blood. "Down home," remarked one of Frankel's informants, "they don't let you cook anything till after the [postpartum] bleeding stops. They say you're not clean during that time. If you touch food it will spoil it" (1977:69). In rural Virginia "several persons believe that women should not cook or prepare food while bleeding, whether following delivery or during menstruation. In contemporary America, of course, many women must cook at these times and know this is an accepted cultural norm. Nevertheless, several study participants said they do not 'feel clean' at this time, and in some families it is still taboo to cook when bleeding" (Roberson 1983:129). The fact that the new mother was considered "nasty" was one of the reasons that Marya Smith learned to cook at a very early age; as the oldest daughter she had to help out as best she could:

> And I was around during that time [my mother] had the baby and afterwards. There's a certain length of time that you allowed to go outside to be seen by anybody else; there's a certain length of time that you could walk down the steps and go outside into the yard. You could walk around *in* the house, but there's a length of time that they would allow you before you could walk down the stairs. And there was a length of time before you just was more and more with the peoples, because they was sayin' like, you know, "This woman is *nasty!*" She not 'lowed in the *kitchen,* she wasn't 'lowed.

"So she couldn't cook?"

> Not at that time. They had to be done with that. You know, I 'magine some cases a woman didn't have a *husband,* then maybe [if] they havin' a period it be a different story. But not right after a baby, not havin' a period. They couldn't cook. Nobody'd want to eat that *food. That's* how *I* ended up learnin' how to cook at a very young *age,* be-

cause my mother couldn't cook in a few days, you know. So I had to
cook. She wasn't allowed to *lift* a skillet, [or] anything heavier than the
baby. So, I don't know, a couple of weeks, six weeks, somethin' like
that. It was a pretty long time before she was able to lift anything.
(Lansing, Michigan; 1982)

There were (in some instances, are) also restrictions involving the
disposition of certain associated products of the pregnancy and birth.
A form of contagious magic makes it dangerous for the membranes,
cord, and placenta to be disposed of improperly lest harm befall
mother and child. "One midwife said she always burned the
afterbirth, either in the fireplace or in the yard, making sure nothing
remained. Because 'salt keeps down infection,' one midwife routinely
'salted the placenta and buried it very deep or buried it in the salty
dirt floor of the smoke house.' Both the burning and the burying
methods were also cited as protection from molestation by animals,
but the belief in magical bonds is clear" (Murphree 1968; see also
Hand 1961:13). "Down South," according to one of Frankel's informants, "the mid-nurse wraps up the afterbirth, then takes it out in
the yard and burns it. If you leaves it lying around, something bad
is supposed to happen—at least that's what the old people believes"
(1977:68). If the burning of the placenta took place in the home the
disposal of the resultant ashes was often put off for a certain length
of time. A taboo against taking the ashes out of the house was often
combined with one against sweeping; both practices have been
described as having African counterparts (Herskovits 1941:188–189;
Holmes 1984); certainly such taboos were in place during slavery
times (Richardson 1912).

In the following passage the elderly Alabama midwife Onnie Lee
Logan speaks of the felicitous effect on her peach trees when she
turned to burial instead of burning when disposing of placentas:

> *I was so glad when they got to the stage that I didn't have to burn it.*
> *If they have a shovel and a backyard, the husband dig a long deep hole*
> *and put it in and bury it. Then right in the city where they didn't have*
> *no place to even bury it, when they was livin in the projects, they*
> *didn't even have places that they could bury it. I wrapped em up in*
> *plastic and carried em home. You want to see me count the many that*
> *are buried in my backyard? There's a million of em buried in my*
> *backyard. A million, million placentas. A million placentas is buried in*
> *my backyard. I have peach trees and whatnot trees back there. I buried*
> *alot of placentas around that peach tree. I had the biggest peaches you*
> *ever did see. . . . (Logan 1989:157–158)*

After the proper number of days had passed, the ashes could be
removed from the fireplace, and the new mother could cook and
sweep the floors and go about her usual tasks. But first she had to
be ritually reintroduced to the outside world. In the following description of earlier postpartum practices in Alabama, a midwife makes

sure that a new mother is safe from the dangers of cold air and internal dirt even as she sends her on a symbolic walk around the periphery of her home:

> *Well, when the midwife came back and she took me up and I remember her giving me a dose of medicine and it was some castor oil to get all the filth and stuff out of you, so they told me. And then you had to walk all the way around the house and come back. It would be up in the day [late in the day]. If it was in the wintertime, they would make sure it would be a nice warm day. The coldest time I had a baby was in March. The midwife would not let me go outside on that day. She waited till she found a better day. She came and she got me up, but she made sure I was back in the bed before she left. . . . It would be a month before they threw the ashes away. If you smoked a cigarette in there, you couldn't take it out of there. You couldn't take no fire out of the fireplace where they burned the afterbirth.* (Holmes 1984:390)

Did *she* do that when she had her babies in Mississippi, I asked Marya? "Yeah, they'd go around the house so many times and then they'd walk back into the house," she said. "You go around the house *nine* times."

The treatment of the umbilical stump is also important in the traditional system. In earlier times—and perhaps today in some home births or after an infant is taken home from the hospital—substances were placed on it in order to stop bleeding and promote healing. Burned cotton, lard, soot, fresh animal manure, and cobwebs have all been used in such a manner (E. Parsons 1923:197; Hand 1961:55).

Cobwebs have a long history of use in stopping bleeding; in the nineteenth century they were "asserted to have been advantageously employed as a styptic in wounds, and a healing application in superficial ulcers" (King 1855, quoted in Morton 1974:165). From the vantage point of the twentieth century, dressings with products such as cobwebs and manure are more likely to be linked to cases of neonatal tetanus (Waring 1967:62, footnote). Deas-Moore suggested that such use of cobwebs by granny midwives in the Sea Islands of South Carolina was largely responsible for a midwife retraining program in the 1930s; cobwebs gathered from stable walls were linked to the deaths of infants from "'nine-day fit,' so-called because convulsions would occur usually about nine days after the tetanus germ had been introduced into the navel with the cobwebs" (1987:474–485).

The use of fresh animal manure on the newly cut umbilical stump seems even more likely to have introduced tetanus bacteria into the infant's system (Hughes 1963); Anna Perry told me sadly that the last of her babies had died a few days after birth, and the death was "of the belly button." "Back home," she said, it was recommended that a fresh manure poultice be applied to the newborn's navel area—since "cows eat all the herbs" she felt that their droppings were the distillation of nature's medicines.

There is also a perceived continuation of the connection between the cord and the infant; this is underscored by beliefs about the proper disposal of the dried fragment that drops off a few days after birth. This bit of flesh represents the months-long link between mother and child so must be disposed of properly to avert danger to the child. One must be careful not to let it drop on the floor, said one of Frankel's informants from North Carolina, "or it will make the baby sick to its stomach, or something like that." It should be burned, according to another, so that "the baby will never slobber" (1977:71–72). As this event usually occurs *after* an infant has left the hospital setting such rituals can easily take place at home.

One summer morning in 1981, for example, I accompanied my friend Jeannie French, a pediatrics nurse practitioner, as she made newborn rounds at a local hospital. She instructed one 15-year-old new mother on the care of her infant's umbilical stump. Did the mother have any questions, Jeannie asked? Yes, there was one. "After it falls off, do I have to burn it up to keep something bad from happening to my baby," the young girl asked anxiously? "That's what my grandmother says." "Doctors and nurses don't think that it is necessary," replied Jeannie after a moment. "But it can't hurt anything. If it makes you and your grandmother feel better, by all means do it." The young girl looked relieved and smiled down at her little daughter as we left the room. As we moved down the hall Jeannie and I agreed that the dried bit of cord would most likely have been burned no matter *what* she had said; it was this new baby girl's great-grandmother who would be making most of the decisions about her care.[1] The old ways do not necessarily die out in the face of modern medical advances, then. As Blake (1979) pointed out, "many of the young people are raised in their early years by grandparents or great-grandparents so that many of the customs [of] the elderly are practiced on the young children." To understand the complex interplay between traditional and orthodox ideas about the care of infants and young children, then, it is necessary to examine childrearing practices as well as health behaviors.

Taking Care of Babies

One morning in the spring of 1991 Bernita Washington invited me to come to her church on Sunday so that I might see her receive a certificate as a teacher/evangelist. The occasion would be doubly special because Josie, her oldest granddaughter, was to sing her first solo as a member of the choir. My most vivid memory from that day is not Bernita's award or Josie's rousing rendition of a gospel song, however, but the sight that greeted me when I walked into the vestibule of the small church a few minutes late. There, waiting for a prayer to be over so that he could go into the church proper, stood a very tall and muscular young man dressed entirely in black.

Black suit; black shirt; black tie; black shoes; black socks. Indeed, he would have looked quite sinister were it not for one incongruous note—he had a pink baby's pacifier in his mouth. He was not in the least embarrassed that I saw this but simply nodded at my greeting, plucked the pacifier from his mouth and popped it expertly into the mouth of the new daughter cuddled in his arms, dressed in a frilly pink dress for what must have been her first trip to church. When the prayer was over the doors opened and we walked in; I reflected on how few men that I have known have been as deeply involved with their babies and very little children when compared to many of the African-American fathers, grandfathers, brothers, uncles, and cousins I have met over the years.[2]

During the church service I observed once again the manner in which infants and toddlers—no few of whom were Bernita and Joseph's own grandchildren and great-grandchildren—were kept content. They were remarkably well behaved considering the length of time (nearly four hours) that they were expected to be quiet. Babies were passed around and the littlest children clambered in and out of the laps of assorted relatives, both male and female, as the adults sang, prayed, and listened to the lengthy sermon.

The fact that many poor African-Americans are members of such an extended kin network was mentioned in the last chapter; nowhere is this more evident than in the arrangements made for the care of the group's newest members. This wider group of kin is particularly important in those instances when the new mother and father do not marry. Formal adoption—in which an infant is lost to the kin group via the courts—has been viewed in a very negative light by these families. What *natural* mother would agree to give away her child never to be seen again? When a 16-year-old girl in the maternity ward where Frankel did her study decided to put her child up for adoption the other new mothers were scandalized; said the roommate of the girl who had made the decision to adopt her baby out in this instance, "If the mother gives a baby away [for adoption] people'd have to think it wasn't no good, and whoever got it would just treat it like a puppy nobody wanted" (1977:60). Robert Hill cited data showing that in 1968 "90 percent of the black children born out-of-wedlock were retained by the extended family, compared to only 7 percent of white children born out-of-wedlock. And, one-fourth of the white unmarried mothers who kept their out-of-wed-lock children had to live apart from relatives, compared to less than 1 percent of the black unwed mothers" (1977:23; see also Felice et al. 1987). In other words, "when all else fails, 'we take care of our own [children], while the white folk give them away'" (Schulz 1969:155; see also Logan 1989:112).

Instead of the finality of the formal—and deeply disapproved—process of legal adoption, African-American extended families have traditionally used the *informal* adoptive practice known as the "giving away" of children. This pattern "has existed in the black com-

munity for generations. In fact, during slavery, the practice of informal adoption of children by grandparents and aunts and uncles
permitted thousands of black children to withstand the ordeals of
slavery—after their parents had often been sold as chattel. Informal
adoption has been especially effective among blacks in providing
adequate adult care to children born out-of-wedlock" (R. Hill 1977:22).
One elderly midwife described what happened after the death of a
brother:

> *My sister-in-law, she stayed around awhile after Elmer died. Finally she*
> *went to Birmingham. She eventually come back and got the chil'rens.*
> *Kep' em about a month or two to see that she couldn't handle 'em and*
> *didn't want em. She just didn't want to take time to handle em. She*
> *brought em back to Mother and Daddy and they was raised up there*
> *with their three last chil'rens. They raised em. Onnie, Lizzie, and Charlie*
> *was raised right there with my younger sisters and brothers. Mother*
> *and Daddy raised em. I don't know how they felt about that cause they*
> *didn't talk that to us with us bein that young. We didn't know what*
> *they thought or was they was thinkin. We was cut out of alot a knowin*
> *and sometimes I think that's best.* (Logan 1989:26)

The practice continues to exist today in response to a variety of
pressures—poverty; illegitimacy; breakup of a marriage or relationship; a too-youthful mother; a mother with too many children to
care for; loss of a job; incarceration of a parent; a parent on drugs,
and so on—so that babies or children may be "given" to another
family member to be cared for (C. Johnson 1934:29–30, 60–61; Ward
1971:26; Ladner 1972:128–129; Stack 1974:46–50, 73–89; Snow 1977:25;
Dougherty 1978:53–54; Lemann 1991:52, 80, 95). The need for child
care "activates the mutual sharing of psychological and material
resources" (Valentine 1978:124). Carole Hill used the term "child-shar-
ing" to describe a pattern in which "older relatives keep the children
of young adults who spend long periods of time away from home
working . . . ," noting that these kinship ties are an important link
between rural and urban life (1988:31, 38).

It must be recognized that the same factors that make it a necessity for children to spend time—temporarily or permanently—with
other family members also affect the families that take them in. The
circumstances of the adoptive family may be only marginally better
than those of the family that has had to give them up. In his study
of informal adoption Robert Hill pointed out that "the families that
are most likely to informally adopt are often the *least* likely that
agencies would seek out for formal adoption. They are more likely
to be female-headed, grandparents, elderly, with children of their
own—and poor. Once again, there is a need to modify or eliminate
regulations that preclude the placement of children with surrogates
who are willing to care and rear these children—given additional
supportive services" (1977:86).

E. Martin and Martin also suggested that the extended family is rooted in rural life and that in urban areas it is "likely to deteriorate. Crime, delinquency, truancy, abortion, the formal adoption of children, the institutionalization of the aged indicate that the extended family is failing to fulfill its traditional functions . . ." (1978:91). Perceived lack of support may be internal as well as external; when Lindblad-Goldberg and Dukes compared 76 "normative" and 50 "dysfunctional" low-income single-parent families, for example, they discovered that though "there was an equal balance of give-and-take regarding emotional and instrumental functions in successful families, dysfunctional family mothers reported unequal exchange in these areas. They felt that they gave more emotional and instrumental support than they received from all network members, especially from family members." There were no differences, however, in "kind of feelings or strength to feelings across all network members or within a network category" (1985).

There is no doubt that the stressors on families with already slender resources have increased in recent years because of the toll taken by crack cocaine, AIDS, and related problems; in cities all over the country grandparents and other relatives who had *not* expected to begin childrearing anew are being asked to do so. In Newark, N.J., one primary caretaker of an HIV seropositive infant explained her initial reluctance to be involved:

> *Well, under the circumstances, because she . . . was a drug abuser, automatically DYES [Division of Youth and Family Services] was brought in. . . . And uh, she didn't have a sufficient place to stay, like I say, she was staying with her boyfriend. They knew the history with him pushing her out the window, whatever. She was saying that she was taking [the baby] home with her. And they said that she couldn't. And the only way he could go home with her, is she had to have somebody supervision over her. That was, that they could depend on. So she said me. But I didn't—I had no knowledge of this. . . . She didn't tell me anything. Because I kept tellin' her, you don't need that baby. Should get an abortion because I'm not taking care of no babies. My daughter is twenty-six years old, that's my baby. But once you see em. Automatically you're going to get involved with it. The baby. And finally, I did go to the hospital to see him. The nurse ask me did I wanta feed him. I said, "no." I didn't want to have no parts of him, because I knew what the deal was going to be.* (Meltzer and Kantor 1990)

And, of course, that's what "the deal" turned out to be.[3]

The positive side of these arrangements is that children are cared for, of course. But there is a darker aspect as well; children may not understand why they are sent away and/or resent the fact that they are (Angelou 1970:3–5, 42–44; Guffy 1971:8–17, 156–157). Babies and children may be sent to households where there are other children and, while these serve as playmates, they are also rivals for the attention of the adults (Schulz 1969:41–42).

Jaleene Jasper, a quiet and plain young woman who lived alone with her small son, brought him to the clinic one day and talked of the party she was going to have for his upcoming first birthday. She was making a fuss of it, she said, as she had never had a birthday as a child. She had lived with her grandparents from the time of her own birth and insisted that she had absolutely no memories of her first six years. Why did she think that was, I asked? Perhaps it was because it was "so peaceful and close to the country," she said. And there were no other children around. But she did remember that unhappy day when she was six years old and her five-year-old brother joined the household; she was used to being the only child and was jealous. He was "not a playmate," she said. "He went his way, I went mine." When Jaleene was eight years old the grandmother died and the two children went to live with a great-grandmother; but two years later this woman died as well, and Jaleene and her little brother were sent to the home of yet another relative. The children were unhappy there and after a year or so the brother ran away. But Jaleene stayed "for eight miserable years." Nor did the presence of a cousin in the home make things bearable; instead, the children were very differently treated. Every year there was a party to mark the cousin's birthday, for example, but for Jaleene each birthday "just passed on by." She had vowed then that if she ever grew up and had children *they* would have birthday parties to remember! Hence the "fuss" for little Tyrone. (Lansing, Michigan; 1985)

Some of these family strategies that have long been so adaptive in the African-American community also produce a number of headaches in clinical settings, of course. This is particularly true in the health care of children. Pediatric medicine is already qualitatively different from adult care in that whatever medical advice is given is necessarily addressed to a third party—the parent or other responsible adult who has brought an infant or child in to be seen. The health professional's assumption is, of course, that this individual will see that instructions are carried out. When childrearing takes place in an extended-family situation, however, such an assumption must be modified. Any discussion of the health problems of the babies and children in these families must take into consideration the fact that they often have multiple caretakers and that they may spend significant amounts of time in more than one household. The person who brings a baby in for an appointment may *not* be the one charged with seeing that instructions are carried out, for example, so that any advice given by a doctor or nurse will still have to be delivered second- or even third-hand to someone else.[4] And the likelihood that instructions will be followed are diminished if, say, the young patient spends days in one home and nights in another. The variety of family constellations in such a client population may be *very* different from the experience of most of the health professionals charged with treating children. In a study of first graders in an area of Chicago in the late 1960s, for example, it was discovered that in their homes "there were no less than 86 different combinations of adults in one school year" (Kellam, Ensminger, and Turner 1977).

Because of "child-tending arrangements and familial relationships that are often not mainstream, and that often involve nonmarital birth," wrote Margaret Boone, "disadvantaged black children can be seen to live in 'households' encompassing several addresses with several heads of household having several different last names . . . " (1987). Both the location and composition of these households may be extremely fluid: People move from one low-rent dwelling to another in search of adequate housing, and friends and relatives come and go in response to the changing events in their lives. Answers to the questions, Where do you live? and, Who do you live with? are rendered almost meaningless unless "right now" is added.

If, as some research suggests, moving from one location to another is a stressful event, then young Josie Washington was under a good deal of stress during the 18 months after she gave birth to her son Mikey in 1982. She lived in no fewer than *seven* different places during that time span. And that does not include the numerous times she went back to stay with her mother—who moved twice in that time period herself—in between moves. Although the families utilizing the Lansing pediatrics clinic were not all *that* mobile, many did in fact move frequently. It was small wonder that the postcards mailed out by the clinic to remind mothers of upcoming appointments for their children were frequently not received.

The delivery of health care is certainly made more difficult by these constantly changing patterns of household composition and location; as well, matters of health and illness must also be examined within the framework of fundamental ideas concerning childrearing. These include beliefs about what babies and children are like and what sorts of techniques must therefore be employed to produce a properly behaving adult. When the opinions of health professionals and the families they serve differ, then the potential for miscommunication is high; what is seen as normal and right by one side may be viewed as neglectful if not downright abusive by the other (see Korbin 1981 re cross-cultural perspectives on child abuse and neglect).[5] And the expectations of the behavior of babies, toddlers, and small children in African-American extended families are frequently very different from those of individuals formally trained in child development or pediatrics.

Babies in these families are greatly desired and greatly indulged in an environment that, as one observer notes, "is almost wholly human. Cribs, baby carriages, and highchairs are almost never seen. The baby is held and carried most of the time, and when it is laid down it is seldom without company" (Young 1970; see also Ward 1971:24–25, and Young 1974). When there is a baby in the house, wrote Dougherty,

> *he is usually the primary focus of attention. He is played with, handled, and talked to and about almost constantly. A familiar person entering the house usually interacts with the baby before greeting or interacting with others present. The central position of babies results in their being contented, smiling, laughing, and responsive. They generally are not shy of strangers and are encouraged to go to the arms of a wide number of adults. Siblings and other children find intense pleasure in eliciting responses from babies. When permitted to, they present him with toys and hold, tickle, kiss, feed, and carry him. (1978:62)*

While I am certainly no expert on the developmental stages of infants and children, I, too, have been struck over the years by how fearless some of these little ones are around strangers. On the occasion mentioned above when I attended church with Bernita's family I happened at one point to catch the eye of the 18-month-old son of Bernita's youngest daughter, Jonell. I had seen him only once before when he was less than a year old and he could not possibly have remembered me; nevertheless, when I smiled at him he promptly got down from his mother's lap and came over and crawled into mine. He sat there quietly for nearly half an hour before he became restless and began to squirm; his grandmother sternly whispered to him to be quiet. When he did not immediately settle down she slapped him smartly on the leg; he did not cry but merely climbed down from *my* lap and and toddled over to sit for awhile in the lap of an uncle. Training in proper behavior obviously begins very early.

Although I thought Bernita's treatment of her little grandson rather harsh, it was based on her culturally grounded belief that small children have a good deal of control over their behavior and so ought to be able to do what they are told. Much control, in fact, is expected even of infants too small to walk or talk. Carrington mentioned "the emphasis black mothers place on wanting their children 'to behave.' In making my postpartum rounds to mothers, I've frequently heard them tell their babies to 'be good now.' Crying excessively is seen as behaving in a 'bad way,' although the new mother's tone of voice is obviously soft and loving . . . " (1978). After the newborn period the admonishments may no longer be soft and loving; I have frequently heard adults scold babies or seen swats delivered to the bottoms of infants in punishment for misbehaving or not minding when (in my opinion) they were *far* too young to understand what was expected of them. When I admired Bernita's latest great-granddaughter on another occasion, for example, I was told that that, yes, Bea Anne was cute but that sometimes she had to be shaken for "cuttin' the fool." What did she mean by "cuttin' the fool," I asked? "Hollerin' when there's no reason for it," said Bernita. Bea Anne was three months old at the time. (1990)

Most health professionals would not have the high expectations of the mother who, when her five-month-old baby urinated in her lap, said to it reproachfully, "You should have gotten down to pee-pee" (Young 1970). Actually, the training of children ought to begin *in* the womb, according to elderly Frances McNair. "A child should be raised before it is born; it ought to be taught," she said, going on to comment that during pregnancy, "What condition you in, the baby be in!" (East Lansing, Michigan; 1983) (See Hand 1961:34, and Newman 1969 for similar beliefs.)

These same small babies who are thought capable of controlling their emotions, their behavior, and their bladders will as toddlers be expected to assume some responsibilities around the home. A small child who has learned to "do for himself" is described with pride, and between the ages of two and three years may be able to accomplish many tasks: "One young mother staying at home with her two-year-old and her sister's infant explained how the baby keeps her tied down. She feels that her daughter is 'no trouble' because she can 'pretty well take care of herself.' When the mother wants to stay in bed in the morning the little girl gets out of bed, goes to the bathroom independently, and then to the kitchen to get her breakfast. She locates crackers or bread to eat and then turns on the television and watches it until her mother gets up. This child is similar in ability to other children of her age" (Dougherty 1978:66).

Before long, in fact, such a child will be able to look after the needs of others as well. After having a baby, I asked 17-year-old Alice Jones—at the prenatal clinic for her third pregnancy in as many years—how long should a woman wait before having another baby? "Three years," she said firmly. "At least three years." *That's* good, I thought to myself; she understands that it's a bad idea to have these children so close together. But Alice went on: "That's so the *first* baby will be old enough to take care of the *new* baby!" (Lansing, Michigan; 1975)

Many small boys and girls learn "adult" responsibilities at a young age, then. They must become independent in caring for physical needs while at the same time aggressively competing with others for attention. African-American adults reared in such families often use the phrase, "when I was old enough to go for myself," in referring to the time when they took full responsibility for their lives. And again such maturity may come markedly earlier than is seen as usual—or "normal"—by the standards of middle-class observers. I can still hear Henry Jackson laughing when I told him that I could not come back and talk to him that evening because I did not have a babysitter. "How old *is* your baby?" he had asked. "He's nine," I had answered. To Henry the idea that a nine-year-old boy would need a babysitter was ludicrous; when Henry was that age he was living alone in a woodshed on the property of a White family. His mother had died, his father had deserted him, and none of his older brothers and sisters wanted to be responsible for him. He had been on his own.[6] (Tucson, Arizona; 1971)

Culturally appropriate gender separation also begins early; even as tiny infants boys and girls are perceived as being different in ways that foreshadow adult behaviors. Talk about baby boys and baby girls reflects the same divisions that are often found between adult men and women. In the view of one very old lady in rural Georgia when speaking of her own children: "All'm but two was girls. I thinked the girls'd be the best. Yes, ma'am! A girl ain't hard to keep up wid. A boy, he'd run away, a boy, he'd be gone. A new dress to put on, that's about the worst trouble a girl is. Boys, they go off and get in devilment, not like a girl. Yeah'm boys is *tough* and mean. Cain't raise 'em, not like the Bible speak of it" (Sh. Thomas 1981:4).

Among Frankel's informants women were about evenly divided in their preference for having a boy or a girl, but there was "almost unanimous agreement on the *reasons* one might have for preferring one over the other, regardless of one's own personal preference" (1977:102). They agreed that boys are "less trouble" in terms of physical care, that is, cheaper to dress and easier in terms of physical grooming, but behaviorally are "more apt to be rough and destructive, as well as more difficult to control than girls." A girl, in contrast, though she may take more of a mother's time because of the task of doing her hair, is "'fun to dress up all pretty,' and is likelier to bring emotional satisfactions to the mother" (pp. 102–103). As the single mother of three boys and two girls in Washington, D.C., put it:

> You know, you just got to act a little bit tougher with boys than with girls, 'cause they just ain't the same. Girls do what you tell them to do and don't get into no trouble, but you just can't be sure about boys. I mean, you think they're OK and next thing you find out they're playing hookey and drinking wine and maybe stealing things from cars and what not. There's just something bad about boys here, you know. But what can you say when many of them are just like their daddies? That's the man in them coming out. You can't really fight it, you know that's the way it is. They know, too. But you just got to be tougher. (Hannerz 1969:123)

When a group of high school student/mothers in Florida discussed perceived differences in male and female babies,

> the idea that boy babies and children are "bad" and "more hard-headed" than girls pervaded the group. All of the mothers had wanted girl babies before their deliveries, only one had given birth to a boy and she strongly verbalized her feeling that after she "got a boy" she "loved him just the same" (as she would have loved a girl). They contended that boys are rougher, "You can beat them and they don't pay attention," and, "They don't be as close as girls to their mothers." Their attitudes about boys and girls were freely and openly discussed, and perhaps, their expectations were self-fulfilling prophesies. They were interested

in and seemed to understand our comments that children grow up to act much the same as they are treated as children—roughly, kindly, lovingly, or indifferently. However, it is doubtful that an understanding of such principles by a few mothers could significantly alter the patterns of behavior that support the social organization of a community. In one sequence the mother of a girl said that she didn't like boys (while holding the boy baby). The mother of the boy retorted, "I'm glad I got a boy because them girls be bringing all them babies to your house, not mine," stressing one advantage of having a male child and her sophisticated internalization of the social order in which the girls live. (Lenocker and Dougherty 1976)

For these young mothers, ideas about discipline "generated little doubt or conflict. . . . They agreed that older infants could have their hands slapped when necessary but other forms of discipline, such as 'switching' or spanking, should occur after 1 year of age when the child is 'into things.' They disciplined their children as they had observed their mothers and grandmothers doing, and they seldom questioned these examples."

The good behavior that is expected of babies, toddlers, and children is brought about by verbal and physical treatment that quite openly links love and aggression (Young 1970; Ward 1971:75–87). Children, noted Ward (p. 26),

are in a separate category from babies. They are seldom held or caressed. In fact, in contrast to babies they appear to be treated rather harshly. They can be screamed at or struck at will. As "children," they have responsibilities: watching another child, going to the store, or helping to clean the house. Needless to say, these activities do not begin immediately at the yard walking stage (eighteen to twenty-four months) but are fully recognized by adults and children by age four. A four-year-old handles money, household tasks, and increasing independence. By this age autonomy outside the house is virtually complete. The children roam at will through the neighborhood. . . . 7

"I love having babies, they are wonderful to have around," is the attitude of mothers in this Louisiana community. "It's the children that get on your nerves" (see also Rainwater 1970:219–220).

The physical punishment that may so unsettle an outside observer is thought necessary to train children, "hard-headed" by nature. The little ones may not appreciate it at the time, say the grownups, but later they will thank them for it. In looking back at their own childhoods many adults compare the disciplinary techniques of parents and/or other caretakers and give special praise to those individuals who loved them enough to "whup" them when they needed it. *They* are the ones who, in retrospect, "made me the man [or woman] I am today!" Old Olive Parsons remembered both of her parents with great fondness, for example, but it was the physically punitive mother and not the permissive father who was given the credit for "raising" her and her siblings in rural Oklahoma so long ago:

> *She was a wonderful mother, but she was strict on us. Our daddy wasn't, he'd get out and play with us just as big! And she'd get after him about it: "All right, play with a puppy, he'll lick your mouth." But that daddy, I dunno, sometime he'd scold some of us, speak short to us. Then if he scold one of us and'd [and we'd] break and cry, why, then he's gonna pet him! Him or her. Hug and kiss 'em, y'know, "Hush cryin', now, hush cryin', now, daddy didn't mean it!" and all like that. . . . We had two parents, but only one of them raised us. She sure raised us; my daddy he didn't. He fed us, but she raised us!* (Tucson, Arizona; 1970) (Snow 1977:53)

It is not surprising that it was Olive's mother, not her father, who came back from the dead for a supportive visit when Olive was concerned about how "spoiled" her great-grandchilden were.

Olive's views are echoed by a college student in a small Southern town, who explains how his "Auntie Sue" disciplined him even though she was not really related to the family:

> *Well, it's like this: whereas Mama would say, "John, make sure you clean up your mess behind yourself," then she'd just go and leave me to do it. Auntie Sue, she won't be standing right over me, but I knew she'd be somewhere watching me. Sometimes I'd try to sneak away, but she'd catch me and say, "Oh, no, you don't do that. Get back there and clean up your mess 'fore I get this dishrag to you." I used to get so mad at her, but I'm glad she was that strict with me. She taught me a lot of things that have stuck with me and made me the person I am today.* (Kennedy 1980:163–164)

"Spare the rod and spoil the child" is believed quite literally by many adults, then, and some see laxity in physical punishment as promoting bad behavior in the young. It was taking prayers out of the schools that gave rise to what Ella Thomas called "juvenile" [delinquency]—that, and rules against corporal punishment in the Arizona schools. "They got a law here you can't whup no child! But I whup mine; he never get too big for me to whup. Ever'body should know how to whup 'em without beatin' 'em and bruisin' 'em up" (Snow 1977:52). And the mother of the young man quoted above says, in regard to punishing his son, her grandson: "Oh! Sometime John tell me I shouldn't beat him so much and so hard. He said I should talk to him more, but I know when to talk and when to use the strap. That's the trouble with the young people these days, folks have forgot how to use the strap" (Kennedy 1980:160). As the pastor of one small Baptist church in Lansing put it, "God doesn't want us to misuse a child—but He wants us to be firm." (1992)

Despite the common belief that physical punishment is a necessary component of childrearing my observation is that it was usually not carried out in the immediate presence of the doctors and nurses at the clinic. There might be a good deal of arm-yanking, hand-slapping, and bottom-swatting in the waiting room, but once babies and children were in the examining room most adults restricted their attempts to control the behavior of little ones to verbal admonishments. The dire consequences that might be promised to a fussy baby "when I get you home" were often as unnerving to new residents as a slap to the infant's face would have been, however, and it took some time for these young physicians to be able to take into account *how* something was said as well as *what* was said.

The terms that adults use to describe babies and children may also horrify middle-class outsiders, and again, tone must be considered as well as content. "I'm really worried about that Mrs. Jones," said one new resident. "She keeps talking about how 'bad' her baby is and he's only three weeks old!" And how was she *handling* the baby while saying it, the clinic director asked? Well, she was cuddling him and looked at him lovingly. (Lansing, Michigan; 1983) The children who are spoken of as "bad," "mean," or even "evil" are not necessarily in danger of abuse and neglect, then. Each of these terms may be used to describe—with fondness and pride—a child who displays boldness and initiative. In her study of family patterns in a Georgia town, for example, Young noted: "There is much talk about babies' meanness. Mothers and nurse children will sigh about how mean a baby was who would not nap, while they are greatly enjoying holding and displaying the mean baby. A four-month-old baby who held tight to a glass of water after drinking was told, 'Uh-uh, stop trying to fight. You's a mean little old girl.' The mother was admiring the baby's assertiveness and attesting to the highly developed character assumed in babies" (Young 1970:279). And it was in a tone of complete admiration that Marya Smith said to me of her first granddaughter, "That Sharleen, she be really *evil* and she only six months old! She pull Mikey and Marcus' hair *both!*" Sure enough, when Marcus wandered by, the baby girl grabbed herself a fistful of hair and would not let go. Little Sharleen wasn't taking anything off of her big brothers![8] (1985)

Babies and Children:
Clean and Warm and Full

Bernita Washington was still a child when her mother died from the hex "put on" her by her husband, Bernita's stepfather, and more than 50 years later she still sometimes laments that she was "raised without a parent." This meant that she did not have her mother around to advise her when as a young girl she gave birth to the first of her ten living children. Fortunately for her there were plenty of other "older ladies" in the neighborhood to help her out when there was something she needed to know:

In my young life I always deal with older ladies when I was havin'
my little kids; I dealt with older ladies. So I would notice what *they*
do for *their* babies and then *I* would know what to do for *mine,* you
know. And if I saw them, if they did somethin' I didn't understand
what they were doin' it for, I would akst them, "Why are you doin'
this?," y'know. "Why are you doin' that?" And they would *tell* me. So
it is *very important* that younger womens that has babies and really
doesn't quite understand, it is really important for them to deal with
an older lady. (Lansing, Michigan; 1987)

Today, of course, Bernita is one of those older ladies herself. And
she is more than happy to pass on the knowledge gained over a
lifetime to younger women. She has plenty to say about everything
from feeding babies to the best ways to prevent worms in small
children. The role of these experienced advisers in extended families
is no doubt important wherever they are found; among Carole Hill's
rural Georgia informants, for example, "most women depend almost
entirely on their mothers and/or other relatives for advice about and
care of their babies" (1988:89).

Much of the advice about keeping babies and children healthy
that is given in the home setting (or settings) revolves around the
same problem areas that have been noted for adults in the traditional
health system. Little ones, that is, must also be protected from the
cold, kept clean inside and out, and properly fed; each of these areas
of concern is exhibited in a lifelong preoccupation with ingestion,
digestion, and elimination that begins on the day that a child is
born. And each of these areas of concern provides potential for
conflict between those who have been formally trained in child
health and those individuals who actually provide care to children
day in and day out. The mothers or grandmothers caring for infants
may consider the solely milk diet suggested by pediatricians to be
a totally inadequate source of nourishment, for example. And since
virtually all meals—whether formula or fast food—are consumed
away from the gaze of professional advisers, unwanted advice can
be freely disregarded.

In general, health professionals view the appropriateness of foodstuffs for babies according to nutritional content and the perceived
ability of the infantile system to digest them properly; different
items are gradually introduced over a period of time until the child
is considered ready to eat the same foods as other family members.
Increases in an infant's height and weight are plotted onto standardized growth charts that provide a quick assessment of whether
development is in the normal range. In contrast, traditional feeding
practices are based on the belief that fat babies are healthy and
contented babies. There is much more emphasis on seeing that babies
get *enough* to eat, that is, than on just what it is that they are fed.
The weight that is seen as perfectly normal by a health professional

may indicate deprivation or illness to the persons caring for the child. And the idea that children (even those unborn) know what they *want* to eat may be just as important as what some outsider says they should eat. Suggestions that a child should not be fed certain things or should weigh more—or less—may thus fall on deaf ears.

The issue of breastfeeding is one in which there is little agreement between health care workers and new mothers. Health professionals, of course, see breast milk as the best possible food in the first months of life. However, data from a number of studies suggest that it is not a popular choice for many African-American women. Although a number of the women interviewed by Frankel agreed that it is the "best thing" for babies, only 2 of the 50 were actually doing so and only 3 or 4 more had ever done so (1977:58, 60). None of the mothers in Ward's Louisiana sample had ever breastfed their infants although it was "actively" encouraged by local health authorities (1971:25). Data from more recent studies provide similar results (Baranowski et al. 1983; Rassin et al. 1984; McLorg and Bryant 1989; Jacobson, Jacobson, and Frye 1991; Ryan et al. 1991). A recent program at Chicago's Cook County Hospital, however, has demonstrated that prenatal education programs can successfully increase the numbers of women who elect to breastfeed their infants (Kistin et al. 1990).

Reasons given *not* to breastfeed vary; a common one is a wish on the part of the new mother not to be tied down (Carrington 1978; Ward 1971:25). One new mother brought her fourth and last baby to the pediatrics clinic for his first postnatal checkup, for example, announcing that *this* time she was going to breastfeed. The infant's grandmother, however, had been piqued at this decision. "How is anyone going to be able to take that child anywhere if you do *that*," the older woman had asked? But with her other babies, "I was out on the streets having too much fun!," the mother said. "And I wanted to try it at least once." (1986) The practice also seems to be viewed with distaste by some women. It was "overtly viewed with revulsion or shame" by several of Frankel's informants; said one who had tried it before and decided against it with a new baby, "I didn't like having a baby sucking on my titty!" (Frankel 1977:104, 58) Over the years I have also noticed that a question about intention to breastfeed often results in a grimace of distaste along with a negative response. Do you intend to breastfeed this time, 20-year-old Josie Washington was asked during her fourth and final pregnancy? Josie made a face and answered in a single word, "Yuck!"

Although most women seem to agree that the milk of a healthy mother is the "best" food for babies—irrespective if they do or do not breastfeed—they also agree that it can rather easily be rendered inedible by the mother's own actions. A breastfeeding mother's diet, says Bernita Washington, cannot contain anything that she had been unable to eat during pregnancy—if the baby did not want it *then*, it should not have it *now*. Breastmilk may also be tainted by factors other than the mother's diet; the idea that it can be "spoiled" by strong emotional states and thereby made poisonous to infants is found among Haitian women (Farmer 1988). It may also carry a variety of contaminants: During the two weeks that the new mother stays in after giving birth she should drink catnip tea daily, according to Anna Perry. This will rid her blood of the "impurities" that built up because she failed to menstruate during the long months of pregnancy; if she does not do so these might be delivered to her baby through the breastmilk and cause sickness. Haitian women living in Miami also fear that breastmilk may cause their infants to have intestinal parasites, a problem which may be avoided if the mother does not breastfeed (DeSantis 1989). In the latest version of this motif it is the AIDS virus that can unknowingly be fed to the innocent child:

> *Another mother, another infant, the same clinic.*
>
> *"Did you ever nurse the baby?"*
>
> *"No, they told me not to."*
>
> *"Good," I say. The current understanding is that breast milk can transmit HIV, so babies who escape infection in the womb could contract it from their mothers after birth. And so, instead of passing out the usual pediatric message (breast-feeding is best), I am saying, good, your child has never tasted your milk.*
>
> *And yet, what a message for a mother to live with: you are dangerous to your child. For that matter, what a message for a pregnant woman. Even if she eats right and stops smoking, even if she stays away from drugs and sees her doctor regularly, she has to live with the fear that along with oxygen, calories and protein her body may be sending through those complex blood-rich interconnections a virus that will one day make her child sicken, and even die. (Klass 1990:26)*

And even "good" breastmilk may not be "enough" food for babies, some say. But if they do not overeat, according to Cassie Seales, at least they are in less danger of contracting "thrash": "If it's a breast baby I don't think you should worry about givin' it too much milk. But if it's a bottle baby I think the mother should be careful not to give them too much milk, because it'll give them the thrash. It's all white; I've seen quite a few babies with it; I don't think they should have too much milk." (Lansing, Michigan; 1973) "Thrash" or "thrush" is moniliasis (an oral yeast infection) in the eyes of health professionals. The whitish growth of the yeast in the baby's mouth resembles curdled milk, however, so the traditional belief that the problem is caused by the baby receiving too much milk is understandable. The mother should also be careful to wipe excess milk off the mouth or tongue, says Bernita:

Some of my babies had thrash. When my kids were little, what happened [was] I wasn't trained enough to *know* that after the baby was through nursin' his bottle or your breast, whatever you had him on, I didn't know that you was supposed to take that little tip and keep his *tongue* cleaned off. O.K., the milk gathers there; you supposed to keep his tongue cleaned off. And if that wouldn't do good then after they, you know, when they urinate in—children *now* wear Pampers but then they wore diapers—O.K., so you supposed to take that wet diaper and wipe off their tongue. And around their mouth. (1986)

It was her great-grandson Mikey Washington's unresolved monilial infection that provided my introduction to the Washington/Smith families, in fact. Her daughter Marya, Mikey's grandmother, had substituted her own treatment of mopping out Mikey's mouth with his own wet diaper for the drops prescribed by his pediatrician. Like her mother, Marya said that it might have been prevented altogether if daughter Josie had only wiped the milk off the baby's mouth with the diaper after feeding him, a practice which Josie refused to follow. Treatment had been negotiated on the third clinic visit for Mikey's infection. Josie was out of the room with the nurse to have Mikey weighed and Marya—who cared for the baby while Josie went to school—was asked if she would be willing to at least *try* the medication for a few days? She was not scolded for the use of the urine-soaked diaper nor was she told to stop using it; instead it was suggested that though it might be an old remedy it did not seem to be working this time. She agreed to give the medicated drops a try, and two weeks later when Josie brought Mikey back in to be checked, the infection was gone. Josie never knew that her mother had not been giving him the medicine all along. And the resident, who had been startled initially by Marya's home remedy, was better prepared the next time he heard it broached. "He's getting too much milk," said another 16-year-old mother who, accompanied by her own mother, brought her three-week-old baby in to be seen for "the thrash." Careful to look at *both* women, he asked if anything was being done for it? The grandmother responded that she had been wiping the baby's mouth out with his wet diaper. "That's fine," said the resident, "but if it doesn't work in a few days, bring him back in and I'll give you some medicine." (1982)

The belief on the part of health professionals that milk—from the breast or from the bottle—will fulfill an infant's nutritional requirements in the first months of life is often not shared by those infants' caretakers. In the Philadelphia maternity ward the mothers "were much preoccupied with the quality and amount of formula brought for them to feed their babies in the hospital, and several pronounced it wanting and vowed to give their babies something 'with more body to it' when they took them home. That this attitude sometimes results in overfeeding seems probable" (Frankel 1977:104–105). It was not likely that they received *only* formula for very long, irrespective of how much "body" it might have. I knew that Janine Jackson was deeply involved in the care of her grandchildren and decided to ask her about her thoughts on infant feeding; she very definitely believes that solid foods should be started earlier than their pediatrician recommends:

> I think you have to do it much earlier than that, uh-huh, because the *milk* just goes right through! And they stay *hungry* for half of the time! I found that out with my oldest child; I was just feedin' her just milk like the doctor said, and she *cried* all the time! And I took her in again, [and] he said, "The baby's *hungry!*" This was earlier; nowadays they tell you to wait six months or whatever. But she must have been three, 'bout four months old. He said, *"Feed the baby!"* And I was feedin' her a little the way it was, and I started feedin' the baby and no more problem! So I think they need *food* along with that milk!

> I told my daughter-in-law [that] at the age of three months, Annie needs some *food!* 'Cause she's one of those babies you can tell love to eat. And she *love,* talk about eatin', she like it! Right. Lots of 'em give 'em this little baby cereal, you know, you get that and you put it in with your milk. Lots of 'em doin' that now. But you can do that *earlier* than the mothers are doin' it! And applesauce, you know that's good earlier for the baby. You know sumpin' like that's good. I'd say at three months you can feed a baby. *Mine* was eatin' from the table at six months! Before then, it didn't *hurt!* Umh-huh. (Lansing, Michigan; 1986)

Many clinic mothers also commented that babies who were given "real food" were less fussy and much more likely to sleep at night. Similar findings were noted in a study where it was found that many maternal grandmothers and male partners encouraged the early feeding of solid foods; when these practices were in conflict with what mothers heard in clinical settings, the "most common strategy adopted by both blacks and whites was to discount health professionals' advice" (McLorg and Bryant 1989). Other descriptions of the feeding of African-American infants also reveal that cereals and other solid foods are introduced earlier than is advised by such professionals (Ward 1971:26; Carrington 1978; A. Ferris et al. 1978; Bowering et al. 1978; Dougherty 1978:60–61). Frankel's comment about probable overfeeding for many infants is also borne out by Lythcott, Sinnette, and Hopkins (1975). A survey of the nutritional status of minority children in 1986, in fact, revealed that though the prevalence of underweight was less than the 5 percent expected, "in most instances, the rate of overweight exceeded the 5 percent expected when compared with the reference population" (Nutritional Status of Minority Children—United States, 1986). It has also been reported that homeless children in Los Angeles exhibit high rates of "health problems such as developmental delay (9 percent) and overweight (13 percent). The diets of homeless children were frequently imbalanced, dependent on food from 'fast-food' restaurants, and characterized by repeated periods of deprivation" (Wood et al. 1990).

It is *underweight* that seems to concern physicians more than obesity, however. New infants who do not gain weight at a rate thought normal by health professionals are worrisome to them, and this concern may result in the infants being diagnosed as demonstrating "failure to thrive." This label often incorporates some sort of emotional lack on the part of the mother as well as her apparent inability to deliver the proper number of calories to her child. Obviously some mothers do *not* "bond" with their children and may be emotionally detached from them—but there are other instances in that there is an explanation for the problem that has nothing whatsoever to do with the mother's psychological state. In one example, a new mother brought her baby boy to the clinic for his first checkup, and it was discovered that he had lost a few ounces since being discharged from the hospital. The mother was only 16 and had no family in the area; she had moved to the city with her boyfriend but he had deserted her when she told him of the pregnancy. As she was inexperienced—and alone—the resident was particularly careful to reemphasize the number of ounces of formula her baby should be consuming each day in order to grow properly. She indicated that she understood; when she returned the following week, however, the baby had lost even more weight and was hospitalized. There the child was given a special formula high in calories and nutrients and gained weight appropriately; he was discharged in a few days. On the mother's *next* clinic visit the beaming resident said to her, "Well, we've solved the problem," and told her that he would write out a prescription for the new formula as it could not be obtained without one. "It's more expensive, but it's worth it!" Instead of being gratified at hearing this news, however, the young woman burst into sobs. A few questions revealed that she had not had enough money to buy formula in the first place and, when told that her baby needed a certain number of ounces/day, she had diluted the bottles to make sure that he got the proper amount. And now she was told that the formula necessary to keep her baby healthy would cost even *more* money! She was eligible for help from social services but had not known how to go about obtaining it; an emergency phone call from the resident set things into motion. On the next clinic visit her baby was no longer "failing to thrive."

On another occasion a six-month-old child was seen as "possible failure to thrive" when it was noted that he was below the normal weight curve for his age. This mother was not inexperienced, however; she had two other children. And when feeding problems had developed with this infant she had simply invented her *own* formula! She had begun by breastfeeding him but had ceased three months earlier when she developed an upper respiratory infection and was given antibiotics; she had taken little Walter from the breast and given him formula instead. But little Walter "didn't like it" and threw it up; even little babies, after all, know what they want to eat. So she thought to herself about what sorts of things are "good" for babies and decided on a combination of 2 percent cow's milk, Karo syrup, cereal, and water—Walter liked his mother's mixture and had been drinking it ever since. She had noticed that he was rather "small" but was not overly concerned; her other two children had also been small as infants. "But when they started to grow they did fine!" And she thought that perhaps her daughter had also been small "because of her metabolism; she just burned it off." She had no reason to think that this baby would not follow the pattern of his older brother and sister. The resident ordered a blood count, recommended a different brand of formula, and instructed the mother to bring Walter back in one week. He had gained five ounces when she returned with him: When given the formula "straight" he had spit it up but she had solved this by mixing it with fruit and cereal. The resident looked at the laboratory report and said, "Well, at least he's not anemic." "Oh, he's not anemic, that's for sure!," the mother broke in. "He's so energetic, when his sister comes in the room he rolls over and starts talking to her!" No child with "low blood" could possibly be so lively. (Lansing, Michigan; 1984)

There is also concern in the home setting if a child is seen as not eating enough, although it is not going to be labeled "failure to thrive." During the first year of his life Mikey Washington was brought to the clinic for regular health maintenance visits, for his "thrash," and on two occasions for mild upper respiratory infections. Once he began to walk, however, his grandmother decided that he was far too thin and he was brought in several times because she was sure that he was "starving." "He's not eating at all," said Marya, who cared for him much of the time. In vain did the resident show her where Mikey fit on a growth chart; *he* might think that he was growing adequately (Mikey was in the 40th percentile for both height and weight) but Marya was certain that he was not. Not only was he *thin*, but he complained of stomachaches; without a doubt he was suffering from worms. The resident pooh-poohed this idea, however, so Marya called her mother. *She* would know what to do. And Bernita did; she, too, had had doctors tell her that a child did not have worms:

> Well, I'll tell you how I suspected [them] in my baby girl. I had kept carryin' her to the doctor. She was *so thin* and I told him, "I believe she's got worms." And her little stomach would hurt all the time, you know! And I *knew* something was wrong and so I carried her to the doctor and I told him. And he didn't believe it. So I got some *nutmeg,* nutmeg, what you put in cake or in potatoes, nutmeg. You can get it

in a little round ball in a box and grate it off. And you can get that and put it in some syrups, cut the worms up. And after that she started *passin'* worms; she started passin' whole worms. (Lansing, Michigan; 1986)

One could also take gunpowder from a shotgun shell and use just the amount that will stay on the end of a paring knife, she said. Gunpowder may not be readily available, she went on, but most people have nutmeg in the kitchen all the time (see Kreig 1964:97–99; Murphree 1968; and Siegel 1976 for warnings as to the serious side effects of overdoses of nutmeg). So little Mikey was given his dose of nutmeg unbeknownst to his pediatrician. But he still continued to complain of stomachaches, and Josie asked advice from one of her aunts as well as her mother and grandmother; the aunt suggested that what he *really* needed was a good dose of Fletcher's Castoria (an over-the-counter laxative preparation for children). Josie misunderstood what it was, however, and on the impression that it was a "vitamin tonic" gave it to the little boy daily for the next six months. "No wonder the poor little kid's got a bellyache," the resident grumbled when he learned of this, "I would, too, if someone gave me a laxative every day!" The laxative was stopped and Mikey began to put on enough weight to satisfy even Marya; perhaps he was just one of those kids who was *supposed* to be kind of thin. (The laxative given by his *mother* was stopped, that is; when he was at his grandmother's she gave him "a few drops" every day and "more if he needs it." On many days he must have been given double doses.)

The delicate systems of infants may also be upset by extremes of temperature. During slavery, according to one author, mothers "could not nurse their babies when they came in from the field until they had rested for fifteen minutes, to prevent babies from getting overheated and colicky" (Harrison 1975/1976). It is cold that is usually the culprit, however, and it may be breathed in or swallowed. If babies take in too much cold air with their food or drink, for example—or are given a cold bottle by someone too lazy to warm it up—the result is likely to be colic or general "fussiness." Failure to protect babies from the weather is also blamed by some. Neither of her children had ever had the colic, one young mother had said in answer to a resident's question. "I never let wind hit their faces. I always bundles them up before I take them out!" (1987) Janine Jackson also believes that cold air is a likely cause of the problem, while noting that cold air is hard to avoid in Michigan. Fortunately it is treatable by one of her favorite all-round remedies:

And then I would think they takin' in too much air when they *young* and that will bring about it. When they very young, like Annie, that's somethin' like two months old or so. When you get out in this air and she would get too much *chill,* and bring it *in!* She'd be cryin' and you

not know what's *wrong*. It the *colic* because she, we always thought
she took in too much *air*. Cold air. So, back *again* to the bakin' soda!
Give her a little pinch of the bakin' soda for the colic. Many time, just
put it in a spoon and drop just a few drops of water, [or] else milk.
Same thing for a stomachache. That bakin' soda; I think that's what my
parents raised us on, bakin' soda. (Lansing, Michigan; 1986)

Another grandmother who came to the clinic with her daughter and
infant grandson had a method of dosage that was simpler yet; when
the baby had "gas," she said, she just dipped the end of her finger
in baking soda and let him suck it off. (1987)

An even more popular folk treatment for colic in babies is catnip
tea; it was this remedy that Patty Ann Thompson's mother had asked
me about at the clinic on the day that the baby had been brought
in for her first shots. I had directed her to a nearby pharmacy where,
according to the owner, it is the "number one seller" among his
"ethnic remedies. The supplier that I buy from is here every two
weeks, and I'm usually buying catnip each time." (Will Upshaw,
Lansing, Michigan; 1986) Catnip (Nepeta cataria L.) is an Old World
plant that was naturalized after being brought to this country by
European settlers; its medicinal uses have been remarkably stable
over the centuries. It was under the dominion of the planet Venus,
according to the great seventeenth century English herbalist Nicholas
Culpeper (whose *Complete Herbal* is widely available in a modern-
ized paperback edition), to be "used in pains of the head, arising of
any cold cause, catarrh, rheums, and for swooning and giddiness
thereof, and is of special use for the windiness of the stomach and
belly" (*Culpeper's English Physician & Complete Herbal*, p. 29). Catnip was an ingredient in a remedy for "the more common pains of
the stomach, arising from accumulating gas, in adults or children"
in the 22d edition of the popular nineteenth-century home health
guide *Dr. Chase's Recipes* (Chase 1865:182). Its use for peevish and
colicky babies was soon taken up by a number of Native American
tribes (Moerman 1986, Vol. 1:303). Its specific use for colic has been
long noted, then, though it is by no means used only for that
particular problem (Van Blarcom 1930; G. Wilson 1967; Waller and
Killion 1972; Morton 1974:101; Tyler 1985:153; Roberson 1983:219;
Fowler 1987). It is also used to treat ailments ranging from colds to
"high-strung children" to hives (M. Bell and Clements n.d.; Hand
1961:53; Jordan 1975; Boyd, Shimp, and Hackney 1984:19; C. Hill
1988:116). Gordon Wilson, in fact, described it as a "cure-all," one of
the ten most commonly used plants (of 139) in a collection of 1,200
home remedies in American folk medicine (1968a).

Catnip does have psychoactive properties, of course—at least for
cats—and has been included in a list of herbs of "undefined safety"
by the Food and Drug Administration (FDA) (Siegel 1976; FDA
Memorandum, November 19, 1975). But whether it is a plant that
should be avoided or, as Moerman says, used as a rich source of

Vitamin C that can be incorporated into a "pleasant after dinner drink" (1982:44–45), it is widely available in the dry form. And, of course, it is also found as a weed in cities as well as rural areas. Janine Jackson knows that it grows in the corner of her yard, for example—if for some reason she cannot get to it there is always Mr. Upshaw's pharmacy right down the street. And if it is not available at all, there is always something else that will work:

> I have it out *here!* Right out there in the corner of my garden plot. And Annie got to cryin' one day, and it was cold, the weather was cold and there was snow. And I went out boppin' around tryin' to find some, and I couldn't find any 'cause of the snow. I was gonna give Annie some 'cause of the bawling. And my daughter-in-law went to the store and she find it there. It was all dried, you know, but you can use that instead. You have to kinda *steep* it, you can boil it just a little bit. And let it sit for a little while. And then you know, strain it out. Whatever you want, put just a *little* syrup in it, just to kinda sweeten it a little bit. If you give 'em that stuff *too* bitter they won't take it. It'll just take that bitterness out of it; a little syrup.
>
> And I remember my oldest sister, when she didn't get ahold of the catnip, she used *ginger* in hot water. 'Cause my daddy, like I say, they was *farmers* and had a bunch of youngsters—they only had 12 kids!—they was such doctors and what not, you know. They couldn't afford it if you *needed* to go to the doctor like that, so he would *always* think of *something* for the com*plaint!* And he would use ginger tea—just put it in hot water, kinda give it a boil, put honey in it. It was good for most anything! For colds, sore throats, or what. [If] you all stuffy-up, they believe in givin' it to you *hot* and then puttin' you to bed. They would say *sweat* it out. And it brought about a difference. (Lansing, Michigan; 1986)

Another popular treatment for colicky babies is tobacco smoke: It may be blown into breastmilk or formula and fed to the infant; blown onto the "mole" of the head where it will find its way down the alimentary tract; blown onto the infant's belly where it will enter the body through the navel; blown into the infant's face to be inhaled; or simply blown up the clothing. Janine Jackson is also familiar with this old remedy but she does not approve of cigarette smoking so has not tried it:

> I know one thing the old people did and I *didn't approve* of it. They thought if you would *smoke* the baby under the coattail, that was *good* for the colic! Blow smoke. And I didn't believe in that. My mom didn't do it, but I heard people say that was *really* good. But I didn't try it 'cause I never had no confidence in smokin'. I didn't smoke myself and I didn't *like* smokin' *around,* so I didn't try it. But I heard lots of people say that was really *good.* Like the baby is cryin', just lay 'em on your lap and if a little skirt is on just blow it on up. I've seen people do it, but I don't know how it reacted. But my mother didn't do it, and I *never* did it 'cause I didn't believe in *smoking!* No smoke for me!

So I can't say that work, that I would recommend that. (Lansing, Michigan; 1986)

Bernita Washington believed colic to be the result of laziness on the part of the person feeding the child; babies are bound to swallow too much air if they are nursed or fed while lying down. Her treatments changed according to the perceived seriousness of the problem: first a postural change; then "azefizitty" (asafoetida); then smoke in the milk. If the baby has swallowed too much air the simplest treatment, she said, is simply to turn him upside down and that air will come right back out:

> You can take 'im, if you've got colic and it's real bad, you can take 'im by both heels and just turn 'im up and just shake 'im once or maybe twice. But not *serious,* you know. Just turn 'im up like that and just turn 'im right back down and just pat 'im in the back a little bit. And just lay him *down,* he's fine! [Or] . . . you can take a spoon, if you're *nursin'* from your breast, you milk just a little milk out of your breast into the *spoon,* and you blow *smoke* into it. Be sure that you smoke it real good, and you give to the baby and the baby will swallow it. That will cure 'im, the colic that he have.

A young neighbor had recently brought her baby to Bernita because she did not know what to do for his incessant crying; she had heard that Bernita knew a lot about babies:

> The baby had the colic and she didn't know what was *wrong* with it. O.K., so with him havin' the colic [he] just cried, cried all day and all night and she didn't know what was *wrong* with him. So I be come to find out that the baby just really had the *colic,* right. [In] other words, what you do you take and *turn* him, turn his stomach down. Lay it across your lap and turn the stomach down, you can pat it. And if he doesn't *burp* or no kind of gas reflection, then that's what's wrong with him, and the gas is hurtin' his *stomach.* So, what *I* did—usually you can use asefizitty, people did—but sometimes they get it too *bad* [and] it doesn't do any good. So what I did was just got some of the milk out of the little bottle they was givin' it and put it in a teaspoon and blew *cigarette* smoke into it! And then after that I *gave* it to it, and it just went to sleep.

The use of tobacco as medicine is like that of catnip in reverse; it is a New World plant that became "'a medicinal wonderplant'" in Europe (Elferink 1983). Domestic tobacco and several species of wild tobacco (all in the genus *Nicotiana*) were used by a number of Native American tribes for both ceremonial and medicinal purposes (Moerman 1986, Vol. 1:303–307); many of these uses were transmitted to the new settlers. Tobacco, in fact—like catnip—became one of the 10 most commonly used plants in American folk medicine (G. Wilson 1968a). The smoke may be used as an analgesic for toothache and earache as well as colic (Brunson 1962:68; Boyd, Shimp, and Hackney 1984:21; Roberson 1983:223, 229), and tobacco juice or a quid of tobacco employed in treating skin ailments from insect stings to boils (Chase 1865:190; G. Wilson 1967; Waller and Killion 1972; Brandon 1976; de Albuquerque 1979; Roberson 1983:226; C. Hill 1988:120). In rural Georgia, in fact, "people talked about tobacco use as if they were talking medicines: 'three or four times a day or half a pack a day and after each meal.' Most believe that chewing and dipping tobacco is healthier than smoking cigarettes and say that these behaviors keep them from smoking too much. Overall, Coberlians classified tobacco use as health promoting rather than as disease causing. Their knowledge of healthy behavior (such as exercise and a good diet) does not extend to tobacco use" (C. Hill 1988:98). It is seen as a valuable antidote to the "hassles" of daily life (Romano, Bloom, and Syme 1991).

Breastmilk does not have to have tobacco smoke in it to be used as medicine—it may be used by itself for earaches or sore eyes. "Down home," says Marya Smith, "for the pinkeye we used milk from *any* lady's breast." Janine Jackson, who uses so many of the old treatments she learned in South Carolina, draws the line at breastmilk as medicine:

> Once I had earache and my oldest sister, she was gonna put some of her milk in my ear. Boy, the thoughts of somebody's milk out of their breast goin' into my ear! And they got it all warm, and I flipped over and it went on the floor! [Laughs] But they used it; it was a remedy for earache pain. I was 16 or sumpin' like that. "Oh, my ear hurts!" Before I knew anything, they was ready to put that in my ear. My mother said, "Hold still, hold still," and I was holdin' real still, and all of a sudden the thought [of it] and I flipped over! "We done went to all of this trouble! And now you didn't let me do it!" So, they did do that for ears, but not for mine! I said, "No, thanks, I'll just let it hurt!"[9]

This particular cure is known not only among the grandparent generation reared in the South: One afternoon in 1985 a young mother called the Lansing clinic for an appointment to have her little daughter's eyes checked. The child had had pinkeye (conjunctivitis), and despite the mother's assurances that she had cured it herself, her daughter's nursery school would not let the child return without a note from a doctor that the problem was gone. "What do you mean, you cured it yourself," a resident asked—"What did you *do?*" Well, said the mother, she had *wanted* to use breastmilk but did not know anyone who was nursing an infant—"and I didn't know if formula would work." So she had put urine in her daughter's eyes instead. "When she gets here I want you to go down and tell her to stop *doing* that," the resident said to me. But when she arrived with the child the eye infection was indeed gone: "Sometimes," the mother observed, "those old remedies work best." But only, in this instance, if the urine is not contaminated; see Alfonso et al. (1983) for an account of ten patients in Miami who developed *Neisseria gonorrhoeae* conjunctivitis when their eyes were treated with urine from someone infected with gonorrhea.

The intake of cold air is also blamed for upper respiratory infections in babies and children just as it is in adults, and the associated mucus is seen as the tangible presence of "cold" in the body. It can be eliminated from the body by a variety of substances taken orally— including cow chip tea or horse urine—or "worked" out by means of laxatives for children too small to be able to cough it up effectively. The 26-year-old mother of two-month-old Akim Jones had brought the baby to the clinic because he was "fussy," and she was puzzled when the resident said that little Akim was suffering from a slight cold. "How could he get a cold when the house be so hot," she asked? She recalled having been given cow chip tea for colds as a child by a grandmother who had been raised in Alabama; but that was not the worst remedy she had ever had to take. Even worse was the time when she was 11 years old and was suffering from a bad cold, and her grandmother had made her drink a whole bottle of castor oil. It made her sick and feel "real hot," she said. "But it really took it out of me!"[10] (1987)

In order to protect them from "catching cold," small babies may be taken outside completely bundled up against the weather irrespective of outside temperature. One 16-year-old new mother—who brought her baby to the clinic fully dressed and wrapped in a blanket—was still quite anxious because the neighbors said she would "kill that baby" by not putting a hat on him as well. It was 87 degrees on that particular afternoon. (1981) It is not unusual for an individual brought up to believe that extremes of temperature are dangerous to babies—and most particularly to sick babies—to be greatly distressed at professional ideas of proper treatment. One grandmother thought that the hospital practice of putting a child into a cool mist tent to bring down his temperature was dangerous; clearly she felt that her *own* treatment would have been preferable:

> She got up from her chair, looked into the tent, and said, "You forgot to give him a blanket. That thing is real cold inside." The nurse again explained that she was keeping him cool because of his high temperature. Mary tried to calm her mother-in-law, seeing that she was becoming hostile. "Mama, it's okay." Mrs. Wilson responded, "What you talkin' 'bout? They got you believing in this foolishness too. I'm gonna put his blanket on him 'cause he is cold. I raised all my nine children and I never put one in no ice box. You know you need to wrap him so he can sweat the fever out. Hot chamomile tea would bring that fever down." (Galanti 1991:100)

If familiar symptoms are attached to new diseases these are rather easily incorporated into existing beliefs; interviews with the caretakers of HIV seropositive children in Newark, N.J., revealed that upper respiratory infections in these children are explained in terms of the traditional model. All of the respondents described the children in their care as healthy, even if they had had several hospitalizations for a variety of health problems such as fevers or pneumonia. The caretakers did not connect these problems with the positive HIV diagnosis; when asked how the health of her child had been, one answered:

> *No problem. The only problem she's been having, last year, she had pneumonia. . . . And she perspires in her head. And the doctor told me that sometimes, it can be, umm, ya know how your body gets wet, you go out into the cold, then that cold gets into your chest. That was how they said she may have. . . . So I didn't pretty much worry about it. And ya know, like I said, I never thought no more about it. 'Cause her mother had one of her lungs removed. So I didn't know whether or not she was, ya know, something hereditary or what. . . . But she just had a chest x-ray, and they said it was kind of cloudy. But Dr. ____ think that she also have slight asthma.*

Said another, when asked about her treatment of the common cold: "I keep her full of water. . . . It flushes her alot. And then, too, when you're dealing with colds . . . some kids all they drink is milk, milk, milk, milk. And milk keeps the cold in you. Cause it's heavy" (Meltzer and Kantor 1990).

Similar findings were reported by Flaskerud and Rush (1989), whose respondents did not discriminate between infection with the AIDS virus and the opportunistic infections resulting from it: "Sometimes they don't know if you have AIDS or you have pneumonia. They say it's like pneumonia," said one. "I think if they have AIDS and somebody coughs at you and your system is low you can get it. It's pneumonia or TB," said another. And, "Even doctors don't know, they say the person has pneumonia and they probably have AIDS."

The normal bodily processes of elimination are also carefully monitored in infants and children. The normal body rids itself of all manner of "impurities" via the skin, the uterus, the kidneys, and the gut. Failure for this to take place means that these impurities "build up" in the body and, as has already been described, a dirty body is a sick body. As tiny infants are by nature relatively weak and delicate it is thought doubly important that their systems be cleansed. If all goes well the system of a new baby will automatically "throw off" the impurities that collected when, *in utero,* the baby shared the blood supply of its mother. These impurities are manifest in the first weeks or months of life by the appearance of "the little red hives." If they do *not* appear then measures must be taken to make sure that they "come out." Heat "brings things out" (just as cold drives them back in) so these measures usually involve feeding the infant something warm: Some say that just warm water or milk will do the trick. If this fails then other remedies will be tried; Janine Jackson's treatment of her little granddaughter to bring out the little red hives has already been mentioned. Anna Perry felt that an infant should be given catnip tea on the day of birth and daily thereafter for two or three months. Initially it brings out the hives and "makes his skin clean and beautiful"; after that it "makes the baby healthy" and keeps him or her from spitting up milk.

As skin eruptions are, in fact, hoped for and expected it is not surprising that they are not necessarily seen as cause for concern. In 1986 one of Bernita's seven daughters had a new baby, and when he broke out in "bumps" it was Bernita that the daughter called, not his doctor:

> My daughter called me night before last. Her little baby, which is about a month and a half old, it came out with some kind of little bumps and she thought it might have been, y'know, measle or hive or something, and she didn't really know what it were. By me bein' home by the phone *I* didn't know what it were, *either.* So I just told her to warm some water and give it him, and whatever it was would just pop right *out,* y'know. And so she warmed some water and put it in the bottle and nursed him with the bottle. And the next morning it popped right out. But it was real thick on his face, so she really doesn't know what it is and I don't *either.*

Did she call the doctor then, I asked? No, said Bernita, "I told her as long as the baby don't come down with a fever don't worry about it, 'cause if it pop right out, it's good. But if it stay inside it'll accumulate a fever and cause sickness."

It is also not surprising to find disagreement when the doctor *is* asked, of course, especially if he or she is not familiar with the old beliefs. One afternoon a resident inquired if I knew about hot water bringing out hives in a newborn infant; the grandmother of an infant he had just examined was concerned because they had not yet "come out." The mother reported that baby Kwame had cried for four hours the night before and her mother, who had come to help out with the other children, wondered if it might be because of the failure of the hives to appear? "And it's not as if she's an *inexperienced* mom," said the resident; "she's *got* four other children!" Did you ask her what she meant by the little red hives, I asked? "Nah, I don't want to get into all that superstition stuff," was the reply. Nor was it noted on little Kwame's chart; "baby starting colicky pattern" was the entry for the day. (1984)

The fact that measles—along with a variety of other skin rashes that physicians would see as having separate causes—are frequently lumped together in the traditional system has already been mentioned. It might have been expected that some of these beliefs would die out with the elimination of measles due to vaccines; unfortunately, there are growing numbers of poor children who remain unimmunized, with concomitant outbreaks in measles and other preventable diseases (Farizo et al. 1991; Schulte et al. 1991). For too many children comprehensive health care is simply not available.

> The impact of vaccines on improving the health of children in this country is substantial. However, thousands of children are suffering from diseases that could be easily prevented. Only four visits to a health care provider during the first two years of life are necessary to protect the vast majority of preschoolers against eight vaccine-preventable diseases. Many children, particularly those living in inner cities, are not vaccinated on time. The health care system itself must assume substantial responsibility, since many opportunities to vaccinate are lost. Barriers in the system serve as disincentives to vaccination. But we believe these are solvable problems that require local, state and federal will to improve the system. By increasing collaboration we can determine effective means to educate and motivate even the poorest parents in this society. All children, rich or poor, deserve protection against vaccine-preventable diseases. (Orenstein et al. 1990)

(See Braveman et al. 1991 for similar inequities in the care of sick newborns.)

The appearance of skin eruptions in infants does not convince women relying on the old beliefs that the little one's system is cleansed once and for all, however. It just means that attention shifts from the skin to the kidneys and the gut. Jacie Burnes' attribution of the "bumps" on her children (seen by the resident as acne and impetigo) to their failure to drink enough water for their "kidneys to act proper" was described earlier. And "constipation" in infants and children is, in fact, a worry frequently expressed by mothers and grandmothers; health professionals must keep in mind that it is a relative term, however. Hughes noted treating one two-week-old infant "with water intoxication secondary to numerous tap water enemas used in an attempt to create more than his usual one bowel movement per day" (1963). Laxatives are frequently used, not only given orally but, in the form of mineral or castor oil, rubbed on externally as well. Just remember to rub them on from *up* to *down* and, if the baby is young enough, a little dab on the mole of the head will "work the baby" as well. You can get more than "cold" out of the body that way.

Bernita had just used mineral oil to treat one of her numerous grandchildren for constipation and told me how it should be done, demonstrating how she had laid him over her knees:

> And you just take and start rubbin' him all the way *down,* from his back, all the way on out to his feet. Let him be real slick in oil. Rub him all the way on out.

"You wouldn't start at the bottom and massage up?"

The *back,* and go *down!* Right, you don't start here and go *up;* you
start here and go down. Then you take and do his stomach with mineral oil. And then [if] that little soft place still on the top of his head,
the tender part of his head, it's the mole of his head—you just put a little mineral oil up there and rub right there. And in a few minutes it
worked. (Lansing, Michigan; 1987)

Caretakers and health professionals may not always agree about
the necessity of treatment for constipation—or what treatments
ought to be employed—but sometimes negotiation is possible. On
one clinic afternoon a 15-year-old mother brought in her baby daughter and reported that her grandfather, with whom they lived, said
little India had constipation and should be given catnip tea with
honey. Would that be all right? Her grandfather had been raised in
Arkansas and knew all sorts of home remedies. The resident explained why she thought that honey was not a good thing to give
to small babies—saying that she thought Karo syrup would be better—but she also did not want to neglect the grandfather's feelings
on the matter. "Ask your grandfather what he thinks about putting
Karo syrup in the catnip tea instead of the honey," she told the
young mother. A few days later the grandfather called to express
his appreciation at the compromise; clearly the resident was *not* "one
of those doctors that knows it all." (1987)

There seems to be less concern with diarrhea than with constipation; better to have "things running" than clogged up. Should it go
on too long, however, flour-water may be given to stop the problem;
it thickens a loose stool just as it does gravy. Said Bernita:

Like kids when they have diarrhea, you know when little babies have
diarrhea? Lot of people doesn't realize that, you know, they go to the
store and get Pepto Bismol, whatever, [but] sometime babies [are too] little and they can't *use* Pepto Bismol. They can't have that 'cause they're
too young to *have* it. But usually babies will have what you call dysen-
tery? And so, only thing you have to do is go in the kitchen and get
yourself a half a teaspoonful of flour, and just mix it in some water
and stir it up and mix it up and pour it into his *milk,* and let him
nurse that! It be thin, just like his milk; see, you puts it into the milk,
don't give it to him by itself, [you] puts it into the milk. It'll go
through because you whips it up until it become *lookin'* like milk. Oh,
a teaspoonful, a half a teaspoonful, fourth teaspoonful, depending on
how old the kid is. That is good for it. (1987)

The concern with the body holding impurities is so great, however,
that diarrhea may not be seen as a problem—better to get them right
out of the system. Says one woman, "They say with AIDS they have
a lot of diarrhea. That makes sense: the body's trying to clean itself
out. That's good" (Flaskerud and Rush 1989).

Conflicts in Treatment

Very different viewpoints about the causes and proper treatments of health problems often results in conflict, of course. "When doctors and patients meet," wrote Weston and Brown, "they each have expectations and feelings about the encounter; if these are at odds or inappropriate, there will be difficulties" (1989). And the source of the "difficulties" may not even be present: The mother of six-month-old Alicia Temple brought her back to the clinic several times for an unresolved middle-ear infection, for example. On the third trip the resident came out of the examining room and said, "That baby's ears look even worse than they did ten days ago! I *know* she is not giving the medicine—see if you can find out why." Alicia's mother was glad to explain; it was "a problem at home," she said. "It's my father." She and Alicia were living with her parents, who cared for the baby while she worked. She had had the prescription for anti-biotic filled the first time she had come to the clinic, but Alicia didn't like the taste and cried when she tried to give it to her. Her father had told her to stop giving it; "*Nobody* is going to make my grandbaby take medicine if she doesn't want to take it!," he had said. And so it had not been given. She was concerned about Alicia's ear infection—and she was even more concerned that her parents would turn her daughter into a "spoiled brat" like her three-year-old niece, who also lived with the family. "But what can I do? I owe my folks so much and I can't argue with my father." It was rather easily solved, in fact. The resident explained to her the possibility of some permanent hearing loss if the infection was not cleared up soon—and that this might affect Alicia's ability to learn to speak normally. He offered to call the grandfather and talk with him about it but the mother, armed with a reason more important that what her child did or did not like, said she did not think it would be necessary. Two weeks later she returned with her little girl; the ear infection was gone. (1980)

Trouble also happens when health professionals are perceived as behaving in a thoughtless and uncaring manner. "Our daughter had an asthma attack," said one of Roberson's informants, "so we took her to the emergency room" (1983:189). There, "we were kept waiting a long time, but we could see doctors and nurses laughing and eating something, so we didn't feel like they were pressed for time. I got aggravated and said so when they finally saw my daughter. The doctor told me she wasn't really an emergency, so I asked why he gave her a shot if he didn't think she had a problem." Another woman reported taking *her* sick baby to three different places in search of care: "I took my baby to Doctor _____ . She was sick and carrying a fever. He gave her some medicine—he never does no exam or nothing. She got sicker so I carried her to the hospital in town and they didn't find nothing either. She kept getting sicker, so I carried her on up to Richmond and *they* did an x-ray. They said she had pneumonia and took care of her" (Roberson 1983:189). Neither mother can have thought that the doctors and nurses had much concern with the health of their little one.

In another example, a woman who had often experienced racial discrimination was quite angry to discover that her ten-month-old grandson's hands and feet had been tied to the bed to prevent him from pulling out intravenous tubing. Her reaction was that he was being treated like an animal: "How come you got the baby tied down? He's not doing anything. He ain't no trouble. Why don't you untie him? He looks like he can't move. He ain't no dog'" (Galanti 1991). She was calmed when it was explained to her just why it had had to be done.

From the point of view of health professionals, such family members may be seen as overly concerned, ignorant people who only interfere with proper care. A parent whose beliefs are *too* different from those of professionals, in fact, may come to be seen as mentally deficient or even deranged (Redlener and Scott 1979; Korbin and Johnston 1982). And when such conflicts reach impasse the real power is on the side of the health professional (Brody 1992). One mother brought her ten-day-old baby to the clinic for her first check-up. Little Carole had weighed just over seven pounds at birth and had gained seven ounces at the time of this visit; the breastfeeding was going well and the resident noted on the chart, "Mother seems happy and is getting adequate help at home." Ten days later she brought baby Carole in to be checked again as she thought that the baby had "caught a cold." The resident was less concerned with this, however, than the fact that the child had only gained three ounces in ten days; the mother was told to bring the baby back in two weeks for a weight check. At this time the infant was found to have lost eight ounces. How could this have happened, asked the mother? "I'm feeding her from a bowl of cereal before I breastfeed her!"

The baby was hospitalized with a diagnosis of "suspected failure to thrive" and now the woman—who only a short time before had been viewed as a happy mother well-bonded with her baby—was suspect as well. "Poor caloric intake and poor maternal interaction suspected," read the nursing notes—and ten days later when weight gain was still slow, "strongly suspect breastfeeding failure." A day or so later there appeared the first real conflict, however, when it was noted on the chart that the mother was "seen feeding infant suspicious looking liquid from bottle." She would tell the nurses only that it was "herb tea." The resident was able to get more information, however; it was catnip tea, "to bring out the little red hives." Little Carole's mother was far more worried about the fact that these had failed to appear than the baby's failure to gain weight. After all, the baby could always gain weight later, but failure of the hives to appear was life threatening. As her concern about the hives increased so did the amount of catnip tea she was giving the baby—and from the hospital staff's point of view the "three or four bottles" a day that she admitted to giving were simply replacing the calories from breastmilk.

She was told that her daughter was not getting enough to eat but the resident did not take the catnip tea away altogether; she believed that the mother's beliefs were important and allowed the baby to be given one small bottle of it each day. Unfortunately, this negotiation was not enough to save the situation. The message to the mother that her baby was "going hungry" was probably responsible for the final failure in communication. As the mother was coming in each day to breastfeed her baby she was given a lunch tray, and one day was seen feeding her daughter a spoonful of cream-of-mushroom soup from her own bowl. "But they said she wasn't getting *enough* to eat," was her response when she was scolded for this; several discussions with a hospital dietician ensued in which she was told that such things constitute "inappropriate" food for small babies. By now the mother had become sullen and withdrawn and there was concern about sending the infant home in her care. Finally a social worker was sent in to see if she had any intentions of changing the way she fed the child. "No," was the answer, "because I don't see anything wrong with it." The hospital authorities did, however, and she was not allowed to take her daughter home.

A few days later another social worker made a home visit to determine if it was a safe setting for baby Carole to go to; there it was found that her five-year-old brother and eight-year-old sister were not in school although classes had started some days previously. Why was this? She had just moved to a new neighborhood and hadn't found the school, was the mother's response. And she had been feeling down over the fact that she had not been allowed to bring her baby home. Now she truly *was* judged to be a poor mother and all three children were put into foster care. The resident called her a few days later and asked how she was getting on. "The house is so quiet," was the answer, "I guess I'll just have to have me another baby." It was a good thing the children *had* been taken from the home, said the resident as she hung up the phone, "She's not playing with a full deck." In this sad story, however, it is hard to say that either side was entirely right or entirely wrong. The mother had certainly done what she thought was best for her newest child—and the health professionals had certainly done what *they* thought was best for the new baby and the rest of the children. Unfortunately, the result was a family torn apart.[11]

Notes

1. There is not space enough to include all of the folk beliefs involving good and bad luck associated with newborn infants. The former include those rituals

done to ensure good fortune in the child's future. The belief that I have heard most often is the practice of pressing a dime into the newborn infant's hand so that he or she will never lack money. Frankel also reported: "Down home, when you comes to the house to visit a new baby the first time, you're supposed to put a dime in the baby's hand to give it good luck" (1977:70). A version reported by Hand, however, is more of a determiner of future character: "If an infant clinches a coin that is put into its hand it will love money. An open-handed baby is generous; a tight fist foretells avarice" (1961:35).

"Don'ts" associated with the first weeks and months of life are numerous. Beliefs with a long history that are still commonly heard today—and found among both African-American and Southern White women—forbid cutting the fingernails, toenails, and/or hair of the child for a certain length of time, often a year (W. Black 1883:178--203; Puckett 1926:338; Van Blarcom 1930; Hand 1961:38--42; Hughes 1963; Emrich 1972:639; Cooper 1972:138--140; Montell 1975:17--18; Dougherty 1978:62). Some of the results of breaking these taboos include bad luck, causing the child to be a thief or "roguish," making it weak or ill, or, most commonly, to die. Cutting anything on the child that grows, that is, cuts the life as well. It is generally said that if the nails grow too long they may be bitten or chewed off; when the child is a few months or a year old they may safely be cut.

To someone trained in orthodox medicine, of course, it is difficult to imagine that someone could truly believe that cutting an infant's hair or nails might do irreparable damage. A few years ago, however, I had a call from a nurse on the maternity floor at a local hospital asking, "What on earth did we do now?" A young woman from the hills of Kentucky who had given birth to a healthy infant the day before had, when it was brought in that morning to nurse, suddenly run out into the hall screaming, "You've killed my baby! You've killed my baby!" Staff members had naturally rushed into the room only to find the infant boy peacefully sleeping; they could not imagine what had caused the mother to be so hysterical. Had anything at all been done to the baby? "Well, the night nurse cut his fingernails because he was scratching his face," was the answer, "but surely it couldn't be *that!*" It was; the young woman was convinced her infant was doomed. The staff now has a policy of asking a mother's permission before cutting a baby's nails.

2. My first job many years ago was as the lab technician in the office of a pediatrician in Wichita, Kansas, whose clientele was almost entirely White and middle-class. Babies and children were almost invariably brought to his office by their mothers. Fathers—or for that matter other relatives—were almost *never* seen. In contrast, one rather striking aspect for me of the Lansing pediatrics clinic was the number of fathers bringing their little ones in for care. In many instances the men are available to help out because they are unemployed or underemployed; in other families both parents work different shifts at a local automobile-manufacturing plant and whichever one happens to work nights helps out with the children during the day. Warren Jackson watches his children daytimes, for example, because his wife is at work then and he works a night shift. He is therefore the parent responsible for getting them to the clinic for well-baby checkups or if they are sick. For any minor health problems, however, he usually calls his mother, Janine Jackson, who always has a home remedy or two available.

It does not seem to matter if the mother and father are married or even living together; in many instances they are still in constant contact (McLorg and Bryant 1989). And such interactions may also include "taking turns" with child care. When I first met her, 24-year-old Sissie Brown was living with her three-year-old daughter and Wanda, her new baby. The little girls have different fathers and Sissie is on good terms with them both; in fact, both men often help out with problems regarding the children irrespective of *which* child is involved. Three-year-old Janice stayed with her own father and his family while her mother was in the hospital to have the new baby, for example. But when Janice developed an upper respiratory infection not long after that her own father was working; the father of the new baby brought her and her mother to the clinic instead. (Lansing, Michigan; 1985)

Not all fathers are so engaged with their offspring, of course. On another clinic afternoon 21-year-old Tommie Ann Stone disclosed how she met rejection from the fathers of her children with considerable sass. "Look what I just bought," she said as I walked into the examining room, handing me a sympathy card. "I'm sorry," I said. "Who died?" No one had. She had bought the card to send to the father of her six-month-old son, Evon. He had called on the previous Sunday to tell her that—although he had gotten married the day before—he hoped that she would "still be his lady." She had no intention of telling him that she had hoped to marry him herself; the sympathy card was to let him know that everything between them was now dead. This was not the first time that this had happened; when the father of her three-year-old daughter, Christine, had married another woman she had sent *him* a box of dog biscuits and a package of stool softener. The dog biscuits were to let him know that he was "no better than a dog," she said. And the stool softener? Well, "that was just to let him know he was full of shit!" (Lansing, Michigan; 1987)

3. In various parts of the country these initially reluctant caretakers are developing support networks to help each other cope. A 43-year-old grandmother in Pontiac, Michigan, has formed a group called "Grandparents Anonymous," for example; she is raising the four children of her two crack-addicted daughters (Coleman 1990). In Oakland, California, a dozen inner-city grandparents gather in a church basement "to learn about psychology and child development, addiction and co-dependency, stress management and nutrition, and other newfangled ideas that barely existed when their sons and daughters were small." They can then fan out in the city, "where one of every five children is believed to be in the care of grandparents, and offer advice and solace to others who have been forced into an unexpected round of child-rearing because their own children are lost to cocaine" (Gross 1991). In New York City, "a city-run program allows family members, overwhelmingly grandmothers, to function as foster parents. The number of children living under such 'kinship' foster care has surged from 150 in 1985 to 17,906 today" (Martin 1991). In these instances the care is still in the hands of family members, irrespective of any expectation that they might have had that their childdrearing days were over.

An even more sensitive indicator of the toll of crack and other recent problems, however, is the fact that many babies are now going *out* of the care of families. The chilling new term "boarder babies"—those infants "remaining in the hospital for home and social evaluation or foster care placement rather than medical needs" (Phibbs, Bateman, and Schwartz 1991)—describes a situation that would have been unthinkable only a few short years ago. But more and more frequently these infants go into nonrelative foster care; though "the number of families willing to take them in is at a standstill," for example, "the number of children needing foster care in Lansing [Michigan] has more than doubled in three years due to drugs. . . . " (Gaudin 1990). Statewide, in fact, with "more and more children needing foster care and a continued shortage of families willing to take them, child-welfare advocates predict a return to orphanages unless new options are developed."

The number of children and youths in Michigan needing foster care has grown by 25 percent since 1986 to 16,982, with only 10,215 currently placed with foster families (McClellan 1991). And this at a time when one proposed solution to the state's fiscal crisis by a conservative new governor is to cut payments to these families (Kresnak 1991). Adoption agencies in Detroit are also "struggling to handle a huge increase in poor, black infants being put up for adoption, forcing them to turn away some women who are near delivery and reject most requests from hospitals to take unwanted babies." According to a supervisor for Catholic Social Services of Wayne County, the increase is believed to be linked to drug use and the inability of some poor women to pay for abortions, which since December of 1988, are no longer covered by Medicaid (Chargot 1990a).

4. The fact that older women—grandmothers and great-grandmothers—are often involved in the rearing of family infants is well known. Adult siblings are also an important source of emotional and financial support, and sisters—especially older sisters—are frequently looked to for help in child care. Barbara Little's five brothers and five sisters all live in the city, for example, and the sisters cooperate in whatever needs to be done. A clinic nurse was very annoyed one afternoon when a sister brought in Barbara's one-year-old son, Morris, to be seen for a cold. "She really ought to send a note if she's not coming," she said crossly. Barbara was sick herself, said the sister, who also had in tow the three-year-old daughter of yet another sister. (Lansing, Michigan; 1984) If a mother is seen as not taking proper care of her babies and children older sisters may take them to task. Twenty-year-old Allie Barnes is one of six sisters, for example, and lives in an apartment right above one of them. This older sister was responsible for Allie coming in with her eight-month-old son, Kareem, for example, after she learned that Kareem had not had his immunizations. "I forgot," said Allie. When the nurse urged Allie to be sure and keep the appointment for his *next* set of shots the sister said, grimly, "She'll be here." She was. (Lansing, Michigan; 1986)

5. I certainly do not mean to downplay the impact of violence—deliberate or accidental—in the lives of these children. Many of them live in households, neighborhoods, and communities where violence is not only endemic (C. Johnson 1934:189–192; Coles 1971b:592–600; Ladner 1971:62–63; Aschenbrenner 1975:74–76; Valentine 1978:29–30), but increasing with the added impact of crack cocaine, homelessness, and so on (Shedlin 1989; C. Taylor 1990; Wood et al. 1990; Lemann 1991). Injuries are a leading cause of death among children in the United States, in fact. Environmental factors play a part in some of these; in 1986 African-American children were found to be several times more likely to die in a house fire than were White children, for example. And in the same year deaths of African-American children due to homicide were approximately five times those for White children (Fatal Injuries to Children—United States, 1986). Statistics do not say it as tellingly as these words from a single child, however. In Kotlowitz's moving account of two years in the lives of two young brothers in a Chicago housing project, for example, "I asked Lafeyette what he wanted to be. 'If I grow up, I'd like to be a bus driver,' he told me. *If*, not *when*. At the age of ten, Lafeyette wasn't sure he'd make it to adulthood" (1991:x). Nonetheless it remains important to remember that the *perception* of potential violence is culturally based; middle-class outsiders may misread verbal and physical cues and fear that a child is in danger when in fact he or she may not be at all.

6. In the case of children living with their mothers in the abnormal social circumstances of a New York welfare hotel it sometimes becomes a case of who is nurturing whom; as Shedlin reported (1989:21), "Children are expected to grow up quickly, to provide child care for younger children, and to be confidants and friends at very young ages. They share their mothers' suffering and are often expected to be little sources of strength and understanding for adults: 'Believe it or not, I talk to my kids (5 children, 6 years to 3 months).' 'I have no close friends, my children are closest to me.' 'He won't leave me; they call him my husband.' 'I go to my kids for advice. . . ; my little H. is the brain in the house . . . the only male.' 'I talk to my kids straight up, tell them how I'm feeling . . . no baby talk. "We gotta stay here, make it our home." I hold them and cry.' (Children were 3, 2, and 1.)" "There appears to be a desperate need for these children in their difficult lives," Shedlin concluded, "but as the level

of desperation increases, the apparent ability of the mothers to care for them decreases. And as the numbers of children increase for these mothers, the chances of individual children's receiving adequate attention and care in an already stressed and precarious situation become less and less."

7. My own discomfort with seeing children with "adult" responsibilities is very deep-seated, even though it is patently obvious that they are capable of far more than I would allow them to do. Some years ago I drove through a busy intersection of the city and saw a small girl, perhaps four or five years old, standing at the corner waiting for the stoplight to change. In one arm she held a small sack of groceries and in her other hand she had gripped tightly the hand of a smaller boy. It was clear that she was seen as responsible enough to be entrusted both with money to go to the store *and* with the care of a smaller child; I couldn't help but reflect that when my son was that age I wouldn't even let him walk to school by himself. And I must confess that on a more recent occasion I was very reluctant to hand a small baby over to the eight-year-old cousin who insisted that it was *her turn* to hold her! This was at the wedding reception of one of Bernita's daughters in the summer of 1990; everyone was enjoying passing around the newest member of the family, six-week-old Bea Anne. After a few minutes the little girl dragged over her own mother, one of Bea Anne's aunts, to assure me that it would be "all right." I had no choice but to hand the baby over. Some hours later it was Bea Anne's 15-year-old cousin Jack who was petting and cooing over her—and remarking wistfully that he wished he had a son or daughter of his own.

8. The potential for misunderstanding is very great when outsiders hear a linguistic style that is unfamiliar; this is expected when an individual who is a native speaker of one language attempts to talk with a speaker of another language, of course. But it may also be true when speaker and listener speak the same language: because they share a common vocabulary they may not recognize that they are failing to communicate. But words or phrases that are familiar to both parties may have entirely different meanings: "Fell out of *what*," I heard a resident say impatiently one afternoon, after a mother reiterated her concern that her small son "fell out twice yesterday." The mother was referring to a fainting spell; the resident assumed that little Johnnie must have fallen out of a window. Similarly, "falling off" refers to weight loss, not a fall from a table, and "bright" may refer to light skin color as well as to intelligence.

One should not expect that words routinely used in clinical settings are understood by all. I believe that the majority of adults understood that there was a problem when a resident looked in a child's ear and pronounced it "red" or "infected"; they often looked puzzled, however, when it was said to look "dull" or, [of the eardrum] "bulging" or "it doesn't move." Weidman et al. (1978:242) cite an instance of a mother who was giving juice and milk to her babies (who had diarrhea) although she had been instructed not to do so: "She showed me the instruction sheet. It read, 'excluding fruit juice, milk, cereal, fruit.' She didn't understand the word 'excluding.' She thought it meant they could have these foods. Their diarrhea is pretty bad. . . . " And in a study of parents who had not complied with medical advice, it was found that there was a tendency "to prescribe a fairly complex, graded feeding regimen with different strengths of formula at different points in time, with variously restricted menus and with detailed instructions about how to prepare one-half skim milk formula or jello water or the like. Some of these were so complex that the research workers found them hard to interpret and were not surprised to learn that parents had floundered" (Francis, Korsch, and Morris 1969).

9. "Mother's milk," wrote Hand (1980:299–300), which is "widely used as a cleansing and healing agent for the eyes of infants, is also used for eye maladies generally. . . . " It may be put into the eyes of the newborn infant (Hand 1961:51)

or squeezed into the sore eyes of a baby (M. Bell and Clements, n.d.). Other scholars report the use of milk for earaches without specifying that it be breastmilk (Waller and Killion 1972; Jordan 1975; Roberson 1983:224). In one example the linkage between eye problems and milk is extended to include the use of *coconut* milk in the treatment of cataracts (Boyd, Shimp, and Hackney 1984:19).

It is tempting to consider that it is not the *content* of breastmilk per se that is seen to have healing properties, but the aura of "goodness" associated with the new mother nourishing her infant. In the history of Euro-American traditional healing other bodily fluids have been ascribed special qualities when they derive from an individual perceived as being especially pure, innocent, or good: saliva or urine from a virgin, a faithful wife, a minister, a minister's wife, and so on. Sometimes it is the very *first* manifestation that is important: a baby's first tears, for example, or urine from a baby's first diaper. Even Mother Nature is included when water melted from the year's very first snowfall is used for sore eyes. Daisy Johnson recalls that her grandmother had always melted this snow and bottled it for use the rest of the year. (1987) Sometimes it was water from *spring* snow that was required to do the trick (Puckett 1926:383; Van Blarcom 1930).

10. Haitian mothers in Miami are reported to believe that colds can be avoided by not giving babies cold drinks, giving them castor oil daily, or not allowing them to be held by menstruating women (DeSantis 1989).

11. Replacing lost children with a new child has also been noted in a recent study of the reproductive decisions of HIV-infected women in a methadone clinic in the Bronx, New York (Pivnick et al. 1991): "The loss of child custody by drug-using mothers is frequently the result of uncontrolled maternal drug use and the consequent removal of children by child welfare authorities and concerned kin. Among HIV-positive women, these separations appear to have particular consequences. Our findings suggest that in the context of HIV infection, mother-child separation has a decided impact on decisions to bear. All of the HIV-positive women who terminated their pregnancies had lived with at least one child for the entirety of the child's life. All of the HIV-positive, pregnant women who had been separated from their children chose to bear, and all had given up or lost custody of their children because of uncontrolled drug use." One study participant, in fact, felt that having another child would "show" authorities that she was responsible and could therefore have her other children returned to her. "'I wanted to get myself together. . . . You know, because I want my kids back. So I figured, you know, if I have this one, I show the authorities that I really want to get myself together and that I want my own kids to be with me.'"

10

The Best Thing to Do Is Get Addicted to God

"There are two ways anybody can go when they come to certain roads in life—ain't about a right way or a wrong way—just two ways. And here we getting down to my way or yours. Now, I got a way for us to help Baby Girl. And I'm hoping it's the one you'll use."

She curls her fingers tighter around his that's holding the ledger and walking cane. "Mine ain't gonna be too hard—really. Back at my coop, there's an old red hen that's setting her last batch of eggs. You can't mistake her 'cause she's the biggest one in there and the tips of her feathers is almost blood red. She's crammed her nest into the northwest corner of the coop. You gotta take this book and cane in there with you, search good in the back of her nest, and come straight back here with whatever you find."

Miranda feels his body go rigid, but she won't let him pull back and she rushes to get through. "Now, I'm warning you, she's gonna be evil so watch out for your eyes. But, please, bring me straight back *whatever* you find—and then we can all rest. You look like you could use a lot of it, son."

—Gloria Naylor, *Mama Day*

"Illiteracy helps superstitions to flourish," folklorist Fanny Bergen commented tartly at the end of the last century, "and it is evident that a very moderate amount of education would banish the belief in hoopsnakes, in voodoo charms, and in lightning-shattered splinters as a cure for toothache" (1899:8). She would be very disappointed in education's failure nine decades later: Hoopsnakes still roll down Southern roads, voodoo charms abound in country *and* city, and a variety of remedies—*sans* dentist—are still to be found to cure an aching tooth. In fact, as medical folklorist David Hufford noted, "in almost a century of intense efforts, bolstered by substantial legal and financial assistance, conventional medicine has not even begun to 'wipe out' non-medical healing practices and beliefs" (1984). If anything, they are more popular than ever (Hufford 1988). What happened? Or, more precisely, what did not?

Part of the reason, unfortunately, is no doubt the fact that many African-Americans—old and young—continue to mistrust doctors and nurses. As one old lady told Gwaltney (1980:220): "Now, my doctor is white, so I tells him some and keeps some. All these doctors want to do is cut you or starve you. Shoot! I works harder than that little young devil I goes to! These whitefolks don' care nothin' 'bout you and me and they don' want to see us flerishin'. That's why so much of that medicine they always after us 'bout takin' is agains' us. These doctors ain' nothin' but whitefolks too." In another instance an obstetrics resident asked a 43-year-old woman, pregnant with her twelfth child, if she had considered having a tubal ligation at the time of delivery? Her answer was a vehement "I ain't gonna have no white doctor messin' with my insides!" (Galanti 1991). The idea that physicians might wish to "experiment" on African-American patients is also frequently heard; in 1986 I was entering the office of Dr. Brooks (Bernita Washington's physician) and held the door open for a young woman on crutches. As we sat in the waiting room she told me that she had injured her leg in an accident at the university laundry. Two university doctors had taken X-rays and said that there was "nothing wrong" with her. But "you can't *see* pain on an X-ray!" So she had come to see Dr. Brooks: "He's not just a doctor, he's a surgeon, too. Some of these doctors at the university probably aren't even doctors! They say about half of them are students, experimenting on people!" If they continued to "mess her over," she said, she would sue.

The fear that doctors will deliberately do harm to people in order to have bodies to experiment on or use in dissection is an old theme in African-American folklore. The "needle doctor," the "gown man," and the "night doctor" are terms that have long been used to describe the individual—often a medical student—who preys on people in such a manner (A. Davis and Dollard 1940:45; Saxon, Dreyer, and Tallant 1945:75–76; Webb 1971; Frye 1975). A variant on the theme is the "black bottle man," also a medical student or physician, who gives the patient poison in the guise of medicine (Cameron 1930:57). Said an elderly midwife:

> They was afraid, honey. Yes, they was really afraid. You know a long time ago black people were treated so dirty and so they was afraid of doctors givin em a dose of somethin just because they was black. They had that in their mind. And from the way they were treated, they had a right to think of such. They use the old sayin, use that word, they may give me the black bottle. That's the word they used I think. Means poison. Somethin like that just to get rid of em. They was afraid of that. That's right—they was afraid of that. Long years ago. They was. You know what? I didn't think nothin about all a this until—all a this really didn't dawn on me, plenty of it, until I just stopped and thinked. Then you realize it and you know it's true. They thought the doctors would do some kinda experiment on em. Removin this and removin that cause it wasn't nothin but a black body. Overall that's the way they felt. And I can see the point. But now it has been some time since they actually felt like that. It has been a change, you know. (Logan 1989:102)

No change for this 45-year old California man in 1970, quoted in the University of California at Berkeley, Folklore Archives:

The black bottle was for Black folks only. Man, if you got sick you went to the hospital and if you acted kinda outrageous, they'd slip you the black bottle. The White folks could perform all kinda autopsies, but if they slip you that black bottle, man, there ain't nothin' they could find out. You learn about the black bottle just from growin up. Me, I was kinda afraid to go to a hospital man, you know, cause when the nurse come around—say "Eddie, take your medicine," I'd look around and wait till she'd leave, you understand, and I'd pass it on to my friends and say—hey man, try some of this here, you know, and I'd watch and see what its gonna do to him, see?

The response of his friends to this offer is not recorded.

It is best to keep in mind the infamous Tuskegee Syphilis Study before deriding such belief. The study, which began in 1932 and continued until 1972, was funded by the Public Health Service. It included a large sample of poor African-American men infected with syphilis; they were not educated about the true nature of their disease but were told that they had "bad blood," the folk term covering a variety of problems. And they were *left untreated* so that researchers might have an opportunity to observe the natural course of the disease until "end point," that is, autopsy (Jones 1981). It has recently been suggested that nearly "60 years after the [Tuskegee] study began, there remains a trail of distrust and suspicion that hampers HIV education efforts in Black communities" (Stephen Thomas and Quinn 1991). Some individuals in one study saw the disease as a form of racial genocide (Flaskerud and Rush 1989): "Otherwise why would so many black people get AIDS?" This belief was also reported from caretakers of HIV seropositive infants in Newark, N.J. (Meltzer and Kantor 1990): "When asked what caused AIDS, many of those interviewed understood this to be a question of the origins of the virus, rather than the mode of transmission. While most answered that they did not know the cause, others answered that they had heard that it was a part of a conspiracy to attack certain segments of the population. One typical respondent said that the 'heads of the economy' put out the AIDS virus 'to eliminate a certain percentage of the people, and after that, then they'll come up with a cure.'"

There is no doubt that there is a significant disparity between the health status of White Americans and African-Americans; one study of mortality rates in New York City, for example, revealed that "black men in Harlem were less likely to reach the age of 65 than men in Bangladesh" (McCord and Freeman 1990). A 1986 national survey of health services usage revealed as well a significant deficit in access to health care for African-Americans, and the fact that when compared to White patients, they are "less likely to be satisfied with the qualitative ways their physicians treat them when they are ill, more dissatisfied with the care they receive when hospitalized, and more likely to believe that the duration of their hospitalizations is too short" (Blendon et al. 1989). The factual basis of feelings of many African-American men and women that they are not receiving the best care is borne out by other studies (Egbert and Rothman 1977; Schiff et al. 1986; S. Johnson et al. 1986; Baker, Stevens, and Brook 1991; Bindman et al. 1991; for some excellent suggestions on ways to improve communication between doctor and patient when racial factors are an issue, see Levy 1985).

The continued—indeed, perhaps increasing—use of home remedies and alternative practitioners is not all due to perceived poor care in orthodox settings, however. Health professionals have also failed to recognize that traditional beliefs are *not* random isolated notions that can be dispelled by simply pointing out that they are incorrect and the believer wrong-headed. Belief systems can and do change, of course, but it is ordinarily not because some disbelieving outsider snips away at single elements. Rather, the individual who has been so admonished quickly learns who can be trusted with "old-time" or "old-fashioned" ideas about alternative treatments, and who is likely to think them quaint, silly, or dangerous. In medical settings individuals frequently must make judgments concerning the wisdom of sharing such beliefs and—when they are withheld—it is all too easy to believe that they are not present at all. (Not *my* patients!) It is difficult, then, to make any kind of accurate estimate of what percentage of African-Americans continue to use traditional means to treat themselves, family members, and friends; suffice it to say that it is probably much higher than we know. My years at the pediatrics clinic in Lansing (1980–1987) certainly provided convincing evidence that the traditional system still functions in the care of infants and children. And my conversations with individuals in the years since have shown that it can be expanded to provide help for the newer problems of drugs and AIDS. Ads by healers claiming to be able to help those addicted to crack appeared in the African-American press as early as 1986. "I am here from Beaufort, South Carolina, to do what so many have failed to do" reads a typical one—going on to list the sorts of things that might be troubling someone: "Are you having problems in love, marriage, sick, voo-doo or witchcraft, need money, losing everything, drug, crack or alcohol. You need to see me and let me use my guaranteed South Carolina old fashion methods" (*New York Amsterdam News,* October 4, 1986, p. 50).[1]

Economic hard times may also play a role in decisions to depend on home treatment. Will Upshaw—whose pharmacy provided a wide array of the "old-time" patent medicines, over-the-counter preparations, and ingredients for home remedies used by Janine Jackson, Bernita Washington, and other neighborhood women—commented on their continued popularity:

Well, basically they're items that we've stocked in the store that our clientele *use*, that they've brought up from the South or have used in the South when they lived there—like the catnip, for example, and the asafoetida tincture. Lot of those sales are to the younger Black generation, recommended to them either by a mother or a grandmother for colic, mainly colic, for their babies. A friend of mine has a store that has a predominently Spanish population, and he has found that the second, third generations come along go away from the old remedies—where *my* experience has been, with the Black clientele, that they still *stay* with it.

Do people ask your advice about health problems, I asked?

> Oh, constantly, yes. We're their first contact, before the physician. I am a high-volume Medicaid pharmacy and I would say initially they would use a medical card for treatment of a problem. But if they're not *satisfied*, then mother or grandmother might mention a home-type remedy and then go that route. I think third-party [insurance] in general, Medicaid included, Blue Cross—people because they *have* that type of insurance would go to a physician first. But, I've noticed that in the past two to three years that the swing is back towards home medication; medicating themselves *first* before going to a physician.
>
> That's basically based on increases in co-payments on their insurance coverage. Increased co-pays, for example; autoworkers that have Blue Cross drug coverage, when those programs first started, they had a two-dollar co-pay. Then, a contract or two down the line, the co-pay got increased to three dollars; then on the last contract the co-pay on their prescription drugs was increased to *five* dollars. So since that co-pay has gone to five dollars the trend is back toward your self-treating first. Personally I think that when the co-pay was two dollars it tended to lead to over-utilization of their insurance; that's my personal opinion. But I think the increased co-pay has led towards a trend back towards self-medicating first, right. (Lansing, Michigan; 1986)

The cultural importance of "old-timey" treatments is underscored by the fact that many people who use few or no old remedies still have vivid memories of earlier times when they or other members of their family did so. They are thus able to draw on a legacy of health-related stories handed down over many generations as part of their family lore; sometimes these family tales have happy endings, sometimes not. But they provide a conscious link between those individuals in the present day for whom the wonders of modern medical technology are at least theoretically available—and all those who came before and used whatever came to hand. As Latishia Simmons put it, the old way of doing things *must* have had "somethin' to it, 'cause those people made the *way* for *us*, that's right." (Detroit, Michigan; 1978)

In some families, of course, the old remedies are more than simply memories. In some instances they continue to be used almost to the exclusion of anything "modern"; in others they are adjunct to over-the-counter preparations and/or prescription medications. They link the experiences of the past to the present in a meaningful way and, more importantly, they allow individuals to have fuller control of decisions about their health. No outsider—particularly an outsider who by reasons of ethnicity and class may be suspect—need be involved. Janine Jackson had never seen a doctor until the accident that injured her leg a year or so before our conversation in 1986; nor did she take more than a dose or two of the medicine prescribed for pain. Better, she believes, to depend on Doctor Jesus. She was raised in a deeply religious family in which it was expected that God would provide the wherewithal to deal with whatever problems there were in daily life. She learned the importance of self-reliance and of making do with whatever was at hand.

The home remedies that she knows about and uses on herself, her children and grandchildren—catnip tea and baking soda and garlic and blessed oil and a goodly dose of laxative now and again—are no different from those used by many of her neighbors. It is her absolute unwillingness to *allow* pain or sickness to interfere with her life that makes her stand out. The fact that she blamed an injury to her leg at work on Satan has already been described; she did not use the suggested elastic bandage or, after a dose or two, take the medication prescribed for pain. (At the age of 64 the first prescription of her life!) Instead, when the pains got bad she simply said, "Begone, Satan," and they disappeared. She also depends on her religious faith to protect her when, at six A.M., she walks from her car to her place of work. The neighborhood may be increasingly dangerous but woe betide anyone who messes with Janine Jackson:

> I walk from my car at six o'clock. They say, *"So* much *happening."* My supervisor say, "So much happening; do you walk?" I say, "Oh, I walk." She say, "So much happenin'; there's a man out there this mornin'!" I say, "Oh, well, don't worry about me; I'm covered with the blood of Jesus!" And when you're not a *believer,* that's kinda make you angry, and she kinda did. See, I don't be*lieve* nothin'll happen to me—and if you don't believe nothin' will happen and you prayin', nothin' will *happen* to you! Ever'body was gettin' broke in around here; ever'body, ever'body. But this house was covered with the blood and it was protected. And I just don't believe anybody is gonna break in, in the name of Jesus. And when I walk by my car? If any-body *start* toward me, *"In* the name of *Jesus,* before you can raise your hand your arm will fall off! You not gonna touch *me!"* That's just the way I feel. I be just as peaceful and it can be half-dark or whatnot; no fear. Hum-uh. (Lansing, Michigan; 1986)

Bernita Washington, who has appeared in so many of these pages, also prefers to avoid health professionals; she occasionally sees a nearby family practitioner in order to hear his diagnosis if she is feeling especially poorly, but she rarely follows his advice. The medications that he prescribes sit in her purse untaken. She never fully trusts the advice—or the medicine—of a person who makes money from his expertise. She echoes an idea that I have heard frequently over the years, that is, that doctors could cure you if they really wanted to. If doctors would just give you the *right* medicine you would be cured, or, if they would just give you enough of it. In the 1970s and early 1980s I also frequently heard people say that doctors' medicine is very "strong"—perhaps *too* strong sometimes—and "too chemical" for some people. And in the last five years or so I have heard people speak of "doctors' medicine" as being addictive as well—several informants, including Bernita—have voiced their concerns about becoming a "drug addict" if they continue to take their prescribed medication.[2]

Drugs and the possibility of addiction to them is much on people's minds these days. Bernita Washington's latest rental house is by an empty lot which is often the scene of drug sales and drug use. Like her neighbor Janine she relies at least in part on faith to help cleanse this area of drug pushers and addicts; each morning she looks out the window facing the lot and prays that such people will move on. As a practical adjunct to this she also—morning and afternoon—picks up used needles to keep them out of the hands of little children. She is also like Janine in that she, too, depends mostly on simple home remedies for herself, her children, and many grand- and great-grand-children. And she too would prefer to give the Lord the chance to heal. Actually, she says, you don't even *need* medicine—be this a doctor's prescription or a simple home remedy—as long as you have prayer. *Every* home has water, she says, and prayer can change a tubful of water into a healing bath. Just pull the plug and your aches and pains will drain away:

> Me myself, I'm saved, O.K.? Me myself, if I have *pains*—if I have any kind of pains, stomach pains, if I have arthritic or most any kind of pains that I have—most people have leg pains, stuff like that, O.K. What I do is I go *into* the bathroom, I turn a tub of *water.* When you turn the tub of water, leave the tub of water run, *I pray* over it. So I ask, "Lord, bless this water because this is *your* water; this is your *healing* water. *You* made this—man didn't make this, y'know—and *God,* I'm askin' You to *bless* this water that my pains will *leave* as I go into there and return out." And when I *does* that, when *I come out,* I have *no pains* about me whatever! I have what you call a pinched nerve in my back, and *I* can get in there in that tub of water and when I come out I can straighten up, I can walk, whatever. And I don't have that pain anymore. The water is blessed by God, so what you have to do is have faith and believe when you go into the water. And God will deliver you from your pain.

Over the years she has called upon God to help with a whole range of health problems, in fact—not just the minor pains that can be washed away in her daily bath. She does not trust doctors and what they might do to you—and she does not trust the alternative practitioners utilized by some of her neighbors (and some of her own children) and what *they* might do to you. If *physicians* sometimes keep patients coming back just to make money, well, so do some of the other sorts of healers. In fact they may make you sick to begin with so that they will have a ready-made clientele, said Bernita:

> O.K., there are peoples if they *want to,* they can do things to you and never come where you *is!* It's *possible!* Right. Because what I'm sayin' is there are people that just *study* those type of things; is some people don't even work. They'll tell you, "I can heal you, come to me; you give me $25 for this treatment," O.K.? Here you go back, say, "Well, you gotta come back to me," for *money.* Each time it's $25, same as a medical doctor, right? Each time you go back it's $25. O.K., say if he got maybe a hundred people doin' that, see what I'm sayin'? He *never* have to *work!* See what I'm sayin'? And sometime they're not *doin'* what they really pro*claimin'* they're *doin!* See what I'm sayin'? They are makin' *money!* If you don't believe me, you listen to the radio sometime; you'll hear people say the same thing! Some of these type of things is really is not *true;* sometime people is just makin' money off you and not doin' any*thing* for you.[3]

Far, far better to depend on God who knows all about her health problems. *He* is aware of her hypertension and is not going to let her have a stroke just because she fails to take a few pills! The Lord *needs* people to be sick, she says, so that He can demonstrate His powers:

> Peoples, saved peoples, get up in church and say, "God doesn't need us, but we need God." But oh yes, He *do!* God *need* us! Say if I was sick here right now, God is not gonna reach His hand down here! What He *do,* he will have somebody come over, say, "Why don't you stop in and check on her?" And when you get there and help, that's God doin' that. He uses our body to do all His good work. To lead us. Now, I could go to the doctor right now and they'd probably put me in the hospital; with my problems that I have now, they probably put me in the hospital. And I get where sometime I'm not able hardly to go to sleep. Blood pressures. I wake up through the night and I can get up and go spit a mouthful of blood out! Every night! I go to the doctor—I goes to Dr. Brooks over here—oh, he get on my case about them pills! [But] I don't like takin' a lot of 'em. I take 'em if I *have* to; if it's serious and really *bad,* you know, and I keep spittin' up a lot of blood, I just take 'em.

I interjected that I thought he was right and she *should* take her medicine; I agreed with her doctor that she was in danger of suffering a stroke. She laughed:

> He is right! I know that! But I'm not gonna let that place in my mind; I'm gonna keep placin' in my mind that God is not gonna let anything

happen to me 'til it's time. I don't want [to] place in my mind sayin', "Well, I gotta stay on this pill as long as I live!" I don't wanta place that in my mind. Listen at this, listen at this: I'm gonna have one [if] I take those pills or not! I'm gonna have it, O.K.? Believe that. *Take* that pill and God intend me to have a stroke, I'm gonna *have* that stroke. If God don't intend me to have that stroke, *I* don't have to lay on no pills. He'll let me know when I—like this mornin' when I got up—I took one this mornin'. Why? Because when I got up I spit out a big mouth of blood, O.K. Really, it just comes right on out of my mouth, you know. But I don't want get it in my mind that I gotta live on pills.

But I don't want be call a dope addict, you know; I don't *want* to take a lot of medicine. You can get addicted to, say if the doctor, O.K., right now—my doctor tell me to be sure to take my blood pressure pill every day. [If] I get angry or sumpin', it's really gone! At my age now, he say I'm gonna have a stroke with it, you know. I gonna go up there and you can't *get* it down, and so he don't want me to go without my tablet. I believe, O.K., if my *mind* said that—if *my* mind said that I *have* to have that every day, *I* would have it every day. My mind says *I* don't have to *have* that every day! And I won't *use* that every day! O.K., my mind is *God's* mind! All right? Knowin' that God *will* take care of me. I don't *believe* God gonna let me have a stroke; I really don't. Not just because I don't take a pill. If I'm gonna have it, I'm just gonna *have* it if I take the pill or don't.

"Gee," I said, "you sound like it's something like smoking crack or shooting up!" "You know what, Lou?," she replied? "You know what really is?" "What," I said? "Here's what," she answered with finality, "the best thing to do is get addicted to God." (Lansing, Michigan; 1987)

Her belief that God can do all and protect all those who love Him allows her to deal with whatever is frightening in her life, be it old or new. On that same afternoon she described a vision she had had a few years earlier in which she was shown a terrible disease without a cure; it was not until later that she knew it to be AIDS:

I usually always, the Lord always usually show me *visions,* and I had saw this vision. The Lord had showed me this vision that what gonna come up on earth about a *disease* that, you know, that nobody—wasn't no doctors, nobody—wasn't goin' to be able to *cure!* I asked the question when I *saw* the vision, I akst the question, "Now, Lord, if this come up here, what are we gonna *do?*" And the Lord replied to me, "There are going to be many things that's gonna happen to let peoples *know* that *I'm* the only strength; I'm the only One that they can *rely* on." And that AIDS, it has come to pass since I *saw* the vision. I done read about it in the papers and stuff like that, and saw peoples *with* it.

You know, I had already *saw* that, because the Lord had already *showed* me and spoke to me and let me know that there is *nothing* that you can trust but *God!* When I *first* saw it, you know, it *really* frightened me. I said, "Well, Lord, suppose I get that? What am I gonna do?" When he first *showed* me the vision about the disease, I said, "Oh

God, what am I gonna do? Why, *I* could get it *myself!* You know I
don't know how it's caught; I don't know how peoples are gettin' it!"

So the Lord said *anybody* that *believes,* you know, anybody that believe upon *Him,* this is not goin' to *happen* to 'em! 'Cause anything
that happen to you, you know—say if you took sick or sumpin'—you
would be *cured!* So if you should happen to get, if *any* of *His peoples,*
if any God's *peoples get* that disease—I'm talkin' about the people that
are *saved*—they will be cured. You got to *believe* that nothin' like that
is gonna happen. You can't think, "This is all bad and I'm scared," and,
"I'm not gonna do this and I ain't gonna do that. I ain't gonna drink behind nobody. I ain't goin' out." Even deadly *poison,* you can eat it and
it won't hurt you. If you just trust in God.

She certainly is not alone in placing the AIDS epidemic in a
religious context; as one physician noted, "We still have not decided
if we are dealing with a crime, a sin, or a disease" (Satcher 1990).
In New Orleans Prophetess Mother Mary had no trouble in deciding,
however. For some years she had been giving several hundred dollars per month to her parish priest to use in his prison ministry;
when she learned that he was using much of the money on the men
in the prison infirmary she instructed him that this had to stop.
"Most of 'em are homosexuals with AIDS," she said, "and if they
have it they deserve it because of unnatural acts." (1988) Two-thirds
of one sample of African-American women in California also suggested that AIDS is the fulfillment of a prophecy in the biblical book
of Revelation regarding plagues (Flaskerud and Rush 1989): "A majority of respondents believed that AIDS was a result of breaking
religious and moral laws—a punishment for sin. 'It's a punishment
for sins—like men with men or fornication or for your parents' sins;
that's why babies get it.' 'The sins of the fathers visited on the
children to the second and third generation. That refers to how you
raise them; but what you do to them, they'll do—like child abuse
and drugs.' Others said, 'Sometimes what parents do, the children
will suffer, like babies born addicted.'"

For those who had contracted the disease but had *not* sinned—if
the virus was transmitted through transfusions, for example—it was
seen to be a test of faith: "'It's a test of faith for you and for other
people; it's a testimony to see if God has healed you.' God allows
some illnesses so that 'He will get the glory'; 'God can put these
things on you so that He can show the people that He could heal';
and 'Right, it has two purposes: to test your faith and to show
someone else that God can heal you.'" As Clatts and Mutchler (1989)
noted, with AIDS we tend to "make something more of affliction
than the merely medical and to make something other of the afflicted
than merely sufferers of disease."

Not everyone has the powerful religious faith that enables Bernita
Washington to serenely believe that she will not contract—or will
have divine protection against—such a disease. Even Reverend Hast-

ings in Grand Rapids, whose own healing ministry he described as being a gift from God, knew himself to be helpless to cure it. When called to the bedside of the young prostitute dying of AIDS (inconsolable as she listened to the weeping of the infants she had aborted) he could only pray for her; indeed, he too thought that she had "to pay" for the sins she had committed. (1987) But not everyone is as scrupulous as the Reverend Hastings and a disease as terrifying as AIDS also provides fertile ground for exploitation. For a year or so an individual advertised in a New York newspaper that he was able to cure it with the "African Bio Mineral Balance" (*New York Amsterdam News,* May 6, 1986, p. 14). He was arrested for fraud in 1987 (Jamison 1988) That summer Myra Green, whose husband had utilized the herbalist's treatment for hypertension, commented bitterly that the arrest was racist: "But you see, I don't know why they didn't do anything when he advertised in the *Amsterdam News.* But when he put the ad in the *Village Voice* they made a big stink about it, and they ar*rested* him for *fraud!* See, they called him a *quack.* He didn't have a *license* and then he was advertisin'. Guess as long as he was around *Blacks* they didn't care!" (New York City; 1987)

In the fall of 1990 I wrote to two individuals who advertised their special abilities in healing to inquire if they might be able to heal an infant infected with AIDS. Reverend Parsons in Flint, Michigan, responded with a photoduplicated form letter that included a series of suggested "freewill offerings" in various amounts. There was a check mark by the sum of $2,000 and a scribbled note that I call him. I asked, when I did so, if the $2,000 would pay for a cure? "Oh no," was the reply, "I just meant if you were blessed by a big amount to support the ministry; if blessed in a big way, support it in a big way." Well, what about the sick baby? He hedged: "I am not a doctor, what do the doctor say? I'm going to do all I can do here spiritually, to enhance things. People tell me about aloe vera; ever hear of that? Aloe vera juice; it's a natural healer. Look into it." He then hung up.

A letter to another individual in Chicago also brought a request that I call; "the Prophet," as he said he prefers to be called, also indicated that a substantial monetary "testimony" of $650 would be required. This would help to pay for the placement of a six-weeks-long ad in the *Globe* newspaper to further his healing ministry: "I *need* that testimony!" As soon as he received the $650—cash or money order only, no personal checks—he could get started on the case. Nor should I doubt that he would be able to help; after all, he had raised his own nephew from the dead only weeks before. "My sister's son was dead, 25 miles from here, when I got there," he told me. "Three girls were standing around the bed. I just prayed over him and laid hands on him and an hour later he was out in the yard eatin' a hot dog." And *how* would he go about curing such a sick infant, I asked? I was not to worry: "I just heal the baby; that kind of work has gotta be did. If I can raise the dead I can heal that baby."

Notes

1. An individual who responds to such an ad is likely to be told only to send money (Snow 1978); although I have been chastised in print (Scheper-Hughes 1990) for referring to such individuals as "charlatans," I continue to hold this opinion. The fact that there are many traditional healers—women and men such as Mother Delphine in Tucson and Reverend Moses Hastings in Grand Rapids—who are *not* in practice simply to extract money from the frightened and gullible does not mean that there not others who are.

2. In the spring of 1988 I spent several hours at the establishment of a well-known healer/adviser in a Detroit suburb. Reverend Rollins is seen by the authorities as a con artist—he evaded charges of practicing medicine without a license a few years ago by declaring he was only following the religious practices of his African ancestors—and by his many admirers as a healer without peer. Certainly he is a successful one; I had to wait a long time to see him on this particular day. The time spent in the waiting room was instructive, to say the least; people freely spoke of the fact that they had come to him because of the failure of their physician—or physicians—to help them. Much of the conversation dealt with two topics: the failure of physicians to prescribe enough medication to cure an individual (thus forcing someone to return and pay for yet another prescription), and the danger involved in taking any medication for too long. Thomas Johnson, a middle-aged man who had driven from Flint for a consultation with the Reverend Doctor, revealed that he had discarded his blood pressure pills a year earlier. "If it was any good it would cure you!" he said. "If you keep taking it you'll get addicted." He was hoping that the healer would give him some herbs for his problem—after all, they are "more natural."

"When my turn to see him finally came, the good Doctor evaded my question about just which herbs would be useful in treating high blood pressure. Did I suffer from high blood pressure, he asked? When I said that I did, he suggested that I might try the white of an egg sprinkled with salt for nine mornings. Or for *really* high blood pressure, he said, *that* can be brought down in 15 minutes if the sufferer eats a raw egg yolk mixed with a tablespoonful of salt" (Snow 1988:6).

3. The problem is two-fold, then—on the one hand, people may *pretend* to have power purely as a money-making ploy. Bernita is quite right in her description of the advertising; individuals proclaim their special abilities by radio, in newspaper ads, in leaflets distributed around neighborhoods, and so on, and some of these are obviously purely money-making ventures (Hannerz 1969:140–144; Snow 1978, 1979). I am on the mailing list of a number of individuals who use religious trappings as a masquerade for their real purpose, to sell the gullible consumer a sure way to hit the numbers. To quote from a few communications received since January of 1991, for example: from Reverend Parsons, of Flint, Michigan, "I have a big red hot blessing for you"; from Reverend Black of Metairie, Louisiana, "God showed me in a vision two red hot lucky numbers hitting straight"; from Reverend Jeremiah of Hialeah, Florida, "Almighty God revealed to me through divine revelation two red hot lucky numbers falling straight"; from Reverend Walls of Chicago, "Yes, rush me the Two Red Hot Blessings God showed you blessing straight on May 10th"; and from Reverend Smith of Miami, Florida, "I will give you these two God revealed numbers on the telephone as soon as you call my lucky number hot line." Their suggested "donation" for a divinely selected hot number ranges from $12 to $25 (see also McCall 1973).

On the other hand, if individuals *do* have power they are no one with whom to trifle. When "falling out" spells are not labeled and treated as "epilepsy" by the orthodox health care system, as Weidman (1979b) noted, these may come to be seen as "unnatural" problems: "Orthodox ministrations then become somewhat irrelevant. Health status may be considerably reduced because of increasing disability from the condition, but the path to reversing this process ordinarily is seen as lying outside the orthodox institution. That route can be a very expensive one to take; consequently, some inner-city persons so afflicted become trapped in an enduring state of illness. They frequently lack the cash required for cure via traditional healing systems; they may be ambivalent about or fearful of the healer's double-edged power; and they perceive the orthodox one as unable to help them."

A young boy in Mississippi left no doubt as to his ambivalent feelings about the local healer: "I have two girls I like to be with, and they'll each say to you they wouldn't know what to do if the healing lady turned against them, and they're right. She's no one to be an enemy of yours, and the best one to have for a friend" (Coles 1971a:532). The reader will recall that it was the failure of Marya Smith's father-in-law to pay the "hoodoo man" that the family believed resulted in the malformation of one infant and the deaths of several others. And as Weidman noted, the fees charged by such individuals may be far more than just the $25 that Bernita cited; it can cost many hundreds of dollars to have a hex removed. Still, people who fear that their problems are the result of malign magic may decide to take no chances; they rely on multiple resources (Roberson 1983:137–138; Scott 1974).

Epilogue

I have been studying African-American health beliefs and practices for most of my professional life. I have listened to the words of healers such as Sister Erma and Mother Delphine and the Reverend Hastings—unique individuals all, dealing daily with the afflictions of body, mind, and spirit among their clientele. But over the years I have been most impressed with the Jacie Burneses and the Janine Jacksons and the Bernita Washingtons—truly extraordinary people using traditional means to cope with illness and all the other problems of everyday life. All of these women embody in large part what it is to be African-American today, and their lives can teach us a great deal more than how they go about maintaining health.

If the reader comes away with anything from this book, I hope it will be that the traditional ways of healing are still to be found because they serve a purpose. They allay the physical ills of the body, of course, but they heal spirit and mind and heart as well. Eating starch and drinking herbal teas and the wearing of charms may ease the anxieties of pregnancy every bit as much as—or more than—any number of prenatal check-ups. Traditional practices are not simply old ways of treating old problems; for better or for worse they are also used to deal with the newer scourges of drugs and AIDS. They may not offer the "cure" sought by biomedicine but they do provide the individual with explanation and accommodation in an increasingly difficult world. They offer empowerment to those who, on the surface, have not much power at all.

I also hope that the reader comes away with a sense of admiration for the intelligence and resilience of those men and women whose voices have been heard in these pages. Choices in problem solving are made within a rational system that continues to function in the face of mounting odds. Children are born and are cared for within the network of an extended family, knowledge continues to be transmitted from generation to generation, and life continues. One would wish for Bernita's grandchildren and great-grandchildren a life free of drugs and guns, violence and death, but that may not be possible. Still, one can know that Bernita—and all the other Bernitas—will continue to use faith and whatever is at hand to insure the survival of the coming generations.

Bibliography

de Albuquerque, Klaus. 1979   Non-Institutional Medicine on the Sea Islands. *In* Implications for Health Policy in Rural South Carolina: Proceedings of a Symposium on Culture and Health. Melba S. Varner and Amy M. McCandless, eds. Pp. 33--79. Charleston, SC: College of Charleston offprint.

Alfonso, Eduardo, et al. 1983   *Neisseria gonorrhoeae* Conjunctivitis. Journal of American Medical Association 250(6):794--795.

Altshuler, Stanley L., and J. Walter Valenteen. 1974   Amenorrhea Following Rifampin Administration During Oral Contraceptive Use. Obstetrics and Gynecology 44:771--772.

The American Heritage Dictionary of the English Language, 2d ed. 1969   Boston: American Heritage Publishing Company and Houghton Mifflin Company.

Angelou, Maya. 1970   I Know Why the Caged Bird Sings. New York: Random House. Bantam Book edition, 1971.

Ansa, Tina McElroy. 1989   Baby of the Family. San Diego: Harcourt Brace Jovanovich.

Armstead, Cheryl A., et al. 1989   Relationship of Racial Stressors to Blood Pressure Responses and Anger Expression in Black College Students. Health Psychology 8(5):541--556.

Aschenbrenner, Joyce. 1975   Lifelines: Black Families in Chicago. New York: Holt, Rinehart and Winston.

Baer, Hans A. 1981   Prophets and Advisors in Black Spiritual Churches: Therapy, Palliative, or Opiate? Culture, Medicine and Psychiatry 5:145–170.

_____. 1984   The Black Spiritual Movement: A Religious Response to Racism. Knoxville: University of Tennessee Press.

Bailey, Eric J. 1988   An Ethnomedical Analysis of Hypertension Among Detroit Afro-Americans. Journal of National Medical Association 80(10):1105--1112.

_____. 1991   Hypertension: An Analysis of Detroit African American Health Care Treatment Patterns. Human Organization 50(3):287--296.

Baker, David W., Carl D. Stevens, and Robert H. Brook. 1991   Patients Who Leave a Public Hospital Emergency Department Without Being Seen by a Physician. Journal of American Medical Association 266(8):1085--1090.

Baldwin, Karen. 1984   Mrs. Emma Dupree: "That Little Medicine Thing." North Carolina Folklore Journal 32(2):50--53.

Bambara, Toni Cade. 1977   A Girl's Story. *In* The Sea Birds Are Alive. New York: Random House. First Vintage Books edition, 1982.

Baranowski, Tom, et al. 1983   Social Support, Social Influence, Ethnicity and the Breast Feeding Decision. Social Science & Medicine 17(21):1599--1611.

Beck, Jane C. 1975   The West Indian Supernatural World: Belief Integration in a Pluralistic Society. Journal of American Folklore 88:235–244.

Bell, Carl C., et al. 1984   Prevalence of Isolated Sleep Paralysis in Black Subjects. Journal of National Medical Association 76(5):501--508.

Bell, Carl C., Dora D. Dixie-Bell, and Belinda Thompson. 1986   Further Studies on the Prevalence of Isolated Sleep Paralysis in Black Subjects. Journal of National Medical Association 78(7):649--659.

Bell, Michael Edward. 1980   Pattern, Structure, and Logic in Afro-American Hoodoo Performance. Ph.D. dissertation, Department of Folklore, Indiana University. Ann Arbor, MI: University Microfilms.

Bell, Michael Edward, and James Clements, Jr. n.d. Roots and Remedies: Afro-American Folk Medicine in Rhode Island. Report of Joint Project: Rhode Island Black Heritage Society, St. Martin DePorres Center, Rhode Island Folklife Project, and Brown University Long Term Gerontology Center.

Bergen, Fanny D. 1899   Animal and Plant Lore. Memoirs, American Folklore Society, Vol. 7, Part 2.

Bindman, Andrew B., et al. 1991   Consequences of Queuing for Care at a Public Hospital Emergency Department. Journal of American Medical Association 266(8):1091–1096.

Black, William George. 1883   Folk-Medicine: A Chapter in the History of Culture. London: Elliot Stock, Publisher.

Blake, Herman. 1979   Utilization of Health Care on the Sea Islands: A Sociocultural Perspective. *In* Implications for Public Policy in Rural South Carolina: Proceedings of a Symposium on Culture and Health. Melba S. Varner and Amy M. McCandless, eds. Pp. 16–27. Charleston, SC: College of Charleston offprint.

_____. 1984   "Doctor Can't Do Me No Good": Social Concomitants of Health Attitudes and Practices Among Elderly Blacks in Isolated Rural Populations. *In* Black Folk Medicine. Wilbur H. Watson, ed. Pp. 33–40. New Brunswick, NJ: Transaction Books.

Blendon, Robert J., et al. 1989   Access to Medical Care for Black and White Americans. Journal of American Medical Association 261(2):278–281.

Block, Eric. 1986   Antithrombotic Agent of Garlic: A Lesson from 5,000 Years of Folk Medicine. *In* Folk Medicine. Richard P. Steiner, ed. Pp. 125–137. Washington, DC: American Chemical Society.

Blockson, Charles L. 1987   "Nowhere to Lay Down Weary Head." National Geographic 172(6):735–763.

Blumhagen, Dan. 1980   Hyper-Tension: A Folk Illness with a Medical Name. Culture, Medicine and Psychiatry 4:197–337.

Boone, Margaret S. 1982   A Socio-medical Study of Infant Mortality Among Disadvantaged Blacks. Human Organization 41(3):227–236.

_____. 1985   Social and Cultural Factors in the Etiology of Low Birthweight Among Disadvantaged Blacks. Social Science and Medicine 20(10):1001–1011.

_____. 1987   Inner-City Black Undercount. An Exploratory Study on the Causes of Coverage Error. Evaluation Review 11(2):216–241.

_____. 1989   Capital Crime: Black Infant Mortality in America. Newbury Park, CA: Sage Publications, Inc.

Bouknight, LaClaire. 1990   Michigan's Black-White Mortality Gap: The Impact of Drugs and AIDS. *In* The State of Black Michigan 1990. Frances S. Thomas, ed. Pp. 29–35. East Lansing, MI: Michigan State University Urban Affairs Programs.

Bowering, Jean, et al. 1978   Infant Feeding Practices in East Harlem. Journal of American Dietetic Association 72:148–163.

Boyd, Eddie L., Leslie A. Shimp, and Marvie Jarmon Hackney. 1984   Home Remedies and the Black Elderly. Ann Arbor, MI: Institute of Gerontology and College of Pharmacy, University of Michigan.

Boyd, Eddie L., and Einar Tjolsen. 1986   Herbal Teas and Remedies: Are They Safe? Journal of Pharmacy Technology (July/August): 153–158.

Boyle, Jacquelyn. Michigan Infant Death Rate Up in 1989. Detroit Free Press, February 23, 1990, 1B, 8B.

Brandon, Elizabeth. 1976   Folk Medicine in French Louisiana. *In* American Folk Medicine. Wayland D. Hand, ed. Pp. 215–234. Berkeley: University of California Press.

Brandon, George. 1988   Regional Variations in Rootwork Symptoms? Some Findings from Folklore, Ethnography and the Clinic. The Griot (Spring):3–11.
Braveman, Paula A., et al. 1991   Differences in Hospital Resource Allocation Among Sick Newborns According to Hospital Insurance. Journal of American Medical Association 266(23):3300–3308.
Brody, Howard. 1992   The Healer's Power. New Haven: Yale University Press.
Brody, Howard, and David B. Waters. 1980   Diagnosis Is Treatment. Journal of Family Practice 10(3):445–449.
Brody, Howard, and Ati Yates. 1990   The Placebo Response. *In* Behavior and Medicine. Danny Wedding, ed. Pp. 333–343. St. Louis: Mosby Year Book.
Brunson, Rose. 1962   Socialization Experiences and Socioeconomic Characteristics of Urban Negroes as Related to Use of Selected Southern Foods and Medical Remedies. Ph.D. dissertation, Division of Social Science, Michigan State University. Ann Arbor, MI: University Microfilms.
Buehler, James W., et al. 1986   Maternal Mortality in Women Aged 35 Years or Older: United States. Journal of American Medical Association 255(1):53–57.
Buescher, Paul A., et al. 1991   An Evaluation of the Impact of Maternity Care Coordination on Medicaid Birth Outcomes in North Carolina. American Journal of Public Health 81(12):1625–1629.
Cameron, Vivian K. 1930   Folk Beliefs Pertaining to Health of the Southern Negro. Unpublished Master's thesis, Department of Sociology, Northwestern University, Evanston, IL.
Camino, Linda Anne. 1986   Ethnomedical Illnesses and Non-Orthodox Healing Practices in a Black Neighborhood in the American South: How They Work and What They Mean. Ph.D. dissertation, Department of Anthropology, University of Virginia. Ann Arbor, MI: University Microfilms.
_____. 1989   Nerves, Worriation, and Black Women: A Community Study in the American South. *In* Gender, Health, and Illness. Dona L. Davis and Setha M. Low, eds. Pp. 203–222. New York: Hemisphere Publishing Corporation.
Cappannari, Stephen N., et al. 1975   Voodoo in the General Hospital. Journal of American Medical Association 232:938–940.
Carrington, Betty Watts. 1978   The Afro-American. *In* Culture, Childbearing, Health Professionals. Ann L. Clark, ed. Pp. 34–52. Philadelphia: F. A. Davis.
Chargot, Patricia. 1990a Increase in Black Infants Crowds Adoption Agencies. Detroit Free Press, July 20, 1990, 1A, 11A.
_____. 1990b Death Rate of Infants Up Slightly. Detroit Free Press, December 7, 1990, 1B, 3B.
_____. 1991   Lack of Mother's Love Linked to State's Ban. Detroit Free Press, February 20, 1991, 18A.
Chase, A. W. 1865   Dr. Chase's Recipes; or, Information for Everybody. Ann Arbor, MI: Published by the author.
Chu, Susan Y., James W. Buehler, and Ruth L. Berkelman. 1990   Impact of the Human Immunodeficiency Virus Epidemic on Mortality in Women of Reproductive Age, United States. Journal of American Medical Association 264(2):225–229.
Clatts, Michael, and Kevin M. Mutchler. 1989   AIDS and the Dangerous Other: Metaphors of Sex and Deviance in the Representation of Disease. Medical Anthropology 10:105–114.
Clinicopathologic Conference Case Presentation (BCH #469861). 1967   Johns Hopkins Medical Journal 120:186–199.
Coleman, Trevor W. 1990   Group Shares the Tensions of Once Again Raising Kids. Detroit News, October 28, 1990, 3C.
Coles, Robert. 1967   A Study of Courage and Fear. Volume I of Children of Crisis. Boston: Little, Brown and Company.

_____. 1971a Migrants, Sharecroppers, Mountaineers. Volume II of Children of Crisis. Boston: Little, Brown and Company.

_____. 1971b The South Goes North. Volume III of Children of Crisis. Boston: Little, Brown and Company.

Collins, James W., Jr., and Richard J. David. 1990 The Differential Effect of Traditional Risk Factors on Infant Birthweight Among Blacks and Whites in Chicago. American Journal of Public Health 80(6):679–681.

Cook, Cheryl, and Denise Baisden. 1986 Ancillary Use of Folk Medicine by Patients in Primary Care Clinics in Southwestern West Virginia. Southern Medical Journal 79(9):1098--1101.

Cooley, Gilbert. 1974 A Collection and Study of Recent Black Folklore. Master's thesis, North Carolina Agricultural and Technical State University, Greensboro, NC.

Cooper, Horton. 1972 North Carolina Mountain Folklore and Miscellany. Murfreesboro, NC: Johnson Publishing Company.

Cothran, Michael C. 1977 Hoodoo: A Belief System Among Self-Identified Blacks in Tuscaloosa County. Master's thesis, Department of Anthropology, University of Alabama, Tuscaloosa.

Courlander, Harold. 1960 The Drum and the Hoe. Berkeley: University of California Press.

Creel, Martha Washington. 1990 Gullah Attitudes Toward Life and Death. *In* Africanisms in American Culture. Joseph E. Holloway, ed. Bloomington: Indiana University Press. Midland Book Edition, 1991.

Croom, Edward M., Jr. 1983 Documenting and Evaluating Herbal Remedies. Economic Botany 37:13--27.

Culpeper's English Physician & Complete Herbal. [1684] 1975 Arranged for Use as a First Aid Herbal by Mrs. C. F. Leyel. North Hollywood, CA: Wilshire Book Company.

Cussler, Margaret, and Mary DeGive. 1952 'Twixt the Cup and the Lip. New York: Twayne Publishers.

Dance, Daryl Cumber. 1978 Shuckin' and Jivin'. Folklore from Contemporary Black Americans. Bloomington: Indiana University Press.

Davis, Allison, and John Dollard. 1940 Children of Bondage. New York: Harper and Row, Inc. 1964 reprint.

Davis, Phillip W., Jacqueline Boles, and Charlotte Tatro. 1984 Dramaturgy of Occult Practitioners in the Treatment of Disease and Dysfunction Entities. Social Science & Medicine 19(7):691--698.

Deas-Moore, Vennie. 1987 Home Remedies, Herb Doctors, and Granny Midwives. The World & I (January):474--485.

DeSantis, Lydia. 1989 Health Care Orientations of Cuban and Haitian Immigrant Mothers: Implications for Health Care Professionals. Medical Anthropology 12(1):69--89.

Diagnostic and Statistical Manual of Mental Disorders. 1987 3rd ed., revised. Washington, DC: American Psychiatric Association.

DiCanio, Margaret B. 1976 Doctor-Patient Communication in the Black Community of a Rural County. *In* The Health of a Rural County. Richard C. Reynolds, Sam A. Banks, and Alice H. Murphree, eds. Gainesville: University Presses of Florida.

Dillard, J. L. 1977 Lexicon of Black English. New York: Seabury Press.

Dorson, Richard M. 1947 Blood Stoppers. Southern Folklore Quarterly 11(2):105--118.

_____. 1967 American Negro Folktales. Greenwich, CT: Fawcett Publications, Inc.

Dougherty, Molly C. 1976   Health Agents in a Rural Black Community. Journal of Afro-American Issues 4(1):61–69.
_____. 1978   Becoming a Woman in Rural Black Culture. New York: Holt, Rinehart and Winston.
_____. 1982   Southern Midwifery and Organized Health Care: Systems in Conflict. Medical Anthropology 6(2):113--126.
Drums and Shadows. 1940   Athens, GA: Georgia Writers' Project.
Dunn, S. Kanu. 1988   A Model of Fertility Decision-making Styles Among Young Mothers. Human Organization 47:166--175.
Durel, Lynn A., et al. 1989   Associations of Blood Pressure with Self-Report Measures of Anger and Hostility Among Black and White Men and Women. Health Psychology 8(5):557–575.
Egbert, Lawrence D., and Ilene L. Rothman. 1977   Relation Between the Race and Economic Status of Patients and Who Performs Their Surgery. New England Journal of Medicine 297:90–91.
Elferink, J.G.R. 1983   The Narcotic and Hallucinogenic Use of Tobacco in Pre-Columbian Central America. Journal of Ethnopharmacology 7(1):111--122.
Emrich, Duncan. 1972   Folklore on the American Land. Boston: Little, Brown and Company.
Farizo, Karen M., et al. 1991   Pediatric Emergency Room Visits: A Risk Factor for Acquiring Measles. Pediatrics 87(1):74–79.
Farmer, Paul. 1988   Bad Blood, Spoiled Milk: Bodily Fluids as Moral Barometers in Rural Haiti. American Ethnologist 15(1):62–83.
_____. 1990   Sending Sickness: Sorcery, Politics, and Changing Concepts of AIDS in Rural Haiti. Medical Anthropology Quarterly (N.S.) 4(1):6--27.
Fatal Injuries to Children—United States, 1986. Journal of American Medical Association 264(8):952--953.
Fatality and Illness Associated with Consumption of Pennyroyal Oil—Colorado. 1978   Morbidity and Mortality Weekly Report 27(51):511--513.
Felice, Marianne E., et al. 1987   Psychosocial Aspects of Mexican-American, White and Black Teenage Pregnancy. Journal of Adolescent Health Care 8:330--335.
Ferris, Ann G., et al. 1978   Diets in the First Six Months of Infants in Western Massachusetts. Journal of American Dietetic Association 72:160--163.
Fingerhut, Lois A., and Joel C. Kleinman. 1990   International and Interstate Comparisons of Homicide Among Young Males. Journal of American Medical Association 263(24):3292--3295.
Flaskerud, Jacquelyn, and Cecilia Rush. 1989   AIDS and Traditional Health Beliefs and Practices of Black Women. Nursing Research 38(4):210–215.
Flowers, A. R. 1985   De Mojo Blues. New York: Ballantine Books.
Food and Drug Administration (FDA). 1975   Herbal Tea: Safe and Unsafe Herbs in Herbal Teas. Memorandum, November 19, 1975.
Forbes, Thomas R. 1966   The Midwife and the Witch. New Haven: Yale University Press.
_____. 1971   Verbal Charms in British Folk Medicine. American Philosophical Society Proceedings 115(4):293--316.
Foster, George M. 1976   Disease Etiologies in Non-Western Medical Systems. American Anthropologist 78:773--782.
Foster, Steven, and James A. Duke. 1990   A Field Guide to Medicinal Plants. Eastern and Central North America. Boston: Houghton Mifflin Company.
Fowler, William E. 1987   Folk Remedies and Beliefs in Maury County, 1936. Tennessee Folklore Society Bulletin 53(1):7–26.
Francis, Vida, Barbara M. Korsch, and Marie J. Morris. 1969   Gaps in Doctor-Patient Communication. New England Journal of Medicine 280:535–540.

Frank, Jerome D. 1977   The Two Faces of Psychotherapy. Journal of Nervous and Mental Disease 164:3--7.

Frankel, Barbara. 1977   Childbirth in the Ghetto: Folk Beliefs of Negro Women in a North Philadelphia Hospital Ward. San Francisco: R & E Research Associates, Inc.

Freemon, Frank R., and Frank T. Drake. 1967   Abnormal Emotional Reactions to Hospitalization Jeopardizing Medical Treatment. Psychosomatics 8:150--155.

Frye, Gladys-Marie. 1975   Night Riders in Black Folk History. Knoxville: University of Tennessee Press. 2nd printing, 1977.

Galanti, Geri-Ann. 1991   Caring for Patients from Different Cultures. Philadelphia: University of Pennsylvania Press.

Gaudin, Kimberly M. 1990   Side Effects of Drug Epidemic. Lansing State Journal, October 26, 1990:1A, 2A.

Genovese, Eugene D. 1974   Roll, Jordan, Roll: The World the Slaves Made. New York: Random House.

Giblin, Paul T., and Marilyn L. Poland. 1985   Health Needs of High School Students in Detroit. Journal of School Health 55(10):407–410.

Giblin, Paul T., Marilyn N. Poland, and Barbara Sachs. 1987   Effects of Social Supports on Attitudes and Health Behaviors of Pregnant Adolescents. Journal of Adolescent Health Care 8(3):273–279.

Glick, Leonard B. 1967   Medicine as an Ethnographic Category: The Gimi of the New Guinea Highlands. Ethnology 6:31--56.

Golden, Kenneth M. 1977   Voodoo in Africa and the United States. American Journal of Psychiatry 134(12):1425--1427.

Gray, Gregory E., David Baron, and Joseph Herman. 1985   Importance of Medical Anthropology in Clinical Psychiatry [letter]. American Journal of Psychiatry 142(2):275.

Green, Jesse, and Peter S. Arno. 1990   The "Medicaidization" of AIDS. Trends in the Financing of HIV Related Medical Care. Journal of American Medical Association 264(10):1261--1266.

Grisso, Jean Ann, et al. 1991   A Population-based Study of Injuries in Inner-City Women. American Journal of Epidemiology 134(1):59–68.

Gross, Jane. 1991   Help for Grandparents Caught Up in Drug War. New York Times, April 14, 1991, 12.

Guffy, Ossie (as told to Caryl Ledner). 1971   Ossie: The Autobiography of a Black Woman. New York: Bantam Books, Inc.

Gunn, J. 1867   Gunn's New Family Physician, or, Home Book of Health. New York: Moore, Wilstach and Baldwin.

Gwaltney, John Langston. 1980   Drylongso. A Self-Portrait of Black America. New York: Random House.

Hahn, Robert A., and Marjorie A. Muecke. 1987   The Anthropology of Birth in Five U.S. Ethnic Populations: Implications for Obstetrical Practice. In Current Problems in Obstetrics, Gynecology and Fertility 10(4). Robert W. Kistner and Robert Barbieri, eds. Pp. 133–171. Chicago: Year Book Medical Publishers, Inc.

Hall, Arthur L., and Peter G. Bourne. 1973   Indigenous Therapists in a Southern Black Urban Community. Archives of General Psychiatry 28:137--142.

Hamilton, Virginia. 1985   The People Could Fly. New York: Alfred A. Knopf.

Hand, Wayland D. 1980   Magical Medicine. Berkeley: University of California Press.

Hand, Wayland D. (ed.). 1961   Popular Beliefs and Superstitions from North Carolina. Volume VI of The Frank C. Brown Collection of North Carolina Folklore, in seven volumes. Newman Ivey White, general ed. Durham, NC: Duke University Press.

Handler, Arden, et al. 1991   Cocaine Use During Pregnancy: Perinatal Outcomes. American Journal of Epidemiology 133(8):818–825.

Handsfield, H. Hunter. 1990   Old Enemies: Combating Syphilis and Gonorrhea in the 1990s. Journal of American Medical Association 264(11):1451--1452.

Hannerz, Ulf. 1969   Soulside. New York: Columbia University Press.

Harburg, Ernest, et al. 1973   Socio-Ecological Stress, Suppressed Hostility, Skin Color, and Black-White Male Blood Pressure: Detroit. Psychosomatic Medicine 35:276--296.

_____. 1978   Skin Color, Ethnicity, and Blood Pressure I: Detroit Blacks. American Journal of Public Health 68(12):1177--1182.

Harrison, Ira E. 1975/1976   Health Status and Healing Practices: Continuations from an African Past. Journal of African Studies 2(4):547--560.

Heiligman, Robert M., LaMont R. Lee, and Deborah Kramer. 1983   Pain Relief Associated with a Religious Visitation: A Case Report. Journal of Family Practice 16(2)299--302.

Henton, Comradge L. 1961   The Effect of Socio-Economic and Emotional Factors on the Onset of Menarche Among Negro and White Girls. Journal of Genetic Psychology 98:255--264.

Herskovits, Melville J. 1937   Life in a Haitian Valley. New York: Anchor Books. 1971 edition.

_____. 1941   The Myth of the Negro Past. Boston: Beacon Press. Paperback edition 1958.

Heurtin-Roberts, Suzanne, and Efrain Reisin. 1990   Folk Models of Hypertension. *In* Anthropology and Primary Health Care. Jeannine Coreil and J. Dennis Mull, eds. Pp. 222--250. Boulder, CO: Westview Press.

Heyer, Kathryn W. 1981   Rootwork: Psychosocial Aspects of Malign Magical and Illness Beliefs in a South Carolina Sea Island Community. Ph.D. dissertation, Department of Anthropology, University of Connecticut. Ann Arbor, MI: University Microfilms.

Hill, Carole E. 1976   A Folk Medical Belief System in the Rural South: Some Practical Considerations. Southern Medicine 16:11--17.

_____. 1988   Community Health Systems in the Rural American South. Boulder, CO: Westview Press.

Hill, Carole E., and Holly Mathews. 1981   Traditional Health Beliefs and Practices Among Southern Rural Blacks: A Complement to Biomedicine. *In* Perspectives on the American South. John Shelton Reed, ed. Pp. 307--322. New York: Gordon and Breach Science Publishers.

Hill, Robert B. 1977   Informal Adoption Among Black Families. Washington, DC: National Urban League Research Department.

Hillard, James R. 1982   Diagnosis and Treatment of the Rootwork Victim. Psychiatric Annals 12(7):709--711.

Hohman, John George. n.d. Pow-Wows, or, The Long-Lost Friend. Published for the Trade. Printed in the U.S.A. (First published 1820)

Holloway, Joseph E. (ed.). 1990   Africanisms in American Culture. Bloomington: Indiana University Press. Midland Book Edition 1991.

Holmes, Linda. 1984   Alabama Granny Midwife. Journal of Medical Society of New Jersey 81(5):389–391.

Institute of Gerontology. 1978   Home Health Care Among the Black Elderly. Final Report. Ann Arbor, MI: University of Michigan offprint.

Hufford, David J. 1982   The Terror That Comes in the Night. Philadelphia: University of Pennsylvania Press.

_____. 1984   American Healing Systems. An Introduction and Exploration. Hershey, PA: Hershey Medical Center offprint.

_____. 1988   Contemporary Folk Medicine. *In* Other Healers. Norman Gevitz, ed. Pp. 228–291. Baltimore: Johns Hopkins University Press.

Hughes, Walter T. 1963   Superstitions and Home Remedies Encountered in Present-Day Pediatric Practice in the South. Journal of Kentucky State Medical Association 61:25–27.

Humphreys Manual. 1967   Rutherford, NJ: Humphreys Pharmacal Inc. Revised and re-copyrighted edition.

Hunter, John M. 1973   Geophagy in Africa and in the United States. Geographical Review (April):170–195.

_____. 1984   Insect Clay Geophagy in Sierra Leone. Journal of Cultural Geography 4(2):2–13.

Hunter, John M., and Renate DeKleine. 1984   Geophagy in Central America. Geographical Review 74(2):157–169.

Hurston, Zora Neale. 1935   Mules and Men. Bloomington: Indiana University Press. Reprint 1978.

Hyatt, Harry Middleton. 1970–1978   Hoodoo, Conjuration, Witchcraft, Rootwork. Five volumes. Hannibal, MO: Western Publishing, Inc.

Infant Mortality Among Black Americans. 1987   Morbidity and Mortality Weekly Report 36(1):1–4, 9–10.

Jackson, Bruce. 1976   The Other Kind of Doctor: Conjure and Magic in Black American Folk Medicine. *In* American Folk Medicine. Wayland D. Hand, ed. Pp. 259–272. Berkeley: University of California Press.

Jackson, Juanita, Sabra Slaughter, and J. Herman Blake. 1974   The Sea Islands as a Cultural Resource. The Black Scholar 5:32–39.

Jacobson, Sandra, Joseph L. Jacobson, and Karen F. Frye. 1991   Incidence and Correlates of Breast-Feeding in Socioeconomically Disadvantaged Women. Pediatrics 88(4):728–735.

Jahoda, Gustav. 1969   The Psychology of Superstition. Harmondsworth, England: Penguin Books Ltd. Paperback edition 1971.

James, Sherman A., and David G. Kleinbaum. 1976   Socioecologic Stress and Hypertension Related Mortality Rates in North Carolina. American Journal of Public Health 66:354–358.

James, Sherman A., et al. 1984   The Edgecombe County (NC) High Blood Pressure Control Program: II. Barriers to the Use of Medical Care Among Hypertensives. American Journal of Public Health 74(5):468–472.

Jamison, Harold J. 1988   A Herbalist Who Claims to Cure AIDS Is Nabbed. New York Amsterdam News, August 13, 1988, 1, 35.

Jeane, D. Gregory. 1978   The Upland South Cemetery: An American Type. Journal of Popular Culture 11(4):895–903.

Joe, Tom. 1987   The Other Side of Black Female-headed Families: The Status of Adult Black Men. Family Planning Perspectives 19(2):74–76.

Johnson, Charles S. 1934   Shadow of the Plantation. Chicago: University of Chicago Press.

Johnson, Shirley M., and Loudell F. Snow. 1979   What Women Do Not Know About the Menopause. The Osteopathic Physician 46(2):28–31, 35–37.

_____. 1982   Assessment of Reproductive Knowledge in an Inner-City Clinic. Social Science & Medicine 16:1657–1662.

Johnson, Shirley M., et al. 1986   Students' Stereotypes of Patients as Barriers to Clinical Decision-Making. Journal Medical Education 61:727–735.

Jones, James H. 1981   Bad Blood: The Tuskegee Syphilis Experiment—A Tragedy of Race and Medicine. New York: The Free Press.

Jones-Jackson, Patricia. 1987   When Roots Die. Athens, GA: University of Georgia Press.

Jordan, Wilbert C. 1975   Voodoo Medicine. *In* Textbook of Black-Related Diseases. Richard A. Williams, ed. Pp. 715–738. New York: McGraw-Hill Book Co.

Joyce, Theodore. 1987   The Demand for Health Inputs and Their Impact on the Black Neonatal Mortality Rate in the U.S. Social Science & Medicine 24(11):911–918.

_____. 1990   The Dramatic Increase in the Rate of Low Birthweight in New York City: An Aggregate Time-Series Analysis. American Journal of Public Health 80(6):682–684.

Kay, Margarita Artschwager (ed.). 1982   Anthropology of Human Birth. Philadelphia: F. A. Davis Company.

Kellam, Sheppard G., Margaret E. Ensminger, and R. Jay Turner. 1977   Family Structure and the Mental Health of Children. Archives of General Psychiatry 34:1012–1022.

Kennedy, Theodore R. 1980   You Gotta Deal With It: Black Family Relations in a Southern Community. New York: Oxford University Press.

Kimball, Chase Patterson. 1970   A Case of Pseudocyesis Caused by "Roots." American Journal of Obstetrics and Gynecology 107:801–803.

King, J. 1855   The American Eclectic Dispensatory. Cincinnati: Moore, Wilstach, Keys and Company.

Kistin, Naomi, et al. 1990   Breast-feeding Rates Among Black Urban Low-Income Women: Effect of Prenatal Education. Pediatrics 86(5):741–746.

Klag, Michael, et al. 1991   The Association of Skin Color with Blood Pressure in US Blacks with Low Socioeconomic Status. Journal of American Medical Association 265(5):599–602.

Klass, Perri. 1990   Mothers with AIDS: A Love Story. New York Times Magazine, November 4, 1990: 24, 26.

Kleinman, Arthur. 1988   The Illness Narratives. New York: Basic Books, Inc., Publishers.

Kleinman, Arthur, Leon Eisenberg, and Byron Good. 1978   Culture, Illness, and Care: Clinical Lessons from Anthropologic and Cross-Cultural Research. Annals of Internal Medicine 88:251–258.

Kleinman, Joel C., and Samuel S. Kessel. 1987   Racial Differences in Low Birth Weight: Trends and Risk Factors. New England Journal of Medicine 317(12):749–753.

Korbin, Jill E., and Maxene Johnston. 1982   Steps Toward Resolving Cultural Conflict in a Pediatric Hospital. Clinical Pediatrics 21(5):259–263.

Korbin, Jill E. (ed.). 1981   Child Abuse and Neglect: Cross-cultural Perspectives. Berkeley: University of California Press.

Kotlowitz, Alex. 1991   There Are No Children Here. New York: Doubleday & Co.

Kreig, Margaret. 1964   Green Medicine. The Search for Plants that Heal. Chicago: Rand McNally and Company.

Kresnack, Jack. 1991   The Cost of Caring. Detroit Free Press, March 5, 1991, 1D, 4D.

Ladner, Joyce A. 1971   Tomorrow's Tomorrow. New York: Doubleday & Co. Anchor Books edition 1972.

Laguerre, Michel. 1987   Afro-Caribbean Medicine. South Hadley, MA: Bergin and Garvey, Inc.

Lazarus, Ellen S. 1988   Theoretical Considerations for the Study of the Doctor-Patient Relationship: Implications of a Perinatal Study. Medical Anthropology Quarterly 2(1)(NS):34–58.

Lefley, Harriet P. 1979   Prevalence of Potential Falling-Out Cases Among the Black, Latin and Non-Latin White Populations of the City of Miami. *In* The Transcultural Perspective in Health and Illness. Hazel H. Weidman, ed. Special issue, Social Science & Medicine 13B(2):115–116.

Lemann, Nicholas. 1991   The Promised Land. New York: Alfred A. Knopf.

Lenocker, Joanne M., and Molly C. Dougherty. 1976   Adolescent Mothers' Social and Health-related Interests: Report of a Project for Rural, Black Mothers. JOGN (Journal of the Nurses Association of the American College of Obstetricians and Gynecologists) Nursing 5(4):9–15.

Levine, Lawrence W. 1977   Black Culture and Black Consciousness. New York: Oxford University Press.

Levy, David R. 1985   White Doctors and Black Patients: Influence of Race on the Doctor-Patient Relationship. Pediatrics 75(4):639–643.

Lia-Hoagberg, Betty, et al. 1990   Barriers and Motivators to Prenatal Care Among Low-Income Women. Social Science & Medicine 30(4):487–495.

Lichstein, Peter R. 1982   Can a Physician Heal a "Hex"? Hospital Practice (November):129–132.

Lieberman, Ellice, et al. 1987   Risk Factors Accounting for Racial Differences in the Rate of Premature Birth. New England Journal of Medicine 317(12):743–748.

Liebow, Elliot. 1967   Tally's Corner. Boston: Little, Brown and Company.

Lindblad-Goldberg, Marion, and Joyce Lynn Dukes. 1985   Social Support in Black, Low-Income, Single-Parent Families: Normative and Dysfunctional Patterns. American Journal of Orthopsychiatry 55(1):42–58.

Logan, Onnie Lee (as told to Katherine Clark). 1989   Motherwit. An Alabama Midwife's Story. New York: Penguin Books USA Inc.

Lyles, Michael R., and James R. Hillard. 1982   Root Work and the Refusal of Surgery. Psychosomatics 23(6):663–667.

Lythcott, George, Calvin H. Sinnette, and Donald R. Hopkins. 1975   Pediatrics. In Textbook of Black-Related Diseases. Richard A. Williams, ed. Pp. 129–197. New York: McGraw-Hill Book Company.

McCall, George J. 1973   Symbiosis: The Case of Hoodoo and the Numbers Racket. In Mother Wit from the Laughing Barrel. Alan Dundes, ed. Pp. 419–427. Reprinted in slightly abridged form from Social Problems 10:361–371, 1963.

McClellan, Barbara. 1991   State Heads into Foster-Care Crisis. Detroit News, February 3, 1991, 1C, 5C.

McCord, Colin, and Harold P. Freeman. 1990   Excess Mortality in Harlem. New England Journal of Medicine 322(3):173–177.

MacCormack, C. P. 1985   Lay Concepts Affecting Utilization of Family Planning Services in Jamaica. Journal of Tropical Medicine and Hygiene 88:281–285.

MacDonald's Farmers Almanac. 1980   Binghamton, NY: Atlas Printing Co.

_____. 1987   Binghamton, NY: Franklin Rury.

McLorg, Penelope A., and Carol A. Bryant. 1989   Influence of Social Network Members and Health Care Professionals on Infant Feeding Practices of Economically Disadvantaged Mothers. Medical Anthropology 10:265–278.

Maduro, Reynaldo. 1975   Hoodoo Possession in San Francisco. Ethos 3(3):424–447.

Marshall, J. S. 1955   A Study of Fifteen Mental Patients at Crownsville State Hospital, Crownsville, Maryland, Who Were Adherents of Voodoo. Master's thesis, Howard University, Washington, DC.

Martin, Douglas. 1991   Now the Work That's Never Done Is Grandmother's. New York Times, May 12, 1991, 6E.

Martin, Elmer P., and Joanne Mitchell Martin. 1978   The Black Extended Family. Chicago: University of Chicago Press.

Mathews, Holly F. 1982   Doctors and Rootdoctors: Ethnomedicine and the American Medical System. Paper presented at annual meeting of Southern Anthropological Society, Boone, NC, April 14, 1982.

_____. 1987   Rootwork: Description of an Ethnomedical System in the American South. Southern Medical Journal 80(7):885–891.

_____. 1988   "Sweet Blood Can Give You Sugar": Black American Folk Beliefs about Diabetes. City Medicine 2(4):12, 14–16.

Meigs, Joseph A. 1982   Choosing Your Baby's Sex—Now and in the Sixteenth Century. Tennessee Folklore Society Bulletin 68(4):111–116.

Meltzer, Alan, and Debra Kantor. 1990   Folk Beliefs and Health Practices Related to Children Seropositive for HIV Infection in an Urban Lower Income Population. Paper presented at Primary Care Research and Development Program, Office of Medical Education Research and Development, Michigan State University, May 1990.

Metraux, Alfred. 1959   Voodoo in Haiti. New York: Oxford University Press.

Michigan HIV/AIDS Report 6(1). 1991   HIV Survey Among Mothers. P. 3.

Mintz, Sidney W., and Richard Price. 1976   An Anthropological Approach to the Afro-American Past: A Caribbean Perspective. Philadelphia: Institute for the Study of Human Issues, Inc.

Mitchell, Faith. 1983   Popular Medical Concepts in Jamaica and Their Impact on Drug Use. Western Journal of Medicine 139(6):841–847.

Moerman, Daniel E. 1975   High-Low, Bitter-Sweet: An American Folk Medical System. Proceedings of the Central States Anthropological Society. Selected Papers VI. Pp. 47–50. Ann Arbor, MI: Braun-Brumfield, Inc.

_____. 1979   Empirical Methods in the Evaluation of Indigenous Medical Systems: Comments on a Symposium. Medical Anthropology 3(4):525–530.

_____. 1981   Masterful Marginals: Black Life on a Carolina Isle. *In* Perspectives on the American South. Merle Black and John Shelton Reed, eds. Pp. 273–305. New York: Gordon and Breach Science Publishers.

_____. 1982   Geraniums for the Iroquois. Algonac, MI: Reference Publications, Inc.

_____. 1986   Medicinal Plants of Native America. 2 volumes. Ann Arbor, MI: University of Michigan Museum of Anthropology Technical Reports Number 19.

Montell, William Lynwood. 1975   Ghosts Along the Cumberland: Deathlore in the Kentucky Foothills. Nashville: University of Tennessee Press.

Morrison, Toni. 1970   The Bluest Eye. New York: Holt, Rinehart and Winston. Pocket Books edition 1972.

_____. 1973   Sula. New York: Alfred A. Knopf, Inc. Bantam edition 1975.

Morson, Donald, Frank Reuter, and Wayne Viitanen. 1976   Negro Folk Remedies Collected in Eudora, Arkansas, 1974–75. Mid-South Folklore 4(1):11–24.

Morton, Julia F. 1974   Folk Remedies of the Low Country. Miami, FL: E. A. Seemann Publishing, Inc.

Mulira, Jessie Gaston. 1990   The Case of Voodoo in New Orleans. *In* Africanisms in American Culture. Joseph E. Holloway, ed. Pp. 34–68. Bloomington: Indiana University Press. Midland Book Edition 1991.

Murphree, Alice H. 1968   A Functional Analysis of Southern Folk Beliefs Concerning Birth. American Journal of Obstetrics and Gynecology 102:125–134.

_____. 1976   Folk Beliefs: Understanding of Health, Illness and Treatment. *In* The Health of a Rural County. Richard C. Reynolds, Sam A. Banks, and Alice H. Murphree, eds. Pp. 111–123. Gainesville, FL: University Presses of Florida.

Murphree, Alice H., and Mark Barrow. 1970   Physician Dependence, Self-Treatment Practices, and Folk Remedies in a Rural Area. Southern Medical Journal 63:403–408.

Nations, Marilyn K., Linda A. Camino, and Frederic B. Walker. 1985   "Hidden" Popular Illnesses in Primary Care: Residents' Recognition and Clinical Implications. Culture, Medicine and Psychiatry 9(3):223–240.

_____. 1988   "Nerves": Folk Idiom for Anxiety and Depression? Social Science & Medicine 26(12):1245–1259.

Naylor, Gloria. 1982   The Women of Brewster Place. New York: Viking Press. Penguin Books edition 1983.

_____. 1988   Mama Day. New York: Ticknor and Fields.

Newman, Lucile F. 1969   Folklore of Pregnancy: Wives' Tales in Contra Costa County, California. Western Folklore 28(2):112–135.

Nguyen, Hoa N., Mary J. O'Sullivan, and Arthur M. Fournier. 1991   The Impact of National Health Service Corps Physicians in the Lowering Perinatal Mortality Rate in Dade County, Florida. Obstetrics & Gynecology 78(3)(Part 1):385–389.

Norbeck, Jane S., and N. Jean Anderson. 1989   Psychosocial Predictors of Pregnancy Outcomes in Low-Income Black, Hispanic, and White Women. Nursing Research 38(4):204–209.

Nutritional Status of Minority Children—United States. 1986   Morbidity and Mortality Weekly Report 36(23):366–369.

Orenstein, Walter A., et al. 1990   Barriers to Vaccinating Preschool Children. Journal of Health Care for the Poor and Underserved 1(3):316–330.

Parsons, Elsie Clews. 1923   Folk-Lore of the Sea Islands, South Carolina. Cambridge, MA: Memoirs of the American Folk-Lore Society, Vol. 16.

Parsons, James S. 1981   Contaminated Herbal Tea as a Potential Source of Chronic Arsenic Poisoning. North Carolina Medical Journal 42(1):38–39.

Payne, Robert B. 1963   Nutmeg Intoxication. New England Journal of Medicine 269:36–38.

Payne, Zelma A. 1980   The Influence of Cultural Patterns on Medical Management. Urban Health 9(19):24–28.

Payne, Zelma A., and W. Dallas Hall. 1978   Folk Medicine Practices in the Control of Hypertension. Abstract A-178. Preventive Medicine 7(1):121.

Pellegrini, Adrian J., and Paul Putman III. 1984   The Amytal Interview in the Diagnosis of Late Onset Psychosis with Cultural Features Presenting as Catatonic Stupor. Journal of Nervous and Mental Disease 172(8):502–504.

Petitti, Diana B., and Charlotte Coleman. 1990   Cocaine and the Risk of Low Birth Weight. American Journal of Public Health 80(1):25–28.

Phibbs, Ciaran S., David A. Bateman, and Rachel M. Schwartz. 1991   The Neonatal Costs of Maternal Cocaine Use. Journal of American Medical Association 266(11):1521–1526.

Pickard, Madge E., and R. Carlyle Buley. 1946   The Midwest Pioneer. New York: Henry Schuman.

Pierce, R. V. 1875   The People's Common Sense Medical Adviser in Plain English: or, Medicine Simplified. Buffalo, NY: The World's Dispensary Printing Office and Bindery. 56th edition 1895.

Pivnick, Anitra, et al. 1991   Reproductive Decisions Among HIV-Infected, Drug-Using Women: The Importance of Mother-Child Coresidence. Medical Anthropology Quarterly (New Series) 5(2):153–169.

Poland, M. L., Joel W. Ager, and Jane M. Olson. 1987   Barriers to Receiving Adequate Prenatal Care. American Journal of Obstetrics and Gynecology 157:297–303.

Poland, M. L., and G. E. Beane. 1980   A Study of the Effects of Folklore About the Body on IUD Use by Black American Adolescents. Contracept. Deliv. Syst. 1:333–340.

Poland, M. L., et al. 1990   Quality of Prenatal Care: Selected Social, Behavioral, and Biomedical Factors; and Birth Weight. Obstetrics and Gynecology 75(4):607–612.

Powers, Bethel Ann. 1982   The Use of Orthodox and Black American Folk Medicine. Advances in Nursing Science 4(3):35–48.

Prince, Isolde. 1989   Pica and Geophagia in Cross-Cultural Perspective. Transcultural Psychiatric Research Review 26:167–197.

Prince, Raymond (ed.). 1982   Shamans and Endorphins. Special issue, Ethos 10(4).

Puckett, Newbell Niles. 1926   Folk Beliefs of the Southern Negro. Chapel Hill: University of North Carolina Press. Reprinted 1969, New York: Dover Publications.

Raboteau, Albert J. 1978   Slave Religion. New York: Oxford University Press, Inc. Paperback edition 1980.

Rainwater, Lee. 1970   Behind Ghetto Walls: Black Family Life in a Federal Slum. Chicago: Aldine Publishing Company.

Rassin, David K., et al. 1984   Incidence of Breast-Feeding in a Low Socioeconomic Group of Mothers in the United States: Ethnic Patterns. Pediatrics 73(2):132–137.

Redlener, Irwin E., and Clarissa S. Scott. 1979   Incompatibilities of Professional and Religious Ideology: Problems of Medical Management and Outcome in a Case of Pediatric Meningitis. Social Science & Medicine 13B:89–93.

Reeb, Kenneth G., et al. 1986   Defining Family in Family Medicine: Perceived Family vs. Household Structure in an Urban Black Population. Journal of Family Practice 23(4):351–355.

Richardson, C. 1912   Some Slave Superstitions. Southern Workman 41:247.

Riva, Anna. 1974   The Modern Herbal Spellbook. The Magical Use of Herbs. Toluca Lake, CA: International Imports.

Roberson, Mildred Hopkins. 1983   Folk Health Beliefs and Practices of Rural Black Virginians. Ph.D. dissertation, College of Nursing, University of Utah. Ann Arbor, MI: University Microfilms.

Rocereto, LaVerne R. 1973   Root Work and the Root Doctor. Nursing Forum 12:414–427.

Rolfs, Robert T., and Allyn K. Nakashima. 1990   Epidemiology of Primary and Secondary Syphilis in the United States, 1981   Through 1989. Journal of American Medical Association 264(11):1432–1437.

Romano, Patrick S., Joan Bloom, and S. Leonard Syme. 1991   Smoking, Social Support, and Hassles in an Urban African-American Community. American Journal of Public Health 81(11):1415–1422.

Ryan, Alan S., et al. 1991   Recent Declines in Breast-Feeding in the United States, 1984 Through 1989. Pediatrics 88(4):719–727.

Satcher, David. 1990   Crime, Sin, or Disease: Drug Abuse and AIDS in the African-American Community. Journal of Health Care for the Poor and Underserved 1(2):212–218.

Satcher, David, and Mary Ashley. 1974   Barriers to Hypertension Control in Urban Communities. Urban Health 3(4):12-13, 18, 34, 61.

Satcher, David, and Ludlow B. Creary. 1984   Family Practice in the Inner City. *In* Textbook of Family Practice, 3rd ed. Robert E. Rakel, ed. Pp. 226–237. Philadelphia: W. B. Saunders Company.

Saxon, Lyle, Edward Dreyer, and Robert Tallant. 1945   Gumbo Ya-Ya. Boston: Houghton Mifflin Company.

Scheper-Hughes, Nancy. 1990   Three Propositions for a Critically Applied Anthropology. Social Science & Medicine 30(2):189–197.

Schiff, Robert L., et al. 1986   Transfers to a Public Hospital. New England Journal of Medicine 314:552–557.

Schulte, Joann M., et al. 1991   Changing Immunization Referral Patterns Among Pediatricians and Family Practice Physicians, Dallas County, Texas, 1988. Journal of American Medical Association 87(2):204–207.

Schulz, David A. 1969   Coming Up Black. Englewood Cliffs, NJ: Prentice-Hall, Inc.

Schwarcz, Sandra K., et al. 1990   National Surveillance of Antimicrobial Resistance in *Neisseria gonorrhoeae.* Journal of American Medical Association 264(11):1413–1417.

Scott, Clarissa S. 1974   Health and Healing Practices Among Five Ethnic Groups in Miami, Florida. Public Health Reports 89:524–531.

—————. 1975   The Relationship Between Beliefs About the Menstrual Cycle and Choice of Fertility Regulating Methods Within Five Ethnic Groups. International Journal of Gynaecology and Obstetrics 13:105–109.

Scott, Clarissa S., et al. 1988   Hispanic and Black American Adolescents' Beliefs Relating to Sexuality and Contraception. Adolescence 23(91):667–686.

—————. 1989   Black Adolescents' Emotional Response to Menarche. Journal of National Medical Association 81(3):285–290.

Shedlin, Michele G. 1989   The Health Care of Homeless Mothers and Children: Impact of a Welfare Hotel. Medical and Health Research Association of New York City, Inc. offprint.

Shiono, Patricia, et al. 1986   Birth Weight Among Women of Different Ethnic Groups. Journal of American Medical Association 255(1):48–52.

Shryock, Richard Harrison. 1966   Medicine in America. Baltimore: Johns Hopkins University Press.

Siegel, Ronald K. 1976   Herbal Intoxication. Journal of American Medical Association 236(5):473–476.

Simons, Ronald C., Frank R. Ervin, and Raymond H. Prince. 1988   The Psychobiology of Trance. I: Training for Thaipusam. Transcultural Psychiatric Research Review 25:249–266.

Simons, Ronald C., and Charles C. Hughes (eds.). 1985   The Culture-bound Syndromes. Dordrecht, Netherlands: D. Reidel Publishing Company.

Singer, Barry, and Victor A. Benassi. 1981   Occult Beliefs. American Scientist 69:49–55.

Snell, John E. 1967   Hypnosis in the Treatment of the "Hexed" Patient. American Journal of Psychiatry 124(3):311–316.

Snow, Loudell F. 1973   "I Was Born Just Exactly With the Gift." Journal of American Folklore 86:272–281.

—————. 1974   Folk Medical Beliefs and Their Implications for Care of Patients. Annals of Internal Medicine 81:82–96.

—————. 1977   Popular Medicine in a Black Neighborhood. In Ethnic Medicine in the Southwest. Edward H. Spicer, ed. Pp. 19–95. Tucson: University of Arizona Press.

—————. 1978   Sorcerers, Saints and Charlatans: Black Folk Healers in Urban America. Culture, Medicine and Psychiatry 2:60–106.

—————. 1979   Mail-Order Magic: The Commercial Exploitation of Folk Belief. Journal of Folklore Institute 16:44–74.

—————. 1988   Herbs, Healers and Hypertension: Examples of Black Traditional Medicine. City Medicine 2(4):4–7.

Snow, Loudell F., and Shirley M. Johnson. 1977   Modern Day Menstrual Folklore. Journal of American Medical Association 237(25):2736–2739.

—————. 1978   Folklore, Food, Female Reproductive Cycle. Ecology of Food and Nutrition 7:41–49.

Snow, Loudell F., Shirley M. Johnson, and Harry E. Mayhew. 1978   The Behavioral Implications of Some Old Wives' Tales. Obstetrics and Gynecology 51:727–732.

Spence, Michael R., et al. 1991   The Relationship Between Recent Cocaine Use and Pregnancy Outcome. Obstetrics and Gynecology 78(3)(Part 1):326–329.

Stack, Carol B. 1974   All Our Kin. New York: Harper and Row.

Stekert, Ellen. 1971   Focus for Conflict: Southern Medical Beliefs in Detroit. In The Urban Experience and Folk Tradition. Anthony Paredes and Ellen Stekert, eds. Pp. 95–127. Austin: University of Texas Press.

Stewart, Horace. 1971   Kindling of Hope in the Disadvantaged: A Study of the Afro-American Healer. Mental Hygiene 55:96–100.

Taylor, Carl S. 1990   Dangerous Society. East Lansing: Michigan State University Press.

Taylor, Lanell. 1986   How Herbs and Plants of the Bible Are Used Today. Offprint.

Thomas, Keith. 1971   Religion and the Decline of Magic. London: Weidenfeld and Nicolson.

Thomas, Sherry. 1981   We Didn't Have Much, But We Sure Had Plenty. Garden City, NY: Anchor Books.

Thomas, Stephen, and Sandra Crouse Quinn. 1991   The Tuskegee Syphilis Study, 1932 to 1972: Implications for HIV Education and AIDS Risk Education Programs in the Black Community. American Journal of Public Health 81(11):1498--1505.

Tinling, David C. 1967   Voodoo, Root Work, and Medicine. Psychosomatic Medicine 29:483--490.

Torrey, E. Fuller. 1972   The Mind Game: Witchdoctors and Psychiatrists. New York: Emerson Hall Publishers.

Tyler, Varro E. 1985   Hoosier Home Remedies. West Lafayette, IN: Purdue University Press.

_____. 1987   The New Honest Herbal, 2nd ed. Philadelphia: George F. Stickley Company. First published as The Honest Herbal, 1982.

Ucko, Lenora Greenbaum. 1991   Who's Afraid of the Big Bad Wolf? Confronting Wife Abuse Through Folk Stories. Social Work 36(5):414–419.

Valentine, Bettylou. 1978   Hustling and Other Hard Work. New York: The Free Press.

Van Blarcom, C. C. 1930   Rat Pie, Black Midwives and Black Magic. Harper's Magazine 160:322–332.

Vlach, John Michael. 1978   The Afro-American Tradition in Decorative Arts. Cleveland: Cleveland Museum of Art.

Vogel, Virgil L. 1970   American Indian Medicine. Norman, OK: University of Oklahoma Press.

Wagner, Edward H., et al. 1984   The Edgecombe County High Blood Pressure Control Program: I. Correlates of Uncontrolled Hypertension at Baseline. American Journal of Public Health 74(3):237–242.

Walker, Alice. 1970   The Third Life of Grange Copeland. New York: Harcourt Brace Jovanovich. Harvest/HBJ edition.

_____. 1973   In Love and Trouble. New York: Harcourt Brace Jovanovich. Harvest/HBJ edition.

Waller, Tom, and Gene Killion. 1972   Georgia Folk Medicine. Southern Folklore Quarterly 36:71--92.

Ward, Martha Coonfield. 1971   Them Children: A Study in Language Learning. New York: Holt, Rinehart and Winston, Inc.

Waring, Joseph. 1967   A History of Medicine in South Carolina 1825--1900. Columbia, SC: South Carolina Medical Association.

Watson, Susan, and Patricia Anstett. 1990   Homicide Reaps City's Young. Detroit Free Press, October 6, 1990, 1A, 8A.

Watson, Wilbur H. (ed.). 1984   Black Folk Medicine. New Brunswick, NJ: Transaction Books.

Webb, Julie Yvonne. 1971   Louisiana Voodoo and Superstitions Related to Health. HSMHA (Health Services and Mental Health Administration) Health Reports 86(4):291–301.

Weeks, John R., and Ruben G. Rumbaut. 1991   Infant Mortality Among Ethnic Groups. Social Science & Medicine 33(3):327--334.

Weidman, Hazel H. 1979a The Transcultural View: Prerequisite to Interethnic (Intercultural) Communication in Medicine. In The Transcultural Perspective in Health and Illness. Hazel H. Weidman, ed. Special issue, Social Science & Medicine 13B(2):85--87.

_____. 1979b Falling-Out: A Diagnostic and Treatment Problem Viewed from a Transcultural Perspective. In The Transcultural Perspective in Health and Illness. Hazel H. Weidman, ed. Special issue, Social Science & Medicine 13B(2):95--112.

_____. 1982 Research Strategies, Structural Alterations and Clinically Applied Anthropology. In Clinically Applied Anthropology. Noel J. Chrisman and Thomas W. Maretzki, eds. Pp. 201--241. Dordrecht, Netherlands: D. Reidel Publishing Company.

_____. 1988 Listen and Learn: Culture and Health Care in the Inner City. City Medicine 2(4):17--19.

Weidman, Hazel H., et al. 1978 Miami Health Ecology Report. Miami, FL: University of Miami offprint.

_____, ed. 1979c The Transcultural Perspective in Health and Illness. Special issue, Social Science & Medicine 13B(2).

Weston, W. Wayne, and Judith Belle Brown. 1989 The Importance of Patients' Beliefs. In Communicating with Medical Patients. Moira Stewart and Debra Roter, eds. Pp. 77--85. Newbury Park, CA: Sage Publications.

Whitten, Norman E. 1962 Contemporary Patterns of Malign Occultism Among Negroes in North Carolina. Journal of American Folklore 75:311--325.

Wideman, John Edgar. 1983 Sent For You Yesterday. New York: Avon Books.

Williams, Carolyn A., et al. 1985 The Edgecombe County High Blood Pressure Control Program: III. Social Support, Social Stressors, and Treatment Dropout. American Journal of Public Health 75(5):483--486.

Williams, Melvin D. 1974 Community in a Pentecostal Church. Reprint. Prospect Heights, IL: Waveland Press, Inc.

_____. 1981 On the Street Where I Lived. New York: Holt, Rinehart and Winston, Inc.

Wilson, Benjamin C. 1985 The Rural Black Heritage Between Chicago and Detroit, 1850–1929: A Photograph Album and Random Thoughts. Kalamazoo, MI: New Issues Press, Western Michigan University.

Wilson, Gordon. 1966 Talismans and Magic in Folk Remedies in the Mammoth Cave Region. Southern Folklore Quarterly 30:192–207.

_____. 1967 Swallow It or Rub It On: More Mammoth Cave Remedies. Southern Folklore Quarterly 32:296--303.

_____. 1968 Local Plants in Folk Remedies in the Mammoth Cave Region. Southern Folklore Quarterly 32:321--327.

Wintrob, Ronald M. 1973 The Influence of Others: Witchcraft and Rootwork as Explanations of Behavior Disturbances. Journal of Nervous and Mental Disease 156:318–326.

Wishner, Amy R., et al. 1991 Interpersonal Violence-related Injuries in an African-American Community in Philadelphia. American Journal of Public Health 81(11):1474–1476.

Wood, David L., et al. 1990 Health of Homeless Children and Housed, Poor Children. Pediatrics 86(6):858--866.

Yankauer, Alfred. 1990 What Infant Mortality Tells Us. American Journal of Public Health 80(6):653--654.

Yoder, Don. 1976 Hohman and Romanus: Origins and Diffusion of the Pennsylvania German Powwow Manual. In American Folk Medicine. Wayland D. Hand, ed. Pp. 215--234. Berkeley: University of California Press.

Young, Virginia Heyer. 1970 Family and Childhood in a Southern Negro Community. American Anthropologist 72:269–288.

_____. 1974 A Black American Socialization Pattern. American Ethnologist 1(2):405--413.

About the Book
and Author

Herb doctors and baby doctors; peach leaf poultice for migraines, penicillin for strep throat; belief in roots and reliance on biomedicine—all these remedies and medical options exist comfortably together for many African-Americans. In a fascinating account based on years of work with herbalists, root doctors, M.D.'s, miracle healers, and just plain believers, Loudell Snow examines these conflicting yet somehow complementary systems from birth to death with a sympathetic eye. The beliefs and practices described here are sophisticated. They are not restricted to love magic and miraculous cures but aim at promoting health and adapting old treatments to the very current problems of drugs and AIDS. *Walkin' over Medicine* portrays a living, breathing folk medicine, invented and used by people of great resourcefulness.

Loudell F. Snow is professor of anthropology and adjunct professor of pediatrics and human development, Michigan State University.

Index

Abortion, 179–182, 216(n6), 262(n3)
Acquired immune deficiency
    syndrome (AIDS), 33, 157, 159,
    242, 256, 273–275
    and African-American traditional
      medicine, 111–112, 253, 268
    beliefs about, 213–215, 267, 273–275
    effect on the family, 231, 264(n11)
    rate among African-American
      women, 172, 216(n2)
Adoption, informal practice of, 229–
    232, 261(n3)
Africa, as source of health practices,
    32–33
African-Americans, 42, 126–127,
    143(n7), 167, 168(n5), 229–230,
    260(n2)
    employment rate of, 175
    health culture of, 31–32, 129. *See also*
      African-American traditional
      medicine
    homicide rate of, 217, 218(n4)
    mortality rates of, 172–173, 215(n1),
      216(n2), 218(n3), 219(n6), 267
    and nutrition, 126, 244–245
    Southern, 84, 90, 93(n6), 97–98, 101,
      108, 110, 112(n2), 118, 135
    and violence, 262(n5)
African-American traditional
    medicine, xi–xiii, 31–32, 44, 139,
    143(n11), 265, 268–269
    and AIDS, 111–112, 253, 268
    and biomedicine, 22, 25, 31, 33, 35,
      147, 265–268, 271, 276(n3)
    and blood, 97, 98–112, 112(n2), 117–
      118, 120, 125, 128, 134–138,
      144(n12). *See also* Blood; High
      blood; Low blood
    and the body, 73–81, 91, 92(n2), 104–
      110, 225, 264(n9)
    and diabetes, 120, 142(n2)

and diet, 78–79. *See also* Diet
    healing powers in, 54–62
    health maintenance in, 69–73, 91–92
    home remedies in, 129, 144(n11). *See*
      also Home remedies
    and magic, 169(n8)
    mental health in, 82–92
    and the natural world, 47–50. *See*
      also Climate
    and reproduction, 145–167, 168(n7),
      182, 186–213, 222–228, 260(n1). *See*
      also Labor; Menstruation;
      Pregnancy
    and sexually transmitted diseases,
      109–110
    spirits in, 50–54
"African Bio Mineral Balance," 275
Ager, Joel W., 183, 184
AIDS. *See* Acquired immune
    deficiency syndrome
Air, as dangerous, 75. *See also* Climate
de Albuquerque, Klaus, 59, 60, 157, 251
Alcohol, 137, 138, 144(n12), 213–215
Alexander, Bertha, 47, 49, 76, 78, 89,
    122, 148
Alfonso, Eduardo, 252
Allen, Shana, 203, 204
Allen, Sister Erma, 21, 36, 39–41, 43, 55,
    57, 71, 83, 93(n5), 113(n3), 136, 148,
    206, 224
Almanacs, use in health care, 48–49,
    64(n7), 80, 105
Aloe vera, in home remedies, 22, 131,
    139
Altshuler, Stanley L., 156
American Heritage Dictionary of the
    English Language, 200
American Indians, 32
American Journal of Public Health,
    215(n1)
Amulets. *See* Charms